Tales from the German Underworld

Tales from the German Underworld

Crime and Punishment in the Nineteenth Century

Richard J. Evans

Yale University Press
New Haven and London

For
Logie and Barbara,
the Bremen bicyclists

Set in Bembo by Best-set Typesetter Ltd, Hong Kong
Printed in Great Britain by St Edmundsbury Press Ltd, Suffolk

Library of Congress Cataloging-in-Publication Data

Evans, Richard J.
    Tales from the german underworld: crime and punishment in the nineteenth century/Richard J. Evans.
    Includes bibliographical references and index.
    ISBN 0-300-07224-4 (cloth)
    1. Crime – Germany – History – 19th century.   2. Criminals – Germany – History – 19th century.   3. Detective and mystery stories, German.
    I. Title.
    HV6974.E95   1998
    364.6'0943'09034 – dc21   97-44612
                                                                          CIP

A catalogue record for this book is available from the British Library.

10 9 8 7 6 5 4 3 2 1

Contents

4. The Life and Death of a Lost Woman 166

Journey to the Sexual Underworld – Demand and Supply – The
Social Origins of Prostitution – The Morals Police and
'Public Houses' – Folk Devils and Moral Panics – The Failure of
Regulation – Legal Problems and Community Protest – Moral
Entrepreneurs and Feminist Campaigners – Narratives of Sexual Deviance

Conclusion 213

Illustrations

Acknowledgments

In the course of collecting the material for this book over a number of years, many debts have been incurred. Much of the work was funded by a Research Fellowship of the Alexander von Humboldt Foundation at the Free University of Berlin in 1981, renewed on two subsequent occasions, and thanks are due to the Foundation for its repeated assistance and generosity over the years. Research was also supported at various times by the German Academic Exchange Service and the British Academy, and made possible with the support of St Antony's College, Oxford, the University of East Anglia and Birkbeck College, University of London. Unstinting assistance was provided by the staff of the British Library, where much of the printed literature cited in this book is located, the German Historical Institute London, the Staatsbibliothek Preussischer Kulturbesitz in Berlin, the Bundesarchiv (formerly Zentrales Staatsarchiv) Potsdam, the Bayerisches Hauptstaatsarchiv München, the Niedersächsisches Hauptstaatsarchiv Hannover, the Staatsarchiv der Freien- und Hansestadt Bremen, the Staatsarchiv der Freien- und Hansestadt Hamburg, the Staatsarchiv der Freien- und Hansestadt Lübeck, the Badisches Generallandesarchiv Karlsruhe, the Staatsarchiv Coburg, the Stadtarchiv Frankfurt-am-Main, the Stadtarchiv Braunschweig, the Mecklenburgisches Landeshauptarchiv Schwerin, the Archiv des Bundes Deutscher Frauenvereine (now housed in the Landesarchiv Berlin) and especially the Geheimes Staatsarchiv Preussischer Kulturbesitz in Berlin. Thanks are also due to the various libraries and archives which kindly gave permission to print the illustrations used in this book. A few parts of Chapter 4 derive from a previously published article, and I am grateful to the Past and Present Society for allowing me to reproduce them here.

The research could not have been completed without the invaluable support of many individual colleagues and friends, especially Hartmut Kaelble and Martyn Phillips in Berlin and Tony and Willy McElligott in Hamburg. Seminar audiences in various universities listened patiently to early versions of these chapters, and forced me to rethink them on a number of points. Helga Stachow provided essential encouragement and suggested the use of

Margarete Böhme's *Tagebuch einer Verlorenen*; Joanna Bourke, Marybeth Hamilton, Philippa Levine and Lucy Riall gave the manuscript a critical reading which led to many improvements. I would also like to thank an anonymous American reader for Yale University Press whose incisive comments led me to incorportate some crucial revisions. Robert Baldock and the editorial and production teams at Yale University Press have been meticulous and helpful in turning a typescript into a book. Michael Burleigh and Tony Nicholls provided vital support for my efforts to fund the research at various times. Christine Corton encouraged and sustained me in the writing, tolerated my absences in the archives and read the proofs with a trained eye. Logie Barrow and Barbara Dabrowski in Bremen provided welcome hospitality during my researches there, as they have done on numerous research trips to Germany over the years. My thanks to all of them.

London, August 1997.

Introduction

This book presents four distinct and varied narratives of crime and punishment in nineteenth-century Germany: the epic adventures of an art teacher transported to Siberia with a gang of violent Prussian felons in 1802 after being imprisoned for repeatedly forging banknotes; the tragic sufferings of a drunken female vagrant subjected to repeated whippings by the authorities in Bremen in the 1820s and 1830s for the crime of persistently returning to the city after having been expelled; the comical and fantastic personal and political deceptions of a professional confidence trickster arrested in the early 1860s for not paying his hotel bill; the ironic career of a young woman who drifts into prostitution in the 1890s after having an illegitimate child and shows by her decline and fall that 'respectable' society is far more cruel and immoral than the 'underworld' to which she finally comes to belong.

These stories fall into the genre, increasingly common in historical studies of recent years, of the 'microstudy': the history of an individual like Martin Guerre told by Natalie Zemon Davis, of a small community like Montaillou recreated by Emmanuel Le Roy Ladurie, of an incident, or alleged incident, like the 'great cat massacre' in eighteenth-century Paris analysed by Robert Darnton.[1] In the 1960s and 1970s, historians of crime and deviance were mainly concerned to make general statements linking crime and penal policy on the one hand, and large-scale historical processes such as industrialization, modernization and the growth of the nation-state on the other. They often used elaborate and highly technical quantitative techniques in doing so. While this produced a great deal of significant research, it did not produce very many readable books. The human dimension tended to disappear beneath a mountain of statistics. Surprisingly, too, perhaps, while the quantitative historians managed to establish a number of key trends and developments in the history of crime, they found it a good deal more difficult to make the large-scale historical linkages they were looking for. Number-crunchers are good at establishing the facts about crime, but they have been much less successful in explaining them.[2]

I

Perhaps this is hardly a cause for astonishment, at least in the case of nineteenth-century Germany, where we still know relatively little about the history of crime and punishment. There is a lot of excellent research on these topics in the sixteenth, seventeenth and eighteenth centuries, but in the nineteenth century the trail peters out, and the early explorations of the German historian Dirk Blasius, the pioneer in this field, have not been followed up.[3] This may be because the ordinary criminals of the nineteenth century are seldom surrounded by the romantic aura that envelops the bandits, poachers and marginal people of an earlier period.[4] Riot and rebellion, 'social protest' and the labour movement, have proved far easier subjects with which historians can identify.[5] Apparently unpolitical sources of resistance to state authority have proved less attractive.

What has particularly drawn modern historians to the period has been not the criminal underworld but the state's attempt to repress it. The nineteenth century has been seen above all as a time when Prussia, followed by states in other parts of Germany, made good the often empty promises of the 'Enlightened Despotism' of eighteenth-century monarchs such as Frederick the Great to establish a thorough police control over German society. Pulling itself together after a series of shattering defeats by Napoleon's armies at the beginning of the century, the Prussian state above all instituted a lengthy series of bureaucratic reforms aimed at transforming the social and political order and equipping it with the efficiency and commitment needed to drive out the French. On the one hand, old social barriers and hierarchies were assailed: the stranglehold of the artisan guilds on industrial and labour production was broken, the rigid network of dues and obligations imposed on the serfs in the countryside torn apart. The way was opened for the transition from a traditional 'society of orders' based on inherited status to a modern class society based on differences in economic power and social consciousness. On the other hand, the state developed a mass of new controlling institutions to master this process of social change: a professional police force and gendarmerie, passports and identity cards, a registration system for known deviants such as ex-convicts and prostitutes, police directories, correspondence networks, lists and information centres for keeping track of deviants and offenders. The penal system was transformed as public whippings and executions gave way to punishment in the decent obscurity of carceral institutions, and the pillory was superseded by the penitentiary.

Historians have seen all these reforms largely in terms of the modernization and rationalization of state controls, in the course of which the state in Germany, and particularly in Prussia, encased the population in a straitjacket of conformity and obedience from which it was subsequently unable to escape. Absolutist ideology conceived of the individual as a subject rather than a citizen; and if research on the seventeenth and eighteenth centuries has amply demonstrated that this remained little more than an ambition in most cases, then research on the nineteenth has suggested that it was in this period that the promise of the police state was fully realized.[6] The die was thus cast for the fateful inculcation of the habit of obedience and the love of authority which were to exert such a terrible price in the collapse of the Weimar Republic and the rule of the Nazi dictatorship.[7] Yet while many historians have regarded this as a uniquely German development, work on other countries has tended to uncover similar patterns there too.

Although it has so far had little influence on German historians, the work of the French philosopher-historian Michel Foucault on the history of crime and punishment in a more general sense in nineteenth-century Europe, and particularly England and France, has reinforced this overall picture of the period as the one in which a 'carceral society' was created by a network of controlling institutions and scientific, classificatory discourses, and the 'tolerated illegalities' so characteristic of early modern European society vanished from the scene. In the course of this development, Foucault argued, the new discursive practices of sociology, criminology, psychology and psychiatry created the image of the 'dangerous classes' against whose constructed deviance the virtues of the bourgeois world could be measured. A permanent underclass was formed, providing the object of continual state surveillance and control, living its life in a network of carceral institutions, from the orphanage and the asylum to the workhouse and the penitentiary. To the citizen who contemplated leaving the paths of conformity, this new, institutionalized underworld posed a continual reminder of what the consequences of such an action could be.[8]

Yet this apocalyptically gloomy view of nineteenth-century authority and obedience was the product of a relatively brief period in Foucault's career, when his ideas on crime and punishment absorbed the wider scepticism of post-1968 radicalism as to the possibilities of thoroughgoing social and political reform. It bore some uncomfortable resemblances to the vulgar Marxist paradigm of the day which saw policing and justice as no more than instruments of capitalist domination.[9] In his other work, Foucault developed a more differentiated and sophisticated view of power. Rather than seeing power as something operating in a simple, 'top-down' way, from state to society, Foucault conceived of it as 'a total structure of actions brought to bear upon possible actions ... a way of acting upon an acting subject or acting subjects by virtue of their acting or being capable of actions.'[10] Power, in other words, is structural, and in most societies involves a two-way, or multilateral process of interaction between people who themselves have varying degrees of freedom of action to exert power as they wish. Putting this in less abstract terms, power in nineteenth-century Germany can be seen, not as a one-way process of the state and its organs of policing and control exerting themselves on society, but rather as a constantly shifting series of structures in which the 'underworld' of deviance and criminality exerted its own forms of power, both influencing the state's discursive practice and evading and manipulating its controlling agencies. It is this perspective that informs the narratives gathered together in this book.

But the narratives are intended to do more than merely present a differentiated view of the operation of power or to question established stereotypes of the orderly and obedient German.[11] Each of them, in its different way, raises a whole series of fundamental questions about the nature of deviance and the purposes of control. Taken by themselves, rather than used as clues to wider historical problems, 'microstudies' too often remain at a level of analysis that is little more than trivial. Going to the margins of society, as this book does, can only provide us with a novel perspective on society as a whole if we are determined to use this vantage-point for a series of more general observations. Each chapter, therefore, while framed at the beginning and the end by an individual story, moves outwards in the middle to reflect on what the story in question has to tell us in a wider sense about crime and punishment in nineteenth-century Germany. These more general reflections lead, broadly speaking, in three directions.

First, and most obviously, each chapter tries to link the individual with the collective. In the first chapter, the story of Wilhelm Aschenbrenner, the forger who was deported to Siberia in 1802, prompts a consideration of who else was deported there at the same time. The biographies of the men who were officially regarded as Prussia's most dangerous criminals at the beginning of the century have much to tell us about life on the margins of society at the time, and the desperate expedients to which some men were driven to survive. The question of why they were deported leads on to a broader survey of the policy of the transportation of felons in nineteenth-century Germany. Britain had its penal colony in Australia, and France its Devil's Island, but though some German states – and not only Prussia – did send convicts overseas, this never became a general policy, and indeed after the middle of the century it effectively ceased, never to be revived, despite attempts from some quarters to start it up again. Penal policy in this instance became intertwined with a whole series of other questions, from the status of Germany's colonial empire to the changing theories of crime and deviance advanced by professional elites, and the story has a good deal to tell us about all of these.

The second chapter begins with the dismaying story of Gesche Rudolph, a vagrant woman who fell foul of the authorities in Bremen in the 1820s and 1830s, with the result that she spent two decades and more being repeatedly whipped and imprisoned, with only brief periods of freedom in between. The story opens up the question of corporal punishment, a penal sanction which was coming increasingly under fire from liberals in the 1840s as a symbol of feudal, authoritarian contempt for the honourable status of the individual citizen. Majority opinion agreed by 1848 that it was ineffective, and it was abolished in the course of the revolutions of that year. Yet the gradual ending of corporal punishment, and the failure of attempts to revive it in the second half of the nineteenth century, cannot be explained solely in terms of the decline of a status-bound, hierarchical society in which patriarchal power was wielded by feudal elites who considered it their right to beat their inferiors with the full backing of the law. Nor was it a case of an ineffective penal sanction being replaced by the more effective instrument of imprisonment, since both its supporters and opponents seemed to agree that prisons were continually overcrowded and did little but create generations of recidivists. Another way of understanding the process, Chapter 2 argues, is to think of it in terms of the disappearance of overt violence from the public sphere and its gradual confinement to the private. The consequences of this change, as the study shows, did not necessarily lead in the direction of a 'civilized society' as the liberals supposed.

In the third chapter, the police interrogation of a confidence trickster in Bremen uncovers a life spent masquerading under a seemingly endless variety of identities in the 1850s and 1860s, as the outwardly respectable gentleman in the police cell is forced to confess that he has earned his living from a career of fraud and deceit. Described by the authorities as a political swindler of the most dangerous sort, Franz Ernst illustrates in his nefarious activities how the political instability of the mid-century years, and the climate of deception and counter-deception created by the conspiratorial activities of the revolutionaries and their counterparts in the espionage and infiltration apparatus of the Prussian political police, provided golden opportunities for the unscrupulous adventurer to make a bit of money on the margins of this deadly game. The ease and skill with which Ernst and many others were able to forge identity papers, or avoid having to carry them, and pass themselves off under many different guises shows the limited effectiveness of the documentation and surveillance machinery which many writers have supposed gave the German police unrivalled control over society in the nineteenth century. Ernst's astonishing life-history, as we shall see, also casts an eccentric light on many other aspects of German society at mid-century, from the continuing difficulties faced by 'dishonourable people' to the psychological dynamics of the bourgeois marriage-market.

The fourth chapter takes as its point of departure the story of a young woman of respectable background who fell into a life of prostitution in the 1890s. Her fate, recounted graphically in a diary discovered after her death, aroused widespread comment, and the diary spawned a number of imitations. But how typical was her story? Prostitution was perhaps the major form of female deviance from bourgeois norms in the second half of the nineteenth century, and historians have argued that the controls exercised by the morality division of the police force in German cities over registered prostitutes created an impenetrable net of rules and regulations which was little short of totalitarian. Yet, on closer investigation, this turns out not to have been the case. As historians like Judith Walkowitz have shown for other countries, it is too simple to view prostitutes merely as the unfortunate victims of bourgeois

society and male sexual hypocrisy. Here, too, conventional portraits and
Marxist myths both need correcting; in German society at the turn of the
century, prostitution was but one of many forms of exploitation to which
working-class and lower middle-class women were subjected – not just by
bourgeois men, but by men of all social classes, including the proletariat – and
at least some women thought it preferable to other alternatives. All this casts
a strongly ironic light upon the moral integrity which respectable society
claimed as its own and denied to the women it cast aside.

In all four chapters, the ties which bound the individual to the collective
turn out to be complex and many-faceted. But there is a second respect in
which these particular case-histories serve as starting-points for wider reflections, and that is through the linking concept of the underworld. In each of
the four studies, police and bourgeois commentators use the concept of the
underworld – and in the case of prostitution, the 'half-world' – to charac-
terize the social milieu of the deviant and the outcast. At the beginning of the
nineteenth century, police, penal philosophers and bureaucrats thought of
law-breaking in terms of the individual moral 'turpitude' of the 'villain', the
culmination of a downward moral career which had begun with neglected
education and childhood disobedience.[12] At the same time, such people were
thought to be especially concentrated among the dishonourable trades, as
indicated by the biographies surveyed in Chapter 1, of a substantial number
of the criminals deported to Siberia. A good number of these people were
vagabonds and beggars, members of Germany's floating population of itinerants, a milieu which supplied a disproportionate number of criminals as well.
Not only the biographies of the deportees, but also the general history of
corporal punishment recounted in Chapter 2, suggest that the lash was a
favoured instrument for dealing with such offenders at this time. Malice and
wickedness were thought to lie at the root of deviance, and harsh physical
punishment was the only remedy, a deterrent which would tame the criminal
will and force its bearer to conform to the law.

By mid-century, commentators were coming to portray these people as
members of an organized criminal underworld, one with its own rules and
regulations, even its own language. In many ways, the confidence trickster
Franz Ernst was also a classic underworld figure, both in his origins and in his
mode of life, as we shall see in Chapter 3. The pimp or procurer was also
thought to be a central figure in this underworld of organized or semi-
organized crime, as the debates about prostitution recounted in Chapter 4
suggest. Marx and Engels reconfigured the notion of the underworld into that
of the *Lumpenproletariat*, and their successors in the German Social Democratic
Party employed the concept enthusiastically in their attempt to demarcate the
respectable working classes whom they represented from the 'rough' elements
lower down the social scale.[13] Here too, therefore, the underworld was
sharply marked off from respectable society. Running through all these
official, bourgeois and even socialist commentaries was the consciousness that

many if not most criminals reoffended; and the nightmare figure of the recidivist, who features in so many of the studies in this book, suggested that imprisonment did not always work. It was ineffective, people began to think, because it wrongly assumed it was dealing with morally weak and thus reformable individuals instead of with an organized social stratum of professional criminals for whom gaol was no more than an occupational hazard. The ameliorative principle in penal theory may have held sway among liberals from the 1840s to the 1880s, but it never managed to get over the fact that none of the measures it implemented produced the desired effect of keeping people from coming back to gaol a second time.

By the early twentieth century, the gradual influx of Social Darwinist concepts and language into the discourse of welfare, criminology and penal reform was leading to a revival of the idea propagated by policemen like Friedrich Christian Benedikt Avé-Lallement in the middle of the century that the underworld was hereditary in nature.[14] But whereas Avé-Lallement had traced the *Gaunerwelt*, the world of the 'knave' and the 'rogue', back to what he perceived as the alien influences of gypsies and Jews, the new criminological theorists ascribed social deviance and criminality instead to individual hereditary defects in all races, including the Germans. Particularly influential here was the Italian criminologist Cesare Lombroso, who thought criminals were 'throwbacks' to an earlier, more primitive human type, recognizable by identifiable physical characteristics which betrayed their hereditary tendency to transgress against civilized norms of behaviour. Not all criminologists in the late nineteenth century accepted everything Lombroso said. But few disputed the thesis that crime was at least in part the product of hereditary factors, activated, it was widely believed, by influences such as the experience of extreme poverty or the excessive consumption of alcohol. It was left to the National Socialists to bring the two strands of racism and hereditarianism together and consign all of these categories of people – Jews and gypsies on the one hand, and German criminals and deviants on the other – to sterilization, the concentration camp and ultimately the gas chamber. The four microstudies collected in this book will pay careful attention to the language used by lawyers, administrators, policemen and bourgeois commentators about the underworld, as it shifted from the ascription of deliberate maleficence to the attribution of personal weakness and finally to the assumption of hereditary damage.[15]

At the same time, such language may well have played its part in helping to create and sustain the very underworld whose existence it formally deplored. It could be visual as well as verbal. Scarring an offender's back, as Chapter 1 shows, or branding a criminal's body, automatically made it difficult for him to pursue an honest occupation afterwards. Consigning deviants to a 'dishonourable' group in society could expose them not only to the assumption, acted on by many of the voices heard in Chapter 2, that they were beyond the reformatory measures to which normal offenders were subjected, but also to ostracism and hostility on the part of respectable society, as Chapter 3 suggests. For women, as the stories recounted in Chapter 4 graphically illustrate, honour could be lost more easily still, through the voluntary or involuntary infringement of sexual norms; few enough commentators made the point that it was the norms, not the behaviour of the transgressing individual, that created the deviant. The language of dress and comportment also subtly but unmistakably marked out the women of the sexual underworld from females of all classes in respectable society. Yet all the studies presented in this book show the limitations of such moral symbolism, as time and again those whom respectable discourse consigned to the underworld managed to conceal their identity or escape from it altogether.

All these studies, in their different ways, raise the question of how far bourgeois society actually created the underworld of its own imagination, in order to have an opposite point of reference by which to define its own respectable norms. Narratives of the underworld which circulated in nineteenth-century German society frequently had the effect of providing a series of negative examples by which norms could be maintained. Thus it may be suggested that the bourgeois public sphere sustained itself in part at least through the depiction of the dire consequences that attended transgression: repeated imprisonment, deportation to the frozen wastes of Siberia, whipping and beating, manhandling by dubious revolutionaries, physical decay and decline, the taint of venereal disease. All these sanctions feature strongly in the narratives presented in this book. The institutions erected by German state and society in the course of the nineteenth century, such as the Morals Police and the state control of officially registered prostitutes, can be interpreted, as we shall see, as being directed just as much at regulating the behaviour of the respectable majority as that of the deviant.

The maintenance of respectability was more than merely an institutional or legal phenomenon. Moral discourse in nineteenth-century Germany was not simply a matter for police regulation. It was backed up by a mass of literary models, from ballads and fairy-stories to novels and autobiographies narrating the life-history of individuals caught up in the drama of moral deviance, crime and sin. Each of the microstudies in this volume serves as the starting-point for reflections not only on the relationship of the individual to the collective fate, and the shifting conceptualization of the criminal underworld, but also, thirdly, therefore, on the nature of narrative and narrativity. For each of the four central stories bears only a contingent and, in the end, to some extent indeterminate and indeterminable relationship to ascertainable historical truth. This is not so much a function of the uncertainties of historical epistemology in general as of the more easily identifiable deficiencies of the particular source material through which we know them. Each of the stories, moreover, is shaped not solely, perhaps not even primarily, by the contours of real events, but by the example of literary and fictional models and structures. These narratives are relativized and set in context by the use of other, mostly archival, sources, which complement them and lead on to more general reflections, so that one important aspect of the book consists in the juxtaposition of literary and other modes of describing past reality.

The autobiography of Wilhelm Aschenbrenner which opens Chapter 1 conforms to many of the structures and motifs of the sensational popular literature of the day. The popular literary genre of the adventure story, the German *Räuber- und Ritterroman*, followed so strikingly by Aschenbrenner's romantic narrative, shaped the perception of many at the outset of the nineteenth century of a life of crime as a life of pleasure and excitement. It reinforced the disapproving official view that criminality was sustained primarily by a positive and evil-minded will to deviance. At the same time, the adventures of Aschenbrenner and other felons deported to Siberia, such as the bandit Johann Friedrich Exner, constituted a story of enterprise, hardship and determination that can fairly be called epic.

The story of Gesche Rudolph which opens Chapter 2 is in fact a plea by her lawyer, cast in the tragic mode: there is no reason to doubt the veracity of those details it does recount; the unknown factor lies in what it omits. But this is nonetheless 'fiction in the archives', in the sense proposed by Natalie Zemon Davis: a deliberately and artfully constructed plea for mercy, a literary creation designed to move the emotions of the reader and to melt the heart of even the most stony-faced official with feelings of compassion.[16] The confidence trickster Franz Ernst's life, on the other hand, could not be portrayed as anything other than a comedy, even by the exasperated policemen whose thankless task it was to interrogate him. As Ernst span one elaborate tissue of truths, half-truths and lies after another, and the police were forced to go to ever greater lengths to winkle out the real facts, it became increasingly apparent that he himself was hardly capable of telling reality from fiction. Here the underworld erupted disturbingly into respectable society, posing the thorny problem of how to tell the one from the other.

The narrative which opens Chapter 4 moves into the ironic mode: the downward career of an innocent woman into prostitution, disease and death, through no real fault of her own: every stage of her decline casts a sharply critical light on the moral pretensions of the respectable society which first casts her out by the heartless rigidity of its conventions and then exploits her in a way that graphically reveals the hypocrisy at its core. Such a depiction varied from traditional criminal biographies, of the sort contained in the popular *Pitaval* series or in the true-crime stories of Paul Anselm von Feuerbach, mainly in its starting-point.[17] Feuerbach's villains were fatally flawed from the outset, and only the gravity of their crimes increased with age. The diary of 'Thymian Gotteball', with which Chapter 4 starts, conforms initially much more to a stereotype familiar from late eighteenth-century literature on infanticide – innocence betrayed and then gradually corrupted by an exploitative and morally flawed society. The chapter goes on to explore other contemporary sources to determine the extent to which the diary reflects what they reveal about the experience of prostitutes in Germany at the turn of the century. But of course it is not enough simply to check such accounts against other sources in order to find out how far they represented historical reality. Just as important is to tease out the ways in which this and other narratives both reflected and helped shape the discursive practice of various social and political groups in nineteenth-century Germany when they came to confront sexual and social deviance. Fictional and non-fictional narratives can be seen in some respects simply as different ways of representing fundamental realities in this society.

Beyond the individual and the collective, the concept of the underworld and the ambiguities of narrative, other threads also interweave and bind together the stories presented in this book: gender and class, the state and civil society, authority and obedience, police, state and society, social and political change. Each narrative focuses on a different kind of underworld figure – the forger, the drunken female vagrant, the confidence trickster, the prostitute. Reflecting the interlinkages between different figures in the German underworld, each story also involves figures present in one or more of the others. Prostitution, the central subject of Chapter 4, also plays a part in the story of Wilhelm Aschenbrenner, the forger who is the subject of Chapter 1. It was also almost the only means which Gesche Rudolph, the woman at the centre of attention in Chapter 2, had of supporting herself. Similarly, corporal punishment, the principal subject of Chapter 2, features not only in Rudolph's life but also in the narrative of the Prussian convicts' journey to Siberia in Chapter 1, just as transportation features in the life of Franz Ernst the confidence trickster in Chapter 3 and again in the story of Gesche Rudolph in Chapter 2. The 'folk devil' of the pimp and procurer puts in an appearance both in Chapter 2, as the object of attempts to revive corporal punishment, and in Chapter 4, as the object of bourgeois anxieties at the turn of the century. Sexual exploitation and the seduction of innocent girls is a theme in Chapter 4, of course, but also, perhaps surprisingly, in Chapter 3, the story of Franz Ernst. Deception, dishonour, the effects of imprisonment, the dilemmas surrounding penal reform, the varying impact of policing and punishment, the exploitation of penal policy for symbolic political purposes on all sides of the political arena; all these form themes which run through every chapter in the book. The individuals who are its focus represented flesh-and-blood incarnations of stock figures in the bourgeois discourse of the underworld, and this discourse changed only slowly over the century, so that similar themes and ideas reappear in different contexts and at different times during the century. This is more, then, than merely a collection of good stories; and at the end of the book, we will return to offer some general reflections on crime and punishment, authority and obedience, in nineteenth-century Germany.

I

The Prussian Convicts' Journey
to Siberia

Aschenbrenner's Authentic History

Criminal autobiographies are unusual at any time and in any form. Among the most unusual of all is a now forgotten narrative penned by the notorious forger and adventurer Wilhelm Aschenbrenner and published in Berlin in 1804 after its author had been deported to the mines of Siberia. Born in Gross-Glogau, in Silesia, the Aschenbrenner presented in this 'authentic', third-person narration is the son of a former Polish officer turned businessman. After serving in the Prussian artillery, he is invalided out and becomes tutor to the son of an officer stationed in Kulm, West Prussia. Here he obtains employment teaching in the army cadet school and acting as its quartermaster. A talented artist, he also gives the cadets private drawing and painting lessons. Marriage is quickly followed by the birth of two children, and all seems to be going well. But the upkeep of a growing family, the need to pay off the debts his father has left to his widowed mother, and the expense of buying books, canvas, artist's materials and other equipment lead inexorably to mounting debts. A new director at the cadet school stops his private teaching activities, and Aschenbrenner's attempts to earn money by painting and selling landscape views of West Prussia cost him more money than they bring in. His wife's parents are also burdened with debt and unable to help. Aschenbrenner's family falls into poverty. 'The blooming, happy and playful children had turned into creeping shadows, whimpering for bread.' Aschenbrenner borrows from friends and pawns his wife's jewels, but all to no avail. Given a 500-Thaler banknote by the cadet school director to take to the bank, he succumbs to temptation, copies it and goes to a bank in Liebstadt to cash it using a false name. 'He aspired to be a father, husband, son, and honest repayer of his debts; he wanted to fulfil his duties as such: noble intention, noble resolve. – But the choice of means – poverty weakened his judgement, his heart alone still acted.'[1]

It is not long, continues the narrative, before the law catches up with Wilhelm Aschenbrenner and he is tried and sentenced to seven years' imprisonment in the fortress in Königsberg, the punishment reserved for high-status offenders as a mild alternative to incarceration in one of Prussia's rotting gaols. Forgery is considered a serious offence and in the worst cases is still punishable by death, so he has in fact got off rather lightly. His wife stands by him, and there is general sympathy for the plight which has led him to commit his crime. The general support he gets from the population is eventually expressed in the arrival one day of a mysterious stranger outside his cell window. Attracting Aschenbrenner's attention through the barred but glassless opening, he passes a parcel through it containing cash, false identity papers and a file. Aschenbrenner loses no time in filing through the bars and climbing out onto the street, whereupon he is met by another mysterious man, wrapped in a cloak, who takes him to the nearby Baltic port of Pillau and puts him on a ship bound for Denmark. Taking up residence in Copenhagen, Aschenbrenner tries to support himself by selling his paintings, but continues to live beyond his means and is soon confronted with a familiar mountain of bills from shoemakers, tailors, grocers and suppliers. Inevitably, he succumbs to temptation and forges some more banknotes. Equally inevitably, the Danish authorities discover the forgeries and he is once more arrested. Again he finds the sympathy of friends, who send him money with which he bribes his gaoler and escapes. Accompanied now by a Danish servant supplied him by the thoughtful prison warder, Aschenbrenner makes his way back to Berlin, hoping to take advantage of a general amnesty issued to offenders on the accession of the new King, Friedrich Wilhelm III. But a lawyer advises him that his case is not covered by the amnesty, and he determines to leave again, this time for France, with the aid of money raised by the simple expedient of altering the figure '100 Thalers' on a banknote to '10,000' and cashing it in.[2]

While Aschenbrenner is putting the finishing touches to his new forgery, he looks out of the window and sees a beautiful young girl being beaten by an older woman outside a house across the road. His landlord informs him the house is a notorious brothel. Driven once more – he asserts in his autobiography – by the noblest of motives, he rescues the girl. Back in his room, the girl, Wilhelmine O., tells him she was being forced into prostitution by indebtedness, even though she is only sixteen. Aschenbrenner buys her out of the brothel with the proceeds of his forgery and decides to take her to her mother in Magdeburg on his way to Paris. The forger's relationship with the prostitute now moves to the centre of the narrative. Aschenbrenner's account emphasizes repeatedly the propriety of his own behaviour in these circumstances, but manages to do so in a way that is both suspenseful and titillating:

As he was approaching the exit from Berlin through the Halle Gate by the lengthy Friedrichstrasse, he began to feel a sense of embarrassment about how he should explain the girl's presence to the duty officer on the gate, and to the landlords with whom they would lodge on the journey. He asked her whether she would prefer to pass as his wife, his sister or his cousin and as which she would like to be treated along the way. She chose the first, and with good reason, for she considered that travelling as his sister or cousin would expose her to the embarrassment of receiving unwelcome attentions from other gentlemen.

Travelling with Wilhelmine as his wife, sleeping in the same room with her and being covered from time to time with her kisses of gratitude, Aschenbrenner confesses that his desire for her is difficult to master. But – he says – he remains true to his wife, and after passing a forged banknote in Leipzig, arranges to send Wilhelmine on to her mother in Magdeburg. However, she now refuses to leave him: 'Say, think what you will,' she says: 'My – ah, I cannot hold back this confession any longer!' *She takes his hand, presses it to her heart, and with an indescribable look and a flush on her face she continues:* 'to my heart you are everything!' Only at this point does Aschenbrenner, in a lengthy and passionate exchange which soon has them addressing each other with the intimate pronoun, '*du*', confess that he is married and in trouble with the law. His companion's response is to declare undying loyalty to him all the same. 'The world', she declares, '. . . must take me for your brother . . . I'm going to cast off my woman's clothing today and change it for a man's.'[3]

Following on the passing of the forgery in Leipzig, the disguised Wilhelmine accompanies the author to Amsterdam, which is at that time occupied by French revolutionary troops, from whom Aschenbrenner obtains work drawing maps. Meanwhile, Wilhelmine falls ill and, thinking she is dying, confesses she is not the innocent her rescuer has taken her for, but a fallen woman who gave birth to an illegitimate child at the age of 14. After further tearful scenes, Aschenbrenner, the narrative relates, generously forgives her deception. More adventures follow, as the two ascend in a balloon to spy out and chart the disposition of the English ships blockading the mouth of the Texel, try to run the blockade with Wilhelmine disguised as a naval cadet, and become involved in a fight with an English warship. Back on land, Aschenbrenner finally succumbs to guilt at having left his wife and family, and to despair at his overall plight:

'My most beautiful dreams are over. – Instead of the fame I wanted to conquer for myself, I will be branded by shame. Instead of enjoying domestic bliss in the quiet circle of my family, I am compelled to flee from country to country, from sea to sea, from one part of the world to another, like a timid, hunted animal; and still to be happy enough when I succeed even in doing that, and avoid pining away amidst all the horrors of the deepest misery of a dreadful dungeon.'

Overcome by melancholy, he picks up a gun and at midnight goes out into the garden of the house where he is staying with Wilhelmine. The latter follows him, worried about his intentions.

> Suddenly he raised his right hand with the pistol up to his face, so quickly that he was able to pull the trigger before she could rush over and prevent him. Terrible was the sight of his face in this moment, lit up by the flash of the powder-flame: it revealed an expression of total desperation. 'Oh God! Oh God!' cried Minna – he sank down, robbed of his senses.

But only the powder has ignited: the bullet has not gone off. Wilhelmine brings the would-be suicide back to consciousness by discharging the gun close to his ear and, recovering the bullet from the tree in which it has embedded itself, wears it suspended over her heart on a silken cord from this moment on.[4]

The pace in no way slackens after fate decrees that Aschenbrenner should live on. Offered a job teaching in America, our hero first travels with his servant and companion back to Hamburg, suffering storm and shipwreck on the way, with the intention of fetching his wife and family for the journey across the Atlantic to a new life overseas. The local newspapers in Hamburg, however, are carrying the story of the forged banknote he has passed in Leipzig, and descriptions of his appearance are circulating. Moreover, Wilhelmine is known to the Prussian ambassador, whom she has previously met in Berlin (where, and under what circumstances, Aschenbrenner, perhaps prudently, does not reveal). Disguising himself as a Polish officer ('all the arts of rendering him unrecognizable were applied'), he goes to the ambassador and succeeds in obtaining a Prussian pass for his further journey to Danzig. At this point, however, his Danish servant – who has long resented having to wait on the 'whorehouse miss', as he calls her, has tried on numerous occasions to seduce her and has had many quarrels with his employer – betrays them to the authorities in the hope of a reward. They are arrested and taken to Berlin, where Aschenbrenner this time is treated as a common criminal of the lowest sort:

> He was given as his night quarters a miserable wooden plank bed without any bedding at all, in a tiny cell, where a base and brutal man swarming with vermin had been lying in chains for months, and because the man was unable to move from the cell, he had an open pail next to him, which befouled the air in the most revolting manner . . . Here he was obliged completely to undress . . . He was only allowed the absolutely minimum necessary covering. . . . He was addressed in the third person, and before he had even been interrogated, he was told as he came in that they were already completely convinced of the veracity of the accusations raised against him; if he contradicted them even in the tiniest respect, he could expect to be whipped.

Only after some time is he finally recognized as one of the *Eximierten*, the legally defined status-group of non-noble gentlemen, and thus treated more leniently than common prisoners – so leniently, indeed, that the friendly prison inspector lets Wilhelmine spend the day in his cell and on numerous occasions even takes him out into the city (disguised in hat and cloak) to see performances of dramas by his favourite playwright, August von Kotzebue.[5]

This situation does not last, however. The friendly inspector dies, and Wilhelmine is imprisoned with a group of women who 'do not belong to the moral classes'. The narrative alternates skilfully between the titillating story of their constant attempts to corrupt her and Aschenbrenner's growing sickness, melancholia and despair. Finally suffering a nervous collapse, he is cared for by the devoted Wilhelmine, who is released from prison and takes up dressmaking to earn money to support him. She brings him food and supplies to his cell and does her best to keep up his steadily declining morale. The story ends with her gradual abandonment of Aschenbrenner and her engagement to 'a well-off young baker's son', and with the forger's continued suffering as he succumbs once more to 'nervous fever' on learning that he has been sentenced to 20 years' in the Spandau fortress for the Leipzig forgery, in addition to having to serve out the rest of the seven years to which he had previously been condemned in Königsberg. His attempts to support himself in Spandau by selling his paintings and drawings and writing plays meet with little success, and his living conditions deteriorate once more after a bankrupt courtier visits him, commissions him to forge another banknote and is discovered by the authorities. Aschenbrenner is deprived of his painting equipment, chained up in a tiny cell, then put to building work with the common criminals and threatened with a beating. 'His lot grew ever more unbearable.' In 1799, he is sentenced to two more years for allegedly forging false papers for the courtier. Unable to make the money to pay for food, light and firewood, he is now constantly ill and only survives thanks to the generosity of a new patron, the land agent and syndic of the Uckermark knighthood, Herr Stilke, who has taken pity on his plight. It is at this point that Aschenbrenner decides to raise money by writing his memoirs, and Stilke may well have been the anonymous friend to whom he eventually entrusted them for publication.[6]

Yet the story's outline is broadly confirmed by the description of Aschenbrenner drawn up by the Spandau fortress authorities in 1801 and based on admissions obtained from him under interrogation. They noted that he had initially been sentenced to seven years for forging banknotes to the sum of 12,000 Thalers, which he then pawned for a considerable sum of money. Aschenbrenner had fled to Copenhagen, 'where he devoted himself to painting and acting', while continuing with his forgeries. Arrested once more in Copenhagen, he had then, according to the official account, again confirming his own story, escaped to Berlin and carried on producing forged

banknotes and swindling merchants in various German towns, notably
Leipzig. The official documents also substantiated his suggestion that he had
eventually been caught in Hamburg, where he had been living under an
assumed name, and sentenced to a further 20 years in prison. All this backed
up Aschenbrenner's basic story, at least in outline, and confirmed that he was
faced with a total sentence of 27 years' fortress arrest, which he had begun
serving in Spandau in 1799. His behaviour in Spandau was said to be 'very
unsettled' and he was alleged to have been the brains behind a number of
'escape plots'. Coupled with the threat he posed to society by his talents as a
forger, this had led to the prison governor's demand for his deportation to
Siberia.[7]

Aschenbrenner's story reveals a good deal about life in Germany in the late
eighteenth century: the role of honour and propriety in relations between the
sexes, the ease with which banknotes and papers could be forged and passed
off as genuine, the fact that such forgeries were bound eventually to be
discovered, the need for an educated criminal to describe his own moral
career in favourable terms, the harshness of imprisonment, and the unequal
way in which offenders of different classes were treated and expected to be
treated. Nevertheless, it does nothing to answer the key question: what was
Aschenbrenner doing in Siberia? The point of the story, and the occasion for
its publication, after all, was Aschenbrenner's deportation there. In suffering
this fate, the forger was in no sense on his own. On the contrary, he was sent
as part of a large batch of convict deportees, the vast majority of whom were
of a class and background which Aschenbrenner had already found objectionable when he had been confined with some of them in the fortress at
Spandau.

The Deportees

Wilhelm Aschenbrenner's name was one of 50 included on an initial detailed
list of convicts for deportation to Siberia drawn up in March 1801, when
prison governors all over Prussia had been instructed to select the most serious
and incorrigible offenders convicted of arson, robbery, theft or deception,
provided that they were healthy and had a strong constitution.[8] According to
the royal order to this effect, issued on 28 February 1801, it had become
necessary to deport

such criminals as must be removed beyond the boundaries of the country
because they have become a threat to the security of the commonwealth,
because they use every kind of violent means to set themselves free from
captivity, and because up to now they have completely frustrated the mission
of penal institutions to reform their fellow-prisoners by their wicked example
and the lessons they impart in pernicious arts. The best people to judge who

belongs among the number of such incorrigible villains are the commanders of the fortresses and the governors of the penitentiaries and workhouses or correctional institutions, so the most appropriate course is therefore to require them via the authorities immediately superior to them immediately to submit a list of the men under their supervision who have been condemned to life imprisonment, with notes on the crimes committed, the age, the physical constitution, and the previous behaviour in prison of each of them.[9]

There was a total of 575 prisoners in all of Prussia's gaols and fortresses put together, of whom 188 were soldiers and the rest civilians. Ninety-eight of them were serving life, 162 over ten years, 292 between three and ten years, and 23 were incarcerated on the King's orders without having undergone a formal legal trial and condemnation.[10] By the end of the year, the list of deportees was having to be revised because some prisoners had 'deserted', some had died, and the friends and relatives of others were pressing the authorities to excuse them because they allegedly lacked the strength for the journey.[11] A longer summary list was drawn up, consisting of 77 names.[12] Sixty-seven of the 77 had been sentenced for robbery, though some (12) had been sentenced for murder, and a handful (four) for deserting the colours, arson (five), fraud (one) or rape (one); a few had been sentenced for more than one of these offences, which accounts for the fact that the figures of crimes add up to more than the total of offenders. The oldest man was 54, the youngest 21; five of them were aged 50 or over, 21 were in their forties; 30 in their thirties; and 20 in their twenties; the average age was just over 35.[13]

The initial detailed list of 50 gives a much clearer indication of the kind of felon selected for transportation than these bare statistics can manage to convey: often the short biographies appended to each name were graphic in detail and redolent of the fears and frustrations of the authorities in the vivid language they used. Among these men, Aschenbrenner was clearly an exception, because of both his educated background and the nature of his crime. Characteristic of the type of prisoner selected for deportation was Johann Friedrich Crantz, aged 40, who had behind him a long career of crime. He had committed 144 thefts before reaching the age of 16, and had been repeatedly imprisoned – in 1780, 1783, 1794 and 1796, the second of the sentences being for ten years. After his last sentence he managed to escape, was rearrested in 1797 and escaped again, subsequently evading capture until 1799, when he was detained at the King's pleasure for robbery with violence. With this record of crime, imprisonment and escape, he seemed an ideal candidate for deportation. There were other violent offenders too, such as Johann Adamski, also aged 40, who had shot a man on a country road for refusing him 'a pinch of tobacco', and Albrecht Sigismund, aged 23, who

in the 20th year of his life robbed and murdered a Jew on the public highway. Since he knew that the same intended to walk to a neighbouring village, he followed him one evening in the darkness, and caught up with him in a spruce wood. He asked the Jew where he was intending to go to, and when the latter had answered him, he seized from him the stick the man was carrying and struck him with it three times over the head with such force that it snapped in two and the Jew fell bleeding to the ground. Thereupon he hit him twice more on the back of the neck with the piece of the stick still in his hand, and robbed him of his purse, which contained three Thalers. He left the Jew lying there, and it was only after several days that pieces of the man's body were found, torn off (by wild beasts).

Sigismund had been condemned to hard labour for life, and was proposed for deportation by the court in Bromberg because of the violent nature of his crime.

Some of the deportees were family men, like the 43-year-old Franz Hübner, who 'ha[d] a wife and four children' and had sought to support them by thieving. A good number of those listed had obviously been marked down as incorrigible by virtue of prolonged careers of thieving and crime. One, the 44-year-old vagabond Franz Schulz, was described as 'a person who has spent his entire life in crime'; another, the 39-year-old vagabond Andreas Conrad Siedentopf, was even more clearly incapable of improvement:

This person, whose brutality makes him extremely dangerous, was already condemned to hard labour for life in a fortress in 1789 for highway robbery and a mass of violent and other thefts. In 1798 he was given remission, and his sentence reduced to 10 years, with the usual threat that if he fell back into his previous criminal ways, he would be imprisoned for life once more. But although his relations took him in after his release and gave him the opportunity to earn a living, he preferred a wandering life, committed several burglaries and break-ins, and tried to rape three female persons on the public highway, for which purpose he struck one of the same on the head with a stone wrapped in a cloth, in order to render her unconscious and incapable of resistance.

On his eventual arrest, Siedentopf had been condemned to 'hard labour for life in a fortress with corporal punishment and certification as unsuited for clemency' and incarcerated in Magdeburg in 1800.

Among the most desperate and violent of the felons selected for transportation were a number of 'dishonourable people', men cut off from respectable society by the dirty and polluting nature of their trade. Such people provided a good number of the criminals who came before the courts in the late eighteenth and early nineteenth centuries as much because of their conspicuousness as because of their criminality. In the hierarchical society of *ancien régime* Prussia, where status was rigidly defined by heredity, there were whole groups of people who were denied the right to guild membership and an honourable occupation because they belonged to 'infamous' clans and families. They were treated as polluting because their jobs, or those of their parents and relatives, involved handling wild or diseased animals, working with dirty and smelly materials, or living far beyond the bounds of civilization, in the remotest depths of the vast forests or upland heaths that covered so much of Central Europe at this time: knackers, skinners, molecatchers, tanners, lepers, prostitutes, shepherds, charcoal-burners and the like. Ethnic and religious minorities such as gypsies and Jews were also included in this category. Even the touch of these people could be polluting, and required a special ceremony to restore the honour of the guildsman or citizen who had been sullied by physical contact with such a person. Although not all of these people were poor – executioners and knackers, for example, though dishonourable, were usually able to make a decent living for themselves – they all lived on the margins of society, usually indeed in a literal as well as a figurative sense, and for the vast majority of them, this meant that they lived their lives on a knife-edge between survival and destitution. They had few rights, and were often the object of widespread social suspicion and distrust which found its expression in the close attention paid to them by law enforcement agencies. All these factors not only encouraged criminal activity when the opportunity arose, but also ensured that they showed up disproportionately among the numbers of those arrested and punished for misdemeanours. Even in prison, moreover, such people were generally segregated from the rest until well into the nineteenth century.[14]

Among people of this sort singled out by the Prussian authorities for deportation to Siberia at the beginning of the nineteenth century was Anton Leikowski, aged 49, who, said the compiler of the list,

> was a slovenly individual from youth onwards, and went into service with a knacker, whereupon he was completely cast out by his family. His brother refused to give him shelter: he concealed himself therefore in a shed, with the intention of murdering his brother. When he was prevented [by circumstances] from doing this, he decided to kill the serving-boy of the lessee in whose shed he was hiding, thought about this plan for two days, and carried it out with a fence-post. He was condemned to death but this sentence was commuted as indicated across the page [i.e. to hard labour for life in a fortress].

Similarly, the knacker's servant Johann Stegemann, aged 31, described as 'a very evil person', had admitted over 50 offences of robbery, mostly with violence. He 'has lived for a long time from stealing, and had connections with the most notorious thieves'. While carrying out a robbery in a village near Stettin, 'together with a certain Stresemann', he had murdered two children aged four and 13. He had only been spared execution because he had withdrawn his confession and denied that the murders were deliberate. This cast an oblique light on the status of confessions in Prussian law. Although judicial torture had been abolished in the course of the eighteenth century, the judicial procedures which accompanied it remained essentially unaltered: criminal trials in Prussia did not take place in public, before a jury, but were held behind locked doors, and consisted mainly of an exchange of documents between judges, lawyers and university legal specialists. Evidence and witnesses were used not so much to prove or disprove a case in the trial itself, as to bring pressure to bear on the accused during the investigatory part of the procedure, when the matter was handled by an 'investigating judge' whose report would form the basis for the main trial decision later on. The object of all this was to bring the offender to confess and, if this failed, legal opinion in Prussia was inclined to the view that the verdict was less than 100 per cent firm. This situation continued, despite mounting criticism, throughout the whole of the first half of the nineteenth century and, as a result, death sentences passed after trials in which the investigating judge had failed to extract a confession from the accused were generally likely to be commuted to life imprisonment by the King on the advice of his Justice Ministry.[15] Hence it was that Johannes Stegemann ended in prison rather than on the scaffold.

As well as the deportees who were regarded as infamous because of their trade or occupation, a number of the prisoners singled out for deportation to Siberia were also treated as dishonourable because they had suffered corporal punishment of various kinds. This would in practice have made it difficult for them to have found work after release. Such punishments were carried out in public, at the pillory, and involved the open degradation of the offender before a crowd, effected both through the touch of the executioner and his servants and through the visible marks left on his face or body afterwards. For Gottlieb Friedrich Breitenfeld, a 27-year-old convict on the Siberian transport who had been sentenced in 1798 to 'whipping, branding and hard labour for life in a fortress', for example, the chances of earning a living other than by thieving would have been small. His dishonour was scorched on his face by the branding-iron. Gatekeepers in every town would see the mark on his cheek and know not to let him in. Prospective employers would recognize him as dishonourable and turn him away. For such men, there were in practice few alternatives to a life of crime. Imprisonment in this period was only one of a number of penal sanctions employed in Prussia, and public corporal punishments were still very much a part of the state's arsenal of crime-control methods. Branding and the public whipping, known as *Staupenschlag*, were regarded as the severest forms of corporal punishment, bar execution.[16] A soldier by trade, Breitenfeld admitted over 30 break-ins carried out as a member of a gang while he was still in military service, which accounted for the severity of his punishment.[17]

Many of the criminals on the list of deportees had military experience, not surprising in Prussia, where the army was the most important state institution. But the nature of their experience often testified to the fluidity of state boundaries and allegiances at this time, before national identities became really influential. The labourer Johann Gottlieb Schulze, aged 30, who had originally been an apprentice shoemaker, had set his master's premises on fire and been condemned to six years in gaol for this offence. On his release, he had met up with some former fellow-prisoners in Berlin and embarked on a career of robbery with violence, which had been ended by another prison sentence. Subsequently he had enlisted in the Swedish army, deserted, and worked as a cattle drover, before returning to Berlin and carrying out further robberies. He had begun a 15-year sentence in Spandau in 1800 and at age 30 was recommended for deportation by the local court. One of his fellow-inmates, Gottfried Ludwig Pfeiffer, a 40-year-old artilleryman who had begun a ten-year sentence in 1794, was another deserter from the Swedish army as well as from the Prussian. He was described as an 'incorrigible and dangerous person'. He had posed as a flower-seller in order to gain the opportunity to commit thefts and was imprisoned for robbery. 'In November 1798, however,' as the official notes on his case recorded, 'he succeeded in escaping from the fortress and thereafter he travelled around the countryside and committed several robberies in company with other notorious thieves.' He was eventually captured and taken 'back to Spandau, where he has committed the grossest excesses'.

A good number of the prisoners had been sentenced by the military rather than the civil authorities. The day-labourer Ludwig Christian Friedrich Bolke, for example, had already been punished in the Prussian army for his 'thefts and other excesses' before being cashiered, and had subsequently been arrested and imprisoned 'for his slovenly way of life'. The prison inspector at Magdeburg described him as 'crafty'. The 46-year-old soldier Johann Albrecht, said the notes on the men selected for deportation, 'is one of the most dangerous and uncontrollable of villains'. He had attacked fellow-prisoners in Danzig with a knife, 'and is said to have sworn even in cold blood that it was his desire to die upon the wheel, provided that he had been able to do still more evil beforehand'.[18] Yet he was certified nonetheless to be 'of completely sound mind'. During his life he had served in the armies of France, England, Spain and Austria. He had ended his service in the Prussian forces by physically assaulting a non-commissioned officer. Such a man was clearly among the most dangerous of the prisoners, far tougher and more violent than the majority of the civilian offenders, most of whom had only been convicted of theft. By contrast, Matthias Wrajewski, aged 30, had served only nine months in the Prussian army before he 'deserted, . . . allegedly out of fear of the coming war'. After his desertion he had lived by theft, but his crimes had involved no serious element of armed violence, perhaps 'because he had cut off the index finger of his right hand, in order to render himself unfit for further military service'. Such a single-minded distaste for military service was considered particularly dangerous in Prussia, the most military of all European states of the period, and it was hardly surprising that Wrajewski was singled out for transportation despite the lack of complaints about his behaviour in prison. It was clear from these and a number of other brief biographies of the deportees that the prison authorities were intent on ridding themselves not only of those malefactors whose behaviour in prison had been particularly disruptive or disobedient, who had a 'very bad reference' from the prison authorities, who had tried to escape, or who had otherwise made a nuisance of themselves, but also of those malefactors whom they felt were likely to reoffend on release, and often in a 'dangerous' (i.e. violent or, in cases such as Wrajewski, morally dangerous) manner.[19]

The vast majority of the prisoners were uneducated, in lowly and often dishonourable manual occupations such as day-labouring, rat-catching, farm work and the like. A few were skilled craftsmen such as cobblers or tailors, but only a couple were higher up the social scale. None was of such high status as Wilhelm Aschenbrenner. The 37-year-old Pomeranian commercial scribe Paul Tarnow was one of the few other educated men on the list. Unusually, he had been convicted and sentenced to death for a crime of passion – the manslaughter of his superior, a civil servant named Truchs, who had treated him badly and aroused his jealousy through his relationship with an officer's widow. Tarnow was on the list because his conduct in prison, at Friedrichsberg, was said to have been poor.[20] These artisans and better-off offenders mostly lacked the long criminal records of the majority of the designated deportees; what got them onto the list was their bad behaviour in prison. Among them was the 49-year-old schoolmaster and tailor Carl Rungenhagen, who had only begun his sentence of life imprisonment with hard labour in a fortress in 1801; it had been commuted from a sentence of death for burning down a house and farm buildings, with the animals in them, belonging to someone who had filed a lawsuit against him, a crime that he was unlikely to have repeated in the future. But although he did not seem to pose a threat to society, Rungenhagen was clearly an irritation to his gaolers, and so he too went onto the list of deportees. Arson was a common crime, easy enough to carry out in a country where the abundance of wood meant that buildings, houses, farms and indeed whole towns were constructed of highly flammable materials. It was therefore considered extremely dangerous, and where it led to loss of life, as it often did, it was punishable by death. This was still carried out in such cases by burning at the stake even after the beginning of the nineteenth century. Although in practice such offenders were given a 'merciful death' by being strangled immediately before the pyre was lit, the authorities continued to consider it necessary to carry out the punishment as a very public and obviously symbolic warning of the fate that awaited murderous arsonists.[21]

In small farming communities arson was frequently the result of jealousies and rivalries over marriages.[22] It was not surprising, therefore, that arsonists often came from relatively respectable backgrounds. According to Prussian judicial officials, another fire-raiser on the Siberian transport, the 26-year-old shoemaker Christian Friedrich Burow,

> intended to marry a somewhat elderly peasant woman, in order thereby to come into possession of her farm. But he was convicted of a theft at a fair, so the widow's relations strongly opposed the marriage. Hereupon he set light to the farm buildings one evening between 9 and 10 o'clock, because he believed that the widow would need a man for the rebuilding and would therefore definitely marry him. In this way he caused 2000 Th[alers'] damage and was malicious enough under interrogation to blame a completely innocent person for inciting his deed.[23]

Other than this admittedly calculated crime and the theft which led to it, Burow had no criminal record and his conduct in prison was not thought bad enough to merit particular mention. Nevertheless, it was probably the fact that his sentence had been commuted from death, and the general threat which arson was thought to pose to life, property and social stability, which led to his name being placed on the list. Another, similar case was that of the 27-year-old farmhand Johann Gottfried, who

> carried out a premeditated act of arson together with a serving-maid, resulting in damage to the sum of over 2000 Th. The two were having a love-affair which was the occasion for frequent reproaches from the farmer's wife who employed her. This caused the maid to run away from her service, but she was brought back. This provided a prime stimulus for resentment against their masters, and led them to decide on the act of arson, incited by Gottfried.[24]

The governor of the fortress at Pillau considered Gottfried eminently qualified for transportation, despite the very particular and probably non-repeatable circumstances of his crime. Arson against a social superior was considered to be especially reprehensible.

In the case of Wilhelm Aschenbrenner himself, the forgery of banknotes was also considered a particularly dangerous offence; Aschenbrenner showed no sign of abandoning his habit of forgery if he was released; and he was also making a nuisance of himself in Spandau with his continual complaints about the conditions under which he was held. It was no surprise, therefore, that the authorities were glad of the opportunity to be rid of him too.

'*Deterrent Examples*'

Aschenbrenner's case reflected a much wider policy that had its origins in the judicial reforms of Frederick the Great in the mid-to-late eighteenth century. Beginning in the 1740s, the Prussian state had gradually replaced capital and corporal punishments with custodial sentences, in the interests of a rational, graded, effective and, as the state argued, humane administration of the criminal law. Many of the old corporal punishments and physical mutilations handed out under the previous law, which loosely followed the *Constitutio Criminalis Carolina* promulgated under the Holy Roman Emperor Charles V in 1532, were thought by 'Enlightened' monarchs such as Frederick to be so cruel as to arouse the sympathy of the watching crowd, and thus to frustrate their deterrent purpose. Only the most serious of offences, it was now argued, should be punished by death. Petty thieving, burglary, even highway robbery, banditry and arson, so long as they were not accompanied by murder or manslaughter, were accordingly removed from the roster of capital offences.[25] In sharp contrast to England, where the 'Bloody Code' continued to require the hanging of a man for stealing a sheep or a sixpence well into the 1830s, the criminal law in most parts of Germany and especially in Prussia had abandoned the death penalty for almost every crime apart from homicide and treason half a century before. While petty offenders in town and country continued to face the sanction of corporal punishment for minor infringements of the law, therefore, serious offenders whose crimes stopped short of murder or first-degree manslaughter now began to be put into custody for lengthy periods of time instead.

The new custodial sentences were designed not only to deter potential offenders and to mete out retribution to convicted criminals, but also to remove offenders from society until they were fit to rejoin it. In the absolutist regime of eighteenth-century Prussia, where there was no parliament and no independent judiciary to raise such awkward questions as the entitlement of the citizen to freedom from arbitrary arrest, to establish such inconvenient principles as the right of *habeas corpus*, or to contest the practice of arrest and imprisonment without trial, it was left to the state to prescribe how this should be done. It proceeded with a fine disregard for all the fundamental civil rights which were being enunciated by contemporaries in other countries, such as the American Declaration of Independence of 1776 or the Declaration of the Rights of Man and Citizen passed by the French Revolutionary Assembly in 1791. The Prussian General Law Code of 1794, the summation of Friederician penal policy, contained provisions not only for the punishment but also for the indefinite detention without trial or formal sentence of thieves and recidivists until they had reformed and could demonstrate their capacity to make an honest living on release. The Code represented the ambition of enlightened absolutism to reshape society along rational lines, and although it had been conceived well before the French Revolution of 1789, the final version reflected increasing concern on the part of the senior bureaucrats who ran the civil administration of the Prussian state that it should eliminate abuses and reorganize the administration of justice in order to help immunize Prussian society against democratizing influence. In this sense, it looked forward to the far more radical reforms which were

pushed through after Prussia's ignominious defeat by Napoleon in 1805–06.
The rights of the individual citizen, however, were accorded scant respect in
the 1794 Code and in the supplementary orders which followed it.[26] In a
Circular Rescript on the Punishment of Theft, promulgated in 1799, the
Prussian state reiterated its policy of gaoling potential recidivists without trial,
basing the right of indefinite incarceration on its claim, characteristic of the
absolutist despotisms of the day, that it had a duty to protect its citizens against
harm. Thieves and repeat offenders were to be detained if they were found
to have a 'criminal cast of mind' and to pose a threat to society, and only
released when they had 'improved themselves' in the judgement of the prison
and state authorities. This so-called 'right of special deterrence', defended by
Prussian legal scholars such as Karl von Grolmann, meant in practice detention on grounds no stronger than suspicion. Although strongly criticized by
other legal theorists, such as the great Bavarian legal and penal reformer Paul
Anselm von Feuerbach, for detaching the punishment from the crime, it
continued to be employed as a policy by the Prussian authorities for many
years to come.[27]

The Circular Rescript of 1799 was designed above all to counter what was
generally agreed to be a crime wave of unprecedented proportions afflicting
Germany in the last years of the eighteenth century. Contemporaries ascribed
this phenomenon above all to the influence of the French Revolutionary and
Napoleonic Wars. Writing in 1801, the Prussian Minister of State Albrecht
Heinrich von Arnim noted with patriotic emphasis that although these wars
had not yet swept over Prussia, their influence was nonetheless beginning to
be felt:

> Our prosperity and culture have increased, while our neighbours and those
> round about us have succumbed to the oppressive burdens of a devastating
> war. It is only too natural that this increased prosperity has attracted not merely
> good and respectable persons but comparatively far more idlers and knights of
> fortune from other lands to our country. They and many others who – partly
> through their own fault, partly not – have been impoverished in the war, wish
> to seek their fortune in a flourishing country. Villains who have become even
> more untamed in the war mingle amongst their number, and under these
> circumstances it is very easy to understand that the total number of criminals,
> and especially of those who commit crimes against the security of property, is
> increasing virtually daily.[28]

But in fact it was only later on that serious problems were posed by armies
sweeping across the country, living off the land, and spreading disorder. As
one observer noted in 1811:

> Every long-lasting war, every conquest and defeat of entire countries, has
> always had not only great and stormy effects, which have transformed the shape

of whole states, but also other, less obvious but just as melancholy influences on the various individual parts of civil society. At such moments, order is completely overthrown, violence alone rules; tranquil trade, industrious activity are robbed of every hope of success, legally acquired riches vanish, fortune favours only those who take risks and commit bold deceptions, and many a man becomes first a beggar and then from desperation a criminal . . . Swarms of dispossessed ruffians follow victorious as well as defeated armies, greedy for plunder . . . Swindles, thefts, highway robberies and murderous deeds multiply, indeed even the general revulsion against such crimes seems for a while to be diminished, for individual atrocities occur in masses . . . The establishment of public tranquillity and the maintenance of good order is most difficult on the borders of great states, above all where the government and its officials have changed . . . Thus it is no wonder that numerous gangs of murderers and robbers . . . have been infesting various localities in the last decade of the past century and the first of the present.[29]

The impact of war and revolution on Prussia in the 1790s was exaggerated by such observers. Prussian civil servants like Arnim might blame disorder on foreign vagrants and 'knights of fortune', but the truth was more complex. Vagrancy and the crime-wave associated with it reflected much longer-term changes in Prussian society east of the river Elbe. Beginning around the 1760s, a number of factors – the new growth of population in northern Germany, the increasing pace of urban expansion in Brandenburg, the growing demand of industrializing Britain for grain and food imports – led to a sharp and sustained rise in grain prices in trading centres such as Danzig. To take advantage of this, Junker landlords and rural seigneurs in Prussia began to expand their demesnes, enclose common land for grain production and replace their serfs with landless labourers whom they could hire and fire at will; for landed peasants gave their labour only with reluctance, and resisted fresh demands on their time with such ferocity that the 1790s saw a rash of peasant uprisings in many parts of Prussia as a consequence.

Between 1750 and 1800, the number of families of landless labourers in the province of East Prussia more than doubled, while that of peasants grew by no more than two-fifths. At the end of the eighteenth century there were twice as many landless labourers in the Kurmark district of Brandenburg as there were landed peasants. The situation in West Prussia was broadly similar. Peasants were losing their land, and were being forced out of common pasture and arable land which was vital to their subsistence. No wonder the number of landless beggars and itinerants was on the increase. Social and economic changes endemic to Prussian society – changes of which the class represented by men such as Arnim and other members of the Prussian aristocracy were taking every advantage they could – were behind the growth in vagabondage. It had very little to do with war and revolution. Neither did the crisis of urban trade and artisanal production which hit Prussia in the

1790s as a series of bad harvests added to the long-term rise in grain prices which forced people to spend yet more of their income on food and cut back on consumer goods. Urban as well as rural trades were represented among the occupations of those felons listed for transportation to Siberia. The crime wave which swept across Prussia in the 1790s hit the towns just as much as it hit the countryside.[30]

The Circular Rescript of 1799 was designed to stop this increase in crime by introducing tougher penal sanctions. Both the new attitude to offenders and the continuing rise in property crime were reflected in the figures for prosecutions for such offences, which increased in Berlin from 423 in 1798 to 623 in 1799 and 637 in 1800.[31] This policy immediately achieved a sharp increase in the numbers of offenders sent to prison. Their numbers had been growing for some time as a result of the legal reforms instituted by Friedrich II. Yet the construction of new prisons had by no means kept pace with the increase in the prison population.[32] Many offenders were incarcerated in *Festungen*, military bases or fortresses, like Spandau, where Wilhelm Aschenbrenner was held. The common, severe punishment of 'hard labour in a fortress for life' (*lebenswierige Festungsarbeit*) simply meant that these offenders were used as a source of cheap labour for repairing the physical fabric of the buildings and fortifications. Much later on, these fortresses were reserved for a very small number of upper-class offenders, for example officers and aristocrats involved in fatal duels, as a way of accommodating them in relative comfort and without the degrading aspects of conventional imprisonment. At the end of the eighteenth century and the beginning of the nineteenth, however, the Prussian state felt it had little option but to employ the fortresses for the purpose of imprisoning violent criminals who in earlier decades would have gone to the scaffold. They were not really designed to hold large numbers of dangerous felons. The buildings had not been constructed with security in mind, and the maintenance of prisoners was only one among a number of different, primarily military functions which these institutions had to carry out. The inmates, therefore, were relatively neglected, and there was no thought of trying to improve or discipline them.

By contrast, purpose-built penitentiaries (*Zuchthäuser*) had been constructed in Prussia and other German states in the late seventeenth and eighteenth centuries with the express aim of educating their inmates through hard work. The shortage of labour in eighteenth-century Germany had turned many of them into institutions resembling factories. During the 1790s, however, in the context of the economic depression which loomed over Europe in that decade, the demand for labour slackened off, and these prisons fell into disrepair. Criticisms began to be raised about the dirty and verminous conditions under which the prisoners lived.[33] Enlightened reformers inspired by the work of the Englishman John Howard demanded a wholesale reform of the prison system, in which imprisonment would become a vehicle for the improvement as well as the punishment of the offender.[34] At the same time as Prussian legal theory and practice were advocating indefinite imprisonment until inmates were fit to return to society, therefore, it was recognized that the conditions of imprisonment were making it less likely that this objective could be achieved. An official report noted:

> Under existing arrangements it has not been possible to realize the benevolent purposes of penal sanctions. Locking up offenders sentenced in this way in fortresses and prisons usually worsens their moral condition to such an extent that they are even more of a threat to public security after they have regained their freedom once more. The scum of the nation and of other countries too is piled up all together in these places, and villains who have reached the highest degree of depravity smother every spark of remorse in the newcomers and destroy the good intentions which some perhaps have otherwise resolved for the future . . . Furthermore it has not up to now been possible to determine the length of time after which it is permissible to set free criminals who have been dangerous to public security in the past, without being obliged to fear that such men will abuse their freedom in order to commit their evil deeds once more. The criminal judge has only been able to set the term of imprisonment in accordance with the severity of the offence.

Moreover, the numbers of offenders incarcerated in the prisons had increased to such an extent 'that there would long since have been a lack of space and a deficit in maintenance cost, if the frequent escape of prisoners had not considerably reduced their number.'[35]

Prison, penitentiaries and especially the ill-adapted fortresses were indeed all too easy to escape from, as Wilhelm Aschenbrenner's experience in Königsberg demonstrated. The official in charge of prisons in Silesia was forced to admit in 1800 that 'a mass of the most villainous and dangerous robbers and thieves' had escaped, set up 'bands' and 'put fear and terror into the heart of the countryman; indeed, even royal treasuries and deposit banks have not remained unscathed.'[36] The Prussian minister Albrecht von Arnim noted in 1801 that 346 inmates were known to have escaped from Prussia's gaols in 1800 alone; the true figure, he thought, was probably a good deal higher. The situation in the fortresses was particularly bad:

> Among others who escaped from Cösel in 1800 were *three* serious offenders, of whom two had been condemned to 12 years' and one to 20 years' imprisonment. The same was also the case in Schweidnitz in 1799 with *five* serious offenders, among whom one faced a 20-year prison sentence and another one of 18 years. Around the same time, an extremely dangerous offender condemned to 20 years' imprisonment absconded from Glatz, and *virtually all the members* of the well-known . . . highly dangerous Dillenburg gang of robbers, who had mostly been condemned to life imprisonment, escaped from Wesel. In the current year, 1801, *four* dangerous criminals have absconded from the

same prison again, and the previous year, *twelve* inmates escaped from Clarenburg in a single night by means of a forcible break-out. – In many penitentiaries and remand prisons the situation is no better. According to a report of 22nd November, among other things it was noted that since the 24th June 1798, no fewer than 35 prisoners had escaped from the penitentiary in Warsaw. On 25th July 1800, *three* notorious thieves liberated themselves from the penitentiary in Stettin by means of burrowing under the foundations, as was also the case with *six* criminals in the Bayreuth penitentiary in 1799. *Three* of the most enterprising villains absconded from the gaolhouse in Brieg in 1800, while *all the prisoners* except one escaped from Gleiwitz in a single night, among them one who had already been condemned to the wheel.[37]

Prisoners also commonly escaped while being transferred from remand after conviction. 'According to the figures, among the prisoners being transferred from the remand prison to the fortresses in Warsaw alone from October 1797 up to 1800,' noted Arnim, *'twenty-one* escaped on the way.'[38]

A major reason for this lack of security was the poor staffing of Prussia's prisons at this time. According to Arnim, there was a serious 'shortage of the necessarily, properly remunerated warders, overseers and other officials':

> In the penitentiary in Herford, where over a twelve-year period there have been on average 41 inmates, on occasion however up to 60, there is – apart from the inspector, who cannot really be counted since he is at the same time city director, and does not live on the premises – only one prison officer, his servant and a nurse in employment. The penitentiary in Magdeburg, where there have often been 80 to 90 criminals in residence at any one time, has to content itself with one manager, one officer and one master-spinner . . . The penitentiary at Königsberg in Prussia, which can hold almost 75 prisoners, has no officials other than an inspector, a scribe, a nightwatchman and a gate-keeper, who is at the same time also the warder.[39]

These were only a few examples from many: the situation, he said, was similar everywhere. Moreover, such posts were so badly paid that they were unable to attract properly qualified or able people. Indeed, they mostly seemed to be occupied by retired soldiers unable to do a proper job and looking for an easy post from which to live in their old age:

> The present gaoler in Schweidnitz, a most upright fellow, who served honestly as a soldier for many years and has occupied his present post most properly, has for some time been so sick and enfeebled that he is no longer able to carry out his duties, and indeed suffered the fate of being overcome by the prisoners, who took the prison key from him and so set themselves at liberty. Yet irrespective of this he is still obliged to stay at his post, and cannot be supported or accommodated anywhere else. – Tasks which in the nature of things

demand young and vigorous men are carried out instead in penal institutions
by old, feeble and worn-out men on whom one can in all fairness make no
demands, and some of whom, like the gaoler at Brieg, can neither read nor
write.[40]

Modest though the lifestyle of such men undoubtedly was, the miserable
salary still forced a large number of them to take other jobs outside the prison
in order to make ends meet.[41] Many also sought to augment their earnings by
selling food, clothing, tobacco, alcohol and other goods to the prisoners, and
not a few appropriated a portion of the prisoners' own earnings as 'payment'
for their maintenance.[42] In all prisons apart from the penitentiaries, inmates
had to pay for their food out of their own pockets. In Glatz at the turn of the
century, however, when the market for prison-produced goods was slack
because of the continuing economic depression, their earnings were so low
that the prison administration actually sent one inmate begging in the town
every Saturday for alms for the prisoners' clothing. All this exposed the
prisoners to the arbitrary power of the prison staff, Arnim thought, as well as
making discipline almost impossible to maintain.[43]

The resulting neglect of the prisons not only made it easy for inmates to
escape, but also made conditions extremely poor for those who remained.
Most prisons were unsuitably constructed for their function of maintaining
substantial numbers of people in a reasonably healthy state over lengthy
periods of time. The fortresses in particular were plagued by damp, and many
cells were small and badly ventilated. There were too many subterranean
dungeons, and heating was generally inadequate in the winter. Above all, they
were dirty and verminous. With the few staff often away on other jobs,
cleaning seldom took place, and prisons in general were well known as
breeding-places for 'vermin of all kinds'. Even in the penitentiaries, prisoners
were neither washed nor given fresh prison clothing on admittance. Scabies
was almost universal among inmates. A senior local administrator described
the prison in Minden as a 'cow-stall', while others were if possible even
worse. As Arnim reported:

> Among others who absconded from the mill-prison in Magdeburg this
> Summer was a dangerous thief who excused his flight merely by reference to
> the prison's filthiness and the excessive number of *vermin* present there. On
> investigation, his claim was found to be true and well-founded. The wood in
> the prison walls had rotted, and the vermin had nested in it and could not be
> removed. – In the Marienwerder town gaol, according to the words of the
> commendable provincial administrator there, the prisoners are covered in
> vermin of every kind, and this is only too easy to understand when one realizes
> that in this prison the warder only gets paid 2 Groschen a *week*, from which he
> has to purchase not only wood – very expensive there – for cooking meals for
> the prisoners, but also straw for their bedding.[44]

Sick prisoners were not isolated from the rest, thus facilitating the spread of disease. Malnutrition – bread was the staple diet of prisoners everywhere – made them more vulnerable to infection.

All these problems were greatly exacerbated at the turn of the eighteenth and nineteenth centuries by a sharp increase in the prison population as a result of the Circular Rescript of 26 February 1799. By 1801, the fortress in Spandau, where the forger Wilhelm Aschenbrenner was incarcerated, held 182 prisoners in accommodation intended for 165; in Colberg there were 34 inmates where the maximum capacity was supposed to be 18; Graudenz held 115 instead of the planned 66; Pillau 110 instead of the proper 50. Arnim complained that 'all our penal institutions are flooded with criminals, so that there is simply no more room there to accommodate them.'[45] There was, then, a real sense of crisis in Prussia's penal and law enforcement system, which gave rise to a considerable debate within the higher echelons of the bureaucracy. Already in 1799, at the time of the Circular Rescript, King Friedrich Wilhelm III had ordered two of his senior officials, Grand Chancellor von Goldbeck and minister von Arnim, to prepare a reform of the prisons, but by 1801 it had become apparent to him that the two men's views on the subject diverged widely from one another.[46] Attacking 'the total anarchy which rules in the management and administration of the prisons' as the root cause of the problems, Arnim proposed a wholesale centralization of penal administration, as well as the construction of a number of large, purpose-built prisons to replace the many small gaols currently in use. He advocated the separation of different kinds of prisoners into different institutions, as well as the removal of the insane, the destitute, the sick and orphans from prison premises. The prisons of his day, he considered, were 'schools of corruption', and it was common for hardened thieves to corrupt their fellow inmates as well as using their captivity to plan fresh robberies at their release. As such he reasoned that the professional criminal had to be separated from the others. He wanted the state to feed, clothe and maintain prisoners properly, but also to make their regime tougher, since he considered that 'idleness, an inclination to an easy life, and a tendency to disorder, are . . . the causes of most crimes.' Too many such prisoners were left to their own devices, he thought, so Arnim proposed an elaborate set of rules based on the ideals of hard work, regularity and orderliness. Moral improvement through education and religion was a lost cause in his view, for it merely encouraged outward conformity and thus hypocrisy among the inmates. Far better was to make them work, and thereby also to assist them to accumulate enough savings to make a proper fresh start on their release. As a preventive measure, Arnim also advocated the speeding-up of prosecutions so that punishment became a sharper and more immediate deterrent. He wanted tougher sentences for theft and complained of the reforms of Friedrich II that 'the softening came too quickly and at the wrong time.'[47]

Arnim proposed the supervision and control of released convicts as well as the reform of the prison. This had already been tried in 1797, when an elaborate official instruction had demanded that such individuals should only be released if they could show that they had a family and a job to go to. Local authorities were told to find them work, and employers instructed to take them on. Yet this would have imposed a considerable financial and administrative burden on the localities, and it is clear that many of them were reluctant to follow it. As for the requirement that prisoners had to return to their families on their release, the circumstances of men such as those included on the lists of Siberian deportees showed that this was impractical. In the main, these people were itinerants, beggars, soldiers, bandits, people who either had no family or had in some cases been rejected by their family. It was among other things their lack of a settled background that had driven them to take up a life of crime in the first place. It was not surprising, therefore, that the 'Instruction' of 1797, though it remained in force for many years and formed the basis, potentially at least, for the creation of an elaborate network of surveillance and control, had little effect in practice, and did nothing at all either to combat the evil of recidivism or to alleviate the chronic overcrowding of Prussia's prisons. But while all could agree on the existence of a crisis and the 'unsuitability of existing forms of punishment',[48] not everyone felt able to accept the solutions which Arnim proposed. In particular, by criticizing the administration of the prison system over which he was supposed to have charge, and by publishing an eight-hundred-page memorandum detailing wide-ranging reforms to improve it, Arnim fell foul of Prussia's top legal official, the powerful Grand Chancellor Julius von Goldbeck, who considered that he was trespassing on his own area of competence and duly forced him to resign.[49] Arnim's proposed reforms, therefore, came to nothing.

Goldbeck's own, rival plan divided prisons into severe and mild institutions, in order to separate out different kinds and degrees of offender. His proposals were typical of the mania for precise ordering and classification that characterized the Prussian bureaucratic Enlightenment. They went into considerable detail. The mild institutions were to be reserved for those improved felons sent there from the more severe prisons, for offenders who were not thought to be a danger to public security and for 'young people who are brought there for correction at the request of their parents or guardians and with the permission of the authorities' − a Prussian version of the infamous *lettres de cachet* which had so angered critics of the judicial system in pre-revolutionary France, and which underlined the power of correction that parents still held over their children in this thoroughly patriarchal society. The 'severe correctional institutions', on the other hand, were to receive not only serious offenders sentenced to be detained in them, but also 'vagabonds' and 'idlers who endanger public security'. Workhouses were also to be constructed for the improvement of beggars and the unemployed.

Even within the severe type of prison, the prisoners should be separated into different classes of 'depravity'. Elaborate precautions were to be taken against 'escapes or mutinies'; for instance, the inmates of the severe prisons were not to be given any work-tools which might be of use to them in either of these respects. The prisoners had to be trained to cleanliness, punctuality, obedience and morality: 'Any utterance of pernicious principles, the narration of disgraceful deeds committed by the prisoner or by others, and in general any behaviour by which the improvement of his fellow-inmates might be frustrated, must be severely punished.' An elaborate system of rewards and punishments was to be instituted, mostly based on gradations of honour: special places in the dormitory were to be marked out as 'shameful', while those who worked hardest were to be given superior rations. 'Unruly inmates' were to be whipped, while the compliant were to be given special uniforms to mark their superior status (the instructions laid particular weight on the prisoners' clothing, 'which provides the opportunity for numerous gradations by which the prison administration can distribute tokens of satisfaction or disapproval'). Prisoners were to be observed closely during Divine Service, and detailed reports were to be made on every aspect of their behaviour. This would enable the authorities to decide from time to time which prisoners had to be classified as incorrigible, and which could be promoted to a milder form of imprisonment prior to release back into the community, once a job had been found for them.[50]

Yet this graded system of imprisonment, which eventually found its way into a General Plan of 1804, backed up by a new set of Criminal Regulations in 1805, was still generally recognized to be insufficient to protect society against the incorrigible offender. The Prussian authorities were forced to admit that

> however much care is taken, it remains impossible to prevent prisoners from escaping. The construction and upkeep of secure gaols would demand very considerable sums of money, and the feeding and maintenance of the imprisoned felons would make even higher demands on the funds. The placing of workshops in the prisons is associated with great difficulties.[51]

Apart from anything else, the possibilities of prisons supporting themselves financially by means of operating as factories which sold products made by the prisoners were now limited because of the objections of the guilds – at a time of severe economic difficulties – that this would undercut them and cause unemployment among journeymen. Aschenbrenner's experience in Spandau had indicated how difficult it was for inmates to support themselves through labour even where they were highly skilled. And 'as soon as a large number of cunning and audacious people who have one aim alone in mind are gathered together in the same place', the chances of escape were obviously high, and those of getting good, productive and remunerative work out of them correspondingly low.

If the prison system was to be tightened up, the 'incorrigible' criminals would have to be placed under special security and treated more harshly, and yet such treatment would have no discernible deterrent effect on potential criminals outside the prisons. 'If one were willing and able in this way to prevent the escape of prisoners who are incapable of improvement,' noted another legal official, one would have to spend 'a very large sum'. As things stood, escaped convicts frequently got together with other 'villains', and 'in this way they form bands of murderous arsonists, robbers or thieves, which spread terror everywhere, and so – as now – necessitate the severest disciplinary measures'. One reasonably inexpensive method of protecting society against incorrigible criminals was to extend the application of the death penalty. Yet this was not allowed by the General Law Code of 1794, and in practice amendments to the Code could not be made quickly (in fact, despite numerous attempts, it was not to be superseded until 1851). Moreover, the 'General Plan' of 1804 was never implemented, and became lost in the general crisis of the Prussian state that followed its heavy defeats by Napoleon's armies in 1805–06.

The only way of protecting society against such offenders, in the view of Prussian officialdom, was to arrange their 'banishment to a remote part of the earth', where the criminals would be compelled to sustain themselves by hard work, which might even improve their character. The distance from Prussia would prevent their return. Thus the punishment would be 'no cruelty' and it would not cost much in comparison to keeping the criminals concerned in high-security prisons for the rest of their lives. And

> [i]t would be the most appropriate measure for the morality of the lower classes of the people if we were to take out of the country heinous villains who made it their profession to nip any remaining seed of good character in their fellow-prisoners in the bud . . . The publication of such an arrangement would keep foreign offenders away from our territory, and offer deterrent examples for inhabitants of our land who might otherwise be inclined to idleness.[52]

The purposes behind this policy were eventually summed up in the official decree promulgated to announce its inception:

> In order as far as possible to secure the property of the loyal subjects of His Royal Majesty of Prussia, our All-Merciful Lord, against the audacious attacks of thieves, robbers, arsonists and similar gross offenders, the All-Highest Same has, to be sure, taken the most emphatic steps to have such villains apprehended; however, experience has shown that this purpose has not been fully achieved by this means, because although the greatest care has been taken to prevent it, from time to time several such malefactors have escaped from penal

institutions to become once more a terror to their law-abiding fellow-citizens.[53]

These felons, it had thus been decided, 'will be transported into a remote part of the world, in order to be employed there in the hardest labours, and without being given any remaining hope of ever regaining their freedom.' This would both protect society and act as a better deterrent than imprisonment in Germany, where the hope of escape undermined the purposes of imprisonment.[54]

For a whole variety of reasons, therefore, the advantages of transportation seemed obvious. Accordingly, the authorities in Berlin recommended that contacts be taken up with Hamburg merchants to see what could be done.[55] Goldbeck added in August:

> The city court in Danzig has suggested among other things in a report submitted to the West-Pruss[ian] administration on 7th April and occasioned by the escape of the warehouse-thieves Basian and accomplices, that instead of being imprisoned for lengthy terms or for life, incorrigible villains should be banished from this country and for this purpose be accommodated in a foreign ship that is already prepared for sailing.

The West Prussian authorities had initially been hostile to this idea. But Goldbeck agreed that at least the most violent and vicious offenders could be transported to a part of the world from which they were unlikely to return. This would not only protect society, it would also be a severe additional punishment which, it was thought, would add considerably to the deterrent arsenal of the authorities in the fight against crime.[56] Moreover, it would create more space in Prussia's gaols.[57] The Prussian ambassadors in Hamburg, Copenhagen, Amsterdam, Madrid and Lisbon were duly contacted and asked to make enquiries about the possibility of deporting criminals to overseas destinations.[58] Soon a variety of possibilities was being canvassed. The idea had taken a significant step towards becoming reality.

The World of the German Bandit

As negotiations about the deportation dragged on, a number of the prisoners on the original list escaped or died, so a further detailed list with another 35 names on it was compiled early in 1802, making a total of 85 prisoners selected for deportation since the beginning of the planning stage. Among those added to the original party in this new list was a bandit of obvious ingenuity and persistence, Johann Friedrich Exner. A 35-year-old man, originally a wool-spinner but by this time a long-term vagrant, born in the Upper Palatinate, Exner, as the Prussian authorities noted, was a notorious thief from his youth onwards, and had been convicted several times of serious and violent robberies. But he escaped from the penitentiary in Pauer and gathered around him several companions in thievery, becoming their leader. According to his own confession he committed 18 serious violent thefts with them. He was, to be sure, frequently arrested, but he usually absconded from prison with great audacity. Even after he had been condemned, he attempted to escape from the prison at Silberberg, where he was usually incarcerated, and then from Glatz, where he threw off the heaviest fetters, burnt large openings through the wooden floorboards, crept through them and then let himself down 40 feet to the ground on a rope made by knotting bedclothes together. At the moment he is back in Glatz in chains that have been completely welded together.[59]

The authorities, not surprisingly, considered that Exner would be less likely to escape from Siberia than from his previous places of imprisonment and so put his name on the new list.

As with the first list, there were several prisoners like Exner who had escaped from gaol often enough to convince the authorities that it was not worth trying to keep them there.[60] One of Exner's band of robbers, Franz Anton Fiedler, was also on the list. Aged 42, he had been left to fend for himself from the age of eight, when his father had gone off to fight in the Austrian campaigns against the Turks, and he had supported himself by thieving ever since. A life of crime that had lasted for over 30 years was enough to persuade the authorities that Fiedler was incorrigible and had to be deported.

Exner and Fiedler were not the only bandits on the transport. Among the new batch of deportees were two further bands of robbers. The first was led by a 'vagabond' from Danzig, Johann Gottlieb Borowski, aged 24. He and his stepbrother, Franz Borowski, aged 34, and two others, said the compiler of the official list of deportees, 'are among those dangerous persons who have afflicted the inhabitants of the West Prussian plain for so long with their robberies and thefts'. They had always lived as vagabonds and had seldom worked. Since 1787 they had committed more than 30 robberies, most of which were break-ins and many of which had been accompanied by violence. 'They formed an organized group amongst themselves and were allied to several other thieves of the district, divided their booty and gave each other thieves' nicknames.' Among their many crimes, they had forcibly entered a farmhouse at night, threatened the farmer with a knife, broken his arm, thereby forcing him to reveal the whereabouts of his savings.

Another entire band of organized robbers, consisting of six men, was also listed for deportation. The leader, Johann Wisniewski, aged 35, the brothers Casimir and Simon Buttkowski, aged 30 and 24 respectively, Matthias Fuhrmann, aged 24, and two others, said the compilers of the list, all belong to the West Prussian vagabonds who, allied and related to other robbers and thieving rabble, steal and plunder as a profession . . . All of them have committed very many thefts, most of them with violence, sometimes on their own, sometimes with a lot of other robbers . . . and lived without any definite occupation, from begging and stealing. In July 1800 these 6 and other accomplices carried out a robbery at night. Armed with cudgels, they came to a farmer's house, broke a window and climbed in. The farmer, an old man of 72, joined with his family in resisting them and tried to fire his gun, so they threw wagon-steps, doors and benches at his head, whereat he fell to the ground. He now hid himself, but the robbers discovered his hiding-place and belaboured him cruelly with blows, continuing this barbaric treatment until he lay senseless on the earth. Then they took everything they could find of value, left the old man bleeding and covered with wounds in the entrance-hall and, after breaking all the windows in the house in addition, made their escape.

In 1801 Wisniewski, the Buttkowski brothers, Fuhrmann and one other had been sentenced to a hundred lashes followed by indefinite imprisonment with hard labour; the sixth member of the gang had received 60 lashes before entering on the same sentence. The nature of their crimes was so self-evidently violent and dangerous that their selection for transportation did not require any other justification. A fourth gang was included in the list, too. This was led by the labourer Carl Gotthilff Fritze, a 42-year-old horse-thief, who had begun an eight-year sentence in Spandau in 1798, the latest in a long series of sentences which had been passed on him since 1783. His crimes had been committed, it seems, with 'slyness and cunning', and the governor of the fortress at Spandau described him 'as a very unruly person and an agitator who incites others to escape'. His 'companion in thievery' Georg Sigismund Schurrbaum, aged 47, who had an equally lengthy record of convictions and was also apparently a difficult prisoner in Spandau, joined him on the list, as did the 'fence' who sold their stolen goods, the 38-year-old 'trader' Friedrich Müller.[61]

Whether it was really wise to send on the same transport men who had been companions in crime for a number of years, no one seemed to question. Gangs of robbers such as these were common in many parts of Germany at the end of the eighteenth century and the beginning of the nineteenth. They were far removed in spirit and reality from the robbers and bandits of Romantic legend. Nor did they really resemble the 'social bandits' studied by the historian Eric Hobsbawm, who – with what justification has been widely disputed – saw the typical Mediterranean bandit as a 'primitive rebel', defending traditional peasant society against the encroachments of the modern world, and articulating its concepts of honour, justice and equality by robbing rich exploiters and attacking the emissaries of the state. Whatever the value of his observations on the Mediterranean bandit, Hobsbawm perceptively remarked that the German bandit was in general a criminal rather than a social type. Criminal bandits in his view were

> likely to consist of members of 'criminal tribes and castes', or individuals from outcast groups. Thus the Crefeld and Neuss gang of the 1790s, like Keil's gang, was composed largely of knife-grinders . . . Criminal vocations were often hereditary; the Bavarian woman robber Schattinger had a family tradition of two hundred years to look back upon, and more than twenty of her kin, including her father and sister, were in jail or had been executed. It is not surprising that they did not seek the sympathy of the peasantry, since they, like all the 'straight' people, were their enemies, oppressors and victims . . . They formed part of large, if loose networks of an underworld which might stretch over half a continent.[62]

This underworld, Hobsbawm noted, formed a separate society or even counter-society which mirrored the world of the peasantry but did not belong to it. The 'straight' occupations they had were not peasant occupations, they spoke a separate criminal argot or *Rotwelsch* (unlike social bandits, who shared the language of the ordinary people), and they were often nonconformist in terms of religion and ideology.[63]

This nonconformism has led another historian, Carsten Küther, who pioneered the serious study of German bandits in the 1970s, to go further than Hobsbawm and to try and reclaim them for the world of the social bandit by arguing that the underworld in which they moved was a genuine counter-society, deeply antagonistic to the rich, hostile to the state, and therefore in a real sense representative of the poor and oppressed majority. Küther was able to point to the extensive popularity enjoyed in German society by robbers such as Johannes Bückler − 'Schinderhannes', as he was popularly known − whose career of robbery in the Rhineland ended on the scaffold in 1803 and was celebrated in numerous ballads and folk-tales, or Matthias Klostermaier, a poacher executed in 1771, who enjoyed a similar reputation among the Bavarian peasantry. The spirit of rebellion nurtured by such men, he argued, eventually found its way into the German labour movement, and Hobsbawm was taking the hostile attitude of contemporary officialdom, on whose sources he largely based his account, too much on trust when he dismissed the bandits as merely 'criminal'.[64] Although they emerged from the world of the itinerants, of people who wandered round the countryside and had no fixed place in peasant society, German robbers and bandits, argued Küther, were accepted by the peasants and were able to articulate many of their resentments against wealthy townsfolk and servants of the state.[65]

This view has in turn come under attack in recent years, especially by the German historian Uwe Danker in his study of three major groups of robbers active around the year 1700. Danker sees no evidence in their attitudes or behaviour of any general or principled hostility to the state, the social order or the modern world. None of the bandits he studies showed any solidarity with the poor and the oppressed. If they mainly robbed the rich, this was simply because the rich, by definition, were the ones with the most money to steal. The vast majority of bandit enterprises, he demonstrates in a painstaking compilation of examples, were break-ins, usually under cover of darkness, to mills, farms or the homes of prosperous peasants, and on such occasions, the robbers were just as likely to torture the farm servants in order to get them to reveal the whereabouts of any hidden treasure as they were to maltreat the farmer or members of his family. Danker confirms Küther's finding that German robbers mostly came from the ranks of the itinerant poor, and underlines Hobsbawm's identification of such offenders as forming a distinct 'underworld' with its own language and customs. But it is clear, too, that such people did not exist independently of ordinary rural society, since in their normal occupations, so far as they had any, they served useful though lowly and often 'dishonourable' functions within it, from knife-grinding to knacking, molecatching to milling. Those who were forced to live mainly by begging also did so openly, as part of the everyday life of rural society, just as beggars had for centuries. Their underworld activities, by contrast, were carried out necessarily in secret, and this was the main reason for their development of a special secret dialect, *Rotwelsch*, by which to communicate with one another. None of this caused them to challenge the state or the existing social order in any principled or fundamental way; on the contrary, when they were brought to the scaffold, they generally expressed repentance and remorse for the life of crime which circumstances had perhaps forced them to adopt.[66]

If they were dangerous to the state, Danker argued, it was because they 'realized in their own lives the secret desire of all for an existence free from rules and constraints'.[67] This helps account for the rise of legends about individual bandits such as Schinderhannes or the Bavarian Hiesl, even where they were far removed from the truth. For if the poacher Klostermaier in some respects articulated the resentments of Bavarian peasant society about the damage noble hunting rights were doing to their livelihood, Schinderhannes was a robber of the normal German kind, who lived mainly off armed burglaries, break-ins and thefts, both planned and opportunistic, often accompanied by casual violence and physical cruelty, and indiscriminate in the choice of his victims.[68] And when it came to the realities of banditry, the mass of people, far from celebrating the malefactor on the scaffold, joined in willingly with the collective ritual of retribution that constituted a public execution in this period. For bandits and robbers threatened them physically as well as psychologically, and they were glad to reaffirm the social norms which had been violated and which, therefore, the bandit on the scaffold was helping to define.

The bandits who were put on the list of Prussian deportees to Siberia in 1802 in many ways conformed to the basic pattern outlined by historians of other bands of robbers in eighteenth- and early nineteenth-century Germany.[69] Many of them were violent, had a long record of offences, or had behaved fractiously in gaol. A good few of them had tried to escape imprisonment, and some, like Exner, had evidently become quite skilled at it. Their crimes ranged from theft and arson to murder and rape. A listing of 60 men who were finally nominated for deportation revealed that 51 of them had been convicted of theft or robbery, 11 of murder, four of arson, three of deserting the colours, and one each of forgery (Aschenbrenner) and rape. Several of them had been sentenced for more than one of these offences. The final selection had been made personally by King Friedrich Wilhelm III himself, following a thorough physical examination of all the candidates which had resulted in a number of the older and weaker felons being weeded out in view of the prospective rigours of a lengthy footslog to Siberia. Others had ruled themselves out because they had escaped, or were taken off the list because of the restricted numbers. There were, however, still several who were relatively old by the standards of the day, including four in their fifties (the oldest deportee was 54; the average age was 34.6).

Heading the list, which gave the felons in descending order of the danger they were regarded as posing to society, was, not surprisingly, the West Prussian escapologist and bandit chief Johann Friedrich (Franz) Exner; at number four was the ex-soldier marked with the branding-iron, Gottfried Breitenfeld, and at number eight the hapless deserter Matthias Wrajewski, whose distaste for military service was once more labelled as extremely dangerous by the Prussian authorities. The knacker's servant Johann Stegemann was placed thirteenth on the list. Wilhelm Aschenbrenner was not far behind, at number 17, probably because of his reputation for plotting escape attempts. Among those apparently regarded as less dangerous were Andreas Siedentopf, Carl Rungenhagen, the Borowski brothers, Johann Wisniewski and his companions in crime Matthias Fuhrmann and the Buttkowski brothers, Franz Schulz, Anton Karaschin, Michael Constantin, Johann Crantz, Franz Hübner and Franz Fiedler.[70] Whether or not these judgements of the deportees' character were accurate would be revealed as the journey got under way.

'A Remote Part of the Earth'

By late November 1800, it was already becoming clear that the idea of deporting Prussia's worst criminal offenders overseas would be far from easy to put into practice. The suggestion of the Danzig authorities that they be handed over to the British for impressing into the navy was rejected as too full of uncertainties. No doubt some of them at least might have made half-decent sailors, and their moral and educational standards would not have been a great deal lower than those of most of the able seamen who manned the

Royal Navy's ships. But however far they might sail out, the fact that British ships eventually returned to port at Spithead meant that there was nothing to prevent Prussian convicts serving on them from coming back home.[71] Most officials seem to have thought at this time that sending the convicts to America would be the best way of making sure that they did not return. Not surprisingly, however, the newly independent United States of America declared firmly that they would absolutely refuse to let them in. In any case, as another official pointed out, the threat of transportation to America to start a new life could hardly be regarded as a deterrent; it seemed more like a reward.[72] Enquiries with the Portuguese, who transported their own criminals to Angola, elicited the response that the Prussian convicts were not wanted because they were unable to speak Portuguese. A similar reply, *mutatis mutandis*, came from the Spanish. The Dutch had lost their colonies in the wars, so they could not help either. As for the French, who regularly sent their own convicts to the West Indian island of Cayenne, the Prussian authorities considered it

> a preposterous idea, which would encounter many objections, to gather the criminals of a revolutionary-democratic state and those of an ordered monarchy in the said place for the said punishment, and beyond this, even if it were possible for such an arrangement to come into being, the unreliability and instability of the current French regime would not provide any guarantee for the continued safe keeping of the prisoners selected for deportation.

It was decided, therefore, that the French should not even be asked.[73]

In all these projects, there seemed to be nothing to keep the convicts from returning to Prussia, since the fact that they had committed no crime under foreign law meant that they would have to be treated as free men when they arrived in America, Australia, Angola or wherever else it was that the government was trying to send them. In this case, predicted one official, it was likely, given their general weakness of character,

> that furthermore, the so-called auction-houses of souls, which would have to be taken into account in our project too, would merely serve to debauch young people in bad houses, and especially to oblige them to enlist as soldiers or sailors to escape their debts, so that they would in many cases gain their freedom and return to their families once they had paid off their debts with their wages.

Apart from such considerations, which seemed to spring mainly from the overheated imagination of Prussian officials, there was the more sober problem of cost – of balancing the expense of keeping the 'incorrigible' prisoners in Prussian prisons for the foreseeable future against that of sending them overseas. An assiduous official in Berlin calculated that the cost of shipping 40 or 50 criminals to France would run to some 2500 Thalers, and that sending them to England would be just as expensive.[74] Moreover, the English government was likely to ask for a substantial extra sum to cover the expense of shipping them off to Botany Bay. All this made the project prohibitively costly. The cheapest possibility seemed to be that of sending them to the Danish island of Bornholm, in the Baltic Sea. This would not cost very much, and the Danes could surely be pressed to keep the convicts there. However, Aschenbrenner's experience had demonstrated how easy it was to escape detention in Denmark and return to Prussian soil, and Bornholm was dangerously close to Prussia. In any case the Danes refused to go along with the idea. So this plan too was quietly dropped.[75]

There remained one last possibility of getting rid of the unwanted malefactors: Siberia. Shipping the convicts across the Baltic to Russia would be cheap, costing a mere 1000 Thalers. And the possibilities of their returning were remote. For during the eighteenth century, the Tsar had acquired the silver-mining district of Nerchinsk, situated over 5000 miles from St Petersburg, beyond Lake Baikal, on the borders of Eastern Mongolia and Western Manchuria. Worked by serfs and convicts, the mines were closely guarded, and escape would be difficult if not impossible. Moreover, as an absolute monarch, the Tsar did not have to worry about the legal niceties which were likely to trouble the Western recipients of the Prussian convicts. He could simply treat them as convict-serfs, and keep them in Nerchinsk for the rest of their lives. This, thought the Prussian bureaucrats, would certainly be an effective deterrent once it became known back home.[76] On 18 January 1801, the Tsar agreed to take them. The only condition that he made was that these dangerous felons should not be allowed to pass through the streets of his capital, St Petersburg.[77]

Delighted with this rapid and favourable response, the Prussian authorities immediately began to make arrangements to put their plan into action. Initially they thought of shipping the convicts off to the Arctic port of Archangel, but it quickly became apparent that very few Prussian merchant ships went there, and that in any case the journey out of the Baltic, up through the North Sea and round the northern tip of Scandinavia would take from eight to ten weeks even with favourable winds. During this time, Prussian officials speculated, there was a serious danger that the prisoners would mutiny, or that the diseases they brought from the insanitary conditions under which they had lived in prison would spread throughout the ship and cause a significant depletion of the crew. A large military guard would be needed and would have to be shipped all the way back to Prussia after delivering their cargo. The costs of feeding and supplying them for a voyage lasting some 20 weeks were considered prohibitive. Nor was the alternative of sending them by land any better, given the need to find a baggage-train and the fact that it would take them just as long as by sea, if not longer. Finally, by the spring of 1801 the idea of sending them via Archangel had been abandoned anyway because of 'the appearance of the English fleet in the Sound, and the death of the Russian Emperor', or in other words the assassination of Paul I, with whom the original agreement had been made. Sending the convicts in a ship sailing under a neutral flag did not seem to improve its prospects of reaching its destination unhindered. So the Prussian authorities were forced to think again.[78]

After some deliberation, it was decided that the convicts should embark at the small Prussian port of Pillau and sail along the Baltic coast into the Gulf of Finland to disembark at the Estonian harbour of Narva, just over a 100 miles west of St Petersburg. This was a good deal further south than Archangel, and so no further from Nerchinsk than the Arctic seaport was. The Russians agreed. Already, however, costs were rising dramatically. The Russian authorities were now requiring the Prussians to pay the daily living expenses of the convicts for the entire journey from Narva to Nerchinsk. 'Two copecks a day', they told the parsimonious Prussians at a later stage in the protracted negotiations, 'are most insufficient.' The journey from Narva to Nerchinsk was some 1124 versts or about 750 miles, which would take the party 285 days if the march went well. Ten copecks a day would be needed to feed and water each prisoner and guard, which made 28 roubles 50 copecks each in total. In addition, every prisoner would need seven roubles and 75 copecks for clothing, and there had to be additional provision for illness, injury and other extraordinary expenses that might be incurred on the journey. Moreover, the guard supplied by the Russians for the journey had to be paid for the return trip as well. For the transportation of 50 convicts, the Russian authorities therefore estimated that the total cost would not be less than 2000 roubles.[79] In addition, the Prussian government felt it necessary to strengthen the fortifications at Pillau, where the prison was felt to be too insecure to contain such dangerous felons. Worried about the possibility of the transportees corrupting the 'better' criminals already there, the authorities undertook substantial building works to ensure that they were kept separate and prevented from escaping.[80] This added further to the expense of the operation. When taken together with the sums demanded by the Russians and the 885 Thalers estimated as the cost of shipping the prisoners to Narva, the whole project now looked as if it would require well over 10,000 Thalers to carry out.[81] At one point, indeed, when the Prussians were considering transporting some 200 felons to Siberia – over a third of their entire prison population at the time – the total cost was estimated at 18,000 Thalers.[82] Not surprisingly, they decided to restrict the initial shipment to no more than 60. Indeed, the Russians were asking for so much money that the Prussian authorities seriously thought of abandoning the whole project altogether towards the end of 1801.[83] Moreover, the negotiations had dragged on so long that the weather was beginning to deteriorate, and it became clear that the transportation could not now take place before the spring of 1802.[84]

After further consideration, however, it still seemed to the Prussian government in the autumn and winter of 1801 that, despite all the problems
associated with it, the transportation plan was worthwhile. After all, by this
time, a considerable amount of money had already been spent, and the
preparations for the shipping were already well advanced. When spring finally
arrived, 60 of the prisoners were moved from their places of confinement.
Fifty-eight of them arrived safely at Pillau in early May 1802. They were
taken on board ship between nine in the morning and 12 noon on 11 June,
under the watchful eye of a guard detachment consisting of one Prussian army
lieutenant, two NCOs, 12 privates and four prison warders, who accompanied them on the journey to Narva. With a favourable, if rather strong, wind
behind them, they set sail across the Baltic. The next day, 12 June, according
to the lieutenant, some of the felons aroused 'suspicion by their very frequently repeated visits to the latrines as well as frequent gatherings around the
hatches', and on 13 June, 'one of the criminals said again that he had noticed
a very dangerous mood amongst his fellow-prisoners.' They were planning
a mutiny, an informer told the lieutenant. They thought the guard was weak,
and declared their intention 'to throw anyone who offered resistance over-
board'. Soon they were testing the resolve of the guard by demanding 'beer
to drink, in the most impetuous manner'. But the lieutenant replied, 'as
coolly as possible, that no beer had been allotted to them in the bill of lading'.
Their misbehaviour would get them nowhere, he told them. Nevertheless,
according to the lieutenant's report, the mood of the prisoners grew more
refractory as the journey progressed. On 15 June, the lieutenant gave the
prisoners 'to understand that he was not a man who would let himself be
frightened.' 'The ringleader of this defiance, Exner', was told by the lieutenant that his intrigues had been observed and stood no chance of success.
After this, the prisoners seem to have abandoned their plans for a mutiny. The
ship reached Narva without further incident on 16 June and the prisoners
were disembarked the following day after the landing formalities had been
completed.[85] It was clear, as the official report on the journey stated, that the
prisoners were indeed a 'dangerous cargo'. If their behaviour on board ship
was anything to go by, the convicts would stop at nothing to try and escape
as they made their way over land to Siberia. It was significant that the leader
of the attempted mutiny had been Franz Exner, the bandit leader from West
Prussia; the authorities had evidently been correct in placing him at number
one on the list of deportees graded by the level of the danger they posed. It
was not to be the last time he caused trouble on the journey.

Up to this point, the enterprise had cost the Prussian authorities the sum of
24,856 Thalers, including the hire of the ship, the payment of the crew and
the provisioning of the prisoners and their guard.[86] In view of the charges
which the Russians were proposing to levy for purchasing clothing for the
felons, the Prussian authorities had few qualms about sending them off to
Narva 'scantily clad'.[87] When they arrived, as the Russians reported, 'each one

was bought to start off with a shirt, a pair of underpants, a pair of long socks and of peasant shoes.' They would need more substantial clothing than this for Siberia. The convicts remained in Narva for a week while the necessary documents were drawn up and provisions collected for their march. Then the column of prisoners finally set off, on foot, under the guard of a detachment of 46 soldiers commanded by a lieutenant from the Narva garrison, starting on 25 June 1802.[88] They faced an overland journey of more than 5000 miles, broken only by the occasional section traversed by convict barge, as for instance along a stretch of the Volga, or by horse-drawn sled, as in the crossing of Lake Baikal, which could only be achieved in winter when the lake was frozen over. Those who survived the journey were estimated as likely to arrive at their destination in April 1803.[89] For the moment we must leave them, setting off from Narva, as we turn to the subsequent fate of the policy that had sent them there from Germany.

Persistence of an Idea

The Prussian government, indifferent to the fate of the prisoners once they had set off for Siberia, was satisfied with the results of the deportation. It had managed to rid itself of a substantial number of serious offenders apparently for good, though at considerable financial cost. Officials were keen on turning the arrangement into a regular one, with a shipment of 50 or 60 felons being sent from Prussia to Siberia annually, a policy that would have stripped Prussia's gaols of virtually all their long-term prisoners within a decade.[90] The prison reforms of the same period were designed with just such an ongoing policy of transportation in mind. In February 1801, King Friedrich Wilhelm III declared his intention of incorporating deportation into the Law Code as a criminal sentence, and in April 1801 Goldbeck ordered:

> In future the period of imprisonment will be used where possible to accustom the former criminals to orderliness and industriousness, and to observe them in such a manner as to reach a conclusion about which of them are to be regarded as rehabilitated and released, and which of them as incorrigible and banished from the country.[91]

In effect, very long prison sentences were set to become things of the past, since all serious offenders would be deported.[92] But in November 1802 it was reported that the new Russian Tsar, Alexander I, was 'completely disinclined' to repeat the operation. The Prussian ambassador in St Petersburg reported that Alexander took this view

> because in the first place the transportation of these people is attended by considerable difficulties, and secondly it contradicts moral sentiment to permit

such depraved persons to stay in his own state; and finally because in any case
the punishment of deportation linked to banishment to Siberia cannot be valid
for Russian felons.[93]

The Tsar evidently felt that the Prussian convicts were being treated unfairly
compared to his own. Moreover, following the renewal of war with France
shortly afterwards, the situation became too precarious for the Prussian government to contemplate moving substantial numbers of dangerous convicts
around the country on a regular basis. The Prussian General Plan for the
reform of prisons issued in 1804–05 proved inoperable for financial reasons,
and the authorities were reduced to trying to cut down on prison break-outs
by offering rewards for the recapture of escaped felons and by providing
military escorts for the transport of prisoners from one gaol to another.[94] In
1804, the Prussian authorities were still complaining about 'the very great
number of criminals who escape every year' and threatening serious action
against warders who neglected their duties.[95]

By the time the wars in Europe were over, in 1815, the climate of legal
opinion had begun to change. The concept of 'special deterrence' which lay
at the root of the deportation policy had come under heavy attack from legal
reformers, most notably the influential Bavarian jurist Paul Anselm Ritter von
Feuerbach. Feuerbach pointed out that arrest and deportation on the mere
suspicion that the offender would continue to commit crimes in the future
was an arbitrary procedure which violated fundamental principles of the rule
of law. Future law codes, such as that prepared by Feuerbach himself for
Bavaria in 1813, would have to restrict themselves to imposing punishments
as part of a policy of general rather than special deterrence, that is, deterring
unknown possible future criminals by the threat of punishment rather than
deterring known existing criminals by locking them up. These arguments
were already influential among legal officials in Prussia by 1815, and were
eventually to inform the principles behind the Prussian Criminal Code of
1851, a document that by the time of its promulgation had already been in
preparation for several decades.[96] Feuerbach's stress on general deterrence
reduced the arbitrariness of incarceration and subjected it much more firmly
than before to court decisions and the strict implementation of legal codes,
but it also led to a widespread neglect of prisons as reformatory institutions,
and an assumption instead that all they had to administer was punishment.
When a liberal penal reform movement emerged in the 1820s, it was on the
basis of the belief that all criminals were in principle capable of amelioration,
if only the right conditions could be provided. But it was to be some time
before such a programme was implemented.

In the meantime, there remained the problem of overcrowding within and,
as we have seen, escapes from gaol. Not surprisingly, therefore, the idea of
transportation did not disappear. The Prussian example encouraged other
states to follow suit. Like the Prussians, they also wished to relieve themselves

of the financial and administrative burden of supporting large numbers of malefactors on a long-term basis. Unlike the Prussians, they made no pretence that an element of deterrence or amelioration was involved. At a time when Germany consisted of hundreds of independent states of varying sizes within the moribund 'Holy Roman Empire' – finally dissolved by Napoleon in 1806 – it had been normal for many centuries for cities and states to punish wrong-doers whose crimes had not earned them the death penalty by expelling them from their jurisdiction (*Landesverweisung*) on pain of death, or some lesser but still serious punishment, should they break their oath not to return. This was still common practice in the early nineteenth century. With the liberation of the Americas from colonial rule between the 1770s and the 1820s, and the advent of safer and faster seaborne communications after the European peace of 1815, a number of states were tempted to extend *Landesverweisung* to expulsion beyond the boundaries of Germany, even Europe, as the most certain way of ridding themselves of unwelcome offenders. Unlike the Prus-sian deportees in 1802–03, these felons would not be sent to a labour colony to work without pay as an additional punishment to their existing sentences of imprisonment. On the contrary, they would in effect be free once they had departed Europe's shores. This indeed was the inducement that was offered to make them go. A characteristic example, from the point of view both of the motives of the authorities and the experience of the offenders, was that of the Grand Duchy of Mecklenburg-Schwerin.

Officials in the Grand Duchy had already been alerted to the possibility of deporting felons to far-off places in the course of the Prussian government's preparations for the Siberian venture in 1801. Evidently acting under a misapprehension, a bureaucrat in Berlin had written to Schwerin asking the Mecklenburg authorities to ask for an account of their experience of sending convicts to Siberia. Mystified, the Mecklenburg officials replied saying they had had no such experience; privately, they noted it was likely to be too expensive for use in the future, too. Some such reservation must have been behind the Grand Duchy's rejection of a more formal proposal put forward to it in 1803. So the matter was laid to rest.[97] But the idea had been planted in the Grand Duchy and only wanted the right conditions to take root. Twenty years later, Colonel Count von der Osten-Sacken, governor of the rural workhouse in Güstrow and one of the officials who had dealt with the original Berlin request, proposed to the Grand Duke that some of the inmates of his institution should be sent off to Brazil. The huge South American state had recently won its independence from Portugal and had just been recog-nized by Mecklenburg.[98] The Mecklenburg government jumped at the opportunity of ridding itself of these 'completely homeless people, whose accommodation threatens to remain a burden on the workhouse for the rest of their lives'.[99] Reducing the state budget was not the only reason for agreeing to the proposal. A major mutiny in the Güstrow workhouse on 4 October 1823 had convinced the governor that the overcrowded conditions in the institution posed a serious threat to order. The military had been called in, and by the time the uprising had been quelled, two inmates had been killed and four wounded, while four soldiers and one warder had received injuries at the hands of the inmates. Nine men had been condemned for their part in these events and sentenced to varying terms of imprisonment in the penitentiary at Dömitz, in most cases along with 15 strokes of the cane.[100] For their part, the Brazilians had strong motives for agreeing to the scheme. Desperate for manpower to build up their economy, they had an agent in Hamburg, Major Schäffer, who was actively engaged in the recruitment of German emigrants, and it was through him that they signalled their willingness to take as many people as wanted to come.

If the arrangement seemed advantageous to the two participating governments, it must also have sounded attractive to the people who were to be transported. The workhouse at Güstrow provided shelter for a variety of the poor, the homeless and the destitute. None of them was there voluntarily. The Mecklenburg authorities used the workhouse to keep the streets free from people they considered a nuisance, such as beggars and tramps. A tramp was officially defined in this largely rural North German state as 'anyone who carries on a forbidden, useless or dangerous trade, who lacks written legitimation or a valid passport, and who seeks to earn his living by illegitimate or insufficient means, including specifically: bear-keepers, puppet-masters, rope-dancers, street musicians, etc, etc.'[101] The workhouse was thus part of a wide-ranging official assault on traditional itinerant trades, many of which, it is true, had long existed on the fringes of the criminal underworld.[102] It was hardly surprising that many of the inmates did not want to be there, or that they resented the conditions under which they were imprisoned to the point where they risked staging a full-scale mutiny. Although the children of such people were usually given into foster-care, there were still a number of families in the Güstrow workhouse in 1823. The Brazilian government agreed that it would be up to the emigrants to decide whether they wanted to practise a trade on arrival in Brazil, to enlist in the army or to become farmers. To prospective immigrants, the Brazilians offered 200 *Morgen* (about 130 acres) of land to colonize in the temperate south of the country, more if there were over three children in the family. They would be provided with cattle, draught animals, agricultural equipment and seedcorn, and a house to live in complete with household goods. The only condition was that they had to accept Brazilian citizenship and stay in the country for a minimum of ten years, after which they would be free to go wherever they wished. The Mecklenburg government accepted this ten-year rule, which meant that it agreed to the possibility that some of the transportees might eventually return. It also undertook to pay the costs of transportation up to the point of embarkation, while the Brazilians agreed to pay the rest.[103] Finally, Schäffer was able to assure the Mecklenburg authorities that the emigrants would be free to practise their Protestant faith.[104] It all sounded too good to be true.

With commendable honesty, the authorities in Schwerin warned the inmates that there would be no means of compelling the Brazilians to keep their end of the bargain once they arrived in Rio. Some were reportedly put off by this rather sobering thought. The fact that a number pulled out at this stage indicates that the authorities were telling the truth when they declared to all concerned that the transportation was completely voluntary. Despite their warnings, however, a substantial number still agreed to go. Most of them were rural labourers, but there were also a few artisans, a scribe and even a 'theological candidate' among them.[105] At four o'clock in the morning on 24 June 1824, nine four-horse open carts carrying 77 men, 23 women and 33 children left Güstrow under military escort for Schwartau, where they arrived, wet through from a day's rain, the same evening. Here they were met by the Brazilian agent in Hamburg, who gave them all new, Brazilian-style clothes to wear. In addition, the Hamburg Bible Society provided each of them with a Bible. Arriving the next day at Boizenburg on the river Elbe, they sailed downstream by barge, past Hamburg to Blankenese, where all, except one who had shown himself on the journey to be 'deranged', embarked on the frigate *Georg Frederic* at seven in the evening of 27 June 1824.[106] Shortly after reaching open sea on the 28th, four of the transportees changed their minds and were sent back. Discipline on the sea-voyage was strict. As one of them later reported,

> any misdemeanour was punished with blows from a twisted rope on the behind. Among the emigrants from this institution it was principally the wife of the huntsman S . . . mann who was beaten several times, once indeed with 500 blows, for stealing, and especially because she had refused to admit it even though she had been caught in the act.

Apart from this, the journey was uneventful, and all except three children and one adult survived the rigours of the long sea-voyage. The ship reached Rio after a 72-day journey, where the transportees were met in person by the Emperor of Brazil, as he styled himself, and made to swear an oath of allegiance to him on the quayside.

They were joined a few months later by a second shipment, which brought a further 32 men, six women and two children from the workhouse. This new contingent also included felons from the penitentiary and the military gaol (*Stockhaus*) at Dömitz as well: 28 men and 13 women from the penitentiary, and 39 male offenders from the military prison (28 of whom were civilians). A further ten men and one woman were sent from the criminal prison at Butzow, where they were awaiting removal to Dömitz after sentencing. This second shipment, totalling 90 people in all, mostly consisted of offenders condemned to periods of imprisonment for theft ranging from six months to life. Two were serving sentences for murder and two for participation in murder, and there were four infanticidal women. One man had been sentenced to two years for 'tumults and excesses'. Perhaps the most serious offender was serving a life sentence for killing his wife. There were also ten soldiers serving time for desertion. Only 'the notorious bandit leader Johan Mehl' had been explicitly excluded by order of the Grand Duke: otherwise, it seemed that any prisoner who wanted to could go.[107] Each of these felons was given a Bible and hymnal on leaving Dömitz and personally warned to work hard and behave well by Osten-Sacken, who shook each one of them by the hand as they departed. On arriving in Rio, they were met by the German merchant Biesterfeld, who had been appointed Mecklenburg's consul in the town on 29 October.[108] They were eventually joined by a third shipment of ten offenders from Bützow, 17 from Dömitz and 41 from the workhouse in Güstrow, who embarked on their voyage on 4 August 1825. These were mostly convicted thieves too, though they also included one man serving time for manslaughter, and another for sodomy.[109] Clearly, once they had made the decision to send convicts and workhouse inmates to Brazil, the Mecklenburg authorities had no intention of stopping until everyone who expressed a wish to go had had their wish granted: 291 sailed to Brazil on the various ships in all. So many offenders had now been transported that the Dömitz prison authorities began to worry that there would not be enough men to keep the prison's various labour projects going. As the responsible official in Schwerin reminded the Grand Duke, however, 'the penitentiary is not a factory, and it would be no misfortune if it was completely empty for lack of any crimes to punish'.[110]

The emigrants could hardly be regarded as ideal citizens of the newly founded state. Those with a trade, such as the carpenter Gierz or the surgeon Meyer, found work easily enough in Rio. Johann Reinaecker, a barber, who was said to be 'almost completely deaf', and half-mad because of his sufferings, was probably an exception among the relatively skilled emigrants: he ended up begging on the streets of Rio. At least a dozen of the married men with families had been given land on the Rio Grando. This was not in the south of Brazil, as promised, but the land was fruitful and there were already German colonists there, which is perhaps why it was selected for the new emigrants too. One of them at least, Heinrich Kruse, sold his land immediately, drank away the proceeds and was later found as a street begger in Rio, where he claimed the Empress had personally promised to send him back to Mecklenburg if he so wished. At least fifteen men ended up as labourers on farms or estates rather than receiving land themselves. One married man, Hans Schrader, had been enlisted in the army, and on the major's orders had divorced his wife 'because of her immorality and drunk-enness', apparently with his consent. She had last been seen as an 'alley whore' in Rio. Another married man had enlisted on his own initiative, and his wife had set up a successful business supplying the troops with food and drink; but they were said to be constantly quarrelling because 'she insists on trying to stop her husband drinking'.

The vast majority of the unmarried men were enlisted in the Brazilian army, which was desperately under-manned. Few of them appear to have been much use as soldiers. Quite a number, after all, had been imprisoned for desertion in the first place. One was known to be frequently in trouble 'because of his tendency to drink, which continued in Brazil', while one of his comrades, Johann Guthoff, was subjected to 'beatings with a rod . . . because of his frequent drunkenness'. Another enlisted man was found to be 'useless . . . because he appeared to be feeble-minded'. One soldier, Johann Kursch, quickly came to a bad end: 'for while he was drunk the negroes stole his clothes and threw him down a well, from which he was pulled out dead.' Fritz Groth, one of the felons from Dömitz, had not been in the army for long when he was sentenced to six years on the hulks in Rio harbour for theft; he could frequently be seen in a chain-gang working on the harbour walls. One Johann Volkmann had been promoted to sergeant, but was said to be trying to leave the army and acquire a farm; other reports noted that he was 'a merry fellow and loves to drink spirits'. Ten or more deserted the colours and tried to make their way back to Europe.

By September 1828, two of the latter, Gunther and Sichtling, were inmates of the Güstrow workhouse once more, where they supplied all these details to the authorities.[111] Two more transportees, the Marlow brothers, were arrested in Mecklenburg in 1830. According to Gunther and Sichtling, there were a number of others who had found their way back to Germany but were not picked up by the authorities. There was in the end nothing much the authorities could do about people such as these, who returned before the ten-year term agreed in the contract was up. There was certainly no question of sending them back to Brazil.[112] On the whole, it is not clear which government got the worst of the bargain, the Mecklenburg or the Brazilian. If the authorities in Schwerin were with hindsight rather foolish to suppose that the people they sent abroad would all stay there, the administration in Rio was perhaps even more foolish to think that the inmates of German workhouses and prisons could furnish them with good soldiers and solid colonists.[113] In retrospect, it is not at all surprising that so many deserted or came to a bad end. Subsequent complaints that the emigrants found it difficult to pursue their Protestant faith in what was constitutionally a Catholic state, despite the promises made to them in Germany, must be taken with a pinch of salt: few of them were likely to have wanted to, and it is highly improbable that more than a handful of them found much use for the Bibles and hymnals with which they were so lavishly provided by well-meaning Christian philanthropists at the outset of their journey.[114] The experience seemed so discouraging that the Mecklenburg government never repeated it, and virtually ignored a suggestion in 1847 that it should agree to send a further batch of offenders to America.[115] Not surprisingly, the Brazilians showed no interest in acquiring any more troops or civilian citizens in this way either.

Mutiny and Brutality on the High Seas

The recruiting activities of the Brazilian agent Major Schäffer in north Germany also convinced another North German state to transport felons abroad in the 1820s. Indeed, it had already done so by the time the first Mecklenburg contingent embarked on its voyage across the Atlantic. In 1824, 36 prisoners from the city-state of Hamburg were among the passengers on two ships, which sailed for Brazil on 23 March and 6 May respectively. The 12 who went on the first ship had been told on being sentenced that they could be transported if they wished, and if the opportunity arose. The other 24 seem to have been more of an afterthought. All of them were allowed to take their savings, and they were provided by the prison governor with some clothing, songbooks, Bibles and other useful or edifying gifts, just like their counterparts from Mecklenburg. The prison authorities reported on the behaviour of the two consignments of felons while the ships were still in port in the most positive and encouraging terms. They were careful to note that

> Among the prisoners who have gone to Brazil there is not one who has undergone a dishonouring punishment such as whipping or branding, not one who has been sullied by the bailiff's hand. A few have stood in the pillory, particularly amongst the first transport, which contains in any case the worst individuals . . . One fellow who was on the last transport, Heinrich Wilhelm Müller, without doubt the most dangerous of them all, stole as soon as he was on board ship, was returned to the police, sentenced to the pillory and transported to Lübeck. The rest have behaved well on board, and various prisoners on the second transport have been made non-commissioned officers, one of them, Rasch, a sergeant.[116]

However, the optimism of the prison authorities about the enterprise turned out to be misplaced as soon as the ships reached the open sea.

One of the passengers on the second ship, Johann Dietrich Holtermann, not a convict himself, reported on 20 November 1825 that the voyage had been an unhappy one. The 24 felons had quickly made their presence felt among the hundred or so passengers. 'At night', wrote Holtermann, 'some of them started to fight and to boast about their crimes.' They became drunk, and the captain confiscated all liquor on board ship. But this was not because he was particularly concerned about the prisoners' sobriety, or the other passengers' safety. On the contrary, the captain turned out to be little better than a criminal himself. Tension mounted, especially between the convict Rasch, who succeeded in making himself popular with the passengers and, as the prison governors had reported back in Hamburg, had been appointed to the post of sergeant while the ship was still in port, and one or two of the ship's officers, who clearly resented his promotion. There were further, noisy quarrels about drink, and the atmosphere deteriorated to such a point that many of the non-convict passengers transferred to another ship that happened to be passing and proved willing to take them on board. Among those who remained, the tension escalated still further, as the captain, who by now had taken one of the younger female passengers permanently into his bunk, doled out the confiscated drinks to his favourites. This unsavoury crew, according to Holtermann, included the 'whorehouse keeper Weimann from Wandsbeck' and 'lieutenant Kiesewetter, an adventurer'. After a furious row, in which pistols were drawn, the captain agreed to return the drink, but only gave them cheap bottles of schnapps instead of the expensive wines and spirits which the passengers had brought on board and which he and his cronies had long since polished off themselves.

Backed by fellow-convicts who threatened to knife anyone who disagreed with him, Rasch now began talking of mutiny and of forcing the captain to veer off towards Lisbon instead of Rio. But the captain got wind of this, and turned up with a group of armed officers to arrest Rasch and his fellow-conspirators on a set of largely trumped-up charges. 'Rasch', reported Holtermann, 'looked the lieutenant freely in the eye. The latter repaid him by cutting his arm off with his hunting-knife . . . All of them were hit several times with rifle-butts.' They were beaten until they confessed to the charges brought against them. Each of them got 60 lashes with a thick rope, and the ship's doctor was threatened with the same punishment when he tried to interfere. After being locked up for a whole night without food or drink, they were all condemned to death by a drumhead court-martial. The captain, Holtermann said, cried 'shoot them all down. The others lent a hand, and so all eight were shot, Rasch last of all. Each one had to witness the others' death.'[117] For the rest of the voyage, the remaining passengers were kept on half-rations, even though there was plenty of food still on board. Holtermann himself now protested, and was put under arrest for his pains, accused of having been a murderer in Hamburg and of carrying poison on his person. He was put on emergency rations and a block of wood was nailed over his arm to immobilize him. A man who tried to help him was beaten up. As they reached Rio, Holtermann's contacts there came on board to try and release him, but they were driven back by the captain and his gang, brandishing sabres. Only when the authorities arrived did Holtermann secure his freedom. The captain and his friends were forced to flee. One of them was beaten to within an inch of his life by the remaining prisoners and thrown over the harbour wall. The Brazilians then tried to press Holtermann into the army, and it was with difficulty that he managed to persuade them to let him pursue his intention of becoming a colonist. Holtermann ended his dramatic tale by advising people not to come to Brazil unless they had a lot of money and good connections there.[118]

The circumstantial detail of Holtermann's account was uncorroborated but convincing. Deportation had proved unsuccessful in this instance as a means of liberating the convicts from their life of violence and brutality. The fate of the Hamburg contingents seems to have been very similar to that of the prisoners and workhouse inmates from Mecklenburg: the main interest of the Brazilian authorities was in acquiring able-bodied men to serve in the armed forces, and one may surmise that most of the men from Hamburg ended up as compulsorily enlisted soldiers or cheap labour on the country's farms and plantations. As with the much larger Mecklenburg contingent, only a small proportion of them was likely to have ended as successful colonists. The idea that any more than a few of them could be reformed or would take a new chance in life if it were offered them seemed unlikely even before they arrived in Rio. However, from the point of view of Hamburg's ruling senate the operation of 1824 had been a success. So it decided to try to repeat the experiment a few years later, though not, in the light of reports of what had happened, to Brazil. In 1832 the Hamburg Chief of Police, Senator Dammert, complained that 'the overcrowding of our correctional institutions' made the transportation of 'some minor offenders' who only had a few years of the sentence left to serve a desirable option. As a result of his initiative, 13 such prisoners agreed to go to the USA. Each of them was given a Bible and an allowance of 61 Marks. Typical of these offenders was

> Johann Martin Fr[ie]dr[ich] Stange, born in Duvenstadt, who is now in prison for the sixth time for theft and violation of his oath [not to return to Hamburg]. His sentence ends on 17 June 1833. It is to be expected that when this man regains his freedom, he will remain in the vicinity of Hamburg without prospects and without means and in a short time become guilty of fresh crimes. Even if Stange is excluded from the transport currently under discussion, it is still greatly to be desired that this serious offender is sent overseas if any fresh opportunity to do so might possibly arise.[119]

Thus the idea of only transporting 'minor offenders' was giving way from the very start to the desire to rid the city-state of 'serious offenders' for good. All the same, the policy seems to have been confined to felons convicted of crimes against property rather than crimes of violence.

Another transportee in the 1832 shipment was Johann Jacob Vogelsang, from Soltau, aged 35, an oil manufacturer who had been sentenced to eight years' imprisonment for setting his own property on fire. Taking into account two years in remand, he was due to be released in 1837. He had lost his lawsuit against the insurance company, which had refused to pay out on his damaged property, and he was in poor health. Nevertheless, he paid for the trip out of his own pocket. News of the impending arrival of this 'notorious arsonist' was sent to the mayor of New York by the American Consul in Hamburg and caused some alarm. However, as things turned out, Vogelsang was far from being the most dangerous of the felons transported on this shipment.

The letters Vogelsang sent back to Hamburg give some idea of the conditions under which the felons were transported, and of what happened to them when they arrived. The voyage to New York, he wrote, began well, and the deportees initially enjoyed 'the best treatment on the part of our ship's company'. But the food on the 67-day sailing was so poor that some of the prisoners 'broke into the captain's larder at night, and not only stole bread, meat and other provisions, but also did not forget to help themselves to the rum and cognac.' The captain interrogated the deportees, among whom the ringleader was Johann Stange, the thief from Duvenstadt, who had, it seems, been included in the transport after all. 'Stange and Tiedemann, who were the most compromised, and had already been thieving from their comrades in all sorts of ways, were subjected to the Spanish goat.' This was a wooden contraption to which offenders were tied so that they could be whipped. Its use had been illegal in almost every part of Germany for years.[120] It is surprising to find it on board a ship at all, let alone as late as the 1830s. Its presence, still more its use, testifies once more to the extreme roughness and brutality often characteristic of life at sea in the era of wooden ships.

The torture failed to elicit a confession from the two men, and the prisoners in general became even more refractory than before. Stange and his gang stole Vogelsang's food, drink and clothes, together with all his savings, and since they were evidently in league with some of the crew, the captain's enquiries failed to uncover any of the stolen goods. Others suffered a similar fate. On arriving in New York, they informed the authorities about the criminals on board, who were thereupon registered at the nearest police station. The sensational reporting of all this in the local press meant they had no chance of getting jobs.[121] Vogelsang therefore made his way upstate, via Albany to Buffalo, which had just been formally recognized as a municipality. The privations of his voyage had left him obsessed with food. Beef was two cents a pound, he reported, and pork was cheap too. Receiving some money from his relatives, he rented a tallow factory and began to make soap and candles, hoping for quick profits.[122] Whether or not he succeeded does not seem to be known. His letters suggest that while some offenders transported to the United States evidently did their best to make a new life, many, like Stange, showed no sign of turning over a new leaf at all. Indeed, Stange and a group of his companions were subsequently sentenced to 15 years' hard labour in New York State for highway robbery.[123]

Emboldened by what was, from his point of view, another outstanding success for Hamburg, Senator Hudtwalcker instructed the city's Consul-General in London in November 1834 to open negotiations with the government of New South Wales for the transportation of minor offenders. 'Our convicts', they said, 'are not so dangerous as the English.' They would be hard-working and respectful of the law. With the blessing of the Australians, who badly needed young, fit and healthy workers, 20 convicts were selected for transportation and told that the climate in New South Wales was 'warm and nice, not exceedingly hot, and healthy'. They were to be given land, small cottages, food and tobacco, and were to be allowed to marry. They would be regarded as volunteers. In fact, the Hamburg Senate was being less than honest, for it selected several serious offenders for the trip, including one murderer and one prisoner who had spent six years working as a Mediterranean galley-slave and had made frequent attempts to escape from his prison in Hamburg. Moreover, the number of petitions sent to the Senate by prisoners who objected to the idea of going to Australia suggests that the much-vaunted voluntary nature of the selection was also a deception. And many of the transportees were neither healthy nor young, since the final quota of 40 was made up by pulling in vagabonds and beggars indiscriminately off the streets. It was not so much these factors which eventually sank the scheme, however, as a growing crisis in the British transportation system. In the new era of political and social reform inaugurated by the Whig governments of the 1830s, the practice of transporting felons was already being wound down. This shift in policy was reinforced by the growing political influence in London of those free colonists who wanted to transform Australia into a quieter and more respectable society. 'Upon a recent occasion', as one of them wrote from New South Wales in 1836, 'I learned there was some project of importing into the Colony a number of Convicts from the State of Hamburg. I remonstrated against so unnecessary an appropriation of foreign Crime, foreseeing that it would be injurious to the Character of the Colony.' The last thing the colonists wanted, he said, was 'New South Wales becoming a general receptacle for Criminals from every part of Europe'. So the project was banned by the Colonial Office in London and never came to fruition.[124]

From this point on, the Hamburg authorities only transported individual felons rather than attempting to send their unwanted criminals off in batches. The scale of these transportations was unknown, but it seems that they occurred on a fairly regular basis during the late 1830s and early 1840s. In 1841, for instance, six individuals were sent off to the USA at various times, including the forger Valerius de Roi, who had served three months of a six-month sentence for counterfeiting coinage. By 1846, however, worries about the possible effects of American hostility to this policy on Hamburg's increasingly lucrative trade in legitimate emigrants had not only put a stop to transportation but was also leading the Hamburg authorities to turn back felons arriving at the harbour from other states too.[125]

Crime Prevention and Penal Reform

Hamburg and Mecklenburg were not the only German states to transport prisoners overseas in this period. The small Franconian principality of

Saxe-Coburg-Gotha also tried this policy out.[126] When in 1826 the Coburg authorities initially took note of the measures adopted by Mecklenburg, they rejected the possibility of employing them for their own purposes:

> Apart from anything else, one has to ask whether a Christian government really should allow such wicked people, indeed the most serious offenders, to be transported in such a manner to a distant part of the world, over which it does not have the slightest influence itself. Every government can and should keep its subjects to the fulfilment of all their civic duties, and punish the refractory in life and limb, with life-long imprisonment and with death; but for it to allow the subjects whom God has entrusted to *it alone* to be torn away from the Fatherland and thus from its own responsibility, and to be transported into a land under a far distant heaven, thus ridding itself of them completely, committing them to a fate that is as monstrous as it is uncertain, and placing them in a situation which it cannot have any knowledge of itself, and in which it is unable to do anything for them at all – that can hardly be justified.

The practice of sending felons to Brazil, the Coburg administration concluded, was neither morally nor legally right.[127] These were powerful arguments for conservative bureaucrats to take note of, and for a time they proved persuasive.

Little more than a decade later, however, such scruples had apparently been forgotten. For in 1837 it was reported from the seaport of Bremen that

> For some time more attention has been paid than previously in the American states to preventing notorious criminals from slipping into the country amidst the general crowd of European immigrants. A numerous company of law-abiding emigrants can thus run the risk of not being admitted if they are transported on the same ship as such people . . . Only today, 13 felons from one of the smaller Saxon states, who found themselves on board a ship ready to sail from Bremerhaven, have been disembarked on the orders of the authorities.

These unlucky 13 were indeed from Saxe-Coburg-Gotha, to where they were now sent back in order to enable the other passengers to be admitted without hindrance into the USA.[128] Now that they had accustomed themselves to the idea, however, the Coburg government did not give up; it merely transported individuals rather than groups, which were obviously far too conspicuous. The evidence is somewhat fragmentary, but there are a number of cases in which this clearly happened, and there were certainly many more which have not come to light. In 1846, for example, the princely government in Coburg considered paying 50 Gulden towards the costs of transporting 'the notorious, completely penniless Elisabeth Tag', who was in prison on account of 'the numerous crimes and misdemeanours' she had committed 'over a number of years'. Tag petitioned the authorities to let her join her brother in the United States. The government thought it a good idea to grant her the money because 'such an expenditure of money is all the more in the interests of the state treasury because, in view of her incorrigible way of life, the said Tag is likely to cause the country disproportionately more if she stays here.' The implication was that it was preferable for the American authorities to bear these costs. The transportation of a 'person who poses such a threat to the property of strangers' would save the state the money it would inevitably have to spend on her upkeep in prison, and was also very much in the interests of public security. Fifty Gulden seemed rather a lot, however, and the government referred back the question of actually raising the subsidy to the local authorities. Whatever happened to Tag in the end, it was made clear in the course of the correspondence that the Coburg police had had a good deal of experience in arranging the transportation of such offenders over the years.[129]

As in the case of Hamburg or Mecklenburg, transportation was not a legally sanctioned punishment or a 'police measure', but an administrative act. If an offender agreed to go overseas to a named destination and never return, the authorities agreed to grant him or her clemency and provide him with the means of travel.[130] The Coburg government claimed that this was purely voluntary, just as it had been in the cases of the other two states. But this was not so. In April 1847 it recommended the transportation to America of the apprentice locksmith Carl August Schuster, who had 'been serving a four-year sentence in the House of Correction to which the court sentenced him in the month of May 1843 for aggressive and impertinent begging, immorality, drunkenness and idly wandering about.' The initiative clearly came from them ('so we have found it suitable that the said Schuster should be resettled in America', the passive formulation indicating clearly that Schuster was not going voluntarily).[131] Like most of these proposals, it was made shortly before the prisoner in question was due to be released. There was no question of granting clemency here: this was an administrative act, based on the perceived need to prevent the offender in question causing fresh problems for the state in future. In this respect, it was more akin to the Prussian transportation of 1802–03. It followed that since clemency was not involved, good conduct in prison was not a qualification for transportation from Coburg either, indeed rather the reverse. In 1845, for example, Johann Lorenz Köhler, who had apparently applied on his own initiative for state support to go to America, was described as 'one of the most dangerous subjects, and most injurious to the common good, who is currently detained in the correction house'.[132] The greater the reputation an offender had for trouble-making, the more likely he was to be transported. Thus Eduard Langguth, transported in 1856, was a young man who had 'already abandoned himself to wandering about and to idleness, and bit by bit made such progress in the ways of depravity that he has caused the police and the courts to take numerous sanctions against him'.

'It must therefore be regarded as highly desirable', the authorities added, 'that this individual, who is as much a burden on the state as a danger to it, should emigrate to America.' Although he had just completed a period of compulsory service in the army and was still in the reserve (which would normally have disqualified him from emigration), he had caused so much trouble here too that it seemed advisable to subsidize his emigration. This time the state's finances were in good order, and the prince approved the expenditure of 70 Gulden on sending Langguth across the Atlantic.[133] The language used in the report suggests that, once more, this transportation was not entirely voluntary.

The practice of transportation has to be seen in the context of the wider policy of the Coburg government of giving financial support to assist the emigration of anybody likely to impose a burden on the state, whether in terms of poor relief or prison administration costs. This was a time of considerable hardship in rural South and Central Germany, and poor people and families were emigrating in hundreds of thousands to America. The files show that the authorities in Coburg considered supporting some 321 individuals and families (some of them quite large) for emigration to America between 1833 and 1855; the vast majority of requests, whether they came from the authorities or (as was the case with the majority of the families) from the prospective emigrants themselves, were granted.[134] Most of these people were poor but respectable. A family such as that of Georg Heinrich Schilling, whose wife and two of whose children had served prison sentences for theft, as indeed he had, was unusual in the extreme. Since there were three other children in the family who seemed destined to take the same path, it was hardly surprising that, as the administration reported in 1855, his local authority 'urgently desires that this family, which is highly dangerous to other people's property, should be enabled to emigrate to America'. As usual in Coburg, it was not least the cost of maintaining these offenders in prison which moved the authorities to arrange for their transportation.[135] As late as 1867, the Coburg authorities were still transporting offenders whom they considered incorrigible. They were sent to America, as usual, on their release from prison.[136] Mostly those concerned were relatively minor offenders, responsible for property crimes, and serving sentences of no more than four or five years. Persons convicted of violent offences do not seem to have been considered for transportation. Nevertheless, though not practised on a very large scale – Coburg, after all, was not a very large state – the transportation of convicted criminals to the United States with help from the public purse was a regular occurrence in Coburg for at least three decades, if not longer. This may well have had something to do with the ruling family's connection with England, whose Queen, Victoria, married to Prince Albert of Saxe-Coburg-Gotha, presided over a state that had taken the lead in transporting felons overseas since the eighteenth century and continued to do so on a considerable, if diminishing, scale until 1857.

The continuation of transportation from other German states, and the administrative memory of the Siberian deportation of 1802, also prompted attempts to revive the idea in Prussia during the 1820s and 1830s. In 1828 the conservative noble assembly of the Silesian Provincial Estates took advantage of ongoing discussions about the drafting of a new Criminal Law Code to declare:

> Undeniably there is no better means of securing the state against further violations of the law by recognized offenders, none which under certain preconditions would be better suited to remoralizing the criminal and thus in both respects would incontestably deserve priority above the long prison sentences dictated by our legislation. While the latter are merely aimed at securing society against further criminal actions, and still achieve this aim only very incompletely, they leave the purpose of moral improvement completely out of account and are therefore bound to fail. On the other hand an appropriate institution of the punishment of transportation can give back to the criminal his lost or at best lowered moral independence by returning to him a degree of freedom, even if it is limited, without endangering the security of his fellow-citizens.

That transportation would protect society in Germany against the threat of recidivism from such felons went without saying. 'Penal colonies' would also allow the criminals to be observed and their moral progress monitored. Moreover, 'incorrigible criminals do not feel the loss of their fatherland as deeply as honest citizens do.' Yet the Prussian authorities considered that the example of 'Newsouthwalis and Vandiemensland' (*sic*) suggested that the end product of such colonies was only more crime and disorder. In true Prussian fashion, they blamed this on 'the inadequate provisions of the government', the failure of the authorities there to punish wrongdoing, the fact that the prisoners were too often left unsupervised and, in short, a general lack of toughness on the part of the British authorities. They were sceptical as to whether the situation would be better anywhere else.[137] The problem, as ever, was the 'overcrowding of penal institutions'.[138] Yet the Justice Ministry found the idea of deporting felons overseas difficult to accept because it would have no control over how they were treated. Nor could foreign governments be trusted to ensure that the deportees never returned.

The idea was eventually rejected by Berlin, but in 1835 the Prussian cabinet discussed the proposal again, in response to renewed concern about levels of crime in the state. It was obliged to conclude that, although it was 'desirable' for criminals to be deported, there was as yet 'no opportunity for accommodating the deported persons'. A memorandum produced as a result of the discussions suggested that the problem of finding somewhere to send them might however be regarded as largely solved if we introduced transportation to America, since we are assured for certain that up to now all foreigners have been accepted in this part of the world without distinction, so long as they possess a few necessary means of support. No one pays any attention to the name, social position or previous way of life of such strangers.

Such a scheme would have the advantage of sparing the Prussian government the cost of maintaining the felons in their new life. Yet two years later, as we have seen, the authorities in Bremen were reporting that the policy was becoming impossible to carry out.

Transportation overseas, of course, if it was to a free life in a new country, had to be seen as a commutation of a more severe sentence and therefore as an act of clemency. The memorandum continued:

> Anyone who has been condemned for example to death or to life imprisonment could under no circumstances ever complain about being transported to America instead of having to undergo such a punishment. But anyone who had been sentenced to five or ten years in prison for a political offence could be entitled to regard transportation in many cases as a much harder sentence. Transportation could be unconditionally permitted therefore in the former case, in the latter, however, only if the offender agreed voluntarily to be deported as an alternative to undergoing the sentence pronounced.[139]

The Prussian cabinet was prompted to reflect on this possibility by reports of the Habsburg government's deportation to the United States of a group of Mazzinian revolutionaries condemned for high treason in Milan.[140] However, it was clear, as the Foreign Ministry pointed out, that this was not the same as transportation, say, to Australia, since it gave the felons a free choice of punishment and effective liberty when they reached the other side of the Atlantic. It was much more like banishment, where the real punishment was removal from one's home. The Austrian government's banishment of the Mazzinians was a special case, both on account of the political nature of the offence, and because it was ordered as a commutation of the originally very severe sentences passed on them as part of an amnesty issued to mark the accession of the Emperor Ferdinand in 1835. Transportation was normally used for common criminals, not political offenders. Moreover, in 1833, when political offenders had been given the choice of either staying in detention in Graudenz, Danzig and Pillau, or going to America, they had chosen the latter and 'had managed to set themselves down partly in England, partly in France, during the voyage'. Transportation to America would therefore only be a punishment if it was carried out against the offenders' wishes. With this conclusion, therefore, the matter was allowed to rest for the moment.[141]

Nevertheless, in April 1837 the Silesian Provincial Estates agitated once more for the renewal of transportation along the lines of the Siberian venture of 1802, stimulated by the fact that other German states had recently undertaken such a policy with, they thought, a considerable degree of success. The senior Prussian administrator of Brandenburg province noted on 23 June 1837 that

> the increasing overcrowding of the penal institutions in the Prussian state is an obstacle to an appropriate treatment and classification of the inmates and in general to the institutions' purpose of rehabilitation. Neither tougher management of penal institutions nor communal after-care for offenders nor police surveillance of these people in their places of domicile has been able to prevent recidivism from growing in frequency.

Half the prisoners in the Spandau and Brandenburg penitentiaries had previous convictions, he said, and some of them had reoffended as many as six to ten times. Concern with criminality reached a peak in the mid-1830s, with a major enquiry ordered by the Prussian monarch into the causes of what he regarded as a massive crime wave sweeping across his dominions; and transportation was actively canvassed as a possible way of helping to deal with it. Legally ordered deportation seemed in the eyes of many the most effective way of ridding the country of incorrigible criminals.[142] On 8 August 1837 the King ordered his ministers to reach a conclusion on the project.[143] A majority expressed scepticism. Criminality, they said, was best combated by increasing the effectiveness of policing and other similar means; sending offenders abroad would be a confession of failure. There were considerable practical difficulties, and many offenders would seem to be unsuitable for transportation, they concluded.[144] So the idea came to nothing.

In the meantime, a new prison reform movement was getting under way. Reforming officials and liberal penal theorists alike had long been troubled by the fact that over two-thirds of prison inmates reoffended, and that the existing system was therefore perpetuating crime rather than preventing it.[145] Eighteenth-century German reformers had placed the major emphasis on the protection of the community from crime through the removal of criminals from its midst and the deterrence of potential offenders by tough sentences. The main innovation of the reformer Heinrich Wagnitz in the 1780s was to demand the moral improvement of the prisoner through education. Like Arnim and Goldbeck, Wagnitz wanted prisoners divided into different classes, but according to their degree of moral turpitude. He had little influence outside Halle, where he was prison chaplain, however.[146] Other proponents of the idea of a classification system based on the degree of moral education of the inmates were similarly limited in the influence they had in practical terms.[147] It was not until the emergence in public debate of the far tougher notion of using solitary confinement as the basis for enforcing the moral improvement of prisoners that the reformers began to meet with any real success. The liberal penal reformers of the first half of the nineteenth century looked to their great English predecessors such as John Howard for inspiration. The English idea, reported Nikolaus Julius in a series of influential lectures in Berlin in 1827, which marked the beginning of the reform movement in Germany, was to remould the offender's spirit by placing him in solitary confinement, imposing a rule of silence, banning all visits, whether of friends or relations, and preventing by any means possible his exposure to the corrupting influence of others. Forced to turn inwards, he would contemplate his soul and repent his crimes, a process which would be aided by frequent religious services and a proper programme of education.[148] Julius urged the adoption of this system in Germany.

Julius was echoed by the leading German penal reformer of the age, Carl Joseph Anton Mittermaier, who consistently advocated the 'separate' system of imprisonment on English lines, and pointed to the example of the new Pentonville gaol, built in 1842, as a model of what was required with its star-shaped construction and wings containing single cells radiating off from a central observation point. In his scheme of things, the aim was 'that the convicts should be accustomed to order, industry and cleanliness', and solitary confinement was the essential means to this end:

> Only solitary confinement provides the guarantees which provide a secure underpinning for the institutions calculated to produce improvement: 1) it alone removes the obstacles which are posed in the way of improvement by the corrupting influence of degenerate fellow-prisoners; 2) it preserves the convict's sense of honour, who in solitary confinement has the privilege of not being forced down into the category of the other common criminals; 3) it can bring the convict, if he is helped in an appropriate way, to reflection and remorse; 4) it facilitates the effectiveness of the factors which according to the above suggestions are calculated through conversation to awaken better feelings in the convict, to imbue him with confidence, to provide him with good advice; 5) solitary confinement makes it possible to apply the appropriate means for the improvement of the convict according to his *individuality*.

In pursuit of this policy, special prisons were to be built with single cells, and existing prisons were to be converted. Prisoners were to be given numbers and forbidden ever to use their own names. Whenever they moved around the prison outside their cell, or were taken to the prison exercise yard, they were to wear a mask, so that they could not be recognized by any of their fellow-inmates. Prison chapels, the central foci of moral re-education, had to be built, or rebuilt, so that the banked rows of pews made each inmate visible from the pulpit at the front, but at the same time provided each inmate with a seat that was blocked off from the sight of those above and below him and on either side of him.[149]

Liberal reformers saw this as a major improvement on what they regarded as the previous lack of purpose and direction in penal policy. 'The idea that the state is obliged to achieve the improvement of the felon in the erection of penal institutions,' wrote Mittermaier in 1834, 'is principally a consequence of the progress of civilization and the ever-widening conviction that the state must replace the raw, physical power with which it used to rule with a spiritual authority and power instead.'[150] German historians, too, have seen this policy as providing the chance for a humane and progressive penal system which was ultimately frustrated by the obstinacy of reactionary aristocratic conservatives and the parsimony of penny-pinching Prussian bureaucrats.[151] Yet the separate system of imprisonment could also be seen as an aspect of the dark side of rationalistic liberalism, along with its radical anti-Catholicism and its intolerance of what it saw as irrational elements in public life.[152] It was part of an attempt to implement a new concept of social order, emphasizing regularity, hard work and self-discipline, the obverse of the liberal insistence on the individual's responsibility for his own actions and hence, in prison, for his own reformation in a process of enforced solitary contemplation and moral reflection. The poor were to be disciplined into submission, made ready for the new world of industry and commerce, detached from the refractoriness which was posing such a widely feared threat to the emerging civil society in a massive upsurge of property crime and social protest in the 1830s and 1840s under the impact of rapid social change, increasing poverty and economic crisis.[153]

Critics of the separate system quoted prisoners' complaints of the mental torture to which they alleged this total isolation subjected them. 'My intellect has become as if confused,' wrote one, 'and the only thing which I have clearly before my eyes is hatred for the human race.' Another complained of the 'harshness and injustice' of the separate system and declared that all it made him do was dream of revenge against the cruel society which had placed him under it.[154] Yet these voices were seldom heard by the 1840s. The proponents of the 'separate system' were slowly winning the argument. Writing in 1834, Mittermaier had bemoaned the 'arbitrariness', 'lack of clarity and conceptual confusion' which he saw in traditional German prison administration at the time; but a few years later, things were beginning to change along the lines he was advocating. Associations for the Improvement of the Prison System gave collective voice to the liberal demand for reform in a manner characteristic of the voluntary pressure-groups which were springing up among the liberal middle classes in Germany at this time. Gradually they began to have an effect on the authorities, as liberal judicial officials and bureaucrats of the kind who played such a prominent role in the 1848 Revolution grew more influential, and as governments became increasingly concerned to stem the rising tide of revolution by timely concessions to liberal opinion.[155]

Thus the pre-revolutionary decades saw an extensive, if slow-moving, programme of prison reform across Germany. Following on the construction of model prisons at Insterburg and at Bützow in Mecklenburg, there were major prison constructions on the Pentonville model at Bruchsal, in Baden, and at Moabit, in Berlin. Moabit, constructed in 1844 for 508 inmates, was a direct copy of Pentonville, and in 1856, the governor ordered 300 younger, 'educable' prisoners into 'solitary confinement' for five years. 'Application of the masks, separation at divine service and in school have been introduced.'[156] In 1838 the small North German state of Oldenburg introduced the separate system in its main prison in Vechta, while in Mecklenburg the inmates of the Dreibergen prison had to spend at least a year in solitary confinement as part of their sentence from 1851 onwards.[157] In 1851 a new prison opened in Münster with 348 cells designed for solitary confinement, and in 1852 prison construction schemes were completed in Breslau, with 244 individual cells, and Ratibor, with 380.[158] By the late nineteenth century, a substantial number of prisons in Germany had been constructed or reconstructed on the star-shaped model of Pentonville.[159] All this suggested a new optimism about the possibility of reforming offenders and reducing the recidivism rate. Hence, by the middle of the nineteenth century the desperation which had led penal and judicial authorities to argue for the deportation of 'incorrigibles' no longer seemed so urgent as it had at the beginning of the century, despite the reluctance of many local authorities to spend money on new prisons.

'Evilly Inclined Persons'

There was one state in which this state of affairs did not seem to obtain, and that was the Kingdom of Hanover. It is surely not fanciful to suppose that – as in the case of Coburg – this had something to do with the ruling family's English connections: the English example could be conservative as well as liberal. United with the British crown until the accession in 1837 of Queen Victoria, who as a woman was ineligible to succeed to the Hanoverian throne, the state was ruled thereafter by the Queen's uncle the Duke of Cumberland, reigning as King Ernst August. The new monarch had spent much of his life in England, and his officials are also likely to have been familiar with the English practice of transporting felons to the colonies. Ernst August was reactionary in the extreme, and under his rule the Kingdom repudiated all forms of liberalism. By the 1850s it was notoriously behind the times in its penal policy. It was, for example, the only large German state to continue using the traditional but often unreliable method of decapitation by the sword for carrying out the death penalty right up to the end of the 1850s.[160] The wave of penal reform that was sweeping across much of the rest of Germany seemed to be passing it by. A report issued in 1860 noted that virtually all the Hanoverian prisons were still based on shared or group cells; overcrowding was common, and there were many problems caused by 'the corrupting community of prisoners amongst themselves'. Even with this recognition, it took two years before the necessary funds were made available to reconstruct the old prisons and build new ones, and much of the rest of the decade before the reform was complete.[161] Thus it is not surprising that, while other states scaled down or abandoned their transportation policy altogether, Hanover continued it obstinately well into the second half of the nineteenth century.

The Hanoverian state practised transportation on a large scale, a fact which duly came to the attention of the American authorities. On 15 December 1847, Dudley Mann, the American government agent in Hanover, wrote to the Hanoverian government reporting that

> Statements have been frequently made at Washington and elsewhere that it was a custom for states, cities, towns and parishes in Europe to furnish facilities to persons charged with and convicted of criminal offences – as well as to those liberated from houses of correction – to emigrate to the United States.

He wanted to know 'whether a practice so prejudicial to the welfare of the American Union at present exists . . . in the Kingdom of Hanover'.[162] In 1845 the American government had actually appointed a Senate commission to look into the matter, following on a previous commission which had met inconclusively in 1838.[163] It had collected a number of affidavits, including one from Moses Catzenstein, who had travelled from Bremen to Baltimore in December 1843 on a ship among whose passengers 'were twenty-eight criminals sent out of the country by their respective governments, and accompanied by a police officer until the ship was fairly at sea.' Catzenstein, who now lived in Baltimore himself, also testified to knowing 'a criminal, exclusive of those mentioned in his statement, who was transported to this country, from the neighborhood from which he [Catzenstein] come [*sic*], for drunkenness and robbery, and that said criminal is now in this city.' His report was confirmed by a Miss Amelia Blogg, who, after being 'sworn on the five books of Moses', reported 'that a man, his wife, two sons, and three or four daughters, were sent from the city of Hanover to New York about four years since, for having committed repeated robberies. The half of their expenses for coming over', she added, 'were paid by the Government of Hanover, and the other half by a congregation in that city.'[164] In effect, according to the Senate commission, foreign governments were subsidizing paupers and felons to go to the USA and become a long-term burden on the state there. Already in 1837, three-quarters of the inmates of Sing-Sing prison in New York State were reported as being of foreign origin, and there was the same proportion of foreigners in New York's poorhouses. 'Our institutions', the commission of 1838 had complained, 'seem to be made alone for the use of foreign paupers and criminals.'[165] The transportation policy was also opposed by organizations of legitimate German emigrants, who feared it would give them a bad name. One report of a German Emigrants' Association in 1845 noted that criminal emigrants always 'turned out badly' when they got to the USA.[166] Dudley Mann's approach to the Hanoverian authorities was thus made against the background of mounting concern about the practice in the USA.

The Hanoverian Interior Ministry thought that, in view of the importance of the practice for the maintenance of public security, it was best to leave Mann's enquiry unanswered. However, it wrote confidentially to the Foreign Ministry reporting for its information that in the 11 years from the beginning of 1836, shortly after the practice seems to have begun in Hanover, to the end of 1846, some 332 convicted criminals had been transported to the United States, not as a punishment, to be sure, but in consequence of royal acts of pardon or clemency decrees issued by the Ministry of Justice. 'This Kingdom has been freed by this measure of a mass of prisoners, some of whom are dangerous, and the public treasury has similarly been relieved of a not inconsiderable amount of expenditure, irrespective of the fact that it has paid most of the emigration costs itself.' The Interior Ministry considered it 'urgently desirable' for this practice to continue, and added that it 'would greatly lament it in the interests of public security, if the resettlement of such pardoned felons should no longer be possible'. It emphasized in a manner familiar from other states which had pursued this policy that the transportation was entirely voluntary. 'Absolutely no influence has been exercised on the convicts on the part of the government in favour of emigration.' Prison and other authorities were also expressly forbidden to exert any pressure on the felons. It claimed that murderers, members of robber gangs and other serious offenders had been declared unsuitable for emigration since 1834, though it also conceded that 'now and again exceptions to this have taken place'. Good conduct in prison had been a prerequisite for pardon, and the transportees had all served the majority of their sentence already before being approved for transportation. Most of the transportees in any case had not been criminals but 'tramps and similar persons who pose a threat to public security or damage the public good'. From 1836 through 1846, no fewer than 563 such persons had been transported, including their 'wives, whores and children', since ridding the Kingdom of the cost of supporting them was 'one of the principal advantages of the proposed procedure'.[167]

The transportation of 895 dangerous persons of various kinds to America in the course of a mere 11 years was an impressive feat. The figure was so high partly because local authorities in the Kingdom were able to act quite extensively on their own initiative in arranging for the transportation to America of 'persons who are a burden to the community, namely those who pursue a vagrant and disorderly way of life'. The police were instructed in a circular issued in 1835 to ask such individuals when they were arrested whether they would rather be transported than imprisoned in a workhouse. Similarly, prison authorities were encouraged to select inmates for transportation and to take the initiative in asking them if they wanted to go. The government's claim that the system was purely voluntary was thus a dubious one, for the initiative seldom came from the offenders themselves, and questioning by the police or prison administration was unlikely to have been entirely neutral. Once they had agreed, the prospective transportees could look forward to their costs being paid by either the local authority or the Interior Ministry if they had no resources themselves, and they could expect the authorities to provide them with money to spend on the journey too. They were to be given clean bedding and clothes for the journey, including 'three good shirts' and two pairs of shoes. They were to be issued with new passports, which were to make no mention of their criminal record – a measure subsequently adopted in the case of dangerous criminals sent to America as well. They were warned to behave themselves on the journey, and the officials who took them to the point of embarkation were to be provided with details of their offences. If they ever returned, they were to be immediately imprisoned.[168]

Other states also followed the practice of paying paupers to emigrate to America. The Grand Duchy of Baden, for example, is known to have sent 422 off to Canada in 1855 alone. They were said to have been dumped on the quayside, 'dirty and run down', without any prospect of employment, and the Canadians complained bitterly that it was quite wrong of German governments 'to flood them with the scum of a foreign pauperism'. They needed the immigration of strong and energetic people, 'and not sickly, feeble men and helpless women and children'.[169] As a result, and prompted by a request from the British ambassador, the Hanoverian government resolved not to send any paupers to Canada.[170] In practice, the vast majority of German emigrants to the United States were poor or destitute – this was the main reason for their departure – and the differences between the Baden contingent and most of the rest were only a matter of degree. The Belgian government was also accustomed to shipping the inmates of workhouses over to the USA, and complained in 1855 that increased vigilance in New York against criminal immigrants, for which they blamed the Hanoverians, was causing them trouble which they did not think they deserved.[171] Once more, the Interior Ministry in Hanover noted that it was best to avoid discussing the matter with foreign governments; if it had to be done, then it was best to avoid saying anything concrete.[172] Far more serious from the point of view of the receiving authorities was the continued immigration of convicted criminals and people transported not because they were poor but because they were dangerous. The Kingdom of Hanover was not the only state to carry on this practice into the 1850s – it continued in Coburg as well, as we have seen – but it was the only state to do it on a large scale, since Coburg only seems to have sent over isolated individuals and their families on an occasional basis.

The Hanoverian government made its arrangements for transportation in the utmost secrecy and steadfastly refused to admit publicly that such a policy was ever carried out. Nevertheless, in 1851 the President of Bremen's ruling council, the Senate, felt obliged to remind the Hanoverians

> that the government of the United States of North America exercises great vigilance, accompanied indeed by a certain irritability, to ensure that the United States does not become a country to which felons and good-for-nothings are deported, so that it has passed the most rigorous legal measures against the importation of criminals and vagrants, even of paupers, under the name of immigrants.

According to immigration regulations passed by Congress on 9 April 1849, the ships and shipping responsible were to be punished, and future immigrants from the states from which felons were discovered to have been transported were to be subjected to increased vigilance at the port of entry. The Bremen senate was therefore worried that the Hanoverians' continued insistence on transporting offenders would lead to sanctions against its merchant marine and compromise its lucrative trade in legitimate migrants. It therefore asked the government in Hanover 'in future not to send any criminals or bad subjects from penal institutions, houses of correction or workhouses by ships departing from the Weser to the United States of North America'.[173] As in the case of the American enquiry in 1847–48, the Hanoverian Interior Ministry thought the best course was not to reply at all; if a reply was thought absolutely necessary, then – again as in 1847–48 – it should be couched in neutral terms, neither acceding to the request nor explicitly refusing it.[174]

It was strengthened in its resolve by a report that the American authorities were in fact doing little to prevent the immigration of criminals. Investigation at the point of entry was said to be mostly the work of crooked lawyers in New York, who used the information they gained to blackmail the captains of the ships in question.[175] It would be better on practical grounds, it was thought, if offenders were shipped elsewhere in future. It had been known for some time

> that in New Orleans there is not so precise a surveillance of immigrants as in Baltimore and New York, and that the authorities of the City of Bremen pay less attention to emigrants to that place, so that the transportation of persons from penal and correctional institutions to New Orleans should be accompanied by the fewest difficulties.[176]

Perhaps they should be sent there, or to Charleston, or even further afield, to Texas.[177] Local authorities were instructed accordingly in 1848.[178] But that they should continue to be transported somewhere in the USA, no one seemed to doubt. Local authorities in particular put pressure on the central government in Hanover not to forbid the practice, since much of the cost of maintaining vagrants and other offenders in workhouses and prisons fell on them.[179] Apart from the occasional brief period such as the last months of 1851, when one local authority declared itself unable to raise the money for transportation, they succeeded in continuing the policy unhindered by any negative intervention from central government.[180] If a convict was found on investigation to possess the means, or to have relatives who had the means, to go to America, the state generally refused to pay.[181] If the offender was Jewish, the Ministry sometimes asked the Jewish community to meet the costs.[182] Only at times of economic crisis in the USA, when it would be difficult for the transportees to find work, did the Interior Ministry in Hanover put a stop to the practice, as in the spring of 1855.[183] As soon as the crisis was over, and with it the danger that the deportees would return to Hanover because they were unable to make a living in the United States, the practice was resumed.

Despite the Interior Ministry's claim to the contrary, those transported included numerous felons convicted of extremely serious offences. However, in such cases the matter had to be approved by the Ministry itself, which generally took a good deal of trouble to ascertain that the person in question no longer posed a threat to society. In 1837, for example, after lengthy consideration, the Ministry approved a subsidy and pardon for the emigration to America of Georg Helmbrecht, who had served 12 years of a life sentence with hard labour 'for intended rape and murder and actual repeated theft'. Perhaps even more serious was the case of the labourer Heinrich Georg Hundertmark, a peasant farmer's son, born in 1810, condemned to death for murder in 1826. He had deliberately shot the servant of a forester as the two men were pursuing him after having caught him poaching. Described by the authorities as 'simple, uneducated, rough', he was shown mercy and received a commutation of his sentence to a lifetime's imprisonment in chains. His brother Wilhelm petitioned the government through a lawyer for his transportation to America as early as 1841, vouching for his good character and warning that, as he grew older, Heinrich would find it increasingly difficult to earn a living as a useful member of society should he be released. At this point, the request was denied; evidently the Ministry felt five years in prison was too insignificant for so heinous a crime, which after all had involved the violent resistance of lawful authority, and King Ernst August himself refused to commute the sentence. It was only after 18 years in gaol and many more appeals that Hundertmark finally secured his release, perhaps because of the milder views of the new King Georg V, who succeeded to the throne in 1852. Hundertmark's conduct in prison was said to be good: he was quiet and hard-working and displayed a 'good nature, which gives rise to the conviction that it was no intention born of inner wickedness and calculation which led him to carry out the criminal deed for which he is paying with his present sentence'. He was finally put on board ship at Bremerhaven, his fare to New York paid by the local authorities in Pyrmont, in March 1854.[184]

The transportation of such serious offenders from Hanover continued well into the 1860s, and was confirmed as a policy by the Interior Ministry as late as 20 July 1866.[185] In March 1864, the painter and glazier Heyko Boelsen, condemned to death for arson in 1858, was pardoned and sent to America after he had served just over a third of the 15-year prison term to which his sentence had been commuted. His brothers had petitioned for his release the previous summer. Fresh doubts had arisen about the soundness of his conviction for a crime which he had always denied committing. His conduct in gaol was said to have been 'model'. Boelsen declared himself willing to go, so long as it was soon; he suffered from rheumatism and feared that, if his transportation was delayed much longer, he would be unfit to make a living for himself in the United States. One of his brothers collected him from the prison and put him on board ship, with strict instructions from the authorities to remind him that, if he ever returned, he would immediately be rearrested and made to serve the remaining nine years of his sentence.[186]

The authorities seemed to harbour no such doubts in the case of Johann Sander, sentenced to death for arson in 1845 at the age of 20 after he had burnt down a neighbour's house because the daughter of the family had spurned his advances. Although the family had been asleep in the house at the time, they had all managed to escape the flames. The prison chaplain argued that Sander had shown 'continual, unmistakable proof of true remorse, as well as a serious desire to improve himself'. After considering numerous similar reports on his character, the authorities agreed to let him go, and he left for America on 15 July 1865 after serving 20 years in gaol.[187] By contrast, the prison authorities opposed the release for transportation of another offender, Heinrich Mundt, in 1865. They were dissatisfied because he had consistently refused to confess to the murder of a gamekeeper which he had been convicted of committing with his brother 25 years earlier while poaching. Heinrich had received a life sentence, while his brother had only had to serve a few months. Heinrich's behaviour in prison in the early years of his confinement had been extremely bad, and he had been punished frequently for 'rough misdemeanours of every kind'. Although he had improved recently, the prison director still considered him a poor candidate for release.[188]

The same year saw another convicted murderer sent to America. Hans Heinrich Kammann had been condemned to death for aggravated manslaughter in 1854. A gamekeeper had been shot dead in the course of a set-to between a group of forest officials and the band of poachers to which Kammann belonged. Kammann swore his innocence throughout, as the priest who had given him his last ministrations testified. Only at the very last minute before the execution had the news of the royal clemency arrived, granted because of lingering doubts as to whether he had actually fired the fatal shot.

Kammann's pastor thereupon took up his cause, convinced that he was innocent of the killing itself, though of course admitting that he bore a share of the responsibility as a member of the gang. With his sentence commuted to a lifetime's imprisonment in chains, Kammann was unable to do anything as his wife and family fell into poverty and sickness. One of his children died of typhus, and his wife died after a long illness in 1862, leaving the remaining children effectively orphaned. In view of these sufferings, the Ministry accepted the pastor's request for his release for transportation to America and a prison official saw him onto a ship bound for New York on 18 December 1865.[189]

In the case of really serious, capital offenders such as these, it was clear that the Interior Ministry did require both a substantial proportion of the sentence to have been served and evidence either of remorse or moral improvement, or of some doubt about the soundness of the conviction. In March 1866, the 44-year-old Ferdinand Noack was paid (partly out of his own earnings in prison) to go to America after serving 21 years of a life term, commuted in 1847 from a death sentence passed on him for a break-in, during which he had attacked and gravely wounded an inhabitant of a merchant's house in Lüneburg with an axe. The prison authorities considered him a model inmate who had made a real effort to improve himself, and warmly endorsed his request to go.[190]

Long-term prisoners knew that a confession of remorse or a claim of improvement offered them the best chance of success in obtaining release to emigrate. Writing from Lüneburg prison on 29 November 1856, Theodor Knoop, who had received a 25-year sentence for theft in 1845 – the latest in a series of sentences that had begun when he was only 13 years of age – told the Justice Minister:

> I was just 20 years old when I was arrested, without a fully developed character and only inadequately educated because of the early death of my father. I don't want in any way to justify myself with this, for I do feel that my punishment was a just one; but the thought of having to spend my best years in the prison, the more because my constitution is weak, as well as the worry about my future existence give me the courage to grasp at every legal method open to me in order to reduce the length of my term. Only the hope of not having to end my perhaps few remaining days of life weighed down by worry, like my unhappy brother, animates me and allows me to dare to bring before Your Excellency the most humble request to commute what remains of my sentence to one of banishment to British North America. My brothers and sisters have offered to gather together the money necessary for this.[191]

But this argument was not the right one to put forward, at least, not at a time when less than half his sentence had been served. Knoop was evidently felt to belong to the more violent and dangerous category of prisoner, where, as we have seen, some evidence of improvement or some doubt about the soundness of the conviction was required before the Interior Ministry would agree to transportation. His request was rejected, as were repeated petitions from his family, all of whom were artisans of one sort or another and therefore relatively well educated. In 1862, the prison director at Lüneburg noted that Knoop had for many years been 'violent-tempered, vehement and mendacious' and had been disciplined several times in 1850 and again in 1858 'for insubordinate behaviour towards superiors'. This also helped explain why the campaign to get him transported had so far failed. However, the prison director continued, 'if he is easily roused, nevertheless his behaviour is good, he does not have a bad influence on his fellow-prisoners, and he is always hard-working.' Despite his character defects he was 'receptive to Good'.[192] It was time for him to be given a chance. The prison chaplain, rather ingeniously exploiting the climate of opinion in favour of solitary confinement that was then making itself felt among Hanover's officials, added that he was certainly capable of moral improvement and would do better in freedom 'than under the unfavourable circumstances of communal imprisonment' in which he had been labouring hitherto.[193] Knoop was finally pardoned and allowed to emigrate to America in 1863.

Less serious offenders were transported because they were deemed incorrigible, and little attention was paid to what proportion of their most recent sentence they had served. Most commonly, they had had a series of short sentences rather than a single long one. Men like the shoemaker Johannes Sommerfeld, who had a long list of convictions for theft, blackmail and burglary, going back as far as 1825, and was sent to America in 1841, were typical of this type of transportee.[194] The clinching argument in favour of transporting Johanne Schweinebart in 1861 was the fact 'that no improvement of the petitioner is likely'. Still only 23 years of age, she was just beginning her 13th prison sentence for vagrancy, at 18 months the longest yet. On 9 September 1861 she was told that she would be given money to go to America immediately provided she never came back. In a little over a month, she was on her way to the United States.[195] The introduction of transportation in the mid-1830s not only acted as a preventive measure in this way, it also enabled the Hanoverian government and local authorities to rid themselves of numerous offenders who had been a trial to them – and a charge on their budgets – for years past and seemed likely to continue being so for many years to come. A typical example was one Johanne Angerstein, who had been in and out of prisons and penitentiaries since 1821. A prostitute who plied the streets of her native Göttingen and other towns for a living, and refused to be registered with the police, Angerstein admitted having had sex with an innkeeper's potman in a stable for money the previous Christmas. The local police reported on 26 February 1836:

She has sunk too low since her last release from the penitentiary for it to be likely in view of her known reluctance to work and her bad reputation, which has cut her off from all intercourse with honest people, for her to take up a legal trade or to improve herself. On the other hand it is to be feared that her shameless importunity will seduce into dissipation many a student who is still too embarrassed to suppose that even a girl who merely gives the appearance of being upright can be tempted into immorality. Her removal from here and the threatened punishment of the dissolute acts she has committed seem all the more necessary because it is only the fear of rigorous punishment that keeps a mass of immoral whores here in check and compels them to observe at least the appearance of demure behaviour.

The police proposed she be put away for a lengthy period.[196] At the suggestion of the Education Ministry in Hanover, however,[197] Angerstein was asked whether she would agree to go to America instead. Given the alternative, it is hardly surprising that she accepted.[198]

The concept of 'pardon' or 'commutation' (*Begnadigung* – the German word is the same for both) as applied to such offenders was a remarkable piece of hypocrisy. Normally understood to apply in cases where there was some slight doubt about the soundness of a conviction, or the presence of clear mitigating circumstances, or evidence of exemplary conduct in prison, in Hanover it was instead applied to offenders who were judged to be difficult or dangerous. In this respect, it was often seen as a cost-free equivalent to life imprisonment, at least from the public's point of view. 'A fundamental improvement', wrote the prison governor in Lingen on 9 March 1856 of one of his most refractory prisoners, Margarethe Schulz, who had served 20 years of a life sentence for slander, arson and assisting in an abortion, 'cannot easily be hoped for in this person, and the wish to see such a creature removed from the country in a suitable way, if she is not to be rendered harmless by life-long incarceration, may well appear justified.'[199] Similarly, recommending the 21-year-old Carl Wilhelm Augustin for transportation to America on 3 September 1841, the Göttingen police declared that he

had already become in his present youthful age such a complete criminal through his unfortunate family circumstances, through the depraved character of his parents, and through his own inborn tendency to evil, that his removal from society appears necessary for its safety and welfare.

In view of his criminal record there was, they added, 'no time to lose' in shipping him off to America.[200] What happened to him after that was not their concern. That some of the transported felons returned is more than likely, though few can have been as brazen as the convicted thief Wilhelm Rettstadt, whose request for transportation to the United States was turned down by the local authority in Gronau in July 1865

> because the said Rettstadt was already resettled in America once, in 1857, at the cost and through the good offices of the town council in Elze, but returned here unimproved, and later immediately used the means once more made available to him by his relatives for emigration to America not for the intended purpose but for wasteful living.

Despite this, however, the Hanoverian Interior Ministry still agreed to put up 20 Thalers, matched by 30 more from the local authority, 'in order thereby to facilitate the resettlement of the useless and dangerous creature in question, a man who has given himself up to drink to the greatest possible extent.'[201] Evidently it was thought worth taking the risk of Rettstadt returning once more in order to rid the Celle penitentiary of the cost of maintaining him. The Hanoverian authorities had no illusions about the prospects of such people changing their ways once they reached the other side of the Atlantic. Indeed, the fact that one transportee, as the prison record put it, 'is a person who does not show the slightest inclination to improve himself' was seen, if not as a reason for sending him to America, then certainly as no reason for not.[202]

As many of these examples indicate, the initiative for transportation often came from relatives of the offender in question. Sometimes it was a brother anxious either to bring to an end the family disgrace of having a close relation in gaol or to assist someone they felt was in prison undeservedly. Less often, perhaps, it was the offender's wife. The case of Katharina Kartjen, who petitioned the authorities on 5 August 1840 about her husband, at that time serving a prison sentence in Hameln, was wholly exceptional. He was an idler and a drunkard, she wrote, he had squandered her hard-earned income, and whenever she had tried to reform him, 'I was beaten up by him in the most outrageous manner.' After several warnings, she had reported his thieving to the police, whereupon he had been sentenced to a year's imprisonment. While he was in gaol, his wife learnt that he had told the warders he intended to kill her on his release. 'He is quite capable of that, and more,' she wrote, 'and I am convinced that he will carry out anything once he has resolved on it.' He was, 'it hurts me to admit it, an extremely dangerous person.' Therefore she was asking the authorities 'to allow him to resettle in America', or, if he should refuse, to admit him 'to some correctional institution or in some other way render him harmless'.[203] The grounds on which her petition was turned down were revealing of more than the state's policy priorities in this area: he could not be sent abroad at the state's expense, she was informed, because that was reserved for those 'who are counted among the most dangerous of all, because otherwise the number of those qualifying would become too great.'[204] Evidently a mere threat to murder his wife was not

considered evidence that a man was dangerous. That the state was simultaneously transporting people simply because they were paupers, or because they
were likely to be a burden to the state or a danger to society in future, does
not seem to have counted. On the other hand, granting Frau Kartjen's request
might have opened the floodgates to popular participation in the policy,
something which the Hanoverian government, with its increasing desire to
keep the matter secret, was anxious to avoid.

By the 1850s, as the example of Hanover shows, the possibilities of using
the Americas as a dumping ground for Germany's unwanted were rapidly
diminishing. Growing nativism in the USA was leading to steadily increased
vigilance. In 1856 Congress established a third commission of investigation
into the matter. The commission reported that more than half the inmates of
America's prisons were of foreign origin, and that this policy of transportation
was therefore causing enormous sums of money to be spent by the American
taxpayer on their upkeep.[205] Finally in 1875 Congress outlawed the immigration of felons altogether.[206] Well before this, however, the practice had come
to a stop. Already by the 1840s, some advocates of transportation were well
aware of the fact that the policy was impracticable on any long-term basis
without overseas colonies, and were urging the temporary creation of penal
colonies within Germany's borders instead. Here convicts would be interned
in what amounted to labour camps, and required to work for their living.
The only real difference from a prison was that these colonies would consist
of a number of individual dwellings with land attached, instead of a single
large building in a town. Not surprisingly, this idea met with little or no
response from those to whom it was addressed.[207] When the opportunity
presented itself, some German state governments, as we have seen, still sent
convicts overseas during the 1850s. In 1852, the governing senate of the
Hanseatic city-state of Bremen took advantage of an offer from the local
merchant house of F.C. and W. Bley to ship nine convicts to Bahia, in Brazil,
on the company's vessel the *Anna*. In this way they managed to rid themselves of three inmates of the city workhouse – all vagabonds – and six
prisoners from the penitentiary – all criminals. The passage was voluntary, and
there was even a waiting list, so that if any of the nine decided to drop out,
others were ready to take their place. The costs were borne by the city senate,
except in one case, where a private charity provided the funds; but so
uncertain had the prospects of acceptance even by a country such as Brazil
now become, that the Bley brothers obliged the senate to agree 'that, if the
ship's captain should be forced to bring these people back home, the state will
also pay the costs of the return passage'.[208] And, as we have seen, the
Kingdom of Hanover and the principality of Saxe-Coburg-Gotha continued
the practice well into the 1860s despite growing difficulties.

In Prussia, however, even in the repressive atmosphere of the decade
following the failure of the 1848 Revolution, when conservative commentators linked common crime with political disorder and anxiously sought a way

to diminish both, the idea of transportation failed to find government support. In 1853 the Legal Administration Commission of the Upper Chamber of the Prussian Parliament noted:

> In fact it has to be recognized as the truth not only that prisons right across the land are overcrowded to a disgraceful degree, but also that a very large number of prison sentences which have the force of law but are only of short duration cannot be carried out because of lack of space both in the prisons and the penitentiaries, and have to be postponed for a lengthy period of time.

There were several thousand cases of this sort, and to clear up the logjam it had been suggested that transportation should be instituted as a policy for dealing with offenders. However, the commission rejected the idea, noting that it had been discussed and turned down on a number of previous occasions, from the Criminal Law Revision Committees of 1826 and 1843 to a Commission of the State Council in 1839 and 1840. The deportations of 1802, it claimed somewhat disingenuously, had merely been a 'police measure' and did not form any kind of precedent.

There were a number of practical and legal grounds which made transportation impossible as a regular policy for the Prussian state. Some of them were reminiscent of the objections raised by the Coburg authorities a few decades before. As the Prussian commission pointed out in 1853:

> All states which practise transportation carry it out in their *own* colonies, belonging to them; no state recognizes any kind of sentence which is passed at home but carried out on foreign territory.
>
> We must control the proper execution of the sentence according to the law ourselves; it must not be left to the arbitrariness of a foreign state, which has the power either to put the felon to the severest and most humiliating of servile tasks, or to prepare a light and pleasant fate for him. In this way the character of the sentence gets lost and the nature of justice is harmed.
>
> The first prerequisite of transportation is therefore the acquisition of an overseas territory suitable for colonization and a substantial navy to protect it; the costs of constructing and maintaining this navy would be in crass disproportion to the savings to be made and the advantages gained by shipping criminals overseas, quite apart from the complications to which it could lead in relations with other sea-powers.

The events which followed the building of a big German navy after 1900 were to bear out the commission's warning about complications in relations with other naval powers. The commission added that transportation would adversely affect the legal rights of the spouses and families of the transportees. And in any case, the reason why the prisons were so full was because of 'the large number of people condemned to shorter custodial sentences', so that the deportation of long-term prisoners, the only ones for whom such a measure would be appropriate, would do nothing to help. Finally, the commission noted that opposition to transportation was growing in England (where indeed the practice was brought to an end four years later, in 1857), and that the numerous executions carried out in Botany Bay showed that it did nothing to improve the character of the criminals subjected to it.[209] Humanitarian penal reformers like Franz von Holtzendorff might argue for the establishment of German penal colonies in South America and praise the educational effects of hard labour in New South Wales, but by the 1860s their views were in almost every respect out of date.[210] Other states were now generally refusing to accept criminals from Europe. In view of this situation, even the local authorities in Hanover, which fell under Prussian control after being on the losing side in the Austro-Prussian War of 1866, formally brought the practice to an end on 21 April 1868.[211] By this time, it was clear that no revival of transportation would occur until and unless German states managed to acquire colonies themselves. This was not really going to be possible unless Germans managed to create a successful, united state equipped with a large navy of seagoing ships, a development which was not to take place until close to the end of the century.

The Penal Colony Project

German unification in 1871 was quickly followed by the establishment of Germany's status as one of the European Great Powers, and with it a seat at the negotiating table when it came to dividing up the spoils of empire in the 1880s. The creation of a German colony in south-west Africa prompted calls for convicts to be transported there.[212] German prisons became overcrowded once more, with construction and expansion failing to keep pace with the massive population growth of the later decades of the nineteenth century, above all in industrial areas. Opinion began in the 1890s to move away from its previous liberal faith in the ameliorative mission of imprisonment towards a darker view of the criminal as hereditarily tainted, a eugenic threat to the racial community and fundamentally incorrigible. Social Darwinism became entangled with racism, and criminological discourse shifted its emphasis from matching punishments to crimes in the interest of rational deterrence, to directing penal measures at criminals in the interest of protecting society and eliminating inherited strains of deviance from the German race. Under the influence of the Italian writer Cesare Lombroso, the emerging discipline of criminology in Germany focused increasingly on what it saw as the hereditary elements in criminality. As in the earlier decades of the century, the evidence of massive recidivism among the prison population seemed to indicate that the reformatory purposes of imprisonment were being completely frustrated by a mass of 'incorrigibles'. By the 1890s, scientific advances in the study of genetics were giving growing credence to the belief that the tendency to reoffend was inherited. To many conservatives and even liberals, the poor in the great cities seemed almost like another race.[213] Building more prisons to contain Germany's growing population of offenders thus appeared an unsatisfactory solution to the problem of recidivism. Transportation would be far cheaper than the construction of new prisons in Germany, declared one newspaper in 1896, at a time of widespread debate on the idea.[214] The right-wing *Hamburger Nachrichten*, a newspaper that in the 1890s was widely regarded as the mouthpiece of the ousted Chancellor Bismarck, came out strongly in favour of transporting felons to the South Seas.[215]

Projects of transportation from the 1890s onwards were tied up with renewed middle-class fears of social upheaval, when the Marxist Social Democrats, most of whose activities had been outlawed since 1878, had become legal once more and were recruiting ever more workers to their cause. The industrialized working class was now a major presence on the social and political scene, and the nature of the perceived threat of crime had changed dramatically since the mid-century years. In place of banditry, wood theft and robbery on the open highway, spread across large tracts of the countryside, a more industrial pattern of crime had emerged, with easily identifiable centres of criminality and disorder in the poorest quarters of great cities such as Hamburg and Berlin, or industrial districts such as Silesia and the Ruhr. Crime, and especially violent crime, did remain higher in the country-side. But this had only a limited effect on the debate on criminality and how to deal with it, which had become highly politicized by the Imperial period. While Social Democrats saw it as the outcome of capitalist exploitation, conservatives, bureaucrats and legal administrators took this to be an excuse or even a justification for lawbreaking and disobedience, and drew even more explicit links between crime and revolution than those which had been made by their predecessors in the aftermath of 1848.[216] At the turn of the century, for example, a state prosecutor in Zweibrücken, who also chaired the local branch of the German Colonial Society, spelled out the reasons why he wanted penal colonies to be set up:

Serious and heinous deeds in every part and corner of the Reich, as continually reported in banner headlines in the daily press, have not only given rise to a feeling of insecurity and discontentment, but from time to time escalate into anarchistic and nihilistic outbreaks, which demonstrate the presence and increase of violent revolutionary activities in our society. On top of this comes the fact that our cities, into which a number of the most dangerous criminals are released every day after completing their sentence, are experiencing the gathering of a mass of riff-raff, who are full of greedy and rapacious longing for the time when the barricades go up and the revolution comes. The only effective measure against such heinous deeds and revolutionary outbreaks is the safety-valve of penal transportation . . . The effect of transportation will be to sustain the state and maintain public peace.[217]

Deportation, he continued, would not only remove such dangerous elements from Germany but would also improve the felons themselves by making them participate in the civilizing mission of the colonial power. So enthusiastic was this particular proponent of the idea of penal colonies that he proposed that virtually all offenders should be sent there, including beggars and tramps, thus ridding Germany of its entire prison population. The Colonial League under-lined these points in a lengthy petition to the Reichstag, stressing the increase of violent crime and the failure of the existing penal system to cope with it.[218] It urged 'optional penal transportation' in 1906,[219] and set up a special committee to prepare plans.[220] During the ensuing debate, some deputies at least spoke out in favour of this project, including the leader of the small Hessian Antisemitic Party, Otto Böckel. But the majority were firmly against.[221]

There were several reasons for the opposition met by the project of a penal colony in the Imperial period. Other colonial nations were becoming increas-ingly reluctant to see new penal colonies emerging near their own spheres of influence.[222] Commentators were already clear in the early 1880s that sending dangerous criminals to Africa or New Guinea would probably lead to con-flicts with neighbouring states and colonies which resented their presence.[223] In parcelling out the South Seas between the imperial powers, the British indeed secured German agreement in 1886 that no felons would be trans-ported to German colonies such as New Guinea or the Bismarck Archi-pelago.[224] Renewed debate on the idea of transporting convicts to German South-West Africa ten years later was quickly taken up by the press in the neighbouring British territory of the Cape Colony, which expressed strong opposition to the idea.[225] The free settlers in the areas under discussion were terrified by the prospect of having to live cheek-by-jowl with convicts. In 1905, indeed, the German colonists in New Guinea and New Pomerania, in the South Seas, actually petitioned Reich Chancellor Bernhard von Bülow against the proposal; the government was obliged to reassure them that it had never given it serious consideration.[226] Moreover, some supporters of the German colonial mission were concerned about the effect which transporta-tion would have on relations with the indigenous peoples of the colonized territories. The Bavarian Ministry of Justice, for example, in discussing the question in 1896, took the view that the presence of German convicts in the colonies would 'damage the reputation of the whites there'. Colonial author-ities tended to agree. The spectacle of white men in chains would hardly be conducive to respect for the European master race. The German governor of Togoland, in a memorandum that reeked of the racist ideologies which sustained the European empires of the day, declared in 1896

that the moment we begin setting up penal colonies, the prestige of the white elements, this principal basis on which the whites' position of power and their standing with the coloured race rest, would be destroyed. The more educated among the natives would certainly ask us how we reconcile the idealistic concept of our cultural mission with the peopling of the colonies which we have undertaken to civilize with criminals, and why we propose to entrust the honourable role of pioneers and bearers of European culture to gaolbirds.

In a thickly populated tropical colony such as Togoland, penal colonies were neither practicable nor desirable; and transporting possibly immoral and incorrigible white women was out of the question. Only where – it was thought – the numbers of indigenous people were small, their 'culture' not very 'advanced', and the climate tolerable for Europeans, was transportation a feasible prospect at all.[227]

Yet as one newspaper remarked, 'if "New Germany" can find no "pioneers" apart from criminals, it is lost.'[228] 'Transportation', another conservative paper remarked in the same year, was 'a short-sighted waste of money . . . Transportation is in the end a failure in terms of colonial policy; no colony can prosper as long as it is a place of penal transportation.'[229] A leading colonial enthusiast, Count Schweinitz, declared: 'Our colonies must not be ruined by criminals . . . In our colonies, we only need people who are willing and able to work.'[230] Moreover, within Germany itself, opposition came both from associations of prison officers, who saw transportation as a threat to their livelihood, and from prison reformers, who viewed it as a vote of no confidence in the institution to which they dedicated their efforts. The Association of German Prison Officers recommended instead the voluntary emigration of prisoners on release, perhaps as a means of ridding themselves from the burden of dealing with the most intractable of their charges.[231] Such a policy might offer the remorseful and deserving ex-convict a better chance of making a fresh start than he would enjoy in Germany.[232] The question was debated in 1908 once more, on the initiative of General Liebert, a former governor of German East Africa.[233] But it all came to nothing. Even this modified version of transportation received relatively little support. The French might still send their prisoners to Devil's Island, but the Germans, in the end, never followed suit. Political pressures at home and abroad had frustrated the realization of this idea. The same racial and hereditarian doctrines which led to a loss of faith in the ameliorative properties of incarceration also, ironically, created an insuperable obstacle to the use of Germany's new colonies as dumping-grounds for the incorrigible.

On the Road to Siberia

It remained the case, therefore, that the only occasion on which transportation to a penal colony was adopted as a specific punishment in nineteenth-century Germany was that of the journey of the Prussian convicts to Siberia in 1802. Nothing is known of the fate of those who eventually reached the mines of Nerchinsk. But we can at least follow them part of the way, and gain some glimpses of the conditions they experienced on the march, through the eyes of a few of the convicts who managed to escape. The route that they followed probably took them via Smolensk to Moscow, which they would not have entered but passed around, and thence to Nizhni Novgorod, Kazan and Perm, travelling the last section partly by barge on the rivers Volga and Kama. Russian convicts travelling to Siberia went on foot, marching usually between 8 and 14 miles a day, and staying overnight in villages, where their escort was usually changed. Roads were muddy and often difficult to pass along, especially in summer, and some 10 to 15 per cent of the 2000 or so Russian prisoners sent to Siberia by the Tsarist government each year in the early nineteenth century died on the way. For river travel, special convict barges were provided, with cages in which the prisoners were penned for the duration of the passage. On land, convicts were usually chained to one another at night. After leaving Perm, they would have to cross the Urals, marching through deep forest and braving the danger of attack by wolves. Passing the towns of Tobolsk, Omsk and Tomsk, they would eventually reach Krasnoyarsk, from where they would cross Lake Baikal when it was frozen over, travelling on large horse-drawn sleds, each of which held several people. From there they would have to tramp through the deep snow and ice of the 'abominable' roads around Irkutsk, across the Yablonnoi mountains, finally reaching Nerchinsk in the spring of 1803.[234]

The party of Prussian convicts who set out for Nerchinsk in 1802, as we have seen, included a number of gangs of robbers who could be expected to act in concert to achieve their freedom. The trouble began after a few days' march, when the brothers Casimir and Simon Buttkowski managed to evade the attention of the party's military escort and made off into the dark. They succeeded against all odds in finding their way back home. Rearrested in East Prussia some 18 months later, in the winter of 1803–04, they forced their way out of custody and effectively disappeared from the record.[235] The remainder of the party skirted round the north of Moscow in the autumn of 1802 and marched on past Nizhni Novgorod towards Kazan. The escape of the Buttkowski brothers spurred the escort to take greater precautions against further attempts to abscond, and the guards locked the prisoners up every night, chaining the hand of one to the foot of another to prevent any possibility of their running off. Around this time, however, a 'Russian count travelling through the area' encountered them on the road and scattered money among the prisoners and their guards. The lieutenant in charge unwisely allowed his troops to spend their windfall on drink in the village of Kostroma, about 34 miles east of Moscow, where the party was spending the night in a barn. The soldiers all got drunk and fell asleep, and one of the prisoners, Johann Borowski, managed to steal their keys and unlock himself and three fellow-prisoners, Johann Wisniewski, Johann Friedrich Exner and Matthias Fehrmann, from their chains. All of them apart from Exner belonged to the same band of robbers as the two Buttkowski brothers who had already made good their escape. The 35-year-old Exner, as we have seen, had also been leader of a 'band of thieves' which had operated in the same area of West Prussia as the Wisniewski gang. He had been sentenced to life imprisonment, and had already been the ringleader in the attempted shipboard mutiny on the way from Pillau to Narva. And he was regarded by the Prussian authorities as the most dangerous of all the prisoners on the transport. Exner's whole history had been one of repeated and persistent attempts to escape imprisonment, and it was no surprise that it was he who led the largest successful break-out of prisoners on the way to Siberia.

Exner and his three companions made off on the 600- or 700-mile journey that would take them back home, retracing the path of their outward journey in case they got lost in the vastness of the Russian steppe, where they neither spoke the language nor understood what people were saying to them. Unable to beg, they were forced to live off the land, stealing food, bread and especially chickens from the villages through which they passed. Recognized by suspicious villagers who had seen the convict party when it was passing through on its way out to Siberia, they were 'fallen upon by peasants' and 'physically chastised' in a village near Novgorod, tied up and left in a barn while the authorities were summoned.[236] But the building was unsupervised, and the felons managed to free themselves, break out and flee. From this point, they travelled only by night. Just outside Novgorod, they came to a bridge, in whose shelter a number of peasants appeared to be spending the night asleep. As the convicts passed across it, however, the peasants woke up and attacked them: Wisniewski and Fehrmann managed to get away, but Borowski and Exner were captured.[237] The two who were still at large made their way on through Opazka and Wikowicz near Kauen to Pren, where they were arrested by some hussars and sent to Marienpohl. Here, however, they persuaded the local (Polish) official that they were Russians who had fled their country to avoid enlistment in the army. The kindly man gave them the all-important passes – which they filled out under false names – and sent them on to Olezko, in Poland, where they spent the winter of 1802–03 supporting themselves by working. The following spring they made their way back onto Prussian territory, and split up. Wisniewski, however, still posing as a Russian deserter, had the misfortune to encounter quite by chance, an official government translator, who became suspicious at his evidently feeble command of Russian and ordered his arrest. As the judicial machinery of the Prussian state began to put him through its mills, he confessed his true identity under interrogation and the whole story began to come out.

Meanwhile, Borowski and Exner had been taken to Novgorod, where they were recognized as part of the convict party, and under the guard of a single armed soldier they once more began to tread the wearisome road out to Siberia, aiming to catch up with the slower-moving main group somewhere on the way. After some weeks, they found themselves back in Kostroma, the

village where they had originally escaped. The soldier who was in charge
of them came from this village, which is presumably why he had been
detailed to escort them; but he was unable to secure them a passage through
the next village on the route because of extra security measures taken after
the escape, so he took them to his house and suggested they earn their keep
by begging. Either he planned to wait with his prisoners until he got the
necessary permissions to continue on the journey, or he had simply decided
that he had had enough of the army, for which the period of enlistment, after
all, was 25 years, and the conditions of service extremely brutal and hard.
Whatever the reason, the soldier kept them in his own home for some time,
and they evidently became fairly successful at begging, for they eventually
gathered enough money to buy sufficient vodka for the soldier to get
insensibly drunk. During his drinking-bout, Borowski and Exner managed to
free themselves from captivity yet again and set off on the long journey back
home a second time. Stopped in a village by suspicious peasants, Exner
escaped and subsequently disappeared. The resourceful Borowski, however,
in custody once more, eventually persuaded the village headman
to release him, and continued on his way alone. His Russian was by now
evidently good enough for him to pay his way by begging, and in the autumn
of 1802 he finally entered Moscow. Here he ran into some fellow Germans,
and he spent the winter with them in the city, before setting off westwards
once again in the spring of 1803. This time, making his way across the
countryside past Smolensk, Vilna and Kauen, he travelled by night because
the peasants were 'very vigilant' and did not treat beggars kindly. He survived
several days in the Polish woods 'by eating leaves and drinking birch-sap',
but was driven by hunger into Kauen, even though he had no pass and was
therefore liable to be arrested at any moment. Here, neatly reversing the tactic
used by his fellow-escapees Wisniewski and Fehrmann, he 'obtained a pass
from a Cossack colonel under the pretence of being a Prussian deserter, in
order to travel freely around Russia. Thus he then [floated downriver] as a
timber-raftsman to Koenigsberg.' Back on Prussian soil, Borowski lost
no time in forming a 'band of thieves' and, using his old contacts, soon built
it up to a formidable size. Eventually, in November 1803, the nuisance they
caused was sufficient for the Prussian authorities to launch one of their
periodic systematic checks of the identity and activities of everyone in
the district. Borowski was picked up as 'suspicious' and taken under military escort to Marienwerder; early in February 1804, seven members of his
gang were also arrested; and by the end of the month, the authorities could
report that their efforts had yielded a total of no fewer than 39 arrests. Armed
with the confession extracted from Wisniewski the previous year, the inter-
rogators had little difficulty in piecing together the rest of the story.[238] The
bandits were eventually confined to a Prussian prison; but at least their fate
here was probably less harsh than it would have been in the mines of
Nerchinsk.

The story was to have a dramatic postscript in the summer of 1805. On the night of 13–14 July, a miller's servant in the village of Harpersdorf, near Glogau, was looking out into the yard when he saw what he thought to be a ghost in the darkness. Shortly afterwards, the figure reappeared outside a window. Dressed in rags, bearded and unkempt, it seemed scarcely human. But it was real enough to start forcing an entry, and the sight of several other, similar figures convinced the servant that the mill was being attacked by a band of robbers. He summoned his master, the miller Gottlieb Meschter, who picked up his hunting-knife and, after a struggle, stabbed the intruder in the left eye. Meanwhile, the servant woke a nearby cottager, the ex-soldier Grüttner, by shouting from the rooftop, and Grüttner armed himself as well and forced his way into the mill. A regular siege followed, as 'the thieves raged and threatened . . . to kill them all.' But a sally by the miller's party was sufficient to scare off the robbers, who ran away into the darkness, leaving the body of their leader behind in the yard.

On the dead man's corpse the authorities found an Austrian pass made out in St Petersburg on 13 May 1804, another document, written in Russian, and a testimonial in French from a 'Countess de Rochechouan', issued on 5 October 1804, which said that the bearer had served her honestly for four months. The man was also armed with a pistol, which could be – and eventually was – taken as evidence that he had physically threatened the lives of the miller and his men. To the doctor conducting the postmortem, the scarring on the dead man's wrists, evidently caused by fetters, was suspicious, and he checked his medical records for felons he had treated in the past. Among these was the convict Johann Friedrich Exner; and Exner's physical characteristics as listed in the doctor's file – bandy legs, a scar on the right cheek from a wound inflicted by a kicking horse, and so on – matched exactly those of the corpse found at the mill in Harpersdorf. Called upon to identify the body, Exner's former mistress confirmed that it was indeed that of the man who had recently been rumoured to have escaped from Siberian confinement. The incident achieved notoriety not just for this reason, however, but because it became the centre of a legal dispute over the right to kill someone in self-defence, after the miller was brought before the courts on a charge of murdering Exner.[239] In the end, the miller was acquitted, and the verdict was confirmed in a rescript of 14 December 1805 signed by Grand Chancellor von Goldbeck, the very man who had initiated Exner's transportation to Siberia four years previously.[240]

The case aroused widespread public interest, and Exner won a good deal of posthumous admiration for his courage and ingenuity. The contemporary legal scholar Karl Grattenhauer, in his account of the affair at the mill, found this completely unjustified:

The circumstance that he escaped his fetters and fled on more than one occasion demonstrates – apart from the carelessness of his guards – nothing more than his physical strength and his mechanical dexterity. There is nothing really outstanding to discover in his criminal career, and his person remains all the more worthy of contempt because he belonged to the common class of people, and his individuality contains no material that is even partially capable of inspiring a psychological analysis from which lessons can be learned, let alone any kind of poetical treatment.[241]

It is notable that Grattenhauer mentioned the robber's lowly social status as a reason for despising him. Such social prejudice was one reason why crime stories designed for the polite reader so frequently presented bandits as nobles by birth, while real popular heroes such as Exner were popular precisely because they were 'men of the people'. Grattenhauer found the whole genre of bandit literature and popular crime stories, despite their 'noble' characters, repulsive. They were fit, he said, for consumption only by the mob. Likewise Exner was not a hero but a 'rogue':

> Only the rabble, the mass of the common people, can regard him as anything other than a totally worthless, deeply contemptible robber and thief, or imagine that he had any spirit, character or soul. The laughable nature of this popular delusion is obvious in itself to anyone with any insight.[242]

Grattenhauer's real point was not to argue the miller's right of self-defence, nor to vilify the popular celebration of bandits and robbers, however, but to advocate the introduction in Prussia of trial by jury in open court. A jury of honest citizens, he said, would never have had a moment's doubt about the miller's innocence, and would have made the convoluted legal reasoning of the final judgment superfluous.[243] As it happened, it would be nearly half a century before his demand was eventually granted.[244]

   Johann Friedrich Exner and his fellow-bandits were not the only deportees who failed to get to Siberia. The forger Wilhelm Aschenbrenner never reached Nerchinsk either. According to a subsequent report, the governor of the Baltic town of Narva went to some trouble to court popularity among the Prussian convicts when they landed there in 1802.[245] He asked them if they had any requests. Aschenbrenner requested the means to draw, and then paint, pictures, and he managed to sell a number of them to the governor and several of his officers. Soon his paintings were so much in demand among the Russian officers in Narva that the governor encouraged him to petition the Tsar for a pardon, which was duly granted. Using the influence of his new-found patrons, Aschenbrenner then successfully petitioned for the pardon of two more of the convicts, Michael Constantin and Anton Karaschin, who, he said, had helped him on the sea-voyage. These two 27-year-olds had been fellow-inmates of Aschenbrenner in Spandau, where they had been serving life-sentences for killing a soldier whom they had suspected of betraying their desertion from the Prussian army. They had obviously been helpful to

Aschenbrenner during his confinement and had been shipped off because of their participation in 'various conspiracies to escape', possibly organized by Aschenbrenner himself.[246] The two had marched on with the other deportees as far as the town of Tver before being called back to Narva to receive their freedom. When they discovered what had happened, the Prussian authorities were furious, and did their best to get the Russians to change their mind, sending them a long list of the crimes and misdemeanours for which Aschenbrenner had originally been convicted.[247] What happened to Aschenbrenner after this is uncertain. In 1804, the friend who edited and published his memoirs reported that he was 'employed as a teacher in the mining school in Omsk, with 500 roubles' salary and 300 roubles' equipment grant, and merely punished by being confined to the town precincts.' However, the accuracy of this report is questionable, since the writer seemed unaware of the events at Narva, and made no mention of the pardon, which – had it remained in force – would surely have made it unnecessary for Aschenbrenner to have restricted his movements in Omsk. Whatever the case, it is more than likely that his class, his education and his skills preserved Wilhelm Aschenbrenner from the fate that awaited most of the other Prussian convicts in the mines of Nerchinsk.

Sitting in his cell at Spandau, and surprised by the news of the impending deportation that would prevent him from selling his memoirs as he had clearly intended when he had begun writing them, Wilhelm Aschenbrenner had been inclined to put the best possible construction on his forthcoming journey. He had consoled himself with a reading of his favourite author August von Kotzebue's *The Most Remarkable Year of my Life*. The success of this book was indeed one of the factors that prompted Aschenbrenner to put pen to paper and compose his own memoirs. For Kotzebue's book appeared as the Romantic era was moving towards its height, the gruesome and the exotic were in vogue, and Gothic adventure stories were being devoured in the salons and drawing-rooms of Europe. Its subject was the year which Kotzebue had spent as a convict in Siberia. Contrary to what readers might have expected from a book about the author's arrest and imprisonment, the book was no diatribe against Russia or the Tsarist regime. On the contrary, Kotzebue was well known as a Russophile. Born in Weimar in 1761, he had pursued his dramatic career while working as an administrator in the service of the Russian Tsar, before taking up an appointment as a theatre director in Vienna in 1797. On his return to Russia in 1800, he had been arrested on the orders of his patron, the unstable Tsar Paul, and sent to Siberia as a prisoner. Restored to the Tsar's grace the following year, he had become director of the St Petersburg theatre, but left for Germany again when Tsar Paul was assassinated. It was in Germany that he penned his account of his confinement.

Kotzebue's subsequent career continued to oscillate between German drama and Russian state service, and he eventually became a political informer to Tsar Alexander I on German affairs, a role that won him the suspicion and hatred of German liberals. This animosity was finally to lead the radical student Karl Ludwig Sand to assassinate Kotzebue in 1819, a deed which caused widespread shock in the chancelleries of Europe and led to the promulgation of Metternich's repressive Karlsbad decrees. But at the beginning of the century it was not for his political services to the Tsar that Kotzebue was famous; it was for *The Most Remarkable Year of my Life*.[248] The book was often reprinted, and prompted criticism from a number of writers who considered its portrayal of Russian society inaccurate.[249] Other writers imitated it in the hope of making a quick profit while the vogue for picaresque stories of convict life in Siberia remained. Among these imitations was a two-volume true-life adventure published in 1804 under the title *The Most Terrible Years of my Life*. Obviously indebted to Kotzebue's example, it was a spurious version of the memoirs of Aschenbrenner, whom the author claimed to have met in a convict settlement in Siberia, and from whom he said he had received the manuscript. If this book is to be believed, Aschenbrenner certainly led an adventurous life. Among his experiences, it seems, were training sessions with magicians, service with the English army and the French navy (the latter in India), the rescue of a prostitute from a Hamburg brothel, travels with a company of itinerant actors, scientific studies with a nobleman in Poland and the attempted forgery of banknotes in Berlin. Finally arrested at the prompting of a bank, Aschenbrenner – according to the book – forged the Prussian king's signature on an order for his own release. When this was discovered, he was been condemned to deportation to Siberia for this criminal act of *lèse-majesté*.[250] As we have seen, this narrative was not entirely without foundation, and indeed in some respects – for example, in its coverage of Aschenbrenner's career as an actor – it conformed more closely to the prison file on the forger than it did to Aschenbrenner's own memoirs. The book combined many of the central features of this great age of sensational popular literature – magic, sex, violence, battle, flight, travel, exotic settings, crime, imprisonment and so on[251] – and did so in a way that far outdid the action contained in the publication by Kotzebue which it was imitating. For August von Kotzebue, a notorious plagiarist himself, it must have been galling to see the success he had achieved with his account of his real-life experiences exploited so shamelessly by a rival.

Not surprisingly, Aschenbrenner found the book even more irritating. Though it showed some knowledge of Aschenbrenner's life, it was, on the whole, said the convict's friend and editor, a mass of lies and distortions. Particularly objectionable was its portrayal of Aschenbrenner's character ('an adventurous mixture of the hateful detritus of every kind of shamefulness and devilish maliciousness, which a human being . . . is simply *not capable* of uniting in *one* person in such multifariousness'). Aschenbrenner's friend therefore now published what he claimed was *Aschenbrenner's Authentic History*, written in the third person, and containing the narrative with which this chapter began. It would demonstrate, he said, that the forger was not the 'immoral monster' portrayed in *The Most Terrible Years of My Life*, but a decent man wronged by fate.[252] *Aschenbrenner's Authentic History*, as we have seen, has its fair share of episodes and devices familiar in popular literature, from poverty, imprisonment and crime to prostitution, romantic love, cross-dressing and disguise. Aschenbrenner probably fell back on such adventures, whatever their basis in fact, to ensure that his book attracted as large an audience as possible. Incarcerated in the fortress at Spandau, he was forced to earn money for his own upkeep and may have thought the manual labour – working on the repair of the fortress, spinning and other trades – which common prisoners undertook for wages was beneath his social station. Instead, he hoped to support himself not only by selling his paintings but also by writing a popular book. Thus, sensational details – remembered, embellished and invented – permeate the text.

Aschenbrenner was also clearly a compulsive forger, which gives further good reason to distrust his narrative. What is fiction, after all, but history written by a forger? At every point, the narrative stresses the propriety of Aschenbrenner's behaviour and the nobility of his motives, with the obvious purpose of winning sympathy for the author's plight. To the modern reader, this character portrait seems as implausible as the author's claim that his relationship with Wilhelmine was never sexual. To a late eighteenth-century readership, an admission of adultery on his part would have been an admission of general moral turpitude and might have alienated whatever sympathy the rest of the book aroused, which indeed was mostly dependent on the presentation of Aschenbrenner's crimes as motivated by the desire to save his wife and family from destitution. Thus it was not surprising that he presented his friendship with Wilhelmine as entirely platonic. The language and action are too firmly embedded in the genre of sensational popular fiction to carry conviction as an authentic account of the author's personal history. The stories of Wilhelmine's cross-dressing and disguise as a man, for example, are only one feature of the narrative among many that smack of pure invention. Moreover, ironically, in view of its origins in Kotzebue's narrative of his exile to Siberia, Aschenbrenner's story ended before its author had even left Germany. In a sense, it was one last confidence trick played by a practised forger: riding high on a wave of interest in exotic stories of convict life in Russia, and mentioning Siberia in its title, it said nothing at all about convict life under the Tsar in the text.

Aschenbrenner's third-person autobiography concluded with the hopeful words:

In May 1802 the journey of the criminals condemned to Siberia began. With remorse and lamentation, but also with wishes for a blessed future, Aschenbrenner left Spandau and his German fatherland. Serious intentions of obtaining again the dignity of an upright man, and the hope of making a second fatherland for himself there, dried his troubled eye and plucked up his courage to new, *noble* deeds . . . If he was passing only from one slavery into another, still, that in Siberia, where according to rumour the deportees were destined, was to be tremendously preferred to that in which he existed at present. Here ruled the polluting air of the dungeon; there he would breathe fresh, pure air under a free sky. Here only dim and guttering lamps relieved the gloom; there the brilliance of the sun would shine down on him. Oh, to be sure! He would gain immeasurably, he would come back to life there! Here he was forced to pine away in oppressive inactivity: there myriad opportunities would open up for him to be active and useful: there, yes, there, he would achieve his desire to recompense the world for his crimes through useful deeds.[253]

Accustomed as he was to deceiving others, however, Aschenbrenner here had been deceiving himself. Kotzebue had not come within a thousand miles of the mines of Nerchinsk, where Aschenbrenner's fellow-convicts were bound, and the relatively mild climate and conditions which he had described were far removed from the situation for which Aschenbrenner was at this point destined. Moreover, Kotzebue had travelled by coach, not on foot as the Prussian party had to, and had enjoyed a pleasant life as an exile in Tobolsk and Kurgan, with rented rooms, permission to go hunting, a circle of friends and a regular supply of paper to write on and provisions to live off. No such fate was in store for the Prussian convicts who followed in his footsteps – or carriage-ruts – in 1802–03.[254]

Surrounded by high mountain ranges, the hilly plateau of Nerchinsk was (and is) extremely inhospitable, sparsely populated, with temperatures rising to 98° Fahrenheit in the summer and sinking as low as −52° in the winter months. Situated 5250 miles from St Petersburg, 480 miles north of the Great Wall of China and 1000 miles west of the Pacific, the area was remote not only from Western Europe but even from the trade routes between Russia and China. As the official announcement of the deportation issued in Berlin in 1802 gleefully reported,

Only a few travellers succeed in penetrating to these remote regions, for deserts, lakes and mountains make the journey thither one of unending diffi-culty. Only a few reports have been received of the fate of the poor wretches who are employed in labouring there, and since this area is surrounded on all sides by desolate steppes and uncultivable mountain ranges stretching for vast distances beyond and serving as a place of habitation only for wandering Tartar hordes, the audacious prisoner who tries to flee this place of punishment can nowhere expect to find either any safety for his person or any satisfaction of the basic necessities of life or any protection against the raw climate of north-east Asia, and any attempt at flight will therefore quickly have as its inevitable result the most terrible manner of death for the unfortunate man who undertakes it.[255]

Its remoteness was only one of the many problems which faced the convicts when they arrived. Conditions in the mines were notoriously bad. One of the few foreign visitors to pass through Nerchinsk in the early nineteenth century, John Dundas Cochrane, a captain in the British Royal Navy and a robust liberal by political inclination, declared roundly:

> I saw nothing at Nertchinsk [*sic*] which could inspire me with any other sentiments than those of contempt and indignation at the inconsiderate conduct of the persons in authority over the poor criminals. It is impossible to conceive the haggard, worn-down, wretched, and half-starved appearance of these victims. Whatever may have been their crimes – and I believe them horrible enough – they never can have authorized the present inconsiderate mode of employing them . . . The man who is sentenced to drag out the remainder of his existence in the mines of Nertchinsk cannot live long. What have become of the many thousands of beings sentenced annually to this place? Where are their wives and families? for here the work is carried on only by the constant arrival of fresh victims.

In the early 1820s Cochrane found 1600 convicts working in 13 different mines, living in 'abject distress and misery' under the guard of 564 troops.[256] He left his readers in no doubt as to the inhumanity of the conditions in which the convicts were forced to exist.

The miners, reported another traveller two decades later, worked 12 hours a day in summer, and six in winter. Unlike the other mines in Siberia, the lead and silver mines of Nerchinsk were very cold.[257] In the 1850s, an American visitor found 'the air chill, damp, and foul' when he went down one of them. They were drained by hand-pumps, manned round the clock by convicts working on four-hour shifts.[258] Still more drastic was the picture painted by a Russian visitor a few years later. Descending into one of the mines, she noted that the only illumination came from a few torches fixed to the walls. 'Under the thin coating of dust which covered the faces of the workmen', she 'observed that their looks were ghastly. The dull leaden hue of their skin' was caused by the 'noxious exhalations' of the silver and lead ore with which they dealt. 'The mortality in these places was frightful; if a man lived two years after his arrival, it was as much as could be expected.'[259] Although conditions were said to have improved by the later nineteenth century, there was still no steam- or even horse-power, and the mining and pumping were still done by the manual labour of the convicts. The American George Kennan, visiting the mines in the 1880s, was told by local technicians that the convicts were constantly beaten and exposed to the chicaneries of corrupt officials. The conditions under which they lived and worked were appalling. 'I can hardly imagine', he wrote, 'a more terrible and hopeless existence than that of a man who works all day in one of the damp, muddy galleries of the Pokrofski mine, and goes back at night to a close, foul, vermin-infested prison like that of Alghachí.'[260] The chances of such a life improving the morality of the Prussian convicts were small. Smaller still, to be sure, were the chances of their ever returning to their homeland as Exner and his companions had managed to do.

The story of Franz Exner, like that of Wilhelm Aschenbrenner, formed an epic narrative whose legitimacy was vehemently contested by those who thought that crime should not pay and criminals should not be romanticized. Neither Aschenbrenner's final optimism about his prospects in Nerchinsk, nor Exner's astonishingly persistent and successful drive to escape confinement was finally borne out by events, though the art teacher's unrealistic vision of a new life in the mines of Siberia may in the end have been at least partially realized in the mining academy at Omsk. Both stories – the one artfully constructed by its subject from a mixture of real-life experience and narrative devices derived from popular literature, the other pieced together by the historian from official documents and legal treatises – present an astonishing picture of human endurance in the face of adversity.

By its very nature, transportation, involving endless journeys over vast distances to strange and unfamiliar countries, was almost bound to generate narrative representation in the epic mode. For those who sent such men overseas, however, the story was a very different one. Transportation was based on an admission of failure. Those who were sent were those whom the state despaired of reforming. The end of transportation coincided with the mid-century high-water mark of Victorian optimism about the perfectibility of human nature, even of the most hardened criminal. Yet imprisonment, even when accompanied by the most radical treatments for character reformation, from solitary confinement to the mask and the treadmill, was never universally accepted as the most effective way of dealing with crime. The 'carceral discourse' never went uncontested. As we shall now see, there were other alternatives to the prison besides transportation, alternatives that were not only actively debated but also widely practised throughout the century.

2

'The Bailiff's Magic Rod'

The Sufferings of Gesche Rudolph

On 21 May 1845, the lawyer Georg Wilhelm Gröning wrote to the governing Senate of the Hanseatic city of Bremen on behalf of an unfortunate woman whose 'personality', he freely admitted, was 'little suited to awakening any sympathy for her, for she is down on the files as a slatternly person, wholly given up to drink, and she has hitherto led a life which in its monotonous repetition is incapable of demonstrating anything positive at all.' The woman in question was one Gesche Rudolph, 'born to very poor parents in Radlinghausen in 1797'. Rudolph's childhood had fallen victim to the tides of war which had washed over Northern Germany during the Napoleonic era. At one time or another, French, Spanish, Danish, French and Russian armies had been active in the area where she grew up, and since all of them lived off the land, widespread poverty and destruction had been the result. As Gröning explained:

> Not only did she receive as good as no education, she soon became well known to the soldiers of all the nations with whom our district was so frequently overrun during the first 18 years of her life. She grew up in such filth that at 20 she hardly had any idea that all was not what it should be with her.

Moreover, Gröning went on, he had 'reason to doubt that she has ever enjoyed proper religious instruction, or that she has been confirmed'. This, he left his readers in no doubt, was a woman of the lowest sort, ignorant, uneducated, irreligious, immoral, poor and dirty.[1] His narrative painted her upbringing and character as a copybook example of the influences which contemporaries considered most likely to lead to a life of deviance and crime.

Yet despite all this, Gröning considered that Gesche Rudolph had been treated with gross prejudice and harshness by the Bremen city authorities.

93

Her sufferings had begun in her 25th year, when she had been expelled from the city as a common prostitute who had refused to be registered with the police. The reasons for her refusal are unknown, but it is at least possible that she rejected the idea of being stigmatized in this way and did not want to be subjected to the very tight restrictions on movement in the city, the regular medical examinations and the constant threat of compulsory incarceration in a hospital ward that registration involved. Whatever the reasons, she had been banned from returning after her expulsion, a measure which Gröning considered 'very hard, one may even say unjust'. This was, he said, the immediate origin of her subsequent misfortunes. Forbidden to return to Bremen, and unable to earn a living for herself through prostitution – the only trade she knew – outside the city, Rudolph had taken up lodging with her stepbrother, on whom she now became completely dependent for her survival. The brother, said Gröning, treated her 'with inconceivable harshness' and struck her 'repeatedly so hard in the face and head that both swelled up – a treatment which is indeed ill-suited to returning a fallen prostitute to good ways'. Her relations with the villagers where she lived were no better:

> Since she had already given herself to so many people, it was only natural that the inhabitants of Woltmershausen, where she was already living at that time, despised her, that no-one spoke with her, no-one gave her work. Treated by strangers like a leper, by her relatives like a dog, she naturally sought out friendlier surroundings, and was unable to find these anywhere except in Bremen, among women who were no better than she was, indeed were even more slatternly and inebriated.

Warned by the police on several occasions to quit the city, and physically expelled from it more than once, Gesche Rudolph was finally arrested on 15 March 1822 and 'sentenced to a prison sentence of three weeks, and to 18 strokes of the cane'.

Although she was once more expelled from the city on her release, Rudolph was back in Bremen by 19 May. She was arrested as 'she was hanging around on the streets late at night', and subsequently 'condemned by the most honourable authorities to six weeks' penitentiary and 50 strokes of the cane'. Even this failed to prevent her from returning to the city, and she was arrested in Bremen again 'on 22 August, this time drunk in a whorehouse', and condemned to three months' penitentiary and 150 strokes of the cane. Thus began a pattern of arrest and punishment, expulsion and return, which was to continue for over two decades. However much she was made to suffer by the Bremen authorities, Gesche Rudolph's desperate situation in Woltmershausen drove her repeatedly back to the city, where all that the police and the courts could think to do was to punish her more severely each fresh time she offended. In 1823, after having been gaoled for six months and received 150 strokes, she tried her luck in Hamburg instead, but by 1826 she was back in Bremen, where she was once more arrested, given 175 strokes and gaoled for 12 months, including six weeks on a bread-and-water diet. On her release, she stayed illegally in the city, and so was rearrested and sentenced to no fewer than 275 strokes and two years' penitentiary, including six weeks on bread and water once again. This steady escalation of the punishments meted out to her predictably failed to have any effect, so when she was rearrested shortly after her release in 1829, the senate ordered that the 100 strokes of the cane which the court had added to her three-year prison sentence should be dropped. If this leniency was intended to have any beneficial effect, it failed, for Rudolph was found in the city once more on 12 March 1833, just a month after her release, and sentenced to five years' penitentiary. Once more, the 100 strokes which the court added to this sentence were dropped, this time by order of the court of appeal. Once more, she reoffended almost immediately on her release, earning herself a six-year sentence, beginning in 1838, the last two months on bread and water. Released at the end of 1844, she was rearrested in Bremen early in 1845, which is when the lawyer Gröning was appointed to represent her. Since her first arrest in 1822, he calculated, she had suffered nearly 18 years' imprisonment 'and 893, that is, just to spell it out, eight hundred and ninety-three strokes of the cane!' Taking into account the time she had spent on remand, the 48-year-old woman had enjoyed only about four years' freedom since the age of 23, and had been beaten so often and so severely, and to such little effect, that the authorities had concluded in the end that corporal punishment was useless in her case.[2]

Georg Wilhelm Gröning was clearly astonished at the number and severity of the canings to which the hapless Gesche Rudolph had been sentenced over the years. They seemed to him not only futile but also savagely immoral. Yet Gesche Rudolph's story was far from untypical of its time. Corporal punishment was used widely and frequently in early nineteenth-century Germany though it should be added that by the time Rudolph's lawyer entered his plea on her behalf with the Bremen senate, the incidence of such punishments had declined and its continued practice was being called into question. Inscribed on Gröning's stark and powerful narrative was a critique of the futility of judicial repression that makes it a characteristic document of the period between the defeat of Napoleon in 1815 and the Revolution of 1848. Although it was a legal petition, it shared the emotive language and stylistic devices of more literary texts of the era, such as the celebrated *Police Stories* (1847) of Ernst Dronke, a radical democrat who collaborated with Karl Marx and Friedrich Engels on their newspaper, the *Neue Rheinische Zeitung*, on the eve of the 1848 Revolution. Like Gröning, Dronke too used repetition to ram home his message of the idiocy and stubbornness of the German judicial authorities of the era – for example, in his (apparently true) account of the experiences of the baker Johann Hanemann, who was expelled from Hamburg in 1832 after the senate had discovered that he had used false papers to gain his citizenship (at this time, a privilege accorded only a minority of the adult male population). Dronke's narrative traces minutely the baker's incessant misfortunes over the following decade. Although Hanemann eventually managed to obtain authentic papers for himself, this conviction led to his subsequent expulsion from Hanover as an undesirable alien. He then opened a business and legitimately gained his citizenship in the neighbouring city of Altona, but was convicted of a minor offence there in 1839. Depriving him of his citizenship on the grounds of his former conviction in Hamburg, the authorities in Altona pushed him over the border into the Hanseatic city-state, where he was promptly arrested and imprisoned for illegal entry. Remaining there secretly after his release, Hanemann was rearrested in 1841 and sentenced to the penitentiary and the treadmill. When the sentence was over, Hanemann was deported to Altona, whence the authorities immediately returned him to Hamburg, only to receive him back from the Hamburg authorities shortly afterwards. Deported to Hamburg yet again, Hanemann was arrested as an illegal immigrant and sentenced to the treadmill a second time. Expelled from Hamburg after having completed his sentence, this time being deposited on Hanoverian territory, Hanemann was arrested in the town of Stade and summarily sent to Altona again, where he was given 25 strokes of the cane and deported to Hamburg. As a last, desperate solution, the Hamburg senate decided to transport him overseas, although, as we saw in the last chapter, they had largely ceased to use transportation as a penal measure by this time; but the Great Fire of 1842, which burned down a large part of the city centre, now intervened, and the plan was dropped. Despite helping the firefighting effort, Hanemann was expelled again, and so the pantomime continued until he managed to get to Frankfurt to present his case to the Diet of the German Confederation.[3]

Though Hanemann was clearly no drunkard, and showed in Altona that he could live by plying a legitimate trade, his story bore many resemblances to that of the unfortunate Gesche Rudolph. Dronke's intention in retelling it was not just to point up the absurdity of the division of Germany into 39 independent states within the loosely organized German Confederation founded in 1815 – the essay which contained Hanemann's story was entitled 'Of the Homeless Fatherland' – but also to pillory the workings of the existing penal system, where someone could be condemned to repeated and escalating carceral and corporal punishments merely for being without the proper papers. Liberals and democrats in the 1830s and 1840s believed passionately in a penal policy based on the principle of amelioration. The purpose of punishment was to remould offenders so that they would be fit to return to civil society and would not reoffend after their release. Mindless violence of the sort attacked by Dronke and Gröning seemed designed more to create criminals than to reform them. Why, these critics asked, did the state waste its time and resources on persecuting relatively harmless people like Gesche Rudolph and Johann Hanemann? In the other chapters of his *Police*

Stories, Dronke told the story of a poor man driven to steal for his starving wife and children, who hanged himself in remorse after his arrest; of a young woman who gave birth to an illegitimate child, and, expelled by the police from the town where she was staying lest she become a burden on the parish, died of starvation with the infant; and of other poor people who, through no fault of their own, fell victim to police spies, indifferent employers and inhuman local authorities. All this went to illustrate Dronke's conviction, and that of most liberals of the day, that poverty – dramatically on the increase in the 1840s – was a root cause of crime, and that the existing system of punishment and law enforcement tended to make things worse rather than better.

In the 1830s and 1840s, the German penal system was in a phase of transition, as some states – such as Bremen – clung to a version of the sixteenth-century *Carolina*,[4] the great but long outmoded law code of Emperor Charles V, others – such as Austria – used law codes framed in the spirit of the Enlightenment, and still others – notably Prussia – had a mixture of different legal systems: Napoleonic law in the Rhineland, and the General Law Code of 1794 in the 'old' Prussian provinces. During the first decades of the nineteenth century, the widespread discussion about the nature and purpose of punishment and the criminal law found its way into a number of new law codes in various German states, of which the Bavarian Criminal Code of 1813 was perhaps the most influential. New criminal codes were promulgated in Saxony in 1839, Hanover and Brunswick in 1840, Hesse in 1841 and Baden in 1845. All this legislation moved penal practice in the direction of the amelioration of the offender. It was backed by a progamme of prison reform and construction – in Bremen, for example, a new prison was built in the late 1820s – undertaken by many states on a quite considerable scale.

Underlying these changes was a gradual shift from a status-bound society of orders (*Ständegesellschaft*) to a class society, in which the institutions which had maintained the German *ancien régime* – guilds, serfdom, patrimonial courts and the like – were slowly being deprived of their power and, in the end, their existence. Honour was the glue which had held this old society together; each status group, from the aristocracy to the artisanate, had its particular code of honour, anchored in law and custom, and many if not most punishments involved the public dishonouring of the offender through physical degradation in front of a crowd. Without 'honour', no one in eighteenth-century Germany could ply a trade, own property or participate in civic ritual and representation. Under the impact of the British Industrial Revolution and the French Revolutionary and Napoleonic Wars, which spread the economics of free enterprise and the doctrines of civil and legal equality across Western and Central Europe, this system began to break down. If the French did not sweep it away during their occupation of territories such as northern Italy or the Rhineland, then their enemies, such as the Prussians, began to dismantle it as a way of reordering economy and society so as to be able to mount an effective challenge to Napoleon's domination of Europe.

In this process of change, the sanction of dishonouring punishments was becoming increasingly ineffective. It was gradually being replaced by a system of punishments aimed, not at the status of an offender, but at his individual character, in conformity with the new doctrines of civil equality.[5] Corporal punishment occupied an indeterminate position in this process of change. As the examples of Gesche Rudolph and Johann Hanemann suggest, far from going the same way as torture, quartering and burning alive in the wake of Enlightenment penal reform, the pillory and public dishonouring were still widely used by German penal authorities well into the 1840s. Nowhere was this more true than in Prussia, the proverbial land of the whip and the cane. Here, the right to administer corporal punishment was associated, as Reinhard Koselleck noted some years ago in his cogent and compelling discussion of the subject, with a specific form of rule, with the patrimonial power which was wielded by superiors over inferiors in a status-bound society.[6] The Prussian General Law Code of 1794 allowed corporal punishment as a sanction applied by police courts, by judicial courts against juveniles for some minor offences and as an additional punishment on top of imprisonment in aggravated cases of other, more serious offences. According to the Circular Rescript issued in 1799 in response to what was perceived as an alarming rise in the crime rate, corporal punishment could be applied by the police in cases of petty theft. This ruling was reconfirmed in 1806.[7] But its most common use was as an instrument of patriarchal power in its widest sense. An attack on corporal punishment was thus not only an attack on a particular conception of justice and a particular penal philosophy, it also constituted an attack on a whole conception of society.[8] Seen from this angle, the history of corporal punishment in the nineteenth century has much to tell us about the changing nature of German, and especially Prussian, society as a whole.

Honour and Shame

The penal system in operation in seventeenth- and early eighteenth-century Germany placed its main emphasis on the public punishment of the offender's body as an act of retribution and a warning to others. The *Carolina*, the law code of 1532 still widely influential at the beginning of the eighteenth century, laid down a variety of capital and corporal punishments, from decapitation, breaking with the wheel, burning at the stake and burial alive, to mutilation of the face, tongue, nose or ears, branding, whipping, beating and exposure to public scorn at the pillory. These were understood as symbolic restitutions of authority in the face of its violation by the offender. More particularly, they attacked the criminal by subjecting him or her to the dishonouring touch of the executioner or bailiff who administered the

punishment and the infamy of possible maltreatment by the crowd.[9] Such
punishments were imposed by a wide variety of judicial authorities; minor
corporal sanctions in particular were widely used by estate-owners against
their serfs without reference to any higher legal body, since noble, serf-
owning estates generally constituted legal and police authorities in themselves
under the patrimonial system of justice. They went together with the widespread, officially sanctioned use of torture to obtain confessions from remand
prisoners under investigation – the principal form of evidence used to convict
offenders under the inquisitorial system. Although torture had been formally
abolished in Prussia as early as 1754, and was phased out in other German
states in the late eighteenth and early nineteenth century,[10] in reality examin-
ing magistrates and police informally continued to apply physical force to
interrogatees. Indeed, a Prussian decree issued in 1802 sanctioned this practice
in the course of trying to regulate it bureaucratically. Provided the necessary
permissions were obtained, the decree stated, it was perfectly in order to
administer a beating, 'so that the stubborn and shifty criminal is not able to
avoid his well-merited punishment by impudent lies and fantasies or through
persistent denial or through remaining completely silent'.[11] The public corporal punishment effectively went together with the private physical torture of
suspects, and when the latter was phased out, the former began to be called
into question as well.

The main motor behind the gradual restriction of corporal punishment in
Prussia during the first half of the nineteenth century, Koselleck noted, was
the drive of the state to limit the judicial powers of private police and
patrimonial estates and arrogate these powers to itself. Already in the 1790s,
Berlin was telling estate-owners to use the whip and not the cane, and to be
moderate in the number of blows they meted out, lest the punishment arouse
hostile reactions among the rural population. During the peasant unrest which
accompanied the Napoleonic Wars in Prussian territory, landowners and local
authorities reached for the cane once more, as well as for a number of
dishonouring corporal punishments whose validity had previously been disal-
lowed by the General Law Code of 1794.[12] Yet this did not stop the state
from continuing to try and enforce the law. Several dishonouring punishments, such as the 'fiddle', the 'Spanish cloak' and 'even more damaging
instruments of chastisement' were reported in 1806 as still being employed on
the land 'as police punishments'. Many of these were wooden or iron devices
attached to the face or body of the offender for a period during exposure at
the pillory and designed to symbolize the offence in question. Like other,
similar punishments also still in use, they were felt by the authorities in Berlin
to be a danger both to health, because they restricted the natural movements
of the body and the 'circulation of the blood', and to public morality, since
'the condemned person becomes the object of the mockery and wilfulness of
the mob', and the return of the offender to society would thus be imperilled.
Because such punishments in this way destroyed any remaining 'sense of

honour among the lower classes', they would in the end be an encouragement to the offender to join the underworld of the criminal and the deviant. Moreover, such dishonouring corporal punishments were sanctioned only 'by custom' and not by law. They should therefore be discontinued.

Such remarks showed how far the thinking of Prussian officialdom was now removed from the original discourse of punishment under the old regime. Of course, the period around 1806, when the Prussian state was in deep crisis following its shattering defeat by Napoleon at the battles of Jena and Austerlitz, was not perhaps the best time to try and enforce these views. Not surprisingly, therefore, reports of the use of dishonouring corporal punishments in the countryside continued to come to Berlin despite the major legislation of 1807 which, along with further measures in 1811, brought about the effective abolition of serfdom in most parts of Prussia. The Superior District Court in the Neumark administrative area noted in 1810 that the cane was still widely used 'for trivial misdemeanours, especially offences against by-laws and resistance to the authorities' and was 'carried out on the spot' by 'village courts or local judicial authorities'. This meant in practice that feudal overlords and aristocratic landowners who possessed jurisdictional and police powers over those serfs who lived and worked on their estates were applying traditional corporal punishments without reference to the codified criminal law. King Friedrich Wilhelm III banned all these punishments outright in 1810, ordering that even patrimonial courts were only allowed to administer the punishments explicitly laid down in the General Law Code of 1794.[13] Yet in 1816, the administrative authorities in Breslau reported that corporal punishments which had 'long been forbidden' remained in use in the area. It was still common for offenders to be publicly displayed in an iron collar outside a church, a courthouse or an inn. The Breslau authorities defended this practice vigorously two years later in 1818, adding 'that the two rescripts alluded to by the Royal Justice Ministry no more apply to the Silesian punishment of caning than did the rescript on the abolition of the Spanish cloak and the Polish goat'. Such punishments were still 'widely used' against male farmhands subject to feudal or semi-feudal forms of employment. The reasons for this were not so much ideological as economic: 'For it is not so much the farmhands who are punished by having to sit in the local gaol . . . as their lords, who are forced to do without their labour.' Imprisonment deprived landlords of the services of their workers; a quick beating did not. As late as 1832 there were reports that the cane was still being used in Silesia. Further west, too, dishonouring public and corporal punishments persisted long after their abolition in formal law. In Wittenberg, the iron collar was reportedly still being employed in 1824. Offenders were also paraded in front of the town hall, with a 'cardboard placard' hung round their neck, which had their name and offence ('fraudster', 'perjured fraudster', etc.) written on it.[14] Honour and shame remained powerful weapons in the penal armoury of local authorities in the 1820s, however much the central bureaucracy might consider them to be outmoded in this context.[15]

All this went to show that any effort on the part of the authorities in Berlin to enforce the idea of equality before the law in the wake of the emancipation of the serfs would inevitably meet with stubborn resistance in the countryside. Indeed, inequality before the law was built into the very idea of corporal punishment itself.[16] In 1804, Grand Chancellor von Goldbeck, Prussia's top legal official, reinforced this inequality by banning the corporal punishment of public officials. 'Physical chastisement', he added, 'is in general to be used mainly for thieves and similar criminals.' To whip civil servants for 'dereliction of duty', he said, was inappropriate.[17] The whip was thus explicitly reserved for the lower orders, a fact underlined by one of the many compromises reached by the increasingly wavering authorities in Berlin during the emancipation of the serfs: for in 1810, the new Servants' Law continued to allow landlords the right to chastise their farm servants, though it forbade them to apply specifically dishonouring punishments. In 1812, the King backed this up by ordering that corporal punishment should only be meted out to 'persons of the lower class'.[18] All this indicated that the steps taken in the General Law Code of 1794 towards establishing the principle of equality before the law in Prussia had not been implemented across the board. On the contrary, the emancipation of the serfs in 1807 and 1811 had been carried out in such a way as to preserve the principle of inequality that had previously sustained the structures and hierarchies of rural society.

These reforms thus failed to still criticism of corporal punishment in Prussia by liberals and reformers wedded to the egalitarian and humanitarian principles spelled out by the French Revolution and espoused in some of the earlier drafts of the 1794 Code. The courts were not slow to point out inconsistencies in the measurement of equivalents between custodial and corporal punishments. For instance, the Decree of 28 September 1808 for the Prevention of Horse-Thefts laid down a sentence of one year's penitentiary as equivalent to 100 lashes, while another rescript, issued on 17 July 1804, laid down a prison sentence of six weeks as equivalent to 60 lashes.[19] As well as inconsistencies such as these, courts were concerned, as the Criminal Division of the East Prussian Superior District Court reported on 6 October 1826, that

> in itself the variability of criminals' physical constitution makes the effect of corporal punishment variable as well, and a beating that might be trivial in itself can mean a hard and painful punishment for those criminals whose previous circumstances have not accustomed them to such treatment, or whose physical constitution is more sensitive to beatings than is that of other offenders.[20]

Considerations such as these prompted further restrictions of corporal punishment by the authorities in Berlin. On 9 October 1833, it was decreed that offenders who voluntarily confessed to a crime before they had been arrested or charged should be spared the rod.[21] Finally, provincial administrators were also instructed by the Ministry of the Interior to deal firmly with abuses of police power in the matter of corporal punishment – widely reported from landed estates in the 1820s – and to press for other sanctions, such as fines, to be substituted wherever possible.[22]

The hesitant and uneven character of the Prussian state's animus against corporal punishment is given expression in the numerous drafts of a new Criminal Code drawn up in this period. As Justice Minister Mühler reported in 1833:

> Many and weighty objections have recently been raised against the corporal punishments which are still employed as legal means of chastising criminals from the lowest classes of people and of punishing minors, and the majority of votes in the deliberations held on the revision of the law up to this point have even been in favour of the complete abolition of this means of punishment.

The draft Criminal Code of 1827 retained corporal punishment only 'as a subsidiary punishment to add to sentences of forced labour and the penitentiary' and 'as a principal punishment against juveniles under the age of 16, and also in certain offences as a substitute for an eight-day to three-month prison or workhouse sentence'. Further drafts in 1830 and 1833 dropped it, but another draft, completed in 1836, at a time when the authorities in Berlin were concerned with rising crime rates, reinstated it 'as an independent punishment and as an additional punishment for the lower classes of the population'. Such fundamental disregard for the principle of equality before the law gave this particular draft a very backward-looking flavour, and it was only slightly diluted in the draft of 1843, which laid down that whipping 'may be carried out on persons of the male sex and indeed not only for the offences and misdemeanours listed in the specific sections but also as a police measure in cases of gross public nuisance'.[23] Already, however, opposition to such proposals among Rhenish liberals was mounting, not least because corporal punishment had been abolished in the Rhineland under Napoleonic law and had not been reinstated in 1815. The publication of the draft of 1843 aroused widespread criticism in the Rhineland, and ensured that the next draft in this seemingly never-ending series, completed in 1845, dropped corporal punishment altogether, 'in consideration of the regard one must have for the maintenance and increase of the sense of honour even amongst the lower orders'. Corporal punishment would dishonour offenders, it was argued again, and so tend to make them more likely to commit crimes, rather than less.[24]

It was only at the insistence of King Friedrich Wilhelm IV that it was written back in to the final draft 'against male criminals who have lost their civil rights as a result of an earlier sentence, if they have been condemned to a period in the penitentiary for robbery, theft or receiving stolen goods'.

However, the United Corporative Committee, a representative body of noblemen called during the gathering crisis of the state in the months leading up to the 1848 Revolution, voted for the complete abolition of corporal punishment 'by a great majority' on 30 December 1847.[25] In consequence, the King and the Justice Ministry were forced to reconsider the matter, and asked Police President Julius Baron von Minutoli to write a report. Minutoli was no hothead, and during the subsequent revolution won something of a reputation as a moderate.[26] However, on the matter of corporal punishment, he was firmly conservative. His report put the case for retention in the strongest possible terms. The objections raised by liberals, Minutoli wrote, could be reduced to the claim

> that this mode of punishment contradicts the moral dignity of the human being in itself, because it is only aimed at the bestial element in his nature, that corporal punishment kills off better feelings in humans; that it therefore only renders the criminal more stubborn, and fails to make him a better person, which after all is the real aim of all punishment.

Minutoli dismissed these objections as 'axioms derived from abstract philanthropic speculation'. They had no basis in the practical experience of real life, he said. He dismissed the claim that corporal punishment was incompatible with human dignity. It was, he said, the *entire point* of any punishment that it was incompatible with human dignity, of which crime and the criminal were themselves direct contradictions. Personal freedom, he observed, was surely the foundation of the dignity of every individual human being, and yet penal reformers had no compunction in depriving the offender of it for lengthy stretches of time. This could be a worse torture than a whipping. Corporal punishment, he said, addressed the animal in man because it was from the animal in man that crime sprang. He allowed that a strict separation had to be maintained between punishments that were dishonourable and punishments that were not, otherwise offenders who were not dishonourable would become so, and it would thus be more difficult than otherwise for them to abandon their life of crime and return to normal human society. For the dishonourable offender, however, corporal punishment was appropriate. Physical fear was the only effective deterrent for such people; they had already lost any sense of morality, and an appeal to the baser emotions was the only way of resuscitating it. 'Anyone who has often had the opportunity of witnessing such corporal punishments being carried out', he remarked, 'will confirm that such punishments almost never fail to leave an impression of a favourable moral transformation of the offender's spirit.' Not imprisonment, but 'the bailiff's magic rod' would bring 'a feeling of true remorse', he declared. Corporal punishment would also be a more effective preventive of crime than imprisonment, he said, implying that the latter held no terrors for hardened criminals.[27]

But these views were already outdated by the time they were committed to paper. Officials in the Ministry of Justice reacted with scepticism and disbelief, and covered Minutoli's memorandum in marginal question marks and underlinings. Very shortly afterwards, in March 1848, the fall of the July Monarchy in France sparked revolutions right across Europe. In Germany, a decade or more of economic hardship and social unrest, expressed among other things in a major increase in property crimes, riots and disturbances through the 1840s, came to a head. Popular uprisings forced monarchs and governments in Berlin, Vienna, Munich and elsewhere to concede liberal reforms or withdraw from the scene altogether. Liberal ministers succeeded conservative ones and prepared to implement wide-ranging measures of social, economic and political change. Among the areas affected were legal and penal reform. Equality before the law, trial in open court, the independence of the judiciary and many other classic liberal demands dating from the era of the French Revolution of 1789 were now on the agenda. Liberal and democratic opposition to corporal punishment came to a head. The case against it was summed up on 24 April 1848 by the Berlin Constitutional Club, one of many voluntary associations set up to debate the shape which liberals and reformers wished post-revolutionary Germany to take. It argued

> that corporal chastisement is a thoroughly immoral punishment, completely contradicting the principle of constitutional monarchy; that the whole land has spoken out against this punishment, which dishonours humanity; that no reason can be found for permitting a punishment which is unknown in the Rhine Province to persist in the old provinces; that the *immediate* abolition of this punishment can be ordered with all the more confidence since according to the Ministerial Rescript of 23 May 1812 it may only be applied to criminals of the *lowest* class of the people, whereas it is a minimum requirement that all classes of the people must immediately be granted equality before the law.[28]

Unable to resist this pressure, the Prussian King, Friedrich Wilhelm IV, was obliged to issue a rescript on 6 May 1848 abolishing corporal punishment throughout the Prussian lands.[29] But it was not only in Prussia that the liberal critics of corporal punishment triumphed. Part of the agenda of 1848 was the creation of a united Germany based on a parliamentary constitution, and the Constituent Assembly which met in Frankfurt following elections held all over Germany immediately began a wide-ranging debate on the fundamental principles on which the new German state was to be founded. Enshrined in the Basic Rights of the German People, these principles included the right to be free from physical chastisement by the state. By outlawing corporal punishment throughout Germany, paragraph 9 of the Basic Rights gave concrete expression to the liberal belief in the exclusive legitimacy of imprisonment as a penal sanction and the inadmissibility of dishonouring and shaming forms of punishment.[30] Of course, this was only a statement of principle, and it had to be implemented in legislative enactments by the individual German states, from Baden and Württemberg to Bavaria and Prussia, before it became law. Nevertheless, under the immediate impact of the events of 1848, most German states did ensure that the courts abandoned corporal punishment for the time being – including Bremen, where it was officially abolished altogether in May 1848.[31] The day of the whip and the cane finally seemed to be over.

The Campaign to Reinstate Corporal Punishment in the 1850s

The triumph of liberalism in 1848 did not last for long. Within a year, the revolution had been reversed. The Frankfurt parliament proved unable to impose its will upon the states. The project of German unification foundered on the intransigence of Austria and Prussia. The liberals were too frightened by continuing popular unrest to use lower-class discontent as a weapon in the struggle for supremacy. By the time Prussian troops broke up the remnants of the Frankfurt parliament, the Basic Rights were a dead letter, soon to be repealed where they had been implemented, forgotten where they had been ignored. Liberal governments and ministers were dismissed and replaced with out-and-out reactionaries determined to reimpose order. The 1850s were a decade of reaction, in which authoritarian policing methods were ruthlessly employed by governments determined to stamp out all vestiges of revolution. In this context, it is not surprising that a major effort was made to reinstate corporal punishment in Prussia. King Friedrich Wilhelm IV himself said in 1852 that he had always believed in corporal punishment for boys and youths and for certain categories of crime. He had signed the law of 6 May 1848 'with the greatest reluctance'. Everything that had happened since 1848, he told Justice Minister Simons, had strengthened his support for corporal punishment.[32] The prison reformer Heinrich Wichern, remarked the monarch, had reported that Prussia's prisons were 'overcrowded' and that the situation was posing a serious threat to the health and morality of the prison population. While Wichern had intended his criticism as a spur to reforming the prisons, the King took it as an encouragement to replace imprisonment with whipping for juvenile offenders, for crimes committed 'wilfully' and for the lesser categories of theft.[33] 'If incidentally', he added, 'the need to reintroduce corporal punishment has been recognized even by a substantial majority of the lower chamber of the legislature in a state such as Württemberg, which has been so thoroughly disrupted by liberal theories for decades, then it surely cannot (be impossible) for Prussia.'

The King's initiative sparked a lively debate within the Prussian governmental and administrative machine. Friedrich Wilhelm's chief supporter was the Interior Minister, Ferdinand von Westphalen, an arch-conservative whose reactionary stance may have been strengthened by the need to overcome the embarrassment of the fact that he also happened to be Karl Marx's brother-in-law, a position which even exposed him on one occasion in the early 1860s to a begging letter from his sister, Jenny von Westphalen, Marx's wife, when the family was in serious financial trouble.[34] Despite his initial scepticism,[35] Westphalen had come round by 1854 to the view 'that moral conditions have deteriorated, not improved, since the abolition of corporal punishment. I even take the view,' he continued, 'that the new penal law system has had a deleterious rather than a beneficial effect on social conditions.' Crime had increased since 1848 because the fear of corporal punishment had been taken away. Prussia's prisons had become overcrowded as a result. In consequence, he went on,

> the intercourse of the convicts with one another produced by this overcrowding cannot be prevented and leads to repeated crimes being committed. The *extension* of prisons and penal institutions and the construction of additional ones will do nothing to alter this disastrous situation, but will only make it worse.

'An impudence of spirit' among the lower orders had resulted from the abolition of corporal punishment, he said. The Rhine province, acquired by Prussia under the Vienna settlement of 1815, might enjoy the dubious privilege of sparing its subjects the rod because it continued to be under Napoleonic law, he reasoned, but the reintroduction of corporal punishment in the rest of Prussia would convince the Rhinelanders of the error of their ways, as they saw crime rates falling elsewhere.[36] Westphalen was influenced in this change of mind by the fact that a survey of opinion among administrators in the 'old Prussian' provinces showed a good deal of enthusiasm for the idea of reintroducing corporal punishment. Only the administrative authorities of Stettin, Bromberg and Münster were opposed; all the others were in favour. In the Rhine province, perhaps predictably, all the authorities apart from Trier were hostile to the idea of a reintroduction of corporal punishment after so many decades without it; but they were very much in the minority in Prussia as a whole.[37] Westphalen could claim the support of the town council of Lützen, the senior administrator and representative institutions of the province of Saxony and 'several petitions, some of which are adorned with thousands of signatures or crosses instead of signatures'.[38] Petitioners were clearly afraid of the cost to taxpayers of a major prison construction scheme and preferred the reintroduction of corporal punishment as a cheaper alternative. They also viewed prison as a soft option. 'For many,' complained one petition, 'prison is a place of rest.' 'Many criminals do not suffer punishment but, as they feel, receive a reward' by being imprisoned. Corporal punishment should be employed, therefore, 'in cases of persistent vagabondage and mendicancy, for petty theft, gross disobedience and impudence on the part of servants, and cruelty to animals'.[39]

A useful sample of opinion among administrators in East Elbian Prussia – the overwhelming majority of them aristocratic landowners, of course – can be found in the returns to the enquiry from the Marienwerder administrative district. The rural adminstrators (*Landräte*) were all in favour of reintroducing corporal punishment for farm servants, who were after all their own employees and those of their friends, neighbours and social acquaintances among the Junkers. As one of them remarked, there were many cases in which 'a few blows work infinitely better than prison'.[40] Another, the district administrator of Neumark, complained, in alarming and no doubt exaggerated tones: 'Through the abolition of corporal punishment it has come to a pretty pass here, for the landowners now fear their servants and their people more than they do [their masters].' He advocated reintroducing it for farm labourers and juvenile servants as well as for criminals and vagabonds, who, he said, had only grown in 'impudence' since its abolition in 1848.[41] 'In areas where the people in general are at a very primitive level of civilization,' wrote another district administrator, meaning his own district, 'the general abolition of corporal punishment can in my opinion only be lamented.' He urged its reintroduction for farm and estate servants, because imprisonment was demonstrably ineffective.[42] It hurt the landowner, as another district administrator remarked, by depriving him of his farm servant's labour, and it hurt the local authority by throwing the offender's family onto the parish. Prison provided the poor and ignorant farm labourer with regular nutrition, frequently better than what he got at home, and it supplied him in addition with the 'interesting company of old villains'. Indeed, convicted East Elbian farm labourers would most probably not want to leave prison at all, 'if bedbugs and other vermin did not replace the slumbering pricks of conscience'.[43] Most farm labourers, one of his colleagues remarked, had no 'sense of honour' and saw imprisonment not as dishonouring, but as simply providing a 'carefree life'.[44] All this of course was a comment as much upon the miserable poverty in which the East Elbian farm labourers lived, as upon the way in which Prussian prisons were run at this time.

Prison sentences, as more than one local official complained, were passed far too long after the offence to which they applied had been committed, due to the cumbersome procedures of the courts.[45] Corporal punishment could be administered immediately, and to instant effect, with or without legal sanction. Indeed: 'In earlier times many petty misdemeanours were not brought to the attention of the courts at all, but immediately punished by the landlord and the police authorities by imprisonment or beating.' This situation had to some extent continued, and one rural district administrator observed that 'corporal chastisement may not have enjoyed validity as a legal criminal sanction since 1848, but it is still widely used as a disciplinary measure by employers.' It was the only thing that the 'roughest popular classes' understood, and indeed they frequently used it amongst themselves, as 'the great number of fights which take place in this area shows'.[46] The rural district administrator for Marienwerder joined the general chorus of complaint about what had happened since the decree of 6 May 1848. The farm labourers and servants, he said, had

> become more defiant, more selfish and more refractory, in that as soon as the spring approaches and work on the land gets under way, they have no compunction about leaving their service in secret, and they also deliberately provoke their employers to administer light corporal chastisements through their disobedience, etc., so that they can find an excuse to sue them and force their release from their service, and in such cases indeed the courts have frequently imposed monetary fines on the employers.[47]

This alarming spectacle of a cunning labour force deliberately provoking the Junkers into beating them in order to sue in the courts for dismissal owed more to the inflamed imagination of the district administrator than to reality. But the same assumption – that the farm servants were not free labourers, but somehow belonged to the Junkers just as they had done in the days of serfdom – was apparent in other returns besides this one. Almost all of them agreed 'that a disturbing loosening of the ties of discipline and order has taken place since 1848'.[48] As the district administrator for Wallenrodt observed, there had been a 'moral decline among the servant classes'. They got drunk, they failed to work properly in the fields and they were not deterred by prison, which gave them what they wanted anyway, by taking them away from hard agricultural labour and supporting them in comfortable and well-fed surroundings without any real work to do. He said it was the fault of the 'superhumanistic tendencies of the recent past and the demands of theoretical world-improvers' that, 'especially amongst the servant classes, disobedience, rebelliousness, coarseness and impudence are now on the agenda'.[49]

The real objection of all these aristocratic landowners and rural administrators was to the breakdown of rural social hierarchies under the impact of market forces – or, as one of them put it, the 'increasing decline in the morality of the lower classes altogether, brought about by the ever-increasing lust for pleasure and the drive to put themselves on an equal footing with the class of people immediately above them'.[50] Corporal punishment, and the right to use it, symbolized the perpetuation of the old social system in the East Elbian countryside. This had been seriously eroded as a result of the emancipation of the serfs, which had been completed in 1848 and which proved in effect to be irreversible. People such as the Polish ethnic minority in the Marienwerder district existed on a 'low cultural level' (in the opinion of the local administrators) and were incapable of benefiting from the same penal sanctions as were applied to people who possessed a 'feeling of higher worthiness and civil honour'.[51] Only a whipping would keep them in order. Serfs they might no longer be, but obedience was still required of them.

Yet there were serious obstacles to the reintroduction of corporal punishment in Prussia in the 1850s. For the defeat of the 1848 Revolution in reality had been less than total. The reactionary governments of the post-revolutionary years realized they could not turn the clock back completely. On the contrary, to re-establish order, they had to reach some kind of compromise with the liberal middle classes. In Prussia, one of the main elements in the post-revolutionary compromise was the promulgation of a new Criminal Law Code in 1851. This conceded a large number of liberal demands, including trial in open court, the ending of public executions and the empanelment of juries or their equivalent in criminal cases. The bourgeois demand for order meshed with that of the authorities, and found expression in harsher custodial sentences for a wide range of offences. These measures meant that the reintroduction of corporal punishment seemed redundant to many. It was significant that the only bourgeois official in the Marienwerder district to send in a return to the Justice Ministry, the mayor of the town of Thorn, sharply opposed it. Whatever the rights and wrongs of the abolition of corporal punishment in 1848, he said, the fact was that it was one thing to leave old customs in being, quite another to reintroduce them once they had been abolished:

> It cannot be denied – after a certain independent political consciousness has been encouraged in that section of the people which is at all capable of developing one, and after it has taken root there – after in the course of five years corporal punishment has been reproved as inadmissible and dishonourable, and a feeling of honour has become fixed in opposition to it even amongst the lower strata – it cannot now be denied that the *general* reintroduction of the same would come into conflict with the moral idea and conception of honour and justice in a large section of the population.

The mayor denied that juvenile crime was on the increase, and argued that the harsher custodial sentences laid down by the Criminal Code of 1851 had had a marked effect in reducing the number of offences committed, except among a hard core of recidivists. 'The criminal law of a people', he said, 'is a mirror of its moral standpoint and its degree of education.' He argued that the reintroduction of corporal punishment 'appears to lower the level of culture, which it is the mission of the government to maintain and to raise.' Reintroduction would simply create popular 'sympathy' with those punished. This did not mean that it should be removed from society altogether, of course, and the mayor went on to argue that as an instrument of the age-old tradition of paternal power, corporal punishment could legitimately be used by the state 'as a disciplinary measure' for juveniles, provided the offender's parents consented. But as a sentence passed on adults by the courts, he firmly believed it had had its day.[52]

With the exception of Interior Minister Westphalen, the Prussian ministers agreed with the mayor of Thorn's point of view.[53] The cabinet warned that, in the new penal climate of the 1850s, it would constitute a 'violation of the basic principles of the criminal law' if 'a dishonouring type of punishment were to be laid exclusively upon certain classes of people'.[54] Formal equality before the law was one of the liberal demands which had been granted as part of the political compromise embodied in the Criminal Code of 1851. Under the King's proposal to apply corporal punishment to offences committed 'out of wilfulness', moreover, its use would be left to the decision of the individual judge in each particular case, and so its application was almost bound to be inconsistent and therefore arbitrary. Whipping would destroy young offenders' 'sense of honour' and so be just as bad as putting them in a prison with older criminals who would corrupt them. The solution was the creation of special custodial institutions for the young. The Justice Ministry added that the increase in crime rates had begun years before the abolition of corporal punishment, in the mid-1830s, and not subsequent to it. The reintroduction of corporal punishment would be retrogressive, putting Prussia behind many other German states in the matter of penal reform. It should, the Justice Ministry urged, be rejected.[55] The opinion of the courts, canvassed by the Ministry in a wide-ranging consultation exercise, was slightly in favour of corporal punishment for juvenile offenders, but on balance came down against it for other classes of offender.[56] Thirteen appeal courts and some 60 courts of first recourse were against any reintroduction of corporal punishment, while seven appeal courts, two criminal senates and some 80 courts of first recourse were in favour, though five of the appeal courts and 40 of the others wanted it applied to juvenile offenders only. Particularly noteworthy in the Ministry's view was the strong opposition of two-thirds of the appeal courts to bringing back the whip. Armed with this information, the Justice Ministry in its draft resolution of 24 March 1854 reiterated its opposition to the plan. Justice Minister Simons saw little prospect of its succeeding in reducing the crime rate, and suggested that those courts and authorities which supported corporal punishment for juvenile offenders did so principally because suitable correctional institutions had not yet been opened in their districts. Prussia's Chief of Police Carl Ludwig Friedrich von Hinckeldey also took the view that corporal punishment 'has been proved by experience to be almost completely ineffectual when applied to hardened and previously convicted subjects, while among people who still retain some sense of honour it blunts this too and in the end destroys it altogether.'[57]

This was not quite the end of the matter, however, for in 1856 the Prussian chamber of deputies also considered the reintroduction of corporal punishment in response to a motion from Rosenberg-Lipinsky and other Prussian Conservatives. The mood among some local authorities, police officers and people of widely varying social standing in Krotoschin, Falkenberg, Glogau, Pommern, Köslin and other parts of old Prussia was strongly in favour of reintroducing the whip for juvenile offenders, tramps, beggars and the 'work-shy'. Crime rates had increased steadily, argued Rosenberg-Lipinsky and his associates, and the prisons were desperately overcrowded. Tougher punishments were needed to remedy the situation. As the commission set up to report on the motion pointed out, the law of 11 April 1854, allowing prisoners to be employed on labour schemes outside the prisons, had alleviated the overcrowding somewhat; yet it had done nothing to tackle the root problem of the long-term increase in the crime rate. In 1836, a wide-ranging enquiry into the causes of the increase in crime rates had highlighted a number of problems, such as deficiencies in elementary education, excessive consumption of spirits and a high degree of morcellization of landholdings, which, 20 years later, had still by no means been overcome. Moreover, the commission went on to observe in a passage that was a masterpiece of bureaucratic grammar and style as well as a revealing example of the links which the Prussian ruling elite was beginning to draw between crime and revolution, new, still more baleful influences on popular morality had emerged since then:

> It certainly seems to be the case that the increase of luxury and the desire for pleasure among the upper classes has found a fateful imitation among the lower classes of the people and has opened the gates of crime to them through gluttony and excessive expenditure. If one further calls to mind the events of 1848 – the depths to which the authority of the administration had sunk at that time, the doctrines of Socialism and Communism with their attitudes of hostility towards property rights – and considers how long the echoes of those events will continue to reverberate, if one adds the deep poverty that has been visited upon many in the last years through the great rise in the price of the basic necessities of life, if one does not fail to forget that poverty and demoralization have always been the most fundamental causes of crime, and finally, if one does not overlook the fact that very many police authorities in the countryside have for years failed to display the energy and activity which one should demand of them above all in the prevention of crime, then it must appear completely beyond doubt that whatever part in the increase of crime one ascribes to the changes which have taken place since 1848 in the types of punishment prescribed by the law, that part can only ever be a very small one.

Moreover, the prisons had been overcrowded before, in the early 1800s for example, and again in the mid-1830s, so that it was hardly plausible to put the blame for the current situation exclusively on the abolition of corporal punishment.[58]

Furthermore, though crime rates had undoubtedly shown a statistical increase, the commission voiced strong doubts as to whether this reflected a real increase in the actual number of offences committed. The abolition of private jurisdictions on 2 January 1849 and the introduction of a new penal

order on 3 January 1849 had brought many offences into the purview of the
state legal system which had previously been outside it. The landowners who
ran the patrimonial courts had sought to keep costs down by minimizing
prosecutions and where possible dealing with offenders on their estates by
other means, as a commentator outside the commission noted on 9 May
1856. This rule, however, did not apply to state-financed courts.[59] Moreover,
changes in court procedure now made it easier to obtain a conviction in the
absence of a confession from the accused. As a result of these new measures,
it was clear in the commission's view

> that many more crimes are prosecuted and punished than was previously the
> case . . . While the prosecution of crime was previously the responsibility of the
> courts, and made up for most of them only *one part* of their official business,
> the institution of the state prosecution service has brought a class of civil
> servants into being whose *sole* profession is the administration of the criminal
> law, and whose particular task it is to ensure that no guilty person escapes
> punishment.[60]

The commission also pointed out that the offences to which the petitioners
wished to apply corporal punishment had been punishable only by imprisonment according to the General Law Code of 1794, so that their arguments
only really applied to areas where the Code was not in force. The real cure
for crime was not to make punishment more severe, but to relieve poverty
and improve education. Penal policy was not just about deterrence, it was also
about the moral amelioration of the offender. A policy based on deterrence
alone would quickly lead state and society back to the barbarism of centuries
past. Nevertheless, the Prussian Criminal Code of 14 April 1851 had tough-
ened penitentiary sentences already, and the resulting increase in the average
length of custody was another factor in the overcrowding of Prussia's gaols.
It was not true, therefore, that serious offenders had an easy life in the
penitentiary.[61]

For vagrants, beggars and the 'work-shy', to be sure, simple imprisonment,
in relatively clean conditions with a reasonably nutritious diet, might seem an
attractive proposition, and the commission agreed that other types of penal
sanction ought to be employed. For some members of the commission this
meant corporal punishment, especially because they thought that its absence
in Prussia, in contrast to neighbouring states, was attracting a large number
of vagrants into its territory. The majority, however, considered that past
experiences had shown

> that criminals have repeatedly fallen back into the same crimes after they have
> been threatened with severe corporal punishment if they should commit them
> again, and irrespective of the fact that they have already suffered serious
> corporal punishment for them. Indeed they have even taught us that criminals

who have been repeatedly whipped or beaten have become so hardened to corporal punishment that they take the blows with indifference and regard it as a kind of matter of honour to mock the law through their contempt for physical pain.

The case of Gesche Rudolph, had they known about it, would surely have provided the commission with concrete evidence for this argument, for Rudolph, as we saw at the beginning of this chapter, seemed – apart from on one occasion – to be completely undeterred by the ever more severe sentences that were meted out to her. Imprisonment may have produced recidivists, but so too did the alternative of the whip and the cane. By the 1850s, cases such as hers had become rare if not completely unknown.

If corporal punishment did have an effect, then it was likely in the majority view of the commission to be 'instead of remorse and amelioration . . . only hatred and embitterment'.[62] Repeating a common argument against corporal punishment, the commission declared that it was 'only directed at the animal element in man', and that it therefore had the effect of depressing 'the nobler impulses of human nature, and in particular deadens feelings of shame and honour'. Its abolition in the army in 1848 had in no way damaged military discipline or effectiveness. The commission denied Rosenberg-Lipinsky's accusation that the opponents of corporal punishment were motivated only by 'impractical humanitarian theories' and insisted that its rejection of the petition was based on sound practical experience. Corporal punishment had not been abolished as a result of the exaggerated liberalism of 1848; rather, as its legislative history showed, abolition had been gradual and had taken place over a lengthy period, beginning with the General Law Code of 1794 and moving on through the decrees of 1811, 1815, 1833 and so forth. It was true that the 1794 Code had allowed moderate corporal punishment for minors, while the Criminal Code of 1851 did not; but to involve the law in all its awesome majesty was inappropriate, and by a majority of five to four the commission decided that the physical chastisement of juveniles was best left to their parents. What the law had to do was to deal with young offenders over whom parental influence had failed, and here it strongly urged the authorities to fulfil the promises of 1851 and launch a proper scheme of construction of special correctional institutions for young people.[63]

The debates of the 1850s therefore ended with the failure of the reactionary forces in Prussia to reintroduce corporal punishment. This did not, of course, mean that other German states immediately dispensed with the whip. As the fears expressed by those who saw its absence in Prussia as a magnet for vagrants and ne'er-do-wells clearly suggested, it continued to be widely used in other North German states in this period. In the Kingdom of Hanover, the law prescribed 50 lashes for vagabonds convicted of another offence apart from vagrancy, and for juvenile offenders between the ages of 12 and 16. It was under this law that the unfortunate Johann Hanemann had been whipped in the 1840s, as we have seen.[64] It was also normal in Bavaria in the 1850s for vagrants to be punished with the cane,[65] and in 1853 the reactionary government in Württemberg formally reintroduced it after its abolition in the course of the revolution.[66] But the days were clearly numbered by the 1860s. Corporal punishment had already been abolished in Hesse-Nassau, Braunschweig and Baden, and it was finally removed in Saxony on 25 January 1868.[67] At the end of the decade, after the Prussian defeat of Austria in 1866 and the formation of the North German Confederation, Bismarck and his ministers piloted through the new North German legislature a Criminal Code which in 1871 became valid over the whole of the newly created German Empire. Basing itself largely on the Prussian Criminal Code of 1851, it did away with corporal punishment as a penal sanction altogether.

Public Decorum and Private Violence

By 1871, therefore, corporal punishment had finally been deleted from German law. Yet this was as little the end of the story as the vote of 1848 had been. For while it is legitimate enough to view the history of corporal punishment in nineteenth-century Germany in terms of the decline of feudal and patriarchal forms of rule, it is also possible to interpret it in a rather different context, that of the changing relations of public and private; and, as we shall now see, in the private sphere it by no means disappeared in the middle decades of the century. Corporal punishment, as Koselleck pointed out, was carried out in the eighteenth century not merely by the law against offenders who had been condemned in court, but also, with the law's explicit approval, by masters against apprentices, husbands against wives, teachers against pupils, parents against children and landowners against farm servants. All these relationships were aspects of the feudal patriarchalism which the reforms of the nineteenth century whittled away and finally effectively destroyed. However, what these reforms were principally concerned with was the construction and regulation of the bourgeois public sphere; a sphere in which equality before the law had to be practised, decorum maintained, and civil rights and freedoms – freedom of speech, mobility of labour, redress of grievances and so on – established. Despite its claims to universality, the bourgeois public sphere was created on the basis of certain crucial exclusions: of women and children, for example, of deviants, criminals and people consigned by law to institutions such as prisons, workhouses and schools. Public opinion as it formed in mid-century was deeply uncertain as to whether corporal punishment should be banned in these marginal or excluded zones as well. Debate continued to rage, as we have seen, around the corporal punishment of juveniles, a group explicitly excluded from participation in the public sphere. A series of compromises between liberal principles and conservative fears of disorder – fears shared by many liberals after 1848 – provided the foundation for the Criminal Code of 1851 and the legal and penal policies associated with it. They included the continuation of corporal punishment, in these zones of exclusion from the public sphere, where many of the principles held to underlie normal penal practice – the rights of the individual, the appeal to reason, the assumption of civic honour, and so on – did not apply.

One such area was the world of Prussia's prisons and their population of convicted felons. Prisoners had few rights and were generally considered to be excluded from the doctrine of equality before the law, since their offences had put them, as it were, into a legally inferior category. It was, for example, customary for offenders condemned to custodial sentences in Prussia to be given a whipping when they arrived in prison, and another immediately before their discharge – the so-called 'welcome and farewell'. The Circular Rescript of 28 February 1799 had ordered increased prison sentences for many kinds of theft, explicitly adding the words 'with welcome and farewell' to many of these provisions.[68] Prussian bureaucratic reformers of the early nineteenth century such as Albrecht von Arnim considered that whipping a prisoner immediately before his release would negate any improvement in his character which might have taken place while he was serving his sentence, and advocated the abandonment at least of the 'farewell'.[69] In 1815, a royal decree ordered 'that in the cases where the sentence has included welcome and farewell, when the condemned person is released from prison, the latter should no longer be carried out.'[70] Thus the 'farewell' was henceforth officially ruled out of order.

On 14 May 1811, King Friedrich Wilhelm III ordered a further restriction of corporal punishment. He declared:

> In cases in which an offender has been sentenced to life imprisonment, I cannot help finding in the corporal punishment of such thieves, which takes place out of the public eye, a futile harshness, for these chastisements, which are witnessed by no one apart from the judge and the bailiffs, cannot function as an *example*, as other additions to life imprisonment in a fortress or peniten-tiary do, such as exhibition at the pillory, public whipping and the like.[71]

In other words, the King thought corporal punishment had a point only if it was carried out in public. In pursuit of the ideal of 'general prevention', he wanted it restricted to exemplary demonstrations before an audience of potential offenders. Whipping a refractory prisoner as a punishment for infringing discipline within prison, and thereby providing an example to the other prisoners, was a different matter altogether. Corporal punishment con-tinued to be used as a disciplinary sanction in custodial institutions for many decades more. Indeed, the 'welcome' and to a lesser extent the 'farewell' also continued, though now as demonstrations of the prison authorities' power over the inmates on arrival and as an informal deterrent to potential recidivists before departure, and no longer as a penal measure ordered by the courts.

Whipping inside prison was used as the last in a series of disciplinary sanctions, which began with a reduced diet and the removal of small comforts such as pillows from the offender's cell and proceeded to tougher measures such as solitary confinement in a punishment cell. The whipping usually took place in the courtyard, before the assembled inmates, unless the prison director considered it advisable for it to be administered behind closed doors. The prisoner was tied to a device, sometimes referred to as a 'beating machine', intended to hold him or her in place while the punishment was carried out. Up to 30 strokes could be given. Female as well as male prisoners could be whipped, though the former only with a birch or with a thin rather than a thick whip, and 'in a specially designated place, or at least in such a manner that the person to be chastised is removed from the sight of the curious, and in the presence only of such persons as have to be present during this act, and with the use of the chastisement machine.' In the cases of both men and women, medical certification of their fitness to undergo the ordeal was required.[72] In the prisons of the Rhine province, according to regulations drawn up in 1827,

> corporal punishment consisting of a minimum of five and an absolute maximum of 15 blows is administered with a whip to men on the back, with a rod to women on the posterior, which is clothed in a tight skirt. The punishment takes place in public in the institution's courtyard and in the presence of the governor.[73]

Here too, whipping or beating in prison formed part of an elaborate arsenal of disciplinary measures, which also included the ball and chain.

Corporal punishment was frequently used against women in late eighteenth- and early nineteenth-century prisons, at a time when the separation of men and women into different gaols, buildings or prison wings had not yet occurred. Other German states were less restrained than Prussia. One woman, Margareta Langreck, imprisoned in the Detmold penitentiary in the principality of Lippe for four years after a conviction for infanticide in 1806, was ordered to be given 15 strokes of the cane every 10 April for the duration of her sentence, 10 April being the date on which she had killed her child. Aged 27 at the time of her committal, she proved persistently disobedient, however, and was given another 16 strokes as a disciplinary measure shortly after her arrival, followed soon afterwards by 30 for a second offence. 'Every time', it was reported, 'that the warder told her how to spin the yarn, she lifted her skirt up high to her armpits and said as she did so, "You can boss lice and fleas about in prison, but not me."' A further sentence of 40 strokes of the cane was followed on 10 November 1806 by one of 50 strokes after Langreck had attacked fellow-prisoners, and it was not long before she received another 45 strokes, delivered over a period of three days, for a further disciplinary infringement. It was only in 1808 that she was finally diagnosed as 'insane' and her physical punishments brought to a stop. According to critics of the practice, the beating of mentally disturbed or retarded prisoners was common in German gaols in the eighteenth and early nineteenth centuries. Nor did the senile escape. In 1802, for example, one Elisabeth Bax, who had previously been committed to an orphanage as an 'imbecile', was sent to the Detmold penitentiary for begging. Aged 70, she was given six lashes with an oxhide whip for a disciplinary infringement a few months before she was recorded as dying of 'enfeeblement owing to old age' in 1804. To be sure, the beating of such prisoners was relatively uncommon, and male convicts were beaten more frequently than female. Altogether, 52 male prisoners and 17 female were whipped or beaten in the Detmold penitentiary between 1801 and 1826. The practice of using corporal punishment as a disciplinary sanction was also on the decline, in this prison at least.[74] Nevertheless, it was still widely practised in prisons across Germany in the 1820s, as this and other examples show.

The permissibility of public whippings of female convicts in prison contrasted sharply with the fact that the corporal punishment of women as a penal sanction ordered by the courts had been banned a good 15 years before the 1848 Revolution. On 19 March 1833, Prussian Justice Minister Mühler had ordered that females over the age of ten were no longer to be whipped in public, because this punishment 'violates modesty'. The whipping of adult female offenders in prison was explicitly sanctioned at the same time, however, as King Friedrich Wilhelm IV declared, so long as it was 'without violating modesty'.[75] What was happening here was a shift in policy undertaken to accommodate the emergence of a public sphere that was not only class-bound but gender-specific, not only linked to the idea of bourgeois respectability but also predicated on the assumption that women were to be confined to the private realm of home and family. Public punishments, if they continued at all, were increasingly envisaged as occasions for the display of collective solemnity by top-hatted and frock-coated gentlemen, and women began to be seen as an embarrassment, both as viewers and as viewed. At the same time, in the early decades of the nineteenth century, the number of women executed in public in Prussia fell sharply until it constituted less than 10 per cent of the total, and hostile comments began to be heard on the presence of women as spectators at these occasions. By 1847, indeed, the Prussian government had drawn up plans – eventually put into effect in the 1850s – for executions to be held in prison courtyards instead of public spaces, and before a hand-picked public consisting solely of men.[76] The audience for corporal punishment within prisons was different to the extent that it included the other prisoners, whereas in the case of capital punishment it did not. Even so, however, the evidence seems to point to the fact that by the 1830s the authorities, starting with the King himself, were worried about the possibility of the whipping of female prisoners in front of an audience which, however small, was bound to include a number of male officials, infringing hard-won feelings of sexual propriety among the respectable classes.

In 1848, the liberal Prussian government which had been placed in office as a result of the Revolution insisted that the order of 6 May abolishing corporal punishment applied to everyone, including the inmates of Prussia's gaols.[77] But a year later, when a reactionary ministry had been installed in Berlin, things were very different, and pressure mounted from prison administrations for corporal punishment to be restored. On 6 December 1849, the Criminal Division of the Superior Appeal Court in Königsberg wrote to the Justice Ministry in Berlin urging the reintroduction of whipping as the only effective means of restoring discipline within Prussia's prisons, and noting

> that rather, in the knowledge that the same is not allowed, the most impudent scorn and derision is heaped upon the prison officers, and that only just recently through a conspiracy of the prisoners in the gaol here, such a terrible disturbance was caused in a cell used for plucking birds, that it could only be quelled with armed assistance, and not without wounds being inflicted either.[78]

These complaints were echoed by the Breslau town council, which complained in December 1849 that the revolutionary spirit had infected the inmates of the local prison and given rise to an 'inclination, helplessly documented every day, in people who find themselves in remand prison or serving sentences to commit acts of insubordination and excesses of every kind'. Previous attempts to improve discipline, such as a rescript of 24 October 1837, had failed to give prison governors the powers they needed:

> The prisoners now declare without any inhibitions: *'that they won't put up with it'*, and defy all the orders of the inspectors of these institutions, since the overcrowding of the prisons means that the latter are not in a position to introduce effective disciplinary measures and break the defiance of the inmates.

The reason for this, in the view of the Breslau town council, was the abolition of corporal punishment within prisons by the 1848 Revolution. As a result, there had been frequent 'outbreaks of the most dangerous felons from the prisons, wilful damage to the prison utensils', and other similar incidents. 'Threats against the persons of the officers are daily occurrences.' The only remedy was whipping, at least 'against such prisoners . . . who belong to the second class of the military or have been stripped of the national cockade'.[79]

This last point was now taken up by the reactionary government in Berlin, which replied that in its view the decree of 6 May 1848 had only banned whipping as a punishment to be prescribed by the courts. Corporal punishment was 'not ruled out' as a disciplinary measure against 'disturbances of the peace' and other infractions of the rules within prisons.[80] As the Appeal Court in Magdeburg pointed out, the main concern of the decree had been to eliminate the inequalities inherent in the rule that only the lowest class of offender could be subjected to corporal punishment. Prisoners did not enjoy the same civil or political rights as ordinary citizens, so were therefore not covered by the precept of equality before the law and not covered by the provisions of the decree.[81] The ruling of 1850 was strengthened three years later, when the Justice Minister repeated the assurance that prison authorities were not breaking any laws by enforcing their traditional custom of giving escaped prisoners a whipping on their recapture.[82] On 6 September 1855, the Prussian Justice Ministry confirmed:

> Corporal punishment may be used in *penal institutions* (penitentiaries) and *Rhenish houses of correction* as a disciplinary measure in the case of infringements of the prison rules according to the criteria of the rules laid down for these institutions and only against *condemned* prisoners held therein.

It was not permissible, the Ministry added, referring to previous rules drawn up in 1827, to use it against remand prisoners.[83] In 1862, the Justice Ministry confirmed that 'corporal punishment is not permitted as a disciplinary measure against persons who have only been admitted as a result of police measures'.[84]

Reactionary forces had thus succeeded in reinstating corporal punishment for a significant segment of the population who were thought to be beyond the boundaries of the respectable bourgeois public sphere. The post-revolutionary settlement indeed represented a series of negotiated compromises between bourgeois liberals and the old order. In return for guaranteeing protection against the kind of riot, rebellion, disorder and crime which had so frightened middle-class liberals as well as conservatives at the time of the 1848 Revolution, the Prussian administration had conceded a number of crucial demands such as equality before the law and trial in open court. In exchange for a more open and accountable judicial system and the abolition of unequal laws such as the prescription of corporal punishment for the lower orders, liberals had conceded, for the moment at least, the reinstatement of the death penalty – formally abolished by the Frankfurt parliament in 1848 – so long as it was not carried out in public any more. This concession opened the way for a parallel if only partial reintroduction of corporal punishment on the same terms.[85] Neither measure was wholly accepted by the liberals, of course, and by the mid-1860s the campaign to abolish the death penalty had revived once more. Just as the defenders of capital punishment argued that it was an exceptional sanction against people who had put themselves beyond the pale of normal human society by committing the heinous crime of murder, so the defenders of corporal punishment argued that it was an exceptional sanction against people who had put themselves beyond the pale of normal human society by committing less heinous crimes, to be sure, but ones which nonetheless made it impossible to treat them as honourable citizens any more. The concept of honour was still crucial here. Everyone seemed agreed that corporal punishment was dishonouring, and that it should therefore no longer be applied to people who could be said to be honourable. Right through the second half of the nineteenth century, however, the advocates and defenders of corporal punishment maintained that for those who had no civil honour or rights, punishments which appealed to the finer feelings and aspirations of self-worth, self-respect and self-improvement were useless. Here was another area where the ameliorative principle of imprisonment did not seem to apply. Where disputes arose was over the definition of who was honourable and who was not, and over who might be deemed capable of responding to attempts to restore a lost sense of honour through re-education.

If any group in society could be regarded as dishonourable, it was the convicted prison population. Liberals, as alarmed as anyone about what were generally perceived as high crime rates at this time, were on weaker ground here than they were in the case, say, of farm servants exposed to corporal punishment under the provisions of the Servants' Law (*Gesindeordnung*). They not only made no real effort to prevent the reintroduction of the whip in Prussia's prisons, but were also relatively disinclined to campaign for its removal even at the height of their influence, in the late 1860s and 1870s. The abolition of the death penalty, by contrast, was a central plank in the liberal platform at this time, because since 1848 it had become a crucial symbol of political sovereignty. Liberals believed in a contractual theory of the state, in which, therefore, it should be impossible for the state to destroy the life of one of the people – citizens – who had constituted it in order to protect their own lives in the first place. Conservatives, on the other hand, held to an organic theory of the state, according to which it was the sovereign's God-given right to protect the community and its institutions by whatever means he chose, including the execution of serious offenders, and it was the sover-eign's right of clemency which should determine in the last instance whether the offender was actually executed.[86] Corporal punishment, by contrast, carried a rather lighter symbolic political baggage. Its public use by patrimonial and other courts had signified the continuation of patriarchal, feudal forms of authority in the first half of the century. Its employment under the Servants' Law continued to be controversial for this very reason. To liberals and Social Democrats, farm servants were employees who had entered into voluntary contracts and were therefore equipped with rights in the public sphere, unlike, say, prison inmates or schoolchildren, to whom such principles clearly did not apply.[87] Given such public hostility, the use of corporal punishment against farm servants probably declined in the decades leading up to the First World War. By 1900, indeed, landowners who used the rod against their employees were quite likely to end up in court.[88]

In other areas, including prison life, corporal punishment altogether lacked this signification, especially after the attenuation and then abolition of patrimonial justice and the introduction of trial in open court. Felons were now in gaol because a judicial system which largely conformed to the bourgeois concepts of Rhenish liberalism had put them there. What happened to them in gaol became primarily a matter of penal policy and lacked any larger political importance. Corporal punishment therefore continued to be used in prisons long after the middle of the century. By the 1860s, gender-based concepts of honour and shame had strengthened to the extent that such punishment was no longer supposed to be used against female prison inmates. In 1865, when the Ministry of Justice learned that women were still being whipped in prison in Stettin, despite an order banning the practice, it told the prison authorities there to stop.[89] Such injunctions were widely ignored by prison governors, who were subject to few restraints in the exercise of their power over the offenders in their charge. Critics claimed that some prison governors ordered virtually daily whippings of the prisoners in their charge. In one institution, reported a local newspaper, the *Breslauer Zeitung*, in 1882:

> The then director of this institution, now deceased, took such pleasure in beatings, that even as a young trainee, long before he ever thought of becoming a prison director, he hired a well-built labourer, whom he personally beat for his private enjoyment a few times every week in return for substantial sums of money.

In the prison over which this man held sway, warders were said to take it in turns to subject the inmates to savage beatings. The bodies of prisoners who had died were so badly scarred by these whippings that the Anatomical Institute of the local university, to which they were delivered, made a formal complaint about their condition.[90] Even without such sadistic governors in charge, beatings in Germany's prisons in the late nineteenth century were common enough. In the prison at Ichtershausen in the 1890s, for example, refractory inmates were put in drill-shorts, tied to a bench and beaten with a rod over four feet in length and half an inch thick with such force that blood was usually drawn after the second blow. Women as well as men were subjected to this treatment, and newspaper reports also recorded that one prisoner accused of 'insubordination' had been put in chains and dragged down a stairway by his hair before being given a beating.[91] Some prison governors were opposed to the use of the whip,[92] but the majority continued to use it as a disciplinary measure long after this time.

The directorate of the penitentiary in Rawitsch, accused in 1894 of possessing a specially constructed 'beating machine', was forced to admit 'that in the penitentiary in Rawitsch an apparatus does exist, to which the malefactor is tied fast; then the middle part of the malefactor's body is moved by means of a screw into such a position that the buttocks are pulled up tightly into the air.' Whipping was then administered at the rate of one lash a minute, and up to ten blows were struck in a session; the maximum punishment was 30 lashes, administered in three sessions over two days.[93] In Prussia and Saxony the leather whip was still used; in most other states in which the custom continued, such as Mecklenburg, Oldenburg, Hamburg, Schwarzburg-Rudolstadt and Lübeck, the cane was preferred.[94] In Bavaria, corporal punishment in prisons had been outlawed by the Criminal Code of 1861. By the late 1890s it had been banned in Baden, Württemberg, Brunswick, Bremen, Saxe-Coburg-Gotha and Sachsen-Weimar.[95] But it continued in Prussia right up to the end of the First World War. In the state of Oldenburg, corporal punishment was reintroduced in the 1860s as a disciplinary measure within prisons. The 'welcome and farewell' was used in Hamburg's prisons as a matter of course in the 1860s.[96] Moreover, the director of Hamburg's prisons, Dr Gennat, later came out strongly in favour of it, and received the support of the Prison Deputation, the controlling authority which consisted of a mixture of lay and judicial members, including two members of the city's ruling senate. Other prison officials spoke out in favour of its extension beyond prison walls, to deal with 'crimes of brutality'.[97] They supported their arguments with reference to the supposed fact 'that the most brutal and unbridled criminals in our penitentiaries become extraordinarily tame once they have been given a sound beating'.[98]

Prisons were not the only institutions in which corporal punishment was practised. For instance, it continued in workhouses long after 1848. The workhouse in Gera did not officially lose the right to beat its inmates until 1882 and was actually employing it as late as the mid-1860s.[99] Even in 1900, according to the veteran socialist leader August Bebel, one workhouse in Saxony was using the traditional 'welcome' on people admitted there for a second or subsequent time.[100] The law in Imperial Germany allowed parents, guardians, schoolmasters and even teachers in further education colleges to beat their charges, so long as the beating did not pose any danger to their health – and the courts had ruled that 'bleeding caused by weals or skin lacerations' did not endanger schoolchildren's health, since the wounds generally healed within a fortnight.[101] The memoirs of Germans educated in the late nineteenth and early twentieth century are full of stories of savage beatings administered by ferocious schoolmasters.[102] In the 1860s, corporal punishment in schools was said to be very widespread, not merely as a disciplinary sanction, but also as an 'encouragement to industriousness'.[103] In East Prussia, teachers were even reported to beat their young charges with a knout, a Russian whip with a number of leather thongs attached, rather like the English cat-o'-nine-tails.[104] At the same time, however, opposition to the use of corporal punishment in schools was growing.[105] A widespread public debate on a new Education Bill being prepared in the late 1860s produced a number of tracts arguing that beating schoolchildren was arbitrary, brutalized the pupils and made the teachers lazy. 'Force replaces reason in this case.'[106]

Fear was not the right method to use in education.[107] The threat of the rod would only drive pupils to lies and deception in order to avoid it; it would create an unnecessary antagonism between pupil and teacher. Such opposition persuaded the Reich government to restrict the use of corporal punishment in schools; but no legislation was forthcoming to abolish it altogether.[108]

Even those who argued for the abolition of corporal punishment in schools did not think it should be done away with in society as a whole. One such writer, for example, conceded that it was necessary to break the 'self-will' of young children: 'Corporal punishment has a beneficent influence only in the parental home of small children under nine years of age. In this case, the rod is only spared too much by the doting parents, above all by the weak, doting mother!'[109] Such weakness on the part of parents only stored up trouble for school later on. Another writer went even further:

> We must not spare the rod as long as a beastly and confused moral conscious-
> ness exists in children, in other words during their earliest years, a conscious-
> ness from which self-confidence eventually springs, and which obliges us to
> influence their spirtual life by external impressions, for in such an undeveloped
> state, no real intercourse between humans is yet possible. It follows that we do
> not completely reject corporal punishment as an educational tool, but allow it
> in the earlier and earliest years of childhood, the first year of life not excluded
> but indeed emphatically included.[110]

So widespread were such views that proponents of corporal punishment as a judicial sanction were quick to claim, as one of them said in the Reichstag in 1900, that 'even the gentlemen of the extreme left are supporters of the rod at home'.[111] Critics of corporal punishment in other spheres continued to defend its use within the family. Confronted with the argument that official beatings led to the brutalization of the bailiffs whose job it was to administer them, for instance, the Reichstag's leading proponent of corporal punishment at the turn of the century, the Conservative deputy Oertel, riposted that the average paterfamilias was surely not brutalized when he administered beatings to his own children. Characteristically, the National Liberal deputy Ernst Bassermann responded to this point not by arguing against the use of the cane in the home, but by declaring that 'the hand of the father or mother who undertakes the beating really cannot be compared with the brutal work of the minions who are called upon to carry out legally ordained corporal punishment.'[112]

All this suggests that it is taking too narrow a point of view to see the decline of corporal punishment in nineteenth-century Germany exclusively as an aspect of the transition from a status-based to a class-based society. Corporal punishment was not abolished, it was simply banished from the public sphere. Here, it may be suggested, we are witnessing not only social change but also a change in culture and mentalities. Interpreting and

accounting for this change is by no means a simple matter. The sociologist
Norbert Elias and his disciples would view it, of course, as an aspect of the
'civilizing process'. With the rise of the modern state came the gradual ending
of the 'spectacle of suffering', in which the sovereign exacted revenge for
crimes on behalf of the victims through the public mutilation of the offender's
body. People stopped enjoying such spectacles because the process of
'conscience formation' and 'interpersonal identification' fundamental to the
creation of a state system based on the sovereignty of the nation meant that
they started to empathize with the criminal at the pillory. Thus, the violent
punishment of the body had to stop and give way to impersonal character
reform in the penitentiary. The decline of public violence appears in this view
as part of a wider process in which people learned to control violent
emotions, such as hatred and revenge, and to live with one another in peace
and harmony.[113]

Elias first advanced his general theory of civilization as an attempt to
explain the long-term origins of Nazi barbarism. The civilizing process, he
thought, had failed in Germany. Nazism was able to murder millions because
the Germans had not learned to live with one another in peace and harmony.
The process of 'conscience formation' was deeply flawed in the German case.
Germans had never managed to control their violent and destructive urges
properly. The ultimate result was the rapid descent into uncivilized behaviour
in the twentieth century.[114] Elias's theory is complex and sophisticated, and
more subtle than it is possible to convey in a few sentences. Yet the history
of corporal punishment in nineteenth-century Germany only gives partial
support to it. To begin with, there is the problem that right up to the First
World War and beyond, decades after it had been formally abolished as
a legally prescribed punishment for offenders in Germany, it continued to
be administered by order of the courts in England, a country which Elias
regarded as so civilized that he spent most of his life there after 1933.
Secondly, there is the problem that even when it was widely administered, in
the eighteenth century and before, it could in no way be seen as an outbreak
of insensate hatred and lust for revenge on the part of the spectators or the
populace at large. On the whole, crowds did not usually vent their anger on
criminals at the pillory, though very occasionally this did happen. In general,
corporal punishment in Germany was strongly bound up with the concept of
honour. What was important in the eighteenth century, and in the minds of
some, as we have seen, long afterwards too, was not the physical pain
administered by the whip, but the dishonour it supposedly brought: the
dishonour of having one's bodily integrity violated, the shame of having one's
suffering exposed to the public view. The public administration of corporal
punishment was an ordered and ritualized affair. The decline of public
corporal punishment mirrored, as we have seen, the decline of the importance
of honour in society in the nineteenth century. Beyond this, it also reflected
changing attitudes to the human body, and here Elias's arguments are of some

help. The nineteenth century saw the spread of squeamishness and embarrassment at the open performance of bodily functions among the emerging middle classes. Prudery in public was an important aspect of bourgeois culture, and would certainly have been violated by the continuation of corporal punishment at the pillory. Such changes were important in bringing public executions to an end in the 1850s and 1860s, and operated in the same way with respect to public whippings and beatings. What mattered, however, was that such punishments should no longer take place in the open, before an indiscriminately assembled crowd. Once banished behind prison walls, they could be monitored and controlled. While dispute raged between liberals and conservatives on the issue of corporal punishment itself, therefore, everybody was agreed that, if it did take place, it should not be in public.

'Gruesome Sexual Desire'

Thus the spirit of the whip continued to live on in some quarters of German society. Driving it out of the public realm did not mean expunging it altogether. Proponents of corporal punishment were never content to see it confined to the margins of the public sphere, and all the way up to the First World War there were periodic demands for it to be reinstated there. These emanated mainly from conservatives. They had never fully abandoned their traditional support for the whip as a convenient and, they thought, effective means of chastising unruly subjects. They were increasingly despairing at what they believed – often wrongly – to be a continual rise in the crime rate, signifying the breakdown of the old social order which they saw it as their mission to maintain. In 1880, for example, Otto Mittelstaedt's wide-ranging tract *Against Custodial Sentences* attacked the ameliorative principle of penal policy as a failure, and urged forced public labour, transportation, execution, fines and corporal punishment as alternatives, based on the principle of deterrence.[115] An official from the Prussian Ministry of the Interior told prison officers in Bremen in 1880 that 'drunkenness is more and more gaining the upper hand' and causing such an increase in 'all those crimes and misdemeanours that can be ascribed to a deep demoralization and moral decadence of the common people'. The return of corporal punishment, he declared, was the only answer. Backing up this view, one conservative newspaper criticized the 'dubious humanitarian ideas' of the Criminal Code, and particularly its citation of drunkenness as an extenuating circumstance in crimes of violence. It then went on to argue, somewhat implausibly, that the real reason for the growth of such offences was 'the complete undermining of all authority in state and community' by Germany's 'satirical magazines'.[116]

In 1885, conditions in Germany's 'Wild West', the new mining and industrial town of Bochum, gave rise to renewed calls for the reintroduction of corporal punishment. A petition to this effect declared:

The statistics of brutality indicate the most troubling situation in our industrial areas. A roughess and lack of restraint, a moral depravity, has spread across these areas, which makes a mockery of every law, despite the praiseworthy toughness with which the courts there punish such excesses and refuse to allow any softening of penal sanctions. The trial and condemnation of persons guilty of the most frivolous acts of assault and wounding have for a long time been occupying criminal courts and lay assessors from the early morning until late at night, and the relevant judges have long since become convinced that even the toughest sentences allowed by the law no longer suffice.[117]

Yet what sparked this petition was a series of brutal sex-murders, for which one would have thought that conservatives would have been content with demanding the rigorous application of the death penalty. A similar confusion was apparent in a call from the conservative newspaper the *Kreuzzeitung* for the reintroduction of 'corporal punishment' as 'a matter of necessity'. There was, declared the paper,

no time to lose in making this effective and, in cases of brutality and murder, most appropriate disciplinary measure once more an integral part of our penal code. Our prisons and penitentiaries are constantly reporting a shockingly full complement of inmates, a large number of rough characters are whiling away their time behind prison walls free of all cares and costing the state thousands and thosands of marks in expenses every year. Custodial sentences in prisons and penitentiaries have for such elements no deterrent character, and therefore it is high time to back up these sentences with a further disciplinary measure in the form of regular corporal punishment.[118]

Presumably this meant that the paper wanted convicted murderers to be whipped before they went to the block – a measure which would have aroused massive public criticism, but which would surely have added little to the deterrent effect of the axe or the guillotine, if indeed there was one.

Fear of violent crime was an important impulse in prompting calls for the reintroduction of the whip in the 1890s:

Year in, year out the newspapers are compelled to report on numer- ous . . . dreadful deeds, among which the defilement and murder of children is, alas, by no means to be numbered among the rarest of such occurrences. The frequent brief reports under the headline 'sex murder', the frightful cases of cruelty to animals, which satanic villains commit from revenge, from jealousy, from demonic destructiveness and gruesome sexual desire, the . . . devilry with which the fragile and the helpless are slowly tortured to death, the systematic torments which in numberless cases unhappy children have to endure from their dehumanized parents and which not infrequently drive them to a volun- tary death, are examples of the despicable state to which the creature which according to rumour God has made master of the world has brought itself. Since such cases have occurred and continue to occur every day, it seems incomprehensible to a normal understanding of such things that jurists, sociologists and moral philosophers are still quarrelling amongst themselves over whether it is permissible or not in view of such abominations and such inhumanity to introduce corporal punishment as an addition to custodial sentences.[119]

As these sentiments suggest, such arguments, based on cultural pessimism and despair at the passing of the old social order, were increasingly cast in a new, populist tone. Conservatives now seldom proposed that corporal punishment should be applied in the traditional manner to servants, labourers and the lower orders, but to no one else. By the 1890s, proponents of corporal punishment conceded that 'differences of class or status would of course be excluded in the application of corporal punishment'. Thus the objection that it violated the principle of equality before the law no longer counted.[120]

Reluctance to reintroduce the whip began to be dismissed in this new discourse as 'sentimental humanitarianism'.[121] 'Anyone who behaves like an animal should be treated like an animal.' This was a paradoxical demand indeed, coming as it did from a quarter which frequently demanded the introduction of corporal punishment for cruelty to animals.[122] The right began to launch a more populist appeal in other areas during the 1890s, frightened by the continued growth of working-class support for the Marxist Social Democrats now that they had been freed from the restrictions imposed by the Anti-Socialist Law of 1878–90. In such circumstances it was no longer possible to rely on traditions of deference and obedience to authority. Even the Junker-dominated Conservative Party turned to the employment of anti-semitic and other populist doctrines at this time in a bid to broaden its electoral base. So the right also turned to new, populist arguments in support of its drive to reintroduce the whip: 'We are convinced', as one right-wing newspaper put it in 1898, 'that, if a referendum were held on the reintroduction of *corporal punishment*, the overwhelming majority would declare itself in favour.'[123] A generation before, as the conservative press pointed out, the weight of political opinion had been firmly against the death penalty; now, however, in the early 1900s, it was firmly in favour. 'Capital punishment has been reintroduced despite the yelling of the sentimentalists,' remarked one conservative newspaper: 'Corporal punishment will, we are convinced, experience the same fate as capital punishment.'[124] 'Fortunately,' another newspaper declared, 'the influence of the liberal apostles of humanity who are combating the idea of bringing in corporal punishment as an excrescence of medieval barbarity is declining more and more from year to year.' It was only a matter of time before majority opinion accepted that punishment was not about reforming the offender but about retribution and deterrence. 'Thugs with knives', pimps, anarchist bomb-throwers, rapists, child abusers – all these, as anyone possessed of 'healthy common sense' surely agreed, should be given 'a sound beating'.[125]

Such demands were symptomatic of a feeling on the far right of the German political spectrum in the Wilhelmine era that liberal penal policies had failed. They expressed a simplistic, demagogic desire to cut through the complexities of crime and deviance and deal with them by the application of violence. The rabble-rousing language in which such desires were expressed was a testimony to this sense of frustration. In 1903, the ultra-conservative *Hamburger Nachrichten* recommended corporal punishment as a remedy for the 'increasing number of rowdies' and pointed to its recent reintroduction for crimes of violence in Denmark.[126] The Germans' 'exaggerated humanitarianism' and 'vague professorial ethics', thundered another right-wing newspaper, had hitherto prevented the support for corporal punishment among peace-loving citizens from being heard by the legislature.[127] Corporal punishment continued to be used in England, a state customarily regarded by Germans of all political persuasions as exceptionally liberal and progressive. 'Over there,' one commentator declared roundly, 'anyone who deserves a thrashing is thrashed.'[128] 'In Norway,' added another writer in 1900, 'children between ten and 15 are very frequently whipped . . . In 1892 some 3000 boys in England and 335 in Scotland were condemned to a whipping.' Yet critics warned that England's record in penal policy was nothing to be admired. People needed reminding 'that imprisonment for debt still existed in Great Britain in the second half of the nineteenth century and that the death penalty was even applied to certain property crimes, at a time when in Germany these draconian punishments were a thing of the past.'[129]

Commenting on the campaign of the far-right newspaper the *Deutsche Tageszeitung* for the reintroduction of the whip as an addition to what it constantly portrayed as the soft option of imprisonment, the left-wing Berlin daily *Vorwärts* was biting in its sarcasm:

> According to reports of the *Deutsche Tageszeitung*, prisons are veritable holiday camps. You get good shelter, huge earnings from labour and better food than in our army barracks. If you compare this situation for instance with the poverty of our landowners, who, shivering from hunger and cold, patch up their thatched roofs with mortgages, then you will understand that the men behind the *Deutsche Tageszeitung* are considering the idea of selling off their unprofitable estates and settling in prisons and penitentiaries for the rest of their days.[130]

In fact, the paper went on, conditions in prison were bad. The diet was poor, certainly insufficient to sustain a man engaged in hard physical labour.[131] The Socialist August Bebel, who had himself spent time in gaol for political offences, and who was in touch with many members of his party who continued to suffer the same fate, concurred: prison food was awful, and the accommodation was dirty, unheated and verminous.[132] What was needed was a reform of the prison system so that it became an effective vehicle for rehabilitation. In keeping with their continued faith in the ameliorative principle in penal policy, opponents of the whip continued to argue that corporal punishment destroyed the sense of honour which was the first precondition of moral improvement.[133] 'It is a moral death sentence,' one newspaper commented in 1890.[134]

Opponents pointed out that, whereas the demand had been for corporal punishment to be applied for minor offences such as vagrancy and begging a few years previously, it was now raised with reference primarily to serious crimes of violence, largely because that was where Danish law applied it. In fact, therefore, opponents suggested, the supporters of the whip wanted it to be used practically universally.[135] Among judges, lawyers and criminologists, the weight of opinion was against it.[136] The draft Criminal Code of 1909 rejected the reintroduction of corporal punishment on the grounds that majority public and expert opinion held it to be 'a means of punishment that no longer corresponds to the German people's circumstances of life or level of civilization.' Since its reintroduction in Denmark, there was no evidence that it had had any noticeable effect on crime rates there.[137] By 1910, critics were able to point out that the Danish law of 1905 had only been applied a total of 14 times, since the courts had refused to use corporal punishment as a regular sentence, and that its existence on the statute book had had no effect whatsoever in stemming the continuing increase in the rates of incidence of the crimes to which it applied.[138] Moreover, the government minister who had introduced the measure was by this time himself sitting in prison after having been convicted of massive pecuniary fraud.[139] Not surprisingly, the law was not renewed when it lapsed at the beginning of 1911.[140] Moreover, opponents of corporal punishment were able to employ racist analogies from Germany's African colonies, where excessive use of corporal punishment created a nationwide scandal in the early 1900s and led to restrictions being placed on its use. Already by the turn of the century, it was officially forbidden to beat Arabs or Indians in German East Africa, and the use of the whip was confined by law to offenders from the black population. Politicians in Berlin were quick to point out that it would be an insult to the German race to reintroduce it in the fatherland when it was only used against what they regarded as the most backward and ignorant of all the various racial groups in the German colonies.[141]

All this only served to make the far right even more frustrated. It was not simply a question of looking back to the days when the aristocratic landlord on any East Elbian estate had been able to keep unruly farm servants in order by giving them a good thrashing every now and then. By the early 1900s, the advocates of corporal punishment were arguing for new, democratic and egalitarian forms of violence, as we have seen; and they were quite prepared to modernize the method as well as the purpose. A National Liberal newspaper, the *Berliner Börsen-Zeitung*, argued in 1911 for the introduction of corporal punishment in the form not of the old-fashioned whip, but of the modern means of electric shock treatment:

> Anyone who has ever felt the effects of a strong electric induction current knows what dreadful pain is caused by it. A shackled malefactor who is only forced to endure this pain for five minutes will certainly not offend again. A whip is nothing in comparison, and the idea of having to expect this torture at a pre-arranged hour every morning is horrific.[142]

This was far from being the product of a diseased or eccentric imagination. In late nineteenth-century England, for example, 'galvanization' was used against prison inmates suspected of malingering, an addition to the conventional arsenal of corporal punishments in prisons which does not seem to have been adopted in Germany.[143] What the far right in Germany, and elements even of the moderate right, increasingly wanted was the re-export of corporal punishment back from the private sphere into the public realm once more. In arguing for this, however, they were opening a Pandora's box far more potent and dangerous than they could possibly realize.

For one of the effects of the privatization of corporal punishment since the 1840s had been to transform it into an illicit source of private pleasure. One of the major concerns of the opponents of corporal punishment had been its impact not on those who suffered it, but on those who watched it being administered. Violence against the body as a form of judicial punishment, it was frequently argued, would encourage the spread of violence against the body in other areas of society. This was why it would be inadvisable to reintroduce the kind of cruel physical punishments which had been common in the Middle Ages, even if they would undoubtedly make an effective deterrent in some cases. It was one thing to clip a child round the ear immediately after it had been naughty:

> But every blow that the official bailiff strikes on the back or the behind of a defenceless malefactor, days, weeks or months after his crime, will also have a powerful projective effect on the sensibility of the bailiff, the prison officers, the judges who have passed the sentence and the whole public, from whom the carrying-out of the sentence may not be withheld. If we reintroduce corporal punishment, we will depress the level of sensibility in substantial parts of the public to hardness, roughness and finally to brutality.[144]

The *Berliner Börsen-Zeitung*, in advocating electric shock treatment for offenders, also considered that while administering a whipping was likely to lead to the brutalization of the officers who carried it out, the same would not be the case if they came to administer electric shock treatment; a view that seems to have derived from the fact that electric shocks would not cause the offender's blood to flow.[145] Another writer remarked:

To avoid the inevitable brutalization of the servants of our state through administering corporal punishment, to prevent everyone involved in carrying out the punishment from becoming bailiffs and bully-boys, and to stop them losing the people's respect, we must on this account protest with every means at our disposal against this regression into the barbarism of times past.[146]

The Liberal deputy Ernst Müller-Meiningen, speaking in the Reichstag in 1900, commented: 'It is really horrifying how the inmates of penitentiaries are corrupted by being allowed to take part in this flagellation through being permitted to be present at whippings.' For the spectacle of corporal punishment, he said, 'arouses the prisoners who are present at whippings . . . [and] encourage[s] cruelty and brutality in them; they are overcome by a strange feeling of longing to witness and rejoice in such a bestially brutal punishment.'[147] Emphasizing the degrading effects of corporal punishment on the audience, while at the same time describing it in graphic, often sexually laden, physical terminology, only served to transform it into a forbidden pleasure of the sort fantasized about by the Marquis de Sade. Thus, as it disappeared from public view, so corporal punishment gained power in the private imagination. It was indeed in the late eighteenth century that sexual flagellation began to become a central element in English pornography, and it was above all in the 1840s, as the liberal campaign against the whip was reaching its height in Germany, that sadistic violence, though not unknown before, began to become a major pornographic element in German popular literature.[148] At the same time, the memoirs of prostitutes began to report that clients were demanding to be whipped with birches in the larger and more sophisticated brothels in which they worked.[149]

By the end of the century, Krafft-Ebing's *Psychopathia Sexualis* was describing in considerable detail the variety of private sexual pleaures which involved the infliction of pain, while Leopold von Sacher-Masoch's pornographic novels purveyed the same kind of fare in less scientific form. Even the description of real, past corporal punishments could now be directed to a readership in search of pornographic pleasures, as the pseudo-historical works of Rudolf Quanter demonstrated.[150] An entire publishing house, H. Dohrn in Dresden, later transformed into the Leipziger Verlag, existed at the turn of the century on the proceeds of printing and publishing sado-masochistic pornography by Sacher-Masoch himself, Carl Felix von Schlichtegroll (author of *Satan's Daughters*, *The She-Wolf* and many similar works) and a number of lesser authors. Sometimes these were cast in pseudo-scientific form, as in *Corporal Punishment in a Medical Light* by 'Doctor of Medicine Wilhelm Hammer',[151] but more often they did not trouble to dignify themselves in this way and advertised their contents with obvious titles such as *The Severe Woman Piano-Teacher*, *Aunt Anna's Disciplinary Rod*, *Rod and Cane in Action*, *My Sweet Cruel Riding-Crop* and so on.[152] This was a time, as one pseudo-scientific compiler of such stories observed, 'in which sadism and masochism are making rapid progress (and that this is indeed the case is proven by the fact that the literature dealing with these subjects has increased sharply in the last four–five years)'.[153] Others agreed:

> In numberless works, stories are told about men who are beaten with canes until the blood runs, in order to be driven by pain into a state of sexual pleasure. Nowadays every prostitute is familiar with this unhappy passion, which has spread considerably, especially among the better classes of society. Canes and dog-whips have become daily tools of the trade in brothels . . . Do not believe that such things only take place in old stories from the year dot; this evil is far more widespread in our own time.[154]

By the early 1900s, therefore, as Müller-Meiningen's remarks in the Reichstag suggested, opponents of corporal punishment were no longer as innocent as they had been half a century before, when hardly anybody had worried about its effects on those who administered or watched it. The volume of such publications had become too great to overlook, and educated middle-class Germans like Müller-Meiningen were now frequently as familiar with the work of Krafft-Ebing, Freud and other specialists in the psychology of sexuality as they were with law codes and penal policies.

By advocating the reimportation of corporal punishment from the private into the public sphere, the far right and their sympathizers in Wilhelmine Germany were inevitably, therefore, advocating not the reinstatement of a ritualized form of physical punishment whose accent was on the shame and dishonour it did to the offender, but implicitly also the release of violent impulses which by now had strong sexual overtones. In the early 1900s, these were predominantly masochistic; the pornography of violence was over-whelmingly a pornography of women inflicting violence on men. The figure of the powerful, seductive and destructive woman, central to Sacher-Masoch's work, featured not only in other novels of the time, such as Heinrich Mann's *Dr Unrat*, first published in 1905 (later filmed as *The Blue Angel*, with Marlene Dietrich in the leading role), in plays of the 1890s, such as Frank Wedekind's *Pandora's Box*, and in *fin-de-siècle* art.[155] These fantasies of violence were an aspect of the fascination of the new modernist art of the day with the marginal and the forbidden. They also represented among other things a masculine reaction to the emergence of a powerful, prominent, active and radical Feminist movement in the public sphere of Wilhelmine Germany from the middle of the 1890s onwards.[156] But liberal contemporaries such as Müller-Meiningen were aware, too, that the violence could be exerted in the other direction, as indeed it frequently was in the private sphere. Defeat in the First World War and the collapse of the Wilhelmine empire hastened the process of reversal towards the – real or imagined – exercise of violent and sadistic impulses against women carried out in the name of an injured masculinity.[157] In the civil disturbances which followed the revolution of 1918, the ultra-right Free Corps finally brought these impulses out into the open, both in their writings and to some degree also in their practice.[158]

The End of the Story

All this has taken us a very long way from the sufferings of the unfortunate Gesche Rudolph in Bremen in the more innocent historical context of the pre-1848 period of the nineteenth century. Of little direct historical significance in itself, Rudolph's story, as related by her lawyer Georg Wilhelm Gröning, was one among many which showed that corporal punishment was common in early nineteenth-century Germany not only as a penal sanction, but also in the private sphere, including the home. What drove her repeatedly to return to Bremen despite the likelihood of a whipping there was the violence shown to her by her stepbrother at the family home in Woltmershausen, violence which was just as much a response to her deviant and drunken lifestyle as was that of the authorities in Bremen. Corporal punishment, like imprisonment, tended to be repeated; it was not a question of a single, 'short, sharp shock', but of prolonged and, as Gröning argued, pointless and purposeless private and, crucially in this case, official violence exerted against a woman who was not really in a position to help herself. Condemned to yet another lengthy prison sentence, of a further seven years, in 1845, Gesche Rudolph was advised by Gröning, who held out no hope at all of a successful appeal against the sentence on legal grounds, to throw herself on the mercy of the Bremen Senate. 'If this unfortunate woman is now locked up in the penitentiary again,' he told the Senate, 'she will be lost without hope of redemption for the whole of the rest of her life':

> She will find there male and female criminals, most of whom she already knows from her earlier periods of imprisonment. Up to now, she has not committed any theft or indeed any offence other than that of coming from Woltmershausen to Bremen, where, to be sure, she was slovenly and inclined to drunkenness. At the moment she still has some physical strength left, even if her health has already suffered a good deal from almost 20 years of imprisonment. But if she is once more forced to return to the penitentiary, her strength will soon be at an end, she will be unable to resist the influence of a thoroughly depraved milieu, she will probably quit the site of her sufferings as a fully developed criminal. Even if she does not become any worse than she already is, she will most certainly not experience any improvement in prison. After her release, she will not depart from her previous way of life, but will soon fall into the hands of the law for a last time and end in a penitentiary a life whose story everyone will turn away from with grief and revulsion.

Such a fate, Gröning declared, was 'terrible beyond description'. It was necessary to make one last attempt to rescue her. It might be possible to return her to human society if she was 'placed under the care of a guardian'.

Gesche Rudolph herself had indeed declared her willingness to take this step.[159] On 20 May 1845, she put her mark ('+++Gesche Rudolph, having no knowledge of writing') on a legal document which made her Gröning's ward.[160] He in turn proposed to the Senate that her new seven-year sentence be suspended and declared his intention of sending her into the countryside, where she would be lodged 'under the strict supervision of a competent countryman' until she was fit to return to society. The Senate accepted this plan on 21 May, adding, however, that it would immediately reimpose the sentence should Rudolph return to Bremen without her guardian's permission.[161] After that, Gesche Rudolph disappears from history; perhaps, since there is no further record of her in the Bremen files, Gröning's plan succeeded; perhaps it did not, and she moved elsewhere; we simply do not know. What her story shows is both the power of the humanitarian narrative in the 1840s, and its limitations in suggesting real solutions to the problems of crime. Corporal punishment created and perpetuated deviance as much as, or possibly even more than, suppressing it. But so too did imprisonment. Gröning framed his story in terms of the futility of repeated imprisonment as well as repeated beatings. Recidivism, as his proposed solution for Gesche Rudolph's troubles made clear, required strict educational measures to overcome, and scepticism about the effectiveness of incarceration unaccompanied by a proper scheme of amelioration shone through many other contributions made from all quarters of the political spectrum to the debate throughout the century, as both this chapter and the previous one have demonstrated. There was no undisputed 'carceral discourse' framing people's approach to the question of deviance in nineteenth-century Germany. The optimism with which penal reformers like Gröning discussed these questions in the 1840s appears in retrospect to have been exaggerated. Yet it was not the defeat of the 1848 Revolution which consigned their efforts to impotence. On the contrary, as prison building and rebuilding continued during the second half of the century, individual prison cells increasingly became the norm. As the discontent articulated by critics of custodial sentences towards the end of the century indicated, the spread of the 'separate system' based on the Pentonville model of solitary confinement, hard and monotonous labour, strict education and enforced moral and religious contemplation, was no more successful than other systems of imprisonment had been in reducing the number of reoffenders.

Other alternatives were still available, however. If neither isolation nor harsh discipline within prisons could control the deviant impulses of offenders, then perhaps tighter checks and controls could be imposed on them in the world outside. An essential part of the move towards a 'carceral society', as outlined by the French philosopher Michel Foucault in his account of penal policy and practice in the nineteenth century, was the creation of a network of classificatory and supervisory devices by which ordinary citizens could be disciplined. In this process, a distinctive underworld emerged, by whose deviant character the moral and social conformity of the quiescent majority could be measured. Almost permanent surveillance by police and bureaucratic authorities became a standard experience of the nineteenth-century deviant. How this was achieved, and how the deviant dealt with it, is the subject to which we now turn.

3

The Many Identities of Franz Ernst

The Story of an Adventurer

On 31 May 1864, an outwardly respectable gentleman calling himself Franz von Vietinghoff was arrested in the Hanseatic city of Bremen after having failed to leave the town as ordered on the 29th. He was subsequently described as follows:

> Age: 44 (born 1820); height: 66 (inches), stocky, powerfully built, corpulent; hair: brown; eyes: grey; teeth: good; beard: brown moustache; face: round, full, healthy. He usually wears a black coat with one row of buttons and a stand-up collar of the sort clergymen wear.[1]

The resemblance to a clergyman was a nice touch. It helped give the gentleman an air of unimpeachable rectitude. But von Vietinghoff had failed to pay his bill at the Hôtel du Nord, and when the landlord had called in the police, he had proved unable to produce proper identity papers. All that was found on him were clothes and a few personal effects. He had evidently lived well, for the final bill from the Hôtel du Nord, included in the police file, shows he had stayed there for nine nights and consumed eight dinners, with two glasses of beer.[2]

Under interrogation by the police, Vietinghoff produced details of his personal history which were as dramatic as they were unusual. He came, he said, from a more than respectable background. Initially, noted the police report,

> he called himself Dr of medicine v[on] Maltzahn; soon afterwards he gave the following personal details: his name was Franz Alex[ander] Nap[oleon] v[on] Vietinghoff, born in 1822 on the landed estate of Hoff in Walterkehmen and a son of Joh[ann] Mich[ael] Balthasar von Vittinghoff, who had been marshall of the court in Stuttgart from 1826 to 1832 and died in 1836 as a retired Pruss[ian] colonel in Berlin, and his wife Johanne Friederike Alexandrine, née v[on] Maltzahn, widow of Major v[on] Puttkamer.

The aristocratic status provided by the noble prefix 'von' – of vital importance in German society in the 1860s – was supported by circumstantial
evidence of high-ranking connections with the major Prussian Junker family
of the von Puttkamers and other details. 'According to the files of various
authorities in Switzerland,' added the police report, 'v[on] Vietinghoff comes
from a respected family which is said to be related to the Russian family v[on]
Krudener.' This indicated connections with the Baltic German family of the
von Vietinghoffs. However, the man under interrogation had not followed a
conventional aristocratic lifestyle. Vietinghoff told the police that he had
attended the grammar school in Neu-Ruppin. According to the record of the
interrogation, he went on to narrate a life-history that was as dramatic as it
was picaresque:

> I studied medicine, namely in the years 1837 to 1840 in Halle, Jena, Göttingen,
> Berlin, obtaining my doctorate in the last-named place. In the following year
> I obtained my doctorate of philosophy in Königsberg. I am single and have
> never been married. In the years 1841 and 1842, I carried out the functions of
> a physician under the supervision of *Medizinalrat* Korn in Berlin. Out of a
> partiality for the study of foreign lands and peoples I betook myself to America
> in 1843, first to New York, passed my scientific examinations in Philadelphia
> in 1844 and signed on as a doctor in the American navy.

He had then, he said, served for two and a half years on an American warship
engaged in the suppression of the slave trade off the African coast, eventually
obtaining his discharge in New Orleans. Vietinghoff told the Bremen police
that he had gone off next to take part in the great gold rush in California. His
life as a 'forty-niner' evidently did not last very long, however, and he failed
to find the nugget that would have made his fortune. 'In 1850 I returned
to New York and embarked on a journey to the Orient, where I visited
Alexandria, Cairo, Jerusalem (from Easter to Whitsun 1851). From there I
went to Constantinople and in 1851 back to America.' There he obtained a
post as ship's doctor on a regular service to Australia, a position he continued
in for five tours of duty until deciding to settle in Australia for a year. Here,
he says, he obtained 'a fortune', with which he returned to New Orleans to
set up a private hospital (costing 36,000 dollars), further evidence of his
philanthropic inclinations. 'During the Civil War and the siege of New
Orleans I lost all my possessions and fled to Cuba.' From March to October
1862 he was in England, 'where I gave scholarly lectures in London, Bristol,
Birmingham and many other cities'. Then he travelled via Paris to Switzerland, before setting out on another lecture tour, this time in Heidelberg,
Esslingen, Tübingen, Stuttgart and other South German cities, finally arriving
in Bremen.

This was indeed a remarkable career. It had brought Vietinghoff into
contact with many different places and involved him in some major events in

world history in the middle decades of the nineteenth century, though not of course the 1848 Revolution, which it would have been impolitic to have mentioned during a police interrogation. He was clearly something of a world citizen with rich social, professional and political experience. He portrayed himself as motivated purely by altruistic considerations – science, medicine, travel, philanthropy – and a man, at times, of considerable means. He was by now, he said, an American citizen; during the upheavals through which he had passed, he had unfortunately lost the papers relating to his previous Prussian citizenship. Nevertheless, now that he had been arrested, he had some vital information to impart to the Bremen police. For his purposes were not only scientific and philanthropic but also conservative and patriotic. His lecturing tour in South Germany had naturally put him in contact with workers' educational associations, and although these were at this time – in the 1860s – less revolutionary in character and composition than they had been before 1848, they were still full of radicals. From them he had learned that there was to be a major international congress of democrats in Brussels. He discovered that it sought 'the violent overthrow of existing state institutions in Germany'. As a freemason he could not agree with this. 'So I considered myself under an obligation to bring these plans to the attention of the King of Prussia as the Grand Master of this Order.' Not only this, he had also stumbled across a plot to kill the Emperor of France. In Geneva, he said, 'I opposed this plot, with the result that I had to take flight with the loss of my papers and effects, after having been placed under suspicion in Switzerland of being a spy and suffering being beaten and shot at so that my hat was full of holes.' He did not offer his hat as evidence of these claims, but he did show the police an anonymous pamphlet on the Brussels congress which mentioned his name. Vietinghoff said that he had determined to expose the revolutionary movement, had published the pamphlet himself and had come to Bremen in order to discuss its sale and distribution. He was, he said, travelling under an assumed name for fear of the democrats and possible wanted notices issued by the Swiss authorities in his real name after the democrats had prompted them to accuse him of espionage.[3]

The pamphlet certainly made no bones about its hostility to the revolutionaries. Its author wrote that he had attended numerous secret meetings of the democrats and become appalled by the violence of their aims and tactics:

> The immediate aim of the revolutionaries is in general to establish the rule of the mob, in order thereby to secure the essential basis of physical power for themselves. After the mob have steered the ship of state for some time during the revolution in the most arbitrary way, without any definite direction, the will of the people is to express itself through its representatives in a democracy and take over. In this transitional period from mob rule to democratic rule the leaders of the former will try to gain for themselves as many privileges as

possible at the expense of the common good, in order then to undermine the institutions of the state more and more, for their own advantage.[4]

The meetings at which these aims had been revealed had culminated in the Brussels congress. The leading Italian nationalist and revolutionary Giuseppe Mazzini had sent representatives, and the honorary presidency had been assumed by his even more celebrated compatriot Giuseppe Garibaldi, who had achieved worldwide fame during the Italian wars of unification in 1859–60. Over 300 delegates from various European countries had been present. They had discussed secret statutes which had been voted on by the Central Committee in Geneva:

> Now §12 says explicitly that the freedom of peoples can only be achieved if the people who are an obstacle to it, the princes with their courts, are done away with; in other words, the assassination of princes is sanctioned in cases in which no other means can be found of removing crowned heads of state from office. The most beloved princes are the most dangerous.[5]

But there had been no agreement on these statutes in Brussels, even after five evenings of debate. Nevertheless, the threat posed by paragraph 12 was palpable, said the pamphlet.

The writer then turned to local politics in Geneva, and to an account of the doings of the exiled German 'Democrat' Johann Philip Becker, who had taken a leading part in the radical revolutionary movement in Baden in 1848–49:

> He it was who had his corps of irregulars loot dairies, bakeries and butchers' shops, and who stole the citizens' horses from their stables in order to provide mounts for himself and his comrades. The meanest trick which he wanted to play was the blowing-up of the bridge over the Neckar at Heidelberg, which he was however prevented from carrying out by Prussian troop manoeuvres.

This was history rather than news. More up-to-date was an account of Becker's activities in exile in Geneva, although these did not appear to be sensationally dangerous. The pamphlet went on to describe the activities of Zamparini, who was apparently Mazzini's agent on the Democrats' Central Committee.[6] Then the author went on:

> In the month of December two Germans took part in the sessions of the Central Committee alongside some Italians who were certainly not distant from those who conceived the idea of the assassination attempt on Napoleon. One of these, Doctor of Medicine v[on] Hoff, had participated in the Brussels congress earlier on, and after this had been once more in Geneva. He resigned from the association at the point when its members were supposed to commit

themselves to the secret statutes. His financial situation cannot be brilliant, since he has been obliged to obtain a credit of 460 francs from a merchant here.

He is said to have reported on the doings of the German democrats to German governments, as has emerged from letters which arrived here after his departure.

Later on, this same man, following a baseless denunciation on the part of the Bavarian ambassador, is said to have been arrested in Berne, but released again after seven days. Whether the Bavarian ambassador exceeded his instructions in doing this must remain an open question, but it is clear that the denunciation was the work of Dr von Hoff's democratic persecutors and that the Bavarian ambassador has not found the Council of the German Confederation unreceptive to their insinuations.

In his Bremen prison cell, Franz Alexander Napoleon von Vietinghoff explained that this 'Dr von Hoff' had been none other than himself, taking part in the congress under an alias for self-protection. Just to underline the identity of von Hoff as the renegade who was now doing the governments of Europe the service of revealing to them the murderous intentions of the Democrats, the pamphlet added: 'What I am doing with this pamphlet, Dr v[on] Hoff has already done before me.'[7]

Aristocratic status and background, medical degree, monied past, philanthropic history, scientific activity, patriotic service, conservative politics, American citizenship – surely all this would be enough to bring about Vietinghoff's immediate release with the apologies of the police for troubling him. But none of this counted for very much in Bremen, a self-governing Hanseatic city where bourgeois values obtained and lack of hard cash – and thus unpaid hotel bills – was more important than status. Moreover, among the documents found among his effects left at the Hôtel du Nord was an undated set of 12 'Questions to a German man of honour', to 'Hoff' in Geneva, written by 'a meeting of German citizens'. They cast an altogether different light on the events recounted in his autobiography. Was he, the citizens asked sarcastically, the same Hoff who had stolen some money while a confirmand at the Neu-Ruppin gymnasium, had maltreated his assistant while working as a doctor, had been involved in shady financial dealings in Berlin and had had a lengthy career of cheating and deception? It went on to pose some even more awkward questions:

5. Are you the same Hoff who had himself supported for a year in America by public charities, then protested, in order to make a living for himself with the help of the pious (!)?

6. Are you the same Hoff who joined a band of slave-traders and carried out medical examinations of slaves for the same?

7. Are you the same Hoff who himself owned slaves and had them whipped unbelievably hard?

8. Are you the same Hoff who travelled through America dressed as an Oriental and carried out medical deceptions as a quack?

9. Are you the same Hoff who as a ship's doctor poisoned sick sailors by injecting them with vaccines?

The document claimed that Hoff had fled to Australia when his deceptions had been uncovered, and that the ship on which he served in Africa was in fact a slaver. In the American presidential elections, he had been a paid agitator working for the pro-slavery campaign.

It went on to allege that, when he got back to Germany, he made his family pay him not to use his real name. He had taken money from workers' educational associations and then 'silently disappeared overnight'. He had acted as a paid police informer at the democratic congress, leading to several arrests. The authors added: 'Just as you are unforgettable in the memory of most of the innkeepers of Germany, so we too cannot easily rid our memories of you, since according to recent information you are the Hoff . . . who bought revolutionary pamphlets here and, far from paying for them, sent them on to the German police.' Many of the details, such as his refusal to pay for the literature he had bought and his reputation, now confirmed in Bremen, for failing to pay his hotel bills, were highly incriminating, and did not cast his character in an honest or upright light; it thus seems most unlikely that he wrote the list of questions himself in order to gain sympathy. The document, in other words, has the ring of authenticity. Evidently the exiled German revolutionaries in Geneva had become suspicious of Hoff's activities and instituted enquiries. Radicals and democrats such as these were also able to get a lot of information from their exiled friends and comrades in the USA. The document had been sent to von Hoff by the authors and postmarked Geneva 28 January 1864, and had given him eight days to answer its charges. It was after this, evidently, that the German exiles had attacked von Hoff, beaten him up, possibly shooting a hole in his hat, and made his position in Switzerland untenable. Some of the details of the allegations were clearly fanciful, and none of them was easily verifiable. Nevertheless, they inevitably raised in the minds of the Bremen police a number of questions about the man sitting in their cell which urgently required answering.[8]

Von Hoff or Vietinghoff was therefore told that he would be kept in custody for the time being. Apparently shocked and disappointed by this outcome, he now tried another tactic, declaring: 'I am not making any more statements, just ask Police President v[on] Bernuth in Berlin about me, then you will get some information, and it's now all the same to me how long I stay in custody.' He was clearly hinting as strongly as he could that he had been working as a secret agent on behalf of the Prussian police, much as had been suggested by the 12 questions sent to him by the Geneva exiles. Given the power of the Prussian police across Germany and even beyond, and the well-known fact that they did indeed employ a large number of secret agents who infiltrated themselves into revolutionary and democratic organizations, the best thing the police authorities of the small Hanseatic city could do was to let him get on with his job. The Bremen police, however, obstinately refused to release him, even in the face of this new and disturbing possibility. So the prisoner began to make a nuisance of himself, in order to provoke the Bremen authorities into releasing him because he was causing so much trouble. He complained vociferously about his conditions of imprisonment: 'No one can exist', he wrote to his gaolers in an official protest, 'in the [cell] which has been provided for me.' He claimed to have an eye complaint which the poor light in his cell would aggravate. He demanded to be allowed to send some letters. All this met with a stony silence from the now thoroughly hostile police authorities in Bremen. For, unknown to their prisoner, their investigations and correspondence outside the city were already beginning to cause his entire narrative to unravel in a fashion almost as dramatic as the events of which it had been constructed.

The Art of Autobiography

As soon as von Vietinghoff had been arrested, the Bremen police had begun writing to university, police and other authorities to check up on the details which he had given them.[9] 'V[on] Vietinghoff', they noted, after instituting enquiries in the areas in which he claimed to have been born and grown up, 'is not known to the police authorities in Havelberg and Neu-Ruppin.'[10] They were also able to use the correspondence which they had seized from his hotel room to uncover further details about his life and connections which were strongly at variance with the story he had told them. On 13 July they informed him that they had discovered 'that the statements which he has made up to now about his name, place of birth, etc. etc. have been revealed as throughly untrue by the official communications which have been made to us in the meantime'. Their prisoner still refused to co-operate with them, however, and stubbornly stuck to his original story. But soon they made an important breakthrough. By checking up on his correspondence, the police discovered that he had a half-brother by the name of Kupfer in Breslau. When they told him on 16 July that they would institute enquiries about his identity through this half-brother, he abandoned his previous refusal to alter his story.

The life-history he now gave the police was very different from the one he had originally supplied:

My name is Franz Ernst, born on 12 Nov[em]b[e]r in Friesack, son of Ludwig Ernst, a man of private means, still alive, and his wife Johanna, born Wesenberg. I studied at the grammar school in Neu-Ruppin, then lived off a private income in Berlin and the surrounding areas roughly in the years 1837 to 1839. From 1840 to 1850 I ran a trading business in Berlin and owned a noble landed estate called 'Adlerhof' in the vicinity. In Sept. or Oct. 1856 I obtained a foreign passport from the Pol[ice] Presidium in Berlin and travelled initially to Australia, where I took the name v[on] Vietinghoff, changing it to v[on] Hoff when I betook myself to America in 1858. I studied medical science in Sommerville and then lived as a doctor in New York a[nd] in the states of the American South. In 1862 I came to England. I said in my first interrogation what happened to me later and where I stayed on the Continent. In 1839 I married Maria Buchholz, daughter of a lord mayor, but divorced her in 1851 or 1852. My ex-wife lives in Wittstock with my two children. I have no previous convictions.

Gone from the new narrative, therefore, were the trips to Africa and the involvement in the American Civil War. Gone was the philanthropic participation in the suppression of the slave trade. Gone was 'the study of foreign lands and peoples'. Gone were the university degree and medical qualification. Gone were the Californian gold rush and the service in the American navy. Gone were the aristocratic background and the bachelorhood. After all these deletions, not much remained.

Yet even this watered-down version of his *curriculum vitae* did not satisfy the Bremen police. On 20 July his half-brother in Breslau confirmed that von Hoff, using the name Dr Schulze, had travelled to Australia via Hamburg in 1856, returning in 1859. When given money to go to America by his family in 1860, he had only made it as far as England and had spent the money there. The police noted that he had been forced to go to America by his family on account of his bad behaviour. He was in fact what was known as a 'remittance man', a ne'er-do-well sent off into exile with a 'remittance' to set himself up there on condition he never came back. This cast an altogether different light on his travels than the one suggested by his claims of scientific interest and philanthropic motives. More than this, the Bremen police also discovered that his claim not to have any criminal history was untrue:

In February this year he was deported from Switzerland for failure to produce proper papers, using a false name, espionage and deception . . . In Mannheim he cheated the inkeeper Horn at the 'Black Lion' of a sum of 42 Thalers which he owed to him, while at the same time he cheated a number of printers by obtaining from them considerable advances on the strength of fictitious publishing projects.

Moreover, his claim to be 44 years of age seemed to be an underestimate, as the new documentation revealed that he was at least 50 and possibly even older. Who, therefore, was this man who had landed in a Bremen police cell because he had failed to pay his hotel bill? The police investigations only seemed to have deepened the mystery.

Faced with more documentary evidence, including details supplied by his half-brother, and interrogated once more on 23 July, 'Dr von Hoff' changed his story yet again. Though some of the details were the same as he had supplied a week before, others were significantly different. The new narrative was far less flattering to its author than his previous versions had been, and carried a correspondingly greater ring of authenticity:

> I might have been born in 1816 or 1815; I don't know precisely. My mother, Johanne Sophie, née Wesenberg, was first married to Kupfer, a man of private means in Neu-Ruppin. After this marriage was dissolved, my mother married the small farmer Ludwig Heinr[ich] Ernst in Friesack. I was born in Friesack a[nd] baptized Franz Hermann. I went to school in Fehrbellin, then attended the grammar school in Neu-Ruppin and served as a volunteer in the 20th infantry regiment in Torgau, before living off my money for a few years, without any fixed occupation, in Berlin, until 1837. In 1837 I bought some land in Herzberg to which the rights of knacker and executioner were attached, and in the same year I married the daughter of the knacker and executioner Schulze in Torgau, being divorced from her in the following year. In 1840 I married the widow of the merchant Leppert, Therese, née Buchholz, in Neu-Ruppin, moved with her to Fehrbellin, and after staying there for half a year, moved to Berlin, where I engaged in trading, before being arrested and imprisoned in 1848 for fraudulent bankruptcy. After serving a sentence of six years, and after . . . being divorced from my second wife, with whom I had three daughters, two of whom are still living, I obtained a passport and left for Australia in 1856. In 1858 or 1859 I moved to Boston and in the latter year for a time to Coethen, where I studied medicine in the institute as Dr Lutze. I did not return to America, but, as I have already said, stayed in the Orient.

He now admitted, therefore, to two marriages instead of none. The number of surnames he confessed to having used had now reached six, and he had silently dropped both the noble prefix and the forename 'Napoleon'. His journeys overseas, it now seemed, had been undertaken not for scientific reasons, but in order to flee from the misfortunes of bankruptcy, imprisonment and divorce.

More dramatic still was his confession to a social background which, far from being aristocratic, placed him in the ranks of the 'dishonourable', outcast social groups long ostracized by respectable society. In many cases, such as that of millers, for example, the imputation of infamy had more or less disappeared as the status-bound, strictly hierarchical 'society of orders' (*Ständegesellschaft*) of the seventeenth and eighteenth centuries had given way to the class society of the nineteenth. But this transition was still far from complete, especially in the case of the trade with which Franz Ernst – this seems to have been his real name – was concerned. The son of a peasant farmer (*Öconom*), he had bought land which carried with it the rights and duties not only of acting as a local skinner and knacker but also of officiating as state executioner in any public beheadings which should take place by order of the courts in the district. By the late 1830s, to be sure, the use of the death penalty in Prussia had declined dramatically since the days before the penal reforms of the Enlightenment, so it was extremely unlikely that Franz Ernst would ever have had to have wielded the axe in person. Nevertheless, the other duties attaching to such a property were degrading enough in the eyes of most people – rounding up and skinning wild and diseased animals, removing the corpses of dead animals from farms and butchering them, killing stray dogs, and even in some cases cleaning out the town drains and disposing of human ordure. Of course, the actual possessor of a property or lease which required these duties – which could in practice be fairly lucrative, given the widespread use of animal skins and fur in the age before the manufacture of synthetic fibres – could always hire someone else to do the real work, and many did. This might go some way towards overcoming the ostracism which traditionally attached to the trade. Still, nineteenth-century sources are unanimous in concurring that skinners, knackers and executioners continued to be widely regarded as infamous, obliging them, for example, to confine their social intercourse to one another's families. The marriages of such men were customarily confined to their colleagues' daughters, which created large and ramified dynasties of executioners who continued to dominate the trade well into the twentieth century, and it is no accident that Ernst's first wife was herself the daughter of a knacker-executioner. It was hardly surprising that he had decided to conceal this background with aliases and invent an aristocratic past for himself.[11]

Franz Ernst had now told so many lies that even this new, more downbeat narrative of his life-history could not be accepted at face value. To be sure, it roughly corresponded to the one supplied to the police by the inter-rogatee's half-brother. However, it still did not appear entirely convincing. Consulting the voluminous files at their disposal and taking advantage of the new technique of photography, the Bremen police noted:

The alleged v[on] Maltzahn or v[on] Vietinghoff or v[on] Hoff bears a surprising resemblance to the crook von Ziemitzki, who was described [with a photograph] in the 1859 volume of the Prussian Central Police Circular. Now 68 years of age, he has used the aliases of Friedrich Massen, Masson, von Oppersdorf, etc. etc., and according to item 4178 no. 10 of the Prussian Central Police Circular of 1859 also used the names Maltzahn and von Maltzahn. This person is known to have had two sons and two daughters with the Silesian Countess von Oppersdorf in the years 1818 to 1822; nothing is known here about what happened to them. V[on] Hoff has claimed to have been born in 1822, and the similarity of their appearance leads to the suspicion that he is one of those sons.

Moreover, according to the Prussian police, 'Baron von Maltzahn' had been sentenced to nine months' imprisonment for illegal gambling and repeated illicit use of the noble prefix and another nine months when he failed to show up. He was now wanted for evading both sentences.[12] All these biographical details of his supposed, possibly real father stamped Franz Ernst not only as a professional 'villain' (*Gauner*) himself but actually as a member of a family of 'villains'. Moreover, in checking out his aliases the police discovered that he had run up numerous unpaid bills not only in the hotel where he had been arrested, but also in other businesses in Bremen, and in doing so he had used the name Maltzahn, the very alias employed by his alleged father. The more the police pursued their investigations, the more ramified the network of his deceptions appeared to become.

Criminal Commissioner Pick, of the Berlin police, had already confirmed this impression on 8 June 1864 when he had warned the Bremen authorities that virtually all the information on his personal history which anybody had gathered derived ultimately from Ernst himself and was therefore unlikely to be true. Certainly he had never been registered as a doctor in Berlin. However, the commissioner then went on to make a damaging admission, which indicated just how difficult it was to deal with a man such as this:

> The alleged Baron von Vietinghoff, alias Dr von Hoff, is one of the most dangerous political swindlers of recent times; he has offered his services in various places and used them to carry out all kinds of fraud. Thus he hawked himself around in Frankfurt/M., Giessen, Gotha, etc. this year, arousing attention everywhere with his deceptions and giving rise to all kinds of enquiries. . . . In order to bring his swindles to an end without creating fuss, Police President von Bernuth had a travelling allowance of 113 Marks paid out to v[on] Hoff, and the latter promised to go away to America via Bremen. Hoff preferred, however, to spend the money and stay in Bremen.
>
> I do not believe that President von Bernuth will agree to giving v[on] Hoff a single penny more; there is no reason for it, since no importance is attached to [von] Hoff's swindles here. It would in any event be a great gain simply for public security if such a filthy and degenerate subject could be done away with.[13]

It now appeared, therefore, that the Bremen police were dealing with a professional confidence trickster of a boldness and ingenuity sufficient to persuade the Chief of Police in Berlin to part with his money and drive Berlin police officials to contemplate murder.

Conning the Crowned Heads of Europe

Just how brazen Franz Ernst was became clear when the police began to unravel the political deception in which he had been involved. 'Von Hoff', noted a police circular in July 1864, 'is one of the political confidence tricksters who have emerged in recent times and deserve the particularly close attention of the police.' He had left a trail of deceptions right across Germany and had drawn the attention of the authorities to himself by appearing as a witness in the trial of the editor Rausche and his accomplices in November 1863.

> Most recently he has sought to support himself through swindling and deception. In April 1863 the newspaper *Felleisen* was said to have issued a warning about him . . . From Geneva he moved to Bern, where he used the name D[r] Fischer. On his arrest, papers were found on him which revealed him as a politically treacherous spy. After his deportation from Switzerland, Vittinghoff stayed in Mainz, Frankfurt, Berlin, etc and in the first-named city moved among red republicans and was expelled from Frankfurt as well as Berlin. – In the year 1863 he made contact with the well-known leader of the Social Republican party, Joh[ann] Phil[ipp] Becker in Geneva, and got to know other leaders of this party there, whom he had sought out in Frankfurt and Mainz.

His purposes in these activities, the police realized, were not political but pecuniary: to prove his usefulness to the authorities by winning the confidence of the revolutionaries. He was prompted to pursue a career as a political confidence trickster largely by the obsession of the police and state authorities on the European Continent at this time with the threat of 'democracy'. It was well known that they had developed a widespread network of secret political police and *agents provocateurs* to deal with it. The previous few years had seen massive publicity devoted to this phenomenon, beginning with Karl Marx's denunciation of the machinations, deceptions, forgeries and perjury of the leading Prussian political police officer Wilhelm Stieber in the mass trial of Communists held in Cologne in the autumn of 1852, and continuing with Stieber's riposte, published jointly with the Hanoverian police chief Karl Georg Wermuth in 1853–54, *The Communist Conspiracies of the Nineteenth Century*.[14]

The 1850s were a decade of reaction, in which police officials such as Stieber and Hinckeldey enjoyed a good deal of freedom to pursue their projects without fear of public criticism or opposition. But by the beginning of the 1860s, the atmosphere was beginning to change. The prolonged illness of Prussia's King Friedrich Wilhelm IV brought his brother Wilhelm I to the throne, initially as regent. This inaugurated a 'new course' in Prussian politics, in which a liberal revival, inspired by the example of the successful unification of Italy in 1858–60, began to take place. By 1862, the Prussian Liberals had the upper hand in the legislature and were using their majority to demand that the Prussian army be brought under parliamentary control. The monarch responded by calling the arch-reactionary Otto von Bismarck to office as Minister-President. But although he proceeded to bypass the Liberals by collecting taxes without parliamentary approval, it was a long time before Bismarck was able to bring the political situation under control. During this period, critics of the police won some notable victories. Stieber was brought to trial for perjury and revealed in the proceedings so many embarrassing facts about the corrupt and arbitrary behaviour of his superiors that the Prussian Justice Minister and the General State Prosecutor had been forced to hand in their resignations.[15] Following this, the journalist Wilhelm Eichhoff published a book containing a series of even more damaging and detailed allegations against the senior officers of the Berlin political police. Soon Eichhoff's book was joined by two others, both published in 1862, attacking the Prussian political police's use of spies and secret agents.[16] So widespread was the publicity generated by all these events that anyone who read the newspapers or had access to any of these publications must have been aware of how murky was the atmosphere of lies and spies, agents and double agents, deceptions and fabrications in which the Berlin political police, and their associates in other states such as Hanover, operated: a world full of aliases, concealment and secrecy, in which police and revolutionaries alike operated not only right across Western and Central Europe but across the Atlantic in the United States as well.[17]

It was in this atmosphere that Franz Ernst, 'Dr von Hoff', tried to pull off his greatest political coup in attempting to gain money from European monarchs and police forces by warning them against the assassination attempts allegedly planned by the conspiratorial wing of the 'democrats' at the Brussels congress in September 1863. For the author of the anonymous pamphlet which he carried around with him, the pamphlet that warned against the treachery of 'Dr. v Hoff' and his betrayal of the democrats' plans, was of course none other than 'Dr. v Hoff' himself. The realization of what he was up to had dawned on the police only slowly, but by July 1864 they were certain. 'He claims', they wrote,

> to have been present at the European congress of democrats held in Brussels at the end of September 1863, together with the watchmaker Ph[ilipp] Jakob Schöppler from Mainz and the editor Rausche. Shortly thereafter he wrote a small pamphlet about this congress, which he offered to several governments along with other democratic writings of Becker. Vittinghoff [*sic*] appears to have seen, perhaps possessed, the printed invitation to the Brussels congress, which carried Garibaldi's signature, and the printed provisional statutes of the congress, for he describes both documents correctly. His pamphlet about the Brussels Democrats' congress contains nothing about its main business; it deals

with secondary issues and belittles a number of personalities. It is composed in such a way that it appears to have been written by an unknown person, as if the Dr v[on] Hoff named therein was not its author. Thus the writer says among other things in this pamphlet: 'He is not naming anybody, but v[on] Hoff was judicially interrogated on one occasion in the proceedings against Schöppler, and his evidence must have been advantageous for the latter, otherwise his release would not have been so quick.['] The alleged Vietinghoff is not familiar at all with the activities of the various revolutionary parties; he has not the slightest knowledge of their origins, organization or central direction, or of their connections with one another. A few leaders of the revolutionary parties let him see their cards a little when they were invited to the Brussels Democrats' Congress, and he has exploited this to compose a vacuous pamphlet about it and, as already noted, to offer it freely on all sides.[18]

The record of his effects found in the Hôtel du Nord included letters and documents relating to the Brussels congress, from which he did indeed seem to have obtained such information as was contained in his pamphlet.

The secret resolution to carry out a plan of assassination against European heads of state was purely his invention. The congress really had happened, but it had been organized mainly to protest against the Russian repression of a nationalist uprising which had begun in Poland early in 1863. Karl Marx was aware of its nature and purposes and wrote to Friedrich Engels some months later, during a sensational visit paid by Garibaldi to London, where Marx was living: 'It was decided at the secret Revolutionaries' congress in Brussels (September 1863) with Garibaldi as its nominal chief – that G. should come to London, but incognito, and thus take the city by surprise. Then he was to come out for Poland in the strongest possible way.' In fact, Garibaldi had entered the British capital very publicly and had used his enormous popularity with the British public not to arouse sympathy for the Poles, who were now beyond help, but to put pressure on Palmerston's government to support his planned Italian nationalist march on Austrian-held Venice.[19] The fact that the congress was held in closed session, and had been set up by known democrats and revolutionaries, had ironically made it easier for a political confidence-man such as 'von Hoff' to invent sensational details of its proceedings and sell them to the Prussian political police. The planned or attempted assassinations of heads of state and government ministers, such as had taken place in the case of Friedrich Wilhelm IV of Prussia in 1852, Kaiser Franz Josef of Austria in 1853 and Napoleon III of France in 1858, had caused widespread alarm among the authorities, despite their failure, and the threat of a repetition must have seemed to Franz Ernst the most effective way of persuading monarchs, governments and police forces to sit up, pay attention to what he was saying and give him their money as a reward.[20]

The Brussels Congress documents were not the only incriminating evidence found among the possessions of 'Dr von Hoff' in the Hôtel du Nord.

The effects consisted mainly of 'scholarly books' and hundreds of copies of his pamphlet, which the landlord of the hotel somewhat optimistically claimed as security for the unpaid bill. More revealing were some 'letters addressed in a begging manner to leading persons of the conservative parties' in which Ernst 'portrayed himself as a martyr and as the victim of his own patriotism; further, begging letters to members of freemasons' lodges'. The begging letters – all preserved in the police file – included for example one sent on 20 June 1864 to the King of Prussia asking for 'a special gratification for services rendered with reference to the Democratic congress and the Democratic movement(s) connected with it'. Ernst claimed that he had run out of money and 'in order to survive on the bare necessities I am living in a village near Bremen, where I am occupied with literary works'.[21] In fact, these 'literary works' consisted mainly of still more begging letters. And the 'village' near Bremen was in fact the Hôtel du Nord, from which he was sending out a stream of letters all the while. On 11 July, for example, the police authorities in the Kingdom of Hanover reported that he had tried to get 100 Thalers off them in return for giving them information about the Brussels Congress. They had refused.[22] Although he had met with only partial success in his endeavours, Ernst, to judge from the effects found in his hotel room and the information supplied by other police forces, was clearly a professional confidence trickster of no mean resourcefulness and ability.

Underworld Identities

Such confidence tricksters were far from unusual in mid-nineteenth-century Germany. Rivalling Franz Ernst in ingenuity was one Heinrich Bauer, for example, also known as Charles-Henri-Amedée-Félix de Latoulade, who claimed to be a political refugee from Paris, where he said he had murdered a policeman during the 1848 Revolution. He recounted his (wholly fictitious) life-story in detail in a 60-page manuscript entitled 'Souvenirs. Mélanges. Par un pauvre diable', dated 1854, which he most probably used to gain money from political and other sympathizers. During his interrogation in Bremen it emerged that his real name was Carl Heinrich Linnartz, from Elberfeld. The same year (1854) he broke out of prison, he was last heard of the following year masquerading as a Hungarian count.[23] Around 1850, too, the clerk Friedrich Eduard Fritze earned notoriety by travelling round Germany posing variously as an aristocrat, a doctor of medicine and an army officer, using at least 12 known aliases and a whole wardrobe of appropriate clothing to con unsuspecting citizens out of their money.[24] The files of German police forces contain numerous examples of such men. Police forces were decentralized in pre-unification Germany to an even greater extent than they were after 1871; and, as we have seen, individual states did not think there was anything wrong in simply expelling offenders whose presence they wished to be rid of,

1. 'Justice'. Illustration accompanying the title page of the Prussian General Law Code of 1794, showing the figure of Justitia holding the symbols of justice, with a portrait of King Friedrich Wilhelm II, 'the legislator', King of Prussia from 1786 to 1797. Nephew of Friedrich II, the monarch who had originally inspired this great Enlightenment law code decades before, Friedrich Wilhelm delayed the promulgation of the code until its radicalism had been diluted by a number of conservative amendments.

2. Wilhelm Aschenbrenner, art teacher and forger. Self-portrait, Spandau, 1801. The epigraph reads in full: 'You pure in heart who, perhaps with secret displeasure, witness him stumble, fall — do not deny him a gentle tear of sympathy.' The picture was printed as a frontispiece to Aschenbrenner's picaresque memoirs, which he wrote in the fortress prison at Spandau to earn money to pay for his keep. The project was frustrated by his unexpected deportation to Siberia the following year.

3. German bandits in the Napoleonic era. Members of the Vogelsberg and Wetterau bands of robbers, 1813. These individuals typified the altogether unromantic professional thieves of the age, who were often drawn from the ranks of vagrants, beggars and the 'dishonourable'.

4. In the prison chapel, 1837. Painting by Wilhelm Joseph Heine. The picture illustrates the situation which prison reformers in the first half of the nineteenth century were trying to change: men and women mix promiscuously, some of the inmates are chatting to one another, or failing to pay attention, they are not dressed in prison uniform, and some of them are lolling around in disrespectful attitudes.

5. In the prison chapel, 1892. From the popular magazine *Die Gartenlaube*. The separate system of prison discipline, favoured by many prison reformers in the nineteenth century, demanded that prisoners be strictly isolated from contact with one another, in order to break their collective spirit and encourage each individual to reflect on his wicked deeds. This prison chapel is designed so that the preacher can see all the prisoners, and the prisoners can see no-one but him.

6. 'Where the Blame Lies'. Cartoon illustrating the growth of nativist sentiment in the United States, fuelled by the (justified) suspicion that European countries were using America as a dumping-ground for their unwanted citizens. The practice of several German states in secretly deporting offenders of various kinds to America from the 1820s to the 1860s was one of a number of influences leading to tighter immigration controls later in the century. In this cartoon, dating from 1891, a judge complains to Uncle Sam: 'If immigration was properly restricted you would no longer be troubled with anarchy, socialism, the mafia and such kindred evils.'

7. Convicts on the way to exile in Siberia, towards the end of the nineteenth century. The condition and clothing of the Prussian prisoners forced to walk from the Baltic to the mines of Nerchinsk, near the Chinese border, in 1802–03, is unlikely to have been very different. Note the chains hampering their movements. The Prussian convicts who escaped from such a party in 1802 had to steal the key from their guard and unlock their fetters in order to get away.

8. Examination of convicts' leg-fetters as they leave their overnight prison quarters for their day's work in a mine, Siberia, late nineteenth century. Conditions in the mines shocked foreign observers such as the American George Kennan, from whose book on Siberia the two illustrations on this page are taken.

9. Female inmate of the Cologne penitentiary, 1845. In a regulation dress and uniform, the woman lowers her head to signify her dishonour and humiliation. Gesche Rudolph might have looked something like this during her lengthy and repeated stays in prison.

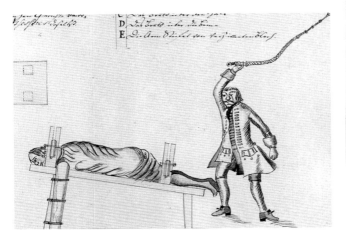

10. 'Sketch of a bench of shame, on which malefactors are whipped and brought to confess', dating from the year 1753, and probably drawn by the Hanoverian executioner Göppel. By the 1820s, whipping was only used as a punishment and was declining in favour in most German states, but the method remained much as shown in the picture.

11. Corporal punishment, cane, and 'violin' or 'fiddle'. Print by J.M. Mettenleiter, late eighteenth century. The brutal or prurient faces of the bailiffs and spectators, and the evident lack of impression made by the punishment on the couple lounging in the window, sum up the enlightened liberal view of corporal punishment as both barbaric and ineffective.

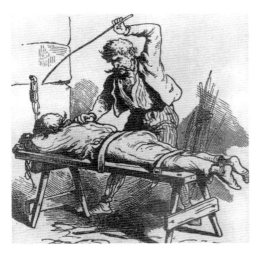

12. (*left*) A whipping in prison. This illustration shows a prisoner tied to a simple wooden bench, with a rough and brutal man administering the beating, apparently without any spectators. In practice the warder or bailiff wielding the whip would have been in uniform, and the whipping would have taken place in the presence of the prison director, warders, probably a doctor, and on many occasions the other prisoners as well. Corporal punishment continued in prisons long after its abolition in public.

13. Discipline in the classroom. From early modern times and through the nineteenth century, teachers used dishonouring punishments, such as the 'ass of shame' and the donkey's cap to encourage hard work and maintain discipline. This teacher is also equipped with two birches for beating his charges; the idle schoolboy is forced to hold one in his hand, as the teacher reaches out for it to administer the punishment; the other hangs from the teacher's desk on the right.

14. Franz Ernst. Photograph found among Ernst's effects in the Hôtel du Nord, Bremen, June 1864, and preserved in the police file. The picture conveys something of his effrontery, as well as the corpulence which evidently lent him a much-needed air of solidity. He has put a globe by his side to draw attention to his experience as a world traveller, allegedly motivated by charitable and scientific interest. It is possible that he may have used this photograph in some of his deceptions.

15. Rogues' Gallery. An illustration dating from the early 1900s, in an edition of Friedrich Christian Benedikt Avé-Lallement's *Das deutsche Gaunerthum* edited by Max Bauer, published in Munich in 1914. Avé-Lallement's great work, published in the late 1850s and early 1860s, sought to classify 'villains' by the methods they used and the guises they assumed. By the early 1900s, interest had shifted to the classification of criminals by their physiognomy, in the belief that hereditary degeneracy found its clearest expression in the criminal's facial features. The editors of the new edition of *Das deutsche Gaunerthum* superimposed this new method of classification on Avé-Lallement's old one. A comparison with the portraits in illustration 3 shows the shift in approach which had taken place.

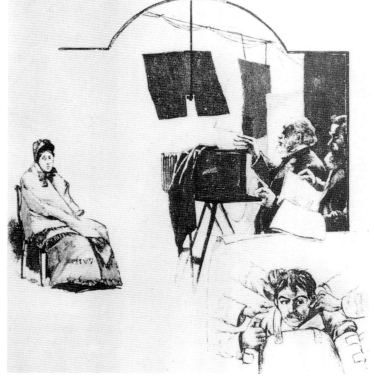

16. The 'Criminals' Album'. Photography was quickly pressed into the service of identifying criminals; this late nineteenth-century illustration betrays typical contemporary gender stereotypes by showing the female offender meekly submitting and the male offender having to be held in place by physical force and mechanical restraint as the police photographer takes the picture.

17. Checking for papers. A policeman asks some vagrants for legitimation. This photograph (*Dufte Kunden bleibt mal stehn, laßt mal eure Flebbe sehn!*) shows how even society's outcasts had to carry some means of identification on them at all times.

18. A Berlin brothel in the 1840s. The artist is concerned to demonstrate the links between alcoholism and prostitution: the male client in the middle is taking a drink from the hands of the elderly and repulsive madam, the client sitting below-right stretches his hand out towards it; beer-barrels serve as seats and tables; and the horizontal line formed by the outstretched arms and the client's heads draws the spectator's eye to the drink being poured from a large bowl on the left. The men appear as victims of their alcoholic and sexual weaknesses; the women to the right and left are portrayed as captors and seducers; only the girl in the centre is shown in a pose of submission.

19. Arrest of a prostitute, under protest. The title-page of the first edition of the satirical artist Heinrich Zille's *Street Kids* (*Kinder der Strasse*, Berlin, 1908) caused such a storm that it was dropped in later editions. Zille's gritty realism offended public taste because it went against conventional stereotypes of the prostitute as a 'lost woman' who had 'fallen' because of her own moral weakness.

20. (*above*) 'From the police report: "The prostitute had already been hanging for several days. Reason for suicide unknown"'. Sketch by Heinrich Zille, 1908, commenting ironically both on the poverty of the woman's existence and the indifference and incomprehension of the police. The picture implies a preceding narrative of downfall and despair, ending in death, common in portrayals of prostitution at this time.

21. Feminists put pressure on the Government. A delegation of thirty-five feminists, led by Anita Augspurg and Marie Stritt visited Reich Chancellor Bernhard von Bülow in the Spring of 1902 to demand the reform of the law on prostitution. Bülow hinted that the feminist crusade to abolish state-regulated prostitution had some sympathizers in government circles, but he himself spoke out in favour of police regulation on another occasion. A special 'Bülow issue' of a satirical magazine here recalls the event two years later.

thus making them the responsibility of other police forces. The most they felt obliged to do was to warn their counterparts that they were coming. Common initiatives were mainly confined to the pursuit of known revolutionaries.[25] To some extent, of course, the police sought to balance out the problems of decentralization and localism by circulating newsletters to other forces with lists, pictures and detailed descriptions of people they were looking for. These 'wanted lists' were sold nationally, and to a degree even internationally, by subscriptions that paid, and possibly more than paid, for their production and distribution. To begin with they were the unofficial creation of individual police officials of an enterprising nature, such as Police Commissioner Merker, in Erfurt, whose newsletter, *Information for the Maintenance of Public Security*, begun in 1819, was one of the first of its kind. It listed 'wanted persons', 'loafers posing a threat to the community' and unsolved crimes, as well as making mention of 'completed cases' which also, of course, served as advertisements for its own success. The wanted people were briefly described by name, trade, place and date of birth, domicile, 'reason for being on wanted list' and 'place of escape'. Cumulative annual indices ensured that the names of those still being sought did not slip the memory of the authorities who read them.

Merker's newsletter was successful, and by the 1850s had been taken over by the Prussian police and transformed into the *Information of the Royal Police Presidium in Berlin for the Furtherance of Public Security*, which contained lengthy lists of offenders recently sentenced in the courts as well as the usual details of wanted individuals. A new feature, characteristic of the post-1848 reaction, was the inclusion of essays on political offenders and refugees.[26] Meanwhile, a second, similar circular, the *General Security Advertiser for the Prussian State*, followed Merker's lead in 1820. It was issued twice a week and consisted of a single sheet, printed on both sides with descriptions of one or two criminal cases and lists of the personal characteristics of the wanted person. Soon there were more periodicals of this kind, issued in a growing number of major cities. One such, *Erhard's General Police Advertiser*, played a role in the case of Franz Ernst. These served to systematize the widespread practice of issuing individual wanted notices circulated about particular offenders, and they were backed up by handbooks describing the underworld and its denizens, and alerting the police to the kind of tactics the latter might use to escape detection. All this burgeoning literature on deviance and deviants in nineteenth-century Germany contributed to building up a picture of criminal society as an organized underworld, with rules and customs of its own. It portrayed confidence tricksters like Franz Ernst not in individualistic terms, but as part of a much wider, highly complex social milieu of the deviant and the criminal.

The classic of this genre was the Lübeck police official Friedrich Christian Benedict Avé-Lallement's *German Villains* published in four volumes between 1858 and 1862.[27] Avé-Lallement thought that criminals in Germany were virtually a race apart, with a language of their own (to which he devoted the whole of the third and fourth volumes of his survey), a repertoire of tricks and a history going back to the decline of random violence and the emergence of states and laws in the later Middle Ages. The German national character, he argued, was fundamentally Christian, and the religious minorities of the Jews and the gypsies had played a major part in the emergence of a criminal underworld, as he thought his study of its language revealed. It was interesting that he singled out as criminal two minority groups which were still substantially disadvantaged in many parts of Germany, lacking in social acceptance and in some cases even proper civil rights, groups which within a lifetime were to form the two principal targets of the racism of Hitler's Third Reich. Yet Avé-Lallement was not an open, theoretical racist, however much he might have encouraged racist attitudes in practice: for he stigmatized gypsies and Jews because they were un-Christian, and therefore, he thought, lacking in the moral principles which made people honest. Moreover, he was clear in his own mind that these criminal elements were assisted by 'outcast Christian elements', such as skinners and knackers and the 'dishonourable trades', and the underworld was growing in size and power as more of these joined its ranks. Indeed, by the time he wrote, he considered that they probably made up a majority of the denizens of the German underworld.

This underworld, Avé-Lallement concluded (though the term 'underworld' was not used, being reserved later in the century for organized crime in the big cities: like his contemporaries, Avé-Lallement spoke of the 'villains' world', the *Gaunerwelt* or *Gaunerthum*), constituted a whole parallel society which imitated and undermined respectable society at every level from top to bottom:

> There can be no question of its being a status-group in itself, a separate sociopolitical stratum, still less a discrete group among the people. From the deposed heir to the throne with a star on his chest, from the cashiered officer, from the unfrocked clergyman, from the burnt-out citizen, down to the poorest beggar, the collectivity of villains represents the criminal proletariat of every level of society, and the princely star of the deposed prince, the honourably modest exterior of the unfrocked clergyman or the unsuccessful citizen is just as much an aspect of the villain's art as the concealed tools of the lock-picker, or the rags and outward poverty of the beggar, which rags and other signs of wretchedness simply serve as the artisanal instruments by which he gets on in his trade.[28]

Avé-Lallement considered that the police were on the whole failing in their duty to combat crime in the middle of the nineteenth century, largely because they consisted mainly of ex-soldiers who were too old to learn the art of policing and used violence instead of intelligence in their dealings with the underworld. The police, he complained, were at war with the whole country instead of just with criminals.[29]

> The history of the German police appears like a great case-history of the sicknesses of the German people, in which one can recognize how the long infirmity of its sociopolitical circumstances has been . . . as often falsely as correctly diagnosed by the examining gaze of those who have been called to cure it, namely the state police.

It was to eliminate such misdiagnoses and help the police become more professional, he claimed, that he was writing his book.

Other writers contributed similar surveys to the picture of an organized underworld in the mid-nineteenth century.[30] The police themselves circulated generalized manuscript descriptions of the underworld as well as accounts of individuals, often drawing on facts learned during the interrogation of suspects. One such description, written in Mannheim in 1856, portrayed a world of 'crooks' that formed a virtual mirror-image of respectable society:

> Most of them are depraved journeymen artisans, but they also travel as hawkers, white-collar workers, students, actors, indeed there are even really well-dressed 'society' crooks who do business as civil servants or officers and only return to their flop-houses in the evenings, to gamble, drink and whore there.

It was impossible, therefore, according to this author, to tell at first sight whether they belonged to the respectable world or not.[31] Like the 'straight' world which it aped, the world of the villain was a male-dominated world. Women appear nowhere in these lists and assessments, except as objects of the villains' lust, as prostitutes, whores and 'thieves' brides'. In conformity with the gender stereotyping of the day, they were thought of as essentially passive creatures, incapable of even active criminality.

Avé-Lallement agreed with the Mannheim document's portrait of the underworld:

> In the practice of the police and the investigating magistracy, one is completely disappointed with the results of physiognomy, and if anyone lacks experience of this, he should cast his eye over the numerous photographs which are printed in such an excellent manner in today's police information sheets, in particular the *Dresden Police Advertiser*, and compare the mostly good-natured faces there with the most sophisticated villainies for which their owners are responsible. . . . The villain is and will remain lost for the ethnographer, his appearance does not go beyond that of the ordinary man in the street, as nature has made him, even if illness, passion and sin have perhaps distorted it. Hence the audacity with which these villains appropriate to themselves all forms of sociopolitical life and attempt to move about within them; hence the difficulty of discovering the villain beneath these forms.[32]

Measured by these criteria, Franz Ernst was clearly a classic example of the 'villain' or *Gauner*.

Like Ernst, such 'villains' wormed their way into respectable society not only through disguise and deception, but also, according to the Mannheim survey of 1856, through the forgery of identity papers, or even the procurement of genuine papers 'through exploiting the authorities' credulity, if not through bribery'. Internal passports, the papers required to move from one German state or statelet to another in the years before Bismarck's creation of the German Empire in 1871, and journeyman's travel passes, the documents which certified them as members of guilds from whom they could then obtain food and shelter, were easily counterfeited, as were the official seals which validated them. In addition, 'even genuine internal passports are not difficult to obtain and offer the advantage over other papers that one does not need to have worked in order to obtain them, and that possession of them makes it easier to forge visas.' How this was done, the document went on to explain in some detail:

> You go to a police station, if possible in a small town or village, and report that your internal passport or journeyman's travel pass has been lost or stolen. In doing this, you declare that your domicile is somewhere a very long way away, if possible outside Germany altogether, in Switzerland or Denmark or Sweden. As the place where your documents were last checked, you give a similarly remote locality, on the assumption that the police either don't care, or want to avoid the expense of arresting you and the effort of writing off to a distant address, and so will issue you with an internal passport valid for a direct journey back to your home. This passport, also known as a reference, has now become a licence for further lengthy travel. Such a pass is almost without exception certain evidence for the possessor being a crook, and in very many, indeed almost the majority of cases, it has emerged that when he has been arrested and his identity checked by correspondence, he has made completely false declarations about his personal circumstances.

Similarly, print workers could easily be bribed to prepare false journeymen's passes or *Wanderbücher*, or impecunious small master craftsmen could be paid to issue certificates. Genuine papers could also be obtained by deception. The variety of methods by which this could be done was manifold:

> A very common tactic is to travel down the Rhine towards Holland on a barge. On the journey you let something drop into the water and then complain that you have lost your internal passport. On the basis of a signed statement by the captain certifying the occurrence of this incident, or even on the basis of a simple declaration that you have lost your papers, you can obtain short-term passports from the Dutch police without any difficulty. The large coat-of-arms, the extremely legalistic form and the foreign language

guarantee anyone who possesses such a document very special peace of mind when it comes to his papers being checked by civil authorities on dry land.

It was so well known, added the document, 'how extremely easy it is to obtain passes from some embassies and consulates' that no further explanation was necessary.

Two years later, Avé-Lallement thought that such deception was becoming more difficult. He admitted that 'the forgery of papers has become ever more serious and frequent in recent times', but also noted:

> The reliability of security papers has increased recently, especially as far as travel documents are concerned. Instead of the previous, sparsely printed blank forms for passports, the latest Prussian, Bavarian and Badensian versions guarantee complete security insofar as they employ an excellent security paper, the whole construction of which makes it extremely difficult, indeed virtually impossible, to copy it or use it for a forgery.[33]

Nevertheless, the 20 pages of his book devoted to detailing the techniques used to forge papers at this time suggested that falsification was still widespread, and that many of the methods described in the Mannheim document were still very much in use. Customary checks and controls on identity remained difficult to enforce, as the case of Franz Ernst showed only too clearly; Ernst, indeed, had managed to get as far as Bremen seemingly without any identity papers at all. Towards the end of the 1860s, one commentator, the prison director Hermann von Valentini, complained in alarming terms that the number of forgers of documents had increased sharply since the 1848 Revolution. Ascribing this trend to the growth of materialism as Germany became more industrialized, Valentini polemicized in unmeasured terms against this 'idol of our times':

> The more this new era directs its aggression against everything for which the common people has preserved some reverence up to now, against moral and religious life, against throne and altar, and the more the filthiest self-interest is elevated into the only ideal of life, the more such an atmosphere in sociopolitical life turns out to be the actual breath of life of the grand order of the knights of industry, and the true, full-blooded matadors of this order are those who finally fall prey to the penitentiaries as forgers of documents.

Such men, Valentini assured his readers from his experience of running a prison in East Prussia, were characterized by work-shyness, lust for pleasure, vanity and lack of character rather than by any deeper or more violent moral defects. They were in some sense, he seemed to think, all too typical of the average inhabitant of the industrializing Germany of his day.[34]

It was small wonder, therefore, that the denizens of the underworld could pass virtually unnoticed through respectable society. Yet despite its invisibility in everyday life, the underworld had a detectable structure and organization, at least in the imagination of those who wrote about it. The Mannheim document continued:

> These crooks constitute a curious state within a state, without however forming a real band as such, without building a structured organization and without indeed any kind of common links except that of being engaged in crimes against property. The struggle they are waging against human institutions has a special attraction for them.

They had a special 'status consciousness', and indeed the whole idea of a German underworld belonged to the 'society of orders' or *Ständegesellschaft*. In an age when most Germans still thought of society as divided into groups whose identity and nature were fixed by heredity and status, it was only natural for them to consider criminals to be, by and large, not individuals who had gone astray, but members of an underworld, with its own rules, customs and hierarchies, which formed a mirror-image of society as a whole and was devoted to subverting and undermining it. Like the 'dishonourable people' who supplied so many of its members, the underworld consisted of large and ramified clans who passed down their knowledge from one generation to the next. Respectability of the sort affected by a Franz Ernst was a mask of deception, which it was the police's job to tear away to reveal the criminal physiognomy beneath. Like the members of the guilds or the secret societies, it was widely believed, the members of the underworld had their own secret ways of recognizing one another, winking with the left eye while glancing to the left, for example, or closing their fists in a particular way. They agreed among themselves to alter the language of the underworld – *Gaunersprache* or *Rotwelsch* – as its expressions became known in respectable society. 'There are numberless "dives", i.e. brigands' inns, thieves' dens, in which the landlord is always "crooked", i.e. belongs to the underworld.' Here indeed the denizens of the underworld were said to stay during their travels, spend their ill-gotten gains on drinking and gambling, make new acquaintances and lay fresh plans for further crimes in the future.

Such places were the centres from which innovations in the language and techniques of the underworld spread:

> Like an army, crooks seek out those localities which offer them the easiest means of making a living and the easiest opportunity of outwitting their enemy, the police, or escaping from a superior enemy force. They look for large, wealthy and remote farms and landed estates, highways lacking in vigilant police posts and the like. They avoid the stretches where it is 'hot', that is, where the gendarmerie is numerous and energetic and where the police

authorities are circumspect. Now and then, individual crooks spy out the lie of the land. If anything strikes them, if they discover any obstacles, they spread the word on their return, and make the area out to be ten times hotter than it really is. If a crook is ever arrested ('buried alive') in any area, no others will go there for a long time afterwards.

Their activities ranged from simple begging, often on the basis of imaginary hard-luck stories, to theft from houses whose inhabitants were foolish enough to invite them in, to pilfering and picking pockets at markets and cheating the peasants at cards when they came to town to sell their wares. There were perhaps 150 such professional thieves at large in north-west Germany, claimed the document, and probably even more in the south and east.[35]

Even the introduction of photography from the 1840s onwards was, as Avé-Lallement pointed out, of little use, given the limited extent to which a person's face betrayed the villainous character beneath. Yet in drawing up elaborate handbooks and dictionaries of means by which the professional criminals could be recognized, the police in the nineteenth century, as the historian Peter Becker has noted, constructed a 'semiotics of villainy' which largely confined itself to the outward signs of an idle and immoral way of life. Criminals were no longer branded in the face as they had been in the early modern period, but physical appearance was still what counted. The authorities were dependent on identity papers which could be forged and confessions which could be lies. One could tell a 'villain' by the language he used, the gestures he employed or the inns he frequented. The biography of a criminal, his background, status and moral career, were thought to hold the key to his true identity, which is why police circulars spent so much time on printing life-histories. But biographies, like identity papers, could be forged, and in an era before the introduction of fingerprinting – a development of the 1880s – and anthropometry, the ingenuity of the 'villain' placed many obstacles in the way of effective detection.[36] As the writer of one police handbook was forced to confess in 1862: 'The enquiries made every day to the Berlin police about the identities of apprehended criminals, and the frequent discovery that they have actually been using aliases, shows how many are sailing under false colours.'[37]

The nature of the underworld had indeed changed since the days of the great robber bands which terrorized western and central Germany in the Napoleonic era and even, as we have seen, found their counterparts in the 'vagabonds' of West Prussia at the same time. Even then, experts had described villains as 'a wandering people, without fixed abode, which is at home everywhere and nowhere' – a description which fitted someone like Franz Ernst almost exactly.[38] But with the restoration of civil order at the end of the Napoleonic Wars, and the creation at about the same time of effective rural policing in the form of the gendarmerie, the age of banditry had come to an end. The underworld had gone underground. Rather than staging robberies on the open highway, hold-ups of stagecoaches or mass assaults on remote farmhouses and mills, criminals had now become more individualistic, more deceitful and therefore, in the eyes of those who sought to apprehend them, more dangerous. The age of the urban-industrial criminal gang still lay in the future. The mid-century villain tended to work on his own, to slip unnoticed into bourgeois society rather than live in an easily identifiable 'criminal quarter' such as grew up in the big cities towards the end of the century. The respectable mid-century obsession with the invisible 'villain' paralleled the contemporary conservative paranoia about the machinations of secret societies, revolutionary plots and democratic conspiracies.

The new image of the underworld expressed the insecurity of the law enforcement authorities at a time when the fragility of the social order, revealed dramatically in the Revolution of 1848, was very much in the forefront of their minds. Politically, too, the Prussian state was on the defensive, with the Liberals refusing to pass the budget since 1862 unless they were given effective control over the Prussian army, and Bismarck, called to office to deal with the situation, pursuing the precarious and illegal course of collecting taxes without parliamentary authorization. The political threat of democracy and revolution was paralleled in the mind of the authorities with the social danger from the organized underworld, a view which Marx and Engels tried to counter with their ascription of the 'dangerous classes' to a *Lumpenproletariat*, the political role of whose members, they thought, mainly exhausted itself in providing a tool for the machinations of reactionaries. Marx and Engels also believed that this class recruited itself from every social group; it was not a social residuum, at the bottom of the class system, but a parallel social world, to which a disaffected journalist and politician like Louis Napoleon Bonaparte, in the years before he became emperor of the French as Napoleon III, belonged just as much as did the vagrant, the drunk, the criminal or the down-and-out. What the two socialist theorists were in effect doing with the concept of the *Lumpenproletariat*, therefore, was to take the contemporary concept of the criminal underworld and give it a political twist, without actually altering it very much in the process. The days when anarchists like Bakunin and police authorities alike would view criminality as directly linked and allied to revolution came later, above all after the Paris Commune of 1871.[39]

The case of Franz Ernst neatly brought together in a single person the various social and political fears of respectable commentators. Here was a member of the underworld acting, as Marx and Engels predicted, as a tool of reaction, bent on infiltrating the revolutionary movement in order to betray it to the authorities; yet the whole manoeuvre was a gigantic deception, preying on the fears of the establishment for pecuniary gain. In the three-cornered relationship between the revolutionaries, the reactionaries and the criminal underworld, only the last-named of the three was meant by Ernst to come out as a winner. There was a pleasing irony in the fact that the Berlin political police, those past-masters of deception, had themselves become the knowing victims of a deception played upon them by a bold and unscrupulous confidence trickster. In the end, after all, Ernst had persuaded Police Chief von Bernuth in Berlin to part with 113 Marks in order to get him to stop pestering his office. The secretive atmosphere in which the democrats operated had similarly been neatly turned from a protective device into a point of political vulnerability by allowing a member of the underworld to invent imaginary plots with which to frighten, or impress, the authorities. The hostility shown to Ernst by the German exiles in Geneva had been evidence enough of the democrats' concern; his arrest on the prompting of the Bavarian ambassador in Bern, however, suggested that someone at least in Switzerland knew the true nature of his game.

'Nothing but a Racket'

Whether or not Ernst had always supported himself by fraud is unclear, though the police record suggests he had begun to do so as early as the 1840s, almost as soon as he had reached adulthood. But the boundaries of the underworld were always more fluid than commentators maintained. Like many of its members, Ernst also engaged in legitimate activities of one kind or another; the life-history he constructed for himself placed him in the world of the private scholar and intellectual to which people like Marx and Engels and some of their associates belonged. At one time, Ernst did indeed seek to support himself not only by political fraud but also by writing. He even planned to publish a magazine called *The Spirit of the Age* (*Die Zeitgeist*), though it never actually seems to have appeared. And unlike many of the details contained in the original narrative he gave to the Bremen police, the claim that he had spent the second half of 1862 in Britain was true. In the British Library in London, indeed, there can be found a copy of a short pamphlet which he wrote about the trip. The 20-page account, published in Mannheim in 1863, carries the somewhat unwieldy title *The German Men of Learning, Merchants, Artisans and Labourers in England, Scotland and Ireland, with their Institutions, in their Life and Activities*. Rather than the social investigation promised in the title, however, it was mainly an attempt to show that Britain was a good place for Germans to find work. They were popular with British employers, wrote 'Dr von Hoff', because they were physically stronger than their British counterparts, worked harder and drank less. However, von Hoff was not impressed with conditions of life in the poor London district of Whitechapel, which he compared unfavourably with those under which the slaves lived in the southern states of the USA (a region of which, he remarked, he had had first-hand experience). It is likely that the pamphlet was used by Ernst as the basis for the lectures about Britain which he gave in various German towns in the course of 1863 under the guise of a scholar specializing in 'the study of foreign lands and peoples'.

All this, however, served another, more important purpose for Franz Ernst, mainly by providing him with the identity of a solid member of the German educated middle class. A curious passage in his pamphlet on the Germans in Britain however, gave the game away. During his stay in London, he reported, he had visited the 'Marriage Bureau' of Herr and Frau Schwarz, a German couple living in a country cottage in Dalston, now a district in north-east London, then a rural area sliding gently into suburbanity. Although the pair had been recommended by a German-language newspaper, said Ernst, he felt it necessary to warn his readers, and any prospective clients of the agency, that it was 'nothing but a racket':

> After I had put my request to [Herr Schwarz], he placed a book before me, in which a number of ladies were listed with first and last names, with the size of their fortune, their own size, the colour of their hair and eyes, and their age (whether or not this last was true) . . . He proved ready to arrange a *rendez-vous* with a lady immediately.

The brazenness of Ernst's complaint about the possibly misleading information concerning the ladies' ages was stunning, given his habit of reducing his own. Had he ever managed to meet one, a delightful comedy of mutual deception might have been in store. But he did not. Charging the very exorbitant fee of £4 per consultation plus 5 per cent of the dowry in the event of marriage, Schwarz promised to arrange a meeting with the lady of his client's choice within three months. 'He claimed already to have obtained wives for princes, counts and barons, etc., in this way.' But the whole business seemed bogus to Ernst. He neither paid the fee nor signed the register.[40]

It seems, indeed, that in the Schwarzes Franz Ernst had at last met his match. For his main business in life, apart from the relatively new line of political deception, was in fact marital fraud. Posing as a well-off, educated, respectable doctor or academic, he would seek out wealthy, single women of almost any age, and persuade them to part with money and property in return for a spurious promise of marriage. 'When he left Frankfurt in Dec[em]b[e]r 1863,' alleged the wanted notice issued for him by the police in July 1864, 'he took Theresia Kammermeyer, to whom he had made a promise of marriage, with him to Geneva; and she was barely able to rescue her possessions, which he tried to sell off.' Among the effects found in the Hôtel du Nord were indeed letters from a Dr Fresenius in Frankfurt and from Theresia Kammermeyer herself, both of whom he had evidently swindled, according to the police, 'the one of his property and confidence, the other of her honour'. The Frankfurt police confirmed these stories on 6 July. The '12 questions' sent to him with hostile intent by the radical German exiles in Geneva also alleged that he had deceived Theresia Kammermeyer out of a considerable amount of money and actually sold her possessions in Geneva without telling her; evidently the questions had been written before she got them back. They added that Ernst had also seduced one girl in Lausanne and another in Mannheim and cheated the landlord of The Black Lion out of 300 Gulden. Was he, they asked rhetorically in their usual relentless way, the same Ernst (or von Hoff) 'who had intended to pay back his deceived fiancée with the ill-gotten gains of espionage . . .'?

Theresia Kammermeyer may have recovered her money, but she had lost her honour, as the police, and no doubt much of respectable society too, saw the matter. The police did their best to be discreet. 'Much of what . . . is already known about him', they noted, 'is not suitable for the public ear.' The effects found in the Hôtel du Nord also included a number of manuscripts and drafts, some relating to 'a fraud which was planned and in part carried out against a family in this town, aimed at enticing the daughter into an engagement'. Among them were letters and certificates forged by Ernst 'with great skill', including his appointment to a professorship at Freiburg University, to impress the family, and of course the documents he needed to get married. The birth certificate he had obtained gives his mother's name as von Pochham, not von Puttkamer; perhaps he preferred to portray himself as related to a relatively obscure noble family which it would not be easy to check up on; whatever the case, it was the noble prefix 'von' that counted. Clearly, he was a man who took a great deal of trouble over the business of marriage and seduction. Yet he was physically unprepossessing, at least to a modern eye. Middle-aged and described by the police as 'corpulent', an impression confirmed by his photograph in the police file, Franz Ernst seemed an unlikely lover. How then did he meet with such success?

Part of the explanation, paradoxically, did indeed lie in his appearance: solid, weighty, the very image of respectability. It went well with his pretended aristocratic background, his medical and scholarly credentials, and his cosmopolitan and adventurous, yet noble and altruistic, personal history – for it is reasonable to assume that the elaborate – and, of course, almost entirely fictitious – narrative which he first told to the Bremen police in 1864 was the one he customarily used for the purposes of wooing the well-off single women who were his prey. Just as he took advantage of the weaknesses of the contemporary Prussian police – above all, its paranoia about revolutionaries – so too he took advantage of the weaknesses of the contemporary German woman. For this was a society in which, for the middle class and the propertied, marriage was all-important. In the burgeoning industrial economy of mid-nineteenth-century Germany, marriage and the family played a vital role in the transmission of fixed and movable capital. No wonder that Herr Schwarz in Dalston put the size, real or imaginary, of his female clients' dowry before their age or appearance in his directory of nubile ladies. Well-off families were always anxious to make a 'good match' for their daughters, and for many a paterfamilias, someone like the well-travelled and well-educated 'Dr von Hoff' must have seemed acceptable enough. Age differences were of little account here; marriages in the German middle class between men in their forties and women 15 or 20 years their junior were far from uncommon.[41]

Unmarried women themselves were as anxious to make a good match as their parents were for them, if not more so. This was a society in which there were virtually no opportunities for middle-class women to support themselves by gainful employment outside the home. Even schoolteaching, virtually the only profession open to them, was at a low and poorly paid level, owing to the absence of any kind of academic schooling for girls and the banning of women from study at Germany's universities. Fear of social ridicule as an 'old maid' vied with fear of destitution, or at the very least forced employment as a governess or companion of more or less menial status, in the minds of women attaining an age where most of their peers had long since walked to the altar. Moreover, romantic literature, the staple reading diet of young educated women, made them particularly susceptible to the kind of appeal which Ernst made it his business to exercise. Here, after all, was a man who claimed to have fought slavers off the West African coast, to have taken part in the Californian gold rush of '49, to have withstood the siege of New Orleans during the American Civil War, to have sailed the Spanish Main off Cuba and to have travelled through exotic parts of the Near East, including (for the pious) a visit to the Holy Land on the way, making sure to call there at Easter and Whitsun, when his religious purpose would be clear to all. Many women must have found such a life-history irresistible. And Ernst knew how to combine it with a plausible epistolary manner which maintained the decorum his contemporaries – and addressees – found so important in relations between the sexes, with tantalizing hints at powerful amatory emotions waiting to erupt from beneath the solid and respectable surface of strictly honourable intentions and the highest degree of social propriety which he presented in his formal dealings with them.

His technique was perfectly represented by a draft letter, dated 18 June 1864, to 'Johanne', his intended victim in Bremen, which the police found among his papers in the Hôtel du Nord. Ernst had surely had a lot of practice by this time, yet the draft is one of several, showing the lengths to which he would go to get the tone and content right. Emphasizing his seriousness – a key nineteenth-century value which he did well to stress – Ernst confessed to Johanne that 'the moment in which I am writing down these words' was 'too earnest' for him 'to lend' his words 'any element of rapture'. For those who knew his real history and intentions, of course, the purpose of his letter was glaringly obvious. Yet to the innocent recipient, it might have seemed genuine enough. He wrote:

My Fräulein, who has become dear to me (*Mein mir lieb gewordenes Fräulein*)! Would you, my dear Fräulein, grant an interview to a man in whom you have awakened slumbering feelings, permit it in such a manner that he may speak openly before and to you? My attentiveness will already have given you proof of what I want to say with the words 'slumbering feelings'. It is unworthy of a man, in my view, to carry with him hopes which are not to be expressed in words of explanation, sincere explanation.

Nor do I count among those who allow feelings to take root when they are not reciprocated, or cannot be reciprocated, and then undergo the certain torments of hell in suppressing them.

If, my Fräulein who has become dear to me, I append the humble request that you will be gracious enough to grant me the interview alone, without the presence of witnesses, please do not see therein anything which violates propriety. Should you nonetheless wish to regard propriety as capable of being violated in this manner, let my holy promises be the guarantee therefore, that every lady will always occupy a position in relation to every man, as to me, which demands humble attention, and especially you, whom I now respect with all my heart . . .

It must have been in similar language that he had wooed Theresia Kammermeyer in Frankfurt, too. Its stress on propriety was an ironic mirror-image of the intentions that lay behind it. Whether he employed such language in other, similar attempts in other places after he left Bremen will probably never be known.

In their final report, on 10 August 1864, the Bremen police summed up what was known of their charge. He had previous sentences in Berlin in 1849, 1853 and so on for using a false name and for fraud, and in 1854 for repeatedly 'insulting public officials in connection with their office' (eight months). It was after that that he had left the country, first for Australia, then for America, which he visited three times. The story of bankruptcy, the police noted, presumably after checks on records of bankruptcies in Berlin had revealed nothing, was probably untrue. He was, they said, a man 'of many-sided but only superficial education, with an enviable memory and quick powers of comprehension', but he was also 'arrogant' and 'stubborn'. Apart from his political activities, he also claimed to be a freemason and used this to get support from masons. The police concluded that he was 'an outragous con-man'. After further correspondence with the Berlin police, the Bremen authorities told him on 8 August 1864 that in view of the weeks he had already sat in gaol, he would not be prosecuted or sentenced, but would be expelled and sent on to Prussia and forbidden to return to Bremen. Arrangements were made for the debts he still owed in Bremen to be paid. Ernst assured the Bremen police that he was going back to the USA. Totally sceptical by this stage about everything he said, the police recorded their view that this was unlikely, since he evidently lacked the money for the trip. They warned their colleagues everywhere to be on the lookout for him. After this, however, he disappeared from the record, and it is at least possible that he did indeed go back to America, to what fate, however, no one will ever know.

The story of Franz Ernst demonstrates the variety of narrative techniques used by a professional confidence trickster to create a fictitious life-history or histories for himself. A man like Ernst most probably had little difficulty in fabricating identity papers, indeed identities, for himself, despite all the progress which the state had made in creating a network of checks and controls over the ordinary citizen in the first half and middle decades of the nineteenth century. Yet sooner or later such men fell into the hands of the police, and their imaginary life-histories did not stand up to the close scrutiny to which they were subjected. Faced with the evidence gathered in Bremen from the records of a number of police forces, Ernst's narrative, with its basis in popular literature and its appeal to the romantically inclined, collapsed, to be replaced with something much more ordinary and prosaic. It was not the first time that this had happened. Ernst had a record of arrest and conviction and was well known to a number of police forces, who were already circulating his description among themselves. However much he renegotiated and reinvented his own identity, they seemed to catch up with him. None-theless, Ernst always seemed to slip out of their grasp and go on to fresh adventures despite everything they knew about him and all the efforts they made to keep him under control. The half-amused, half-despairing resigna-tion with which the Bremen police recorded his departure, ostensibly for America, but probably for somewhere else in Germany, reflected their aware-ness that a network of surveillance created on the basis of the documentary proof of identity was never likely to function perfectly.

Ernst was indeed a member of a stigmatized underclass, from which it was difficult for him to escape entirely; but at various times he was also able to assume the guise of a perfectly respectable citizen. Such people's ability to shape their own lives could often be considerable. As fast as the police tracked down one identity and advertised it in their circulars, Ernst seemed able to manufacture another. In every case, these identities were characteristically bourgeois, whatever their purported political orientation: bourgeois intellec-tual, bourgeois professional, bourgeois philanthropist, bourgeois revolu-tionary. There was just the hint of aristocratic connections in his use of the prefix 'von', rendering him unimpeachably respectable by implication. Only by reinventing himself as a bourgeois could Ernst hope to generate the income to maintain himself – of course, in a lifestyle that was itself similar to that of the many bourgeois who fell on hard times in this uncertain era of emerging capitalism in Germany. His career of impudence and deception showed how easy it could be for an ingenious man to run rings round the police and evade, or even exploit, those checks and controls on social and political deviants which some historians have argued were so effective in nineteenth-century Germany. It also exposed the fragilities of bourgeois identity and the insecurities which could lie beneath the appearance of solidity and respectability which the bourgeoisie so assiduously cultivated. No wonder the authorities found such 'crooks' so dangerous.

Ernst may in the end have escaped the clutches of the police; we do not know. There were many others, however, who were subjected to a network of checks and controls that was even more tight-meshed than that which closed round Ernst in Bremen in the summer of 1864. Perhaps the most stigmatized of all these groups was that of publicly registered prostitutes: and it is to their position in the structures of authority and obedience that framed the everyday lives of the deviant in nineteenth- and early-twentieth-century Germany that we now turn.

4

The Life and Death of a Lost Woman

Journey to the Sexual Underworld

In June 1905 Wilhelmine Germany was shaken by a sensational publication which threatened to lift the lid off the underworld of prostitution and sexual exploitation normally concealed beneath the surface of everyday life. In the *Diary of a Lost Woman (Tagebuch einer Verlorenen)*, the writer Margarete Böhme presented to a shocked public the journal of a professional prostitute in all its raw immediacy, with – as she said in the preface – only the names altered and some 'deletions of passages which were absolutely unsuited for publication'. Böhme said she had found the document among the woman's possessions after her death. 'Nothing is further from my purpose than to add another book to the literature of titillation,' she continued:

> These simple notes do not lay any claim to artistic or literary value; they are, and seek to be, nothing other than an authentic contribution to the debate on a burning social question of our time. More eloquent and more convincing than the most brilliant depictions from the pen of a professional writer, they speak directly to us and cast their lurid light on the world of those who are dead to civil society, the outcasts and pariahs of society.[1]

With this warning, Böhme then presented her acquaintance's account of her descent into the underworld of vice and degradation which lay behind the respectable façade of Wilhelmine society.

The story the diary had to tell was a grim one. The daughter of a respectable apothecary, 'Thymian Gotteball' begins her diary as an innocent adolescent and ends it as a world-weary courtesan, dying of tuberculosis. Her downward descent starts with the death of her beloved mother, after which her father has a string of mistresses whose presence gradually introduces moral corruption into the household. 'It's simply so,' her father's assistant tells her, 'a healthy man in his prime has need of women.' After one of the mistresses, the beautiful Elisabeth, with whom Thymian has become friendly, commits suicide on being told by the apothecary that he will never marry her, Thymian collapses and is raped by the assistant. Far from this leading to the man's arrest, or even sacking from her father's business, however, it is Thymian who gets the blame. Pregnant, she is sent to a private establishment for unmarried mothers. Here she loses her innocence in the company of women more knowing and more experienced than herself. They become her friends. After her baby is born and given away for adoption, Thymian is effectively rejected by her father, who remarries and wants nothing more to do with her. Sent to be 'reformed' by a brutal pastor and his unpleasant wife, she refuses to let her spirit be broken and escapes to rejoin her easy-going friends from the maternity home. They try to persuade her that a woman in her situation has no chance of a respectable life, but must seek her fortune in the company of rich men. When she voices her moral qualms at this doctrine, they tell her that she may be a cut above the average,

> 'but that won't do you any good any more, dearie! You've got a child, and respectable society won't have any more to do with you. You're lost to them, you can do what you want, you'll never be taken again as a proper person, and if you really do succeed in getting back once more, you'll always live in fear of something coming out about your past.'

Struggling with her own conscience, Thymian debates the matter in her diary in pages which, the editor notes, are later taken out and destroyed because they form a painful reminder of a 'time when, with hesitant steps, she crossed the last bridge swaying between two worlds'. The struggle ends with Thymian deciding that she wants the good life offered by the underworld and refusing to pay any more for a sin that is not hers.

Breaking with her family, she moves with her friends to a 'salon' in Hamburg, where she educates herself in the social graces and becomes a high-class courtesan. When the salon degenerates into a brothel, it is raided by the police. The madam, Thymian's friend and employer, is arrested and imprisoned. Forewarned, Thymian flees to Berlin, where she is soon visiting the grand cafés on her own and attracting wealthy men to her room. She gets to know the underworld of prostitution in the capital city and learns how to avoid the attentions of the vice squad. Enrolment on the police list of 'public girls', which she manages to evade, is no great disaster in itself, she says, nor are the regular and compulsory medical examinations for venereal disease which this involves particularly objectionable. However, the landlords of inscribed prostitutes demand exorbitant rents as insurance against the charge of procuring to which their tenants' trade exposes them, given the fact that the women are inevitably known to the police. This is the main reason why Thymian avoids registration. Living on her own, on the other hand, she is exposed to the danger of intimidation by pimps, men who are 'down-and-outs . . . from every class of society', too lazy or too drunk to make an honest living for themselves. So she arranges for a childhood friend, the degenerate aristocrat Count Osdorff, to live with her. They get married, but Osdorff is constantly drunk, sleeps with other women, spends her money, gets himself arrested and finally falls ill and dies. Thymian is thrown back on her own resources once more. Her aim is to climb within the world of prostitution until she becomes the kept woman of a wealthy man. A prosperous doctor with whom she falls in love helps her, but he is married and lacks the necessary wealth. She finally finds the man she wants in Osdorff's former guardian, an elderly widowed count. Giving up her love of the doctor for the prospect of money, she becomes the old man's companion. A period of travel (to Nice and Monte Carlo) follows, but she gets bored and longs for the doctor's company. She resumes her relationship with him and also goes out with other men for money. Even this fails to relieve her sense of futility and *ennui*, so she engages in charitable work, until the association to which she belongs discovers her past and ostracizes her. Plagued by feelings of guilt, depression and worthlessness, and full of regret at not having been able to lead a normal life with a husband and family, Thymian falls ill with tuberculosis and dies.

After the publication of the book, the *Diary*'s editor, Margarete Böhme, reported that she had received 'a never-ending flood of letters from all four corners of the world'; 'and I have almost lost count', she added, 'of those asking for an explanation of or information about this or that matter in the *Diary* . . . The *Diary*'s success has called forth a mass of *Confessions, Professions, Memoirs, Other Diaries*, whose tendency is only too obvious.'[2] The reasons for the book's appeal are not hard to imagine. For the first time in Germany, the problem of prostitution had been discussed from the point of view of the prostitute, who appeared not as a wicked or evil seductress, but as a victim of social hypocrisy and discrimination. 'To be sure,' wrote the *Diary*'s author of her fellow-prostitutes in Berlin, 'there are indeed girls among them who really have come to their present state *only* through their own frivolity, their own fault, but I maintain that none of them has landed in it in full knowledge and consciousness of what she was doing.' All of them, she said, would wish to find their way back to 'orderly circumstances' if the possibility presented itself. The descent into this 'half-world' could be the product of no more than chance. But in the context of social mores as rigid as those of Wilhelmine Germany, once a woman embarked on this path, there was no turning back. The *Diary*'s narrative portrays a downward path from which every attempt to escape – for example, through engaging in charitable work – is blocked by the narrator's previous loss of 'reputation'. The changing language of the entries skilfully mirrors the changing moral constitution of the writer – from innocent adolescent to grasping courtesan to world-weary 'companion' – and allows the reader to follow from outside the inner journey of a lost soul to perdition. At the same time, nobody is left in any doubt as to who is to blame: it is society that is responsible for Thymian's fate, not Thymian herself.

On the face of it, there was no particular reason why 'Thymian Gotteball', by this point in her short life comfortably off and well cared-for, should have contracted tuberculosis and died so rapidly from its effects. But consumption was also a metaphor. It was frequently used in literary representations of prostitution – classically in the *Lady of the Camellias* and *La Bohème*, which belonged among the nineteenth century's most popular texts – to denote, not so much the ravages of other diseases which would be impolitic to mention in a work destined to be read by the respectable classes, as the inevitability of mental and moral decline. Thought to be an aphrodisiac and to give the sufferer considerable powers of seduction, tuberculosis also indicated spiritual poverty and weariness with life beneath the surface appearance of affluence and happiness. The passion with which the tubercular patient burned, in works such as Thomas Mann's *The Magic Mountain*, served to refine and ennoble; the body wasted away, exposing the purity of the soul within. A death from tuberculosis, as in the case of the prostitute Fantine in Victor Hugo's *Les Misérables*, could be the means of redemption from a life of sin. The *Diary of a Lost Woman* is no great work of literature, and the theme of tuberculosis appears only towards the end, almost as an afterthought, rather than playing a role in the plot as such; but the book's audience would have read enough such works in which tuberculosis played a role to have understood its multiple metaphorical resonances all the same. Whether or not tuberculosis was the real cause of Thymian's death was another matter.[3]

Besides centring on the familiar figure of the tubercular courtesan, the *Diary*'s action takes place within a social world that would have been more or less well known to most of its readers. The characters are taken from a limited social range, ascending from the professional middle class of the doctor and the apothecary to the status-bound world of the aristocrat, and the action is set in equally familiar milieus, in hotels, cafés, casinos, opera-houses, comfortable furnished rooms and the solid houses of the bourgeoisie. The working class is nowhere to be seen. The underworld in which Thymian moves is not the world of an underclass, of poverty and deprivation, but a parallel world, cut off from respectable society by an invisible curtain while shadowing it at every level. It is not poverty that is responsible for driving women such as Thymian into prostitution, the book suggests, but the rigidity of social convention, often enforced in public by men who spend their time undermining it in private. The story of a poor working woman led to sell her body to make ends meet would have had far less impact on the book-buying public of the day than a direct attack launched in this way on the hypocrisy and double standards of respectable society. Of course, the uneducated were unlikely to write diaries. More importantly, however, the poor had little respectability to lose in the first place. The downward moral path from innocence to prostitution could only be presented from the metaphorical starting-point of a relatively high social standing. All this raises the question of how representative the experiences of 'Thymian Gotteball' really were, and beyond this, of why it was that this book, rather than others written on the same subject, was the one to arouse public debate in the mid-1900s. For while sexuality and its regulation were topics seldom discussed in the polite society of Wilhelmine Germany, they were not exactly ignored by it either; and a mass of evidence exists, compiled by social investigators, government agencies, police and commentators of various kinds, which inevitably puts the story told by the *Diary* into a rather different light, as we shall now see.

Demand and Supply

In portraying the demand for prostitution as a bourgeois and upper-class demand, the *Diary of a Lost Woman* was echoed by a good many contemporary writers and subsequent historians. It has been commonplace to ascribe the existence of prostitution in nineteenth- and early twentieth-century Germany largely to the psychosexual dynamics of the bourgeois family. This is a view that goes back ultimately to the Social Democrats, indeed to Marx and Engels's *Communist Manifesto* itself, which saw prostitution as the most unspeakable aspect of the exploitation of the proletariat by the bourgeoisie. August Bebel devoted a whole chapter of his widely read book *Woman and Socialism* to demonstrating that prostitution was a specific form of social exploitation, and that it was increasing as exploitation in general increased. The demand came from the bourgeoisie; the supply from the proletariat.[4] Here, therefore, the experience of someone like 'Thymian Gotteball', who grew up in a comfortably off middle-class milieu, already seems extremely unusual. Prostitutes were widely thought of as above all working class. The Social Democratic writer Heinrich Lux even claimed in 1892 that 'almost every self-supporting female labourer who lacks family connections is constantly in danger of being forced to earn the largest part of her living from prostitution at times, either permanently or temporarily, when trade is bad.' Indeed, he went on, it was 'a fact that prostitution is generally regarded as extra income on top of wages, that numerous employers already reckon this "secondary income" in their calculation of wages.'[5] More recently, some historians have gone beyond this to suggest that the demand for the services of prostitutes came almost exclusively from bourgeois men because bourgeois women were expected to be sexually pure before marriage and sexually passive or frigid within it, and often were.[6] The feminist historian Regina Schulte has commented:

> Prostitution hardly played any part in satisfying the sexual needs of the working-class male, because a completely different kind of sexual behaviour and therefore a different kind of sexual morality had developed among the working class than among the bourgeoisie.[7]

Yet this is really far too simple a view, deriving from a Marxist tendency to reduce everything to an epiphenomenon of the class struggle and from the German Social Democrats' desire to portray the main body of their supporters, the men of the industrial working class, as moral, upright, law-abiding and responsible, fit to take power when the revolution came. Alain Corbin's classic study of prostitution in France has revealed a far more complex and differentiated picture, and has pointed to the substantial demand for prostitutes from young working men living on their own in the rapidly expanding cities of the industrial era, from soldiers and sailors, and from married working men with wives worn out by illness or childbearing, or with wives who refused to have sex for fear of conception (*coitus interruptus* being the normal, and highly unreliable, means of contraception in the working class right up to the First World War and beyond).[8] The 'free love' which Regina Schulte maintains was common in the working class was mainly a characteristic of adolescence and early adulthood; informal polygamy was largely confined to areas where shift-work predominated, such as the mining districts of the Ruhr, and where there was a drastic shortage of women, and has in any case been wildly exaggerated by historians.[9] There was in reality just as much sexual poverty among workers as there was among middle-class men, even if it did have very different origins.

Contemporaries in Wilhelmine Germany who knew the prostitution scene at first hand told a very different story from that presented by the Marxists. One such was the writer Hans Ostwald, who published extensively on the subject between the turn of the century and the First World War. Ostwald's intention was to map out the underworld and its institutions in Berlin, to chart the social geography of crime and deviance in all their manifold varieties.[10] His journalism pandered to the voyeuristic anxieties of the bourgeoisie in purveying a kind of pornography of deviance, in which he supplied his readers with detailed descriptions of the houses, streets and quarters they were seldom likely to enter themselves. It also seems to have been very accurate. Almost every volume he published emphasized the importance of the underworld and the institutions, from doss houses to low bars and dives (*Kaschemmen*), that were its haunts. A good number of them stressed the role of prostitution in keeping the underworld together. As one of Ostwald's collaborators, Magnus Hirschfeld, wrote in his volume on male prostitution and homosexual underworlds in Berlin: 'Prostitution and criminality go hand in hand; thefts and break-ins, blackmail and extortion, violent acts of every kind' were all part of the homosexual milieu.[11]

Ostwald and the other contributors to his *Documents of the Big City* were no bourgeois social investigators; all of them had close connections with the worlds they described. Magnus Hirschfeld, for example, was himself homosexual, a pioneer researcher into homosexuality and champion of gay rights and gay identity, who was only too well aware of the risks that men ran when they availed themselves of the services of rent-boys at a time when sexual acts between males were punishable by imprisonment according to Paragraph 175 of the Criminal Code. Hans Ostwald too had experienced low-life in Berlin and elsewhere at first hand. Born in 1873 and a goldsmith by trade, his life as a journeyman had degenerated imperceptibly into that of an unemployed and homeless vagabond. By the early 1900s, he was beginning to make a living by writing about his experiences, encouraged by the writer Felix Holländer, whom he had met by chance in the late 1890s.[12] The *Documents of the Big City* series, which Ostwald launched in 1905, was his most ambitious project, with a planned 50 volumes; after that, Ostwald's amazing productivity slowed down, though he continued to publish occasional works of popular cultural history during the 1920s, and until he died in 1940 devoted himself to the posthumous editing of the work of the popular cartoonist of Berlin life, Heinrich Zille.[13]

Ostwald's portrayal of prostitution in Berlin, planned for publication in no fewer than 20 volumes, of which, however, only half a dozen seem to have appeared, was detailed and specific, and revealed to his readers a world with many social gradations, echoing the observation of 'Thymian Gotteball' in the *Diary of a Lost Woman*: 'In the half-world', confided Thymian to her diary, 'there are just as many layers or circles as in the whole one.' At the top of the social scale, Ostwald noted, were 'the well-known courtesans of Berlin – the flower-girls of the smart restaurants, the singers and dancers of many a theatre.'[14] This was the world to which 'Thymian Gotteball' belonged. These women, who also frequented the broad boulevard of Unter den Linden late at night – a fact not mentioned in the *Diary* – were described by Ostwald as rich, and he did not even dare to hazard a guess at their earnings, which he clearly thought were considerable. Here, prostitution shaded off into concubinage and the phenomenon of the 'kept woman' familiar from novels such as Heinrich Mann's *Man of Straw*, whose anti-hero, the odious Diedrich Hessling, maintains a young girl in an apartment paid for by himself until it becomes inconvenient to continue doing so. Next in social standing were those women who served male clients from the solid, monied or educated bourgeoisie, gentlemen often visiting Berlin on business. Such women gathered after 10 pm in and around another central area where there were many hotels, coffee-houses and places of entertainment. They traditionally wore a hat and shawl, or in the early 1900s 'a raincoat of the type so familiar nowadays', as Ostwald commented, and whistled melodies of obscene songs as men passed by. A prostitute of this class in the latter part of the nineteenth century commonly carried a key in her hand to show she had her own room; but in deference to bourgeois custom, where it was always the man who took the initiative in a sexual encounter, she would seldom approach a customer, instead waiting to be asked.[15] The rooms of this class of prostitute, noted Ostwald, were usually located in the Krausenstrasse, the Schützenstrasse or the Charlottenstrasse, and their services cost 20 Marks a time.[16] 'South of the Leipzigerstrasse,' he continued, 'down to Kochstrasse and Besselstrasse another

type again goes walking, less well dressed and less obvious in her approach.'
Sex with such a woman would cost a man 10 Marks. Many of these,
especially north of the Behrenstrasse, were casual prostitutes, needleworkers
or domestic servants, usually accompanied by an older procuress who made
sure they did not sell themselves too cheaply.[17]

Ostwald went into a good deal of detail about the various kinds of
prostitute in Berlin, from women who 'pose as lusty young widows' to the
young girls who gathered around the Potsdamerplatz on the afternoons when
the garden of the Café Josty was filled with customers; but his main concern
was with the social hierarchies of prostitutes and the social standing of their
clients, and he devoted considerable space to describing the milieu of the
petty-bourgeois prostitute, of whom he took a rather snobbish view:

> Girls who possess all the bad habits of the Berlin petty bourgeoisie are almost
> always tastelessly clothed. They do not wait, like the whores of the
> Friedrichstadt and Potsdamerplatz, until they are spoken too, but press their
> attentions upon prospective clients with 'Come with me, darling!', 'Come
> along, my dear!' and on occasion utter crude curses as well. Their clients
> belong to the lower middle classes. They are those inhabitants of Schöneberg
> and the western districts of the city, who will only give a girl three or five
> Marks for their pleasure, treat her roughly, leave her in an oppressive financial
> situation and subject her to the deepest humiliation.

Such customers included generally students from modest backgrounds, better-
paid manual and skilled workers, and white-collar workers. A similar level
of prostitution was provided in the Turmstrasse, Prenzlauerstrasse and
Zimmerstrasse, and a few other quarters, especially in Berlin's more modest
'entertainment districts', he added. Finally, noted Ostwald,

> A few of the street-walkers' patches are reserved for the poorest among the
> populace. In the sooty Koppenstrasse by the Silesian Station, poor, weather-
> beaten and dissolute creatures wander about at night, mainly on Saturdays,
> without any headgear, wearing blue kitchen-aprons. They depend on drunken
> labourers coming back home, and give themselves to them for one or two
> Marks . . . Near the Tiergarten Station, too, on the footpath going to the
> Zoological Garden, between 9 and 11 whores of the lowest sort stand every
> evening. Old and bereft of any charms, they prostitute themselves under cover
> of the trees.[18]

The lowest, cheapest and most miserable forms of prostitution, Ostwald
reported, were also to be found in the north of Berlin and in Friedrichshain.

Thus prostitution paralleled virtually the entire social scale, some women
earning 20 times as much for a single encounter than others did a variation
which was paralleled by the corresponding resources of their respective

customers. Far from prostitution being an aspect of the sexual exploitation of proletarian women by bourgeois men, it represented, rather, a sexual version of the kind of underworld described by many commentators earlier in the century, shadowing all classes of society from top to bottom. Such commentators, indeed, were just as aware as Ostwald that this was how prostitution operated. In 1846, for example, one writer calculated that there were 500 mistresses in Berlin, 4500 'more refined prostitutes', 8000 'common whores' and 2000 of the lowest sort. These women, he said, served male clients of all social classes, from wealthy wastrels and late-marrying civil servants down to journeymen and labourers. The figures, even for a period strongly marked by mass poverty (which indeed the author considered the principal cause of women falling into a life of prostitution), seem perhaps a little high; the observation of the social structure of prostitution, however, is likely to have been an accurate one.[19]

It was only in the lower reaches of the social scale that prostitution conformed to the model described by the historian Regina Schulte – a 'mass processing' which 'brutalized the forms of sexuality, demanded the continual, soul-destroying readiness of the prostitutes to comply, and the reduction of the sexual act to its quickest and most mechanical performance.'[20] Among working-class men too, however, companionship could be important in the brothel. In 1868, the police in Brunswick reported that two workers accused of theft had spent no fewer than eight hours in a local brothel, from 3 am to 11 am, spending their ill-gotten gains on sex and drink, an allegation confirmed by the girls who worked there. Drinks formed a vital element in the income of such institutions, and customers were encouraged to sit around and talk over a bottle of wine or schnapps even when police regulations forbade it.[21] In 1870, one commentator noted:

> Many men, even among the lower classes, no longer feel fulfilled by a mere satisfaction of their sexual urge, they now place some value on pleasant company and an attractive conversation with the female person with whom they usually carry on a kind of liaison.

In the later decades of the century, too, noted the same writer, 'the coarseness with which good-time girls used to accost potential clients is also beginning bit by bit to disappear'.[22]

Soldiers and sailors were frequent clients, as might be expected. In the Baltic town of Lübeck, for instance, prostitutes were often to be seen walking up and down in front of the army barracks in the 1870s.[23] Half a century before, one brothel in the town was closed down because of a 'bloody fight' involving the 'sailors who habitually visit those premises'.[24] Such traditions continued long after the turn of the century. A police raid on a brothel in Lübeck in 1923, for example, found five sailors present.[25] In 1910, a deputy in the Baden parliament reported that the inhabitants of the Kleine

Spitalstrasse in Karlsruhe, where all the city's regulated prostitutes were quartered, had complained 'how when there is an enrolment of recruits or manoeuvres for reservists, 50 or 60 soldiers come along to the Spitalstrasse with flags flying, like gymnastic clubs'. Schoolboys and students also regularly visited brothels to gain sexual experience, and there were complaints from neighbours of brothels in Karlsruhe about the manner in which 'students depart in the night, bellowing and roaring'.[26] A pastor in Colmar claimed: 'Just to mention one example, I know a grammar school in which all the boys in the fourth year, with one exception, visited a brothel, and one parish in which all the boys about to be confirmed arranged a *rendez-vous* in such a house.'[27] One feminist campaigner reported that a large number of clients had been supplied to the prostitution trade by right-wing ceremonies held at Bismarck's old home near Hamburg, 'the patriotic student celebrations in Friedrichsruh, which found their end in the brothels of Hamburg', along with the similar events which, she claimed, had taken place after a major congress of 'naturalists' in the city. 'Hamburg gentlemen are also said to frequent Hamburg's brothels,' she went on, 'very many *married* and unmarried gentlemen, and also many less wealthy Hamburg gentlemen . . . and many travellers who visit Hamburg from *other parts of Germany*'.[28]

A similar clientele, doubtless, was supplied to prostitutes in Baden, where the police noted between 20 and 30 'street-walkers' at the Ifferzheim races in the late 1900s.[29] Prostitutes also customarily made their appearance in substantial numbers at church-ales (*Kirmes*), popular festivals, fairs and the like.[30] It may be, as Alain Corbin has argued, that as the middle class grew in wealth and size, so the demand for the services of prostitutes did indeed shift up the social scale, stimulating the emergence of luxury brothels that offered the illusion of a home-from-home as well as providing exotic sexual services that middle-class men felt unable to obtain in marriage.[31] Controlled brothels, too, may have catered for particular categories of male client who placed importance on the fact that they were approved by the state, such as students, schoolboys and soldiers.[32] The fact remains, however, that the demand from working-class men, itinerant labourers, soldiers and sailors, and young males of widely differing social background in no way seems to have diminished as a consequence of these changes. If prostitution supplied a variety of services, from the cheapest and most basic to the most costly and elaborate, it was because there was a variety of demand for them from men all the way up and down the social scale.[33]

This conclusion was underlined by an anonymous survey of Hamburg prostitution in the late 1850s, which divided the male clients by social standing. In the up-market brothels of the Schwiegerstrasse, for instance, 'the male public . . . consists of merchants and traders, the more refined of the clerks, officers, civil servants and above all of the numerous travelling salesmen who fill our hotels in summer and winter alike.' In the waterfront district of St Pauli, where there were 20 brothels with a total of 250 girls working in them, the custom, according to the survey, was more varied and by no means so polite:

> There one sees sailors and landlubbers; travelling artisans and grain-workers, their coats covered in dust; tarry Irish sailors, who would stick to a wall if you threw them at it; *sans-culotte* bakers with bare feet, pantaloons and women's skirts; slim, grave Americans, in their Haiti-blue dress; turbaned Bedouins; men from Copenhagen, their jackets proudly ornamented with braid; dirty, bearded Russians; slaughtermen reeking of fresh blood; broad-shouldered, dance-loving East Prussians; men from the Vierlanden, with their knee-breeches; peak-capped pastrycooks; and humble, pitch-black negroes in snow-white costumes.

All currencies were accepted in payment here, he added.[34] In Berlin, the police official Wilhelm Stieber noted in 1846, 'The brothels' customers belong to greatly varying classes of society, but mostly to the lower ones.' Here, too, the notion of a simple exploitation of proletarian women by bourgeois men was a long way from the truth. The most frequent clients, Stieber noted, were drawn from a wide variety of backgrounds:

> Merchants' servants and clerks . . . bargees and coachmen from out of town, who seek a real surrogate for marriage here, and strangers who satisfy their voyeurism and want to enrich their geographical knowledge, students and young persons of higher social standing, who let their high spirits off the leash here, apprentice lads and schoolboys, driven by curiosity and prematurely awakened sensuality, and many regular customers who were once journeymen, usually come in every Saturday night at fixed times, and also seek, and find, a substitute for marriage here.

As for soldiers, Stieber remarked, whether accurately or not, most of them were too poor to afford such pleasures.[35]

Prostitutes naturally favoured some clients over others, insofar as they were able in practice to express preferences. According to what seems to be an authentic set of memoirs of a St Pauli prostitute, published in 1847, the best customers were the Americans, clean-cut and well-heeled; the worst were the English – 'small, coarse-boned, stocky chaps, drunken, smutty, boastful, keen on trade, dirty, indeed not infrequently filthily dressed.'[36] Five years previously, there had been anti-English riots in the city following the Great Fire of 1842, which had been blamed on English navvies working on the construction of a railway line near the city. These prejudices were evidently still very much alive when the memoirs appeared. The variety of clients reflected a market situation in which the prostitute attempted to go for the highest bidder; but the price paid depended on youth and beauty as well as intelligence and the social graces, a factor which reflected the social position of women in the marriage market of respectable society as well. Given the extreme inequalities of nineteenth-century German society, with only a small number of wealthy or even well-off people at the top, it would be reasonable to suppose that the majority of clients came, as commentators indicated, from the working class and petty bourgeoisie rather than from the numerically limited ranks of the educated and professional bourgeoisie. The tiny minority of mistresses and courtesans at the top of the tree catered for a correspondingly tiny clientele of wealthy men from the highest rungs of the social and economic ladder. The social structure of demand for the services of prostitutes was more or less derived from the social structure of the male population of Germany as a whole. In this respect at least, 'Thymian Gotteball', the 'salon', and the professional client and dealing with playing the role of the paid mistress-companion, operated at the top end of the scale.

The Social Origins of Prostitution

If this was the case for the clients, then what of the social origins of the women who served them? According to the Berlin police, 1015 out of the 2224 prostitutes registered in Berlin between 1871 and 1878 were the daughters of artisans (47.9 per cent), 467 of factory workers (22.0 per cent), 305 of minor officials (14.4 per cent), 222 of fathers employed in trade and transport (10.4 per cent), 87 of peasant farmers and rural labourers (4.1 per cent) and 26 of soldiers (1.2 per cent).[37] A study carried out in Cologne before the First World War showed that few registered prostitutes came from solid bourgeois backgrounds on the one hand, but equally few came from the poorest backgrounds on the other. Out of a sample of 70, 19 were the daughters of artisans, nine of factory workers, five of white-collar workers or lower state officials, and six of miners. The fathers of the rest were from a wider variety of working- or lower-middle-class occupations.[38] A similar pattern can be observed in other cities. Of some 2574 clandestine prostitutes known to the Munich police in 1911, 1147 were the daughters of artisans, 944 of labourers and 248 of peasant farmers or rural workers. Similarly, out of 565 prostitutes registered in Stuttgart the same year, the fathers were artisans in 127 instances, day-labourers in 84 and peasant farmers or rural workers in 60.[39] It was common in the larger cities for regulated prostitutes to be immigrants. In 1907, for example, only 10.8 per cent of the 408 controlled prostitutes in Hamburg had been born in the city; 50.2 per cent of the city's population as a whole were native-born.[40] Outsiders may of course have been more vulnerable to arrest than natives; they knew the city and the various opportunities for evading the attention of the police less well, and they may have been more naive, and so more willing to be inscribed. Yet all the same this statistic does seem to suggest that, among the diverse social groups of women who went into prostitution, it was particularly the daughters of rural or small-town artisans who ended up being registered.

The social investigator Kurt Schneider was struck by the frequency of job-changing among registered prostitutes in Cologne in the period prior to registration. He ascribed this to their dislike of hard work, a bourgeois prejudice which mainly displayed his own ignorance of the instability of employment in this class of society in general. Virtually all the prostitutes in his sample of 70 had had a number of previous jobs. No fewer than 50 had worked as domestic servants, 16 as factory workers, 16 as waitresses, 12 as sales-girls, six as needleworkers, four as rural labourers, four as artists or musicians and three as nurses or nannies. One had even worked in one of the most modern of jobs, as a telephonist.[41] A similar survey carried out in Breslau at the turn of the century revealed a similar pattern: 72 prostitutes had formerly worked at one time or another as domestic servants, 37 as factory workers, 13 as waitresses, hairdressers or flower-girls, 14 as sales-girls, 36 as needleworkers and four as dancers.[42] Of the 4560 prostitutes newly registered in Munich in 1909–10, 1261 had been domestic servants, 1102 had worked as 'waitresses, barmaids, etc.' and 513 as factory workers. Of the 2574 prostitutes in the town who were not officially registered but were nonetheless on the police's files, 721 had been domestic servants, 608 barmaids, 255 factory workers and 60 dancers or singers on the stage. Similarly, 431 of the 1200 prostitutes enrolled in Berlin in 1909–10 had been domestic servants, 455 factory workers and 479 seamstresses or laundresses. This pattern was not new to the last years of peace. Out of 279 newly inscribed prostitutes in Hamburg in 1872, 162 had been domestic servants, 28 had been factory workers, 19 garment workers and 16 waitresses.[43] And in Berlin in the 1870s, 794 out of a total of 2224 registered prostitutes had been domestic servants, 355 factory workers, 946 domestic or shop workers and 139 waitresses.[44]

Some of these trades were already situated well within the domain of sexual exploitation. Waitresses in Imperial Germany, for example, were heavily dependent on tips, and in garden cafés often had to hire the plates and cutlery from the owner. One investigation claimed that a majority of them worked between 14 and 16 hours a day.[45] Wages were extremely low. This left them open to demands for sexual services from male clients, who in many cafés, restaurants and bars simply assumed that they were sexually available. In such a situation, the behaviour required of a waitress to earn a good tip could already have strong sexual overtones. Cafés, variety houses and 'tingel-tangels' where the barmaids, singers and performers were expected to earn not just extra money, but the bulk of their income from informal prostitution became increasingly common during the 1890s.[46] Other trades in which registered prostitutes had formerly been engaged were common jobs of the young, uneducated working-class woman of the age. Sewing and dressmaking, carried out at home for piece-rates paid by a middleman, were not only poorly paid but uncertain too, subject to the vagaries of fashion, the season and the market. It was not uncommon for women who depended on these sources of income to be left without work for months at a time.[47] Factory work for women was equally unsteady, with unemployment common in times of depression or even a temporary slackening of demand.[48] In all of these cases, poor and frequently interrupted pay could place young women in a situation where the temptation – or the necessity – to earn money through prostitution was irresistible.[49] There is evidence that in this exploitative situation, many young women took to prostitution as a matter of rational choice rather than out of moral degeneracy or outright compulsion.[50]

The most common previous employment of registered prostitutes was in domestic service. This was the largest single urban occupation for women in the late nineteenth and early twentieth centuries, accounting for about 28 per cent of the female workforce, so it is not surprising that it was also the largest single occupational group represented among registered prostitutes. In two of the above samples, the proportion of domestic servants was indeed larger than the proportion of servants in the female workforce, at 58 and 36 per cent respectively; in the other two it was exactly 28 per cent. The American investigator Abraham Flexner also reported that some 60 per cent of the registered prostitutes of Berlin in 1900 were former servants.[51] Nobody, of course, would argue that these women represented anything but a tiny proportion of those who worked in service in any of these cities; nevertheless, the high proportion of former domestic servants among the registered prostitutes does seem to require some explanation. One feminist writer, Karin Walser, has argued that this predominance of former domestic servants among prostitutes is a figment of the imagination of bourgeois men consumed by fantasies about the sexual availability of servants.[52] This may well have been true of someone like the Berlin police official Wilhelm Stieber, who claimed in 1846 that virtually all the city's domestic servants were secret prostitutes already.[53] But in fact the main proponent of this view has been the feminist historian Regina Schulte, who has concluded from a survey of published statistics that the proportion of domestic servants among registered prostitutes increased sevenfold between 1855 and 1898.[54] From this, Schulte argues that servants were mainly drawn from rural backgrounds, where premarital sex was common. They worked long hours and in poor conditions. Without contacts in the city, they were isolated by the refusal in most cases of their employer to provide the warmth and support of a family atmosphere in which the servants themselves were included. The girls' first sexual experience, to be sure, was generally not with the 'young master' in their employer's home, nor with their employer himself, but with a casual acquaintance of their own social standing made outside. It was a fantasy that such women had been seduced by their employers while working in domestic service, for virtually all the Cologne prostitutes questioned by Schneider said they had lost their virginity to men of their own class. No fewer than 42 out of his sample of 70 had become pregnant before entering upon their life as professional prostitutes, and many had been rejected by their parents as a result.[55] If pregnancy ensued, or if the liaison was discovered by a servant's employer, dismissal was generally the result. Illegitimate motherhood and prostitution really were connected. Prostitution, whether entered into consciously or through seduction by a pimp, was often the only way for such women to make a living. In this sense at least, although she was neither poor nor a servant, 'Thymian Gotteball' went through an experience that was all too typical of the manner in which women drifted into the world of professional vice.

Contemporary statistics did indeed suggest that, while servants between the ages of 16 and 30 constituted about a quarter of the female population of Berlin at the turn of the century, they were the mothers in roughly a third of all illegitimate births. And out of 1531 girls newly inscribed in the city in 1908–10, no fewer than 636 had had children. More important, however, seems to have been the influence of a broken home: fully 64 per cent of the 565 prostitutes registered in Stuttgart in the early 1900s were wholly or partially orphaned, according to one study. This shattered emotional background was present in a high proportion of prostitutes in Victorian England as well. And it was there in the history of 'Thymian Gotteball', too. It was this, rather than some unthinking adherence to country customs and mores, that made them vulnerable in the big city, and drove them to seek the emotional and sexual warmth which, all too often, left them with a child to look after, nobody to support them and no legitimate means of earning a living.[56] Regina Schulte has claimed that they mainly came from peasant societies where premarital sex was accepted, and so were vulnerable in the very different social milieu of the big town or city, where marriage was far less likely to follow than it was in the village. But this seems to be belied by the fact that they were the children above all of artisans, petty officials and factory workers, and not of peasants.

Schulte argues that servants played a key role in the sexual socialization of young men in the servant-employing classes. Because the physical aspects of bringing up children, starting with breast-feeding and toilet-training, were generally left to servants, a bourgeois child grew up associating physical intimacy with social contempt. The upper middle-class mother or father was a remote figure, rarely seen by the child, and still more rarely touched. Indeed, a primary concern of the bourgeois household was the suppression of childhood sexuality and the concealment of sexual realities from children, and parents went to considerable lengths to prevent common practices such as masturbation. This kind of socialization, argues Schulte, produced adult women who were ignorant of and resistant to sexuality, and adult men who sought physical sexual intimacy not with their wives, but with prostitutes. As a contemporary writer put it, prostitution was 'regarded as necessary for young men to retain their health and young girls from better families their virtue'.[57] But these views are in need of some qualification. They explain only a part of the demand for prostitutes, as we have seen. Much if not most of it came from men of the non-servant-employing classes. Moreover, a considerable proportion of prostitutes were not former domestic servants and had not been pregnant. And although the instability of the female labour market must have played a role in leading them to earn a living by selling their sexual services, not all of them were forced into earning their living this way by poverty and destitution.

As we have seen, the earnings of the better-off courtesan were quite considerable. The social investigator Kurt Schneider was struck by the number of prostitutes in his Cologne study who were bold enough to admit to him that they were happy in their job. 'I really like this life up to now,' one of them told him; while another denied that she had any regrets: 'I wanted it this way.' Of course, many did express their unhappiness with their lot, but that was hardly surprising, since all of the women Schneider interviewed were hospitalized with venereal disease, and many of them, used to telling men what they thought they wanted to hear, may well have given this response to Schneider because that was what he seemed to expect. Far from welcoming the positive attitude of many of his interviewees to a life of prostitution, in the belief that it demonstrated their inherent wickedness, Schneider was shocked by it, and considered that it merely added to the medical and social problems which he thought they caused.[58] However, what the responses indicated was that, in the exploitative and unequal society of Wilhelmine Germany, a number of women saw a period of earning their living by prostitution as a positive step. The vast majority of such women came from the lower end of the social scale, though seldom from the very bottom. Prostitutes from a middle-class background, like 'Thymian Gotteball', were extremely rare. Prostitution in nineteenth-century Germany thus has to be understood not in terms exclusively of class, or of gender, but rather of both; of men of all social classes exploiting women who came overwhelmingly from the petty bourgeoisie and proletariat.

The Morals Police and 'Public Houses'

Bourgeois men, according to Schulte, sought to deal with prostitutes by imprisoning them in state-controlled brothels, by regimenting them, driving them off the streets, forcing them to undergo humiliating medical examinations, punishing them with incarceration under a harsh and impersonal prison regime or classifying them as abnormal or mentally diseased in scientific investigations. This reflected a double-standard of morality, based on differing notions of male and female sexuality. Defenders of regulation, indeed, assumed that male desire was 'natural', while condemning prostitutes as 'unnatural' because their sexuality did not conform to the modest female norm. One writer, Robert Hessen, even drew up a chart to illustrate his belief that while 50 per cent of men were 'very sensual', only 2 per cent of women were, while on the other hand 2 per cent of men were 'not sensual at all' in comparison to 50 per cent of women; 48 per cent of each, he concluded with

implausible precision, were 'moderately sensual'. Thus the 2 per cent of
women whom he classified as 'very sensual' formed the group from which
German prostitutes were taken; between them, he argued, pursuing his
strange obsession with sexual statistics, they performed the sex act no fewer
than 60 million times a year in Germany in the period just before the First
World War. Not only for them, but also – far more importantly – for the
50 per cent of men who were 'very sensual', sexual abstinence was an
impossibility.[59]

If they were not allowed to work off their sexual energy on prostitutes,
another writer argued earlier in the century, men would inevitably fall prey
to that sexual terror of the nineteenth century, masturbation, with all the
terrible medical and moral consequences which were believed to flow from
it.[60] Given the relatively late age of marriage in Imperial Germany, argued one
group of supporters of regulation, it was inevitable that men would seek to
satisfy their natural urges in brothels.[61] Prostitutes, wrote an anonymous
commentator in 1870, were not only 'ineradicable' but also necessary, because

> for those individuals who depend on extra-marital sexual intercourse, they
> facilitate the satisfaction of one of their liveliest and most powerful natural
> urges, and thereby prevent numerous unnatural forms of sexual intercourse
> which disgrace human dignity and destroy their vital energy, as well as pro-
> tecting the marital bed from defilement and thousands of honourable girls from
> seduction, and contribute to the maintenance of discipline and morality in a
> large part of the population in that they provide an indirect, if not explicitly
> intended protection for the chastity of married women and the innocence of
> virgins by diverting unchaste lusts and desires towards themselves.[62]

The state had a duty, therefore, to protect honourable women by confining
the dishonourable to state-controlled brothels. Others echoed this argument
advanced on the basis of an ascription of a 'natural' sexual dynamism to men
and a 'natural' sexual passivity to the mass of 'normal' women. 'It is indeed
a fact', a group of male citizens in Hamburg at the turn of the century
confidently pronounced, 'that comparatively few men enter marriage having
had the moral strength to restrain themselves from indulging in any sexual
pleasure beforehand, and in the face of such a truth, the state . . . has the
simple duty to remove . . . the shameful consequences.' The clear assumption
was that the state represented a male electorate, men ran the state, and the
state therefore had the obligation to protect men from venereal disease 'simply
in the interests of its existence'.[63]

'Prostitution', wrote another proponent of regulation in Hamburg, 'is a
necessary evil!'

> What insightful and understanding man could doubt the truth of this sentence?
> We cannot do without prostitution, certainly not in a big city, where a large

number of young men come together, and least of all in a harbour-city like Hamburg, where many thousands of sailors get to see a female face for the first time after months of abstinence ... Anyone who does not want immorality to find its way into families in unsuspected measure, who does not want it to grip our entire population, who does not want a repulsive and disease-ridden generation to people our fatherland, must tolerate the existence of prostitution.

Thus free female sexuality had to be confined to a specific sector of the population or else it would corrupt the whole of it. The writer portrayed in drastic terms the consequences of letting prostitution operate freely across the city. Prostitution, he claimed, 'offers itself to the man, the youth who has scarcely grown out of his short trousers, in a thousand forms and opportunities, it storms him, it persecutes him, it forces itself upon him ... and in the end brings about his fall.' In such a situation, it was no longer men who sought out prostitutes, but the other way round: 'Instead of a need conditioned by natural urges on the one hand, we now have a wild, unbridled competition on the other, repulsive and pernicious!' Women were driven to prostitution not just by hunger or because they had been betrayed in love, but also through 'frivolity' and the 'addiction to vain frippery'.[64] They were 'lethargic, addicted to clothes and jewellery and pleasure ... they do not work, they let themselves be waited on.'[65] According to the Berlin police official Wilhelm Stieber, indeed, prostitutes all had deep voices, and they smelt.[66] Idleness was the cause of their downfall, according to another pro-regulation account.[67] Thus prostitutes were immoral deviants who had to be clearly separated from the normal female majority. It was not female poverty that caused prostitution, but the 'inclination of numerous female persons to live in the pursuit of pleasure and vanity without having to work'.[68]

The consequence of this view was necessarily the imposition of stricter norms of propriety on women in general, with all that implied for the social control of their conduct in public, whatever their moral or social standing. So bourgeois society, in Schulte's words, established 'restricted areas' to protect itself against medical and social infection, confining prostitution to an underworld whose limits were strictly defined. The laws and regulations which allowed women suspected as prostitutes to be arrested and forcibly examined were the tools with which the police carried out this task. Moreover,

A prostitute who was not discovered had 'learned' to conceal herself, not to attract attention, not to contravene the regulations, not to arouse suspicion, not to cause offence – she was no longer visible and thus she was disciplined in the same way as the obedient 'controlled' prostitute.[69]

The Berlin police regulations, for example, covered the dress code which regulated prostitutes had to follow ('decent and simple'), the areas such as the zoo, cafés, bars, various public places and a long list of streets where they were forbidden to appear, and the behaviour expected of them when they did venture into the public domain ('She must not attract the attention of others to herself on the city streets and squares'). Similar prohibitions were in force in other towns, such as Düsseldorf.[70] This leads Schulte to conclude:

> The regulations of the Morals Police (*Sittenpolizei* or vice squad) were the formal basis and the real inception of an all-encompassing grasp over the lives of women who became 'official' in their capacity as prostitutes; they were a net, cast over the entire city, and drawn ever tighter around the prostitute herself . . . The observation of these regulations meant a total disciplining and subjection of the prostitute. On the other hand, they were connected with so tightly meshed a net of possibilities of falling foul of the law, that she was bound to stumble into it every time her vigilance faltered. If she lived with and according to these rules, she moved within the confines of a prison that might have been invisible but was also ever-present.[71]

In Brunswick, registered prostitutes were subject to a curfew, and were forbidden to leave the brothel after seven in the evening during the summer months, or after five in winter.[72] In Frankfurt-am-Main, indeed, the Morals Police went even further and, as well as confining prostitutes to a number of designated streets, divided them into three classes as an additional means of control. 'Those who have been freshly placed under control,' commented a local committee of investigation in 1899, 'as well as those of no fixed abode who have entered the city from outside, are placed to begin with in the IIIrd class, from which good conduct can promote them into the IInd and the Ist class.' While the two lower classes of prostitutes had to go to the police gaol to be examined on a weekly basis, first-class prostitutes were allowed to be examined at home, and at less frequent intervals. The power that this gave the police, who were allowed to define the vital concept of 'good conduct' as they wished, can be imagined.[73]

No less a personage than King Friedrich Wilhelm III of Prussia said early in the nineteenth century: 'Because of the great influence they have on morality and health, brothels are a very important object of police administration.'[74] Backed by such exalted opinion, the police gave four main reasons for their advocacy of the regulation system. First, they argued that free prostitution would encourage the evasion of medical checks and lead to an increase in venereal diseases. Defenders of the system even argued for daily medical examinations of controlled prostitutes.[75] While this was nowhere carried out, the regulations in every city did allow the police to incarcerate prostitutes in locked hospital wards if they were found to be diseased. Opponents of the system argued, however, that it actually spread disease by encouraging men to believe that all regulated prostitutes were free of infection. The numbers of women to be found undergoing an enforced spell in hospital, together with the variety of techniques they used to get a clean bill of health from the often rather perfunctory and careless examinations to which they were exposed, certainly gave credence to this view.

Secondly, the police claimed to be worried at the possibility of public immorality, which was one reason why the regulations forbade prostitutes to appear on the main thoroughfares of cities, such as the Jungfernstieg in Hamburg or Unter den Linden in Berlin, or the town hall, zoo, botanical gardens, theatres and opera houses in almost any large German town. The sight of public prostitution in places frequented by the respectable classes was often felt to damage a city's reputation in the eyes of outsiders. A Bremen Senator, for example, visiting Hamburg in 1862, was shocked by the improprieties he observed in Hamburg's dance-halls and considered that police-controlled brothels would help reduce such public immorality, though he admitted the difficulties of registering every prostitute in the city. He was told by a Hamburg Senator that 'almost all our domestic servants' as well as 'peasant women who come into the town are whores. Women here are in general meretricious.' This caused a 'poisoning of Hamburg's respectable classes'.[76] In Lübeck, the regulations followed this spirit in trying to prevent the prostitutes from leaving the brothels to go to dances at any time.[77] Of the 23 paragraphs of the Hamburg Morals Police regulations for controlled prostitutes, fully ten were devoted to restricting their appearances in public. Vice could flourish in the backstreets and dark alleyways of the older parts of the great cities; but no self-respecting police force could afford to allow the more respectable parts of its city to become market-places for the trade in human flesh if it wished to maintain its claim to be the guardian of public decency and the protector of bourgeois society. Yet the failure of regulation to encompass more than a tithe of those actively engaged in prostitution ensured from the start that this objective stood no chance of being achieved. Indeed, observers were well aware by the 1900s that it was 'a mere fiction' to claim that 'the great mass of prostitutes' was covered by the system.[78]

The third reason given by police authorities and their supporters for the control of prostitution was that it was in the interests not only of society at large but also of the prostitutes themselves. One writer even argued somewhat implausibly that 'brothels often encourage a girl's conversion to a moral way of life ... because of the continual monotony of life in them.'[79] Another claimed they could be used to force the girls to save money with which to launch themselves on a respectable career.[80] More usual was the argument, advanced for example by Senator Carl Petersen, Hamburg's Chief of Police in the 1870s, that regulation would protect the girls against the exploitation of unscrupulous landlords. In Berlin, where police-controlled brothels did not exist at this time, he said, 'the girls are exploited to the most extreme degree'.[81] The police argued that the creation of officially sanctioned brothels took prostitutes off the streets, and they were inclined to deny allegations, made by critics of the system, that brothel-keepers made enormous profits.[82] A police official in Brunswick noted in 1868: 'The rapid accumulation of a fortune is no longer possible for brothel-keepers, as they are at present situated, and indeed most of them get into debt if they have not acquired means beforehand or obtained them later through some particular stroke of fortune.'[83] Opponents in other small towns like Heidelberg countered with claims that brothel-keepers took over 4000 Marks a year in rent from each prostitute, and that houses with an estimated value of 24,000 Marks could change hands for 130,000 if they were designated 'public houses' by the police.[84] In Heidelberg, of course, there were plenty of affluent students to provide custom, even if the consequent earnings were not as great as they were in the upper reaches of the trade in a big city such as Berlin. Nevertheless, given the fact that Germany was predominantly a country of small and medium-sized towns, it is probable that the great majority of brothel-keepers, like the great majority of prostitutes, often found it hard to make ends meet.

Folk Devils and Moral Panics

A fourth reason given by defenders of regulation for the necessity of police controls was that they were an effective means of suppressing pimps and the criminal activities associated with them. As one pro-regulationist argued: 'Brothels are the best means of curbing the activities of those who encourage immorality and of acting against those involved in the procuring businesses.'[85] This, he maintained, was good not only for the girls but also for society as a whole, because pimping and procuring were closely associated with crime and social unrest. In the 1840s, the Berlin police official Wilhelm Stieber reflected widespread official anxieties in the face of mounting social disorder when he wrote:

> There are three terrible enemies which our age has to fight in almost every town and city, and they all threaten to rob us of the fruits of its civilization, however high the level which it has reached, namely: *the proletariat, crime,* and *prostitution.* One meets with all three in particular in Berlin in a threatening superabundance, and all three complement and support one another with an unshakable certainty and assiduity. The penniless *proletarian man* becomes a *criminal,* the starving *proletarian woman* a victim of *prostitution.* Almost all *female criminals* are also *prostitutes* and almost all *male criminals,* after correction in prison, even in the most fortunate cases, become no more than *proletarians.*

Stieber thought this disastrous situation had been exacerbated by the abolition of Berlin's state-controlled brothels under liberal pressure in 1846, and he saw their reintroduction as an urgent task in the maintenance of the fragile social order of pre-revolutionary Prussia. Apart from anything else, he considered them a necessary instrument in the police's fight against crime, and a vital source of information-gathering for the authorities.[86]

Some years later, the police in Danzig advanced the common claim that the removal of controlled brothels drove prostitutes into cheap private rooms in poor areas where the prospect of easy earnings attracted the 'propertyless and work-shy' to take up procuring, so the working classes would be morally ruined as a result. Regulation was the only way to keep the streets safe at night. The Augsburg police complained that prostitutes who lived alone generally had pimps who were a major element in the criminal underworld. The Dresden authorities concurred: controlled brothels kept the numbers of pimps down. Unsupervised brothels, the Hamburg police agreed, would be centres of criminality and disorder.[87] The municipal authorities in Frankfurt-am-Main similarly justified the police regulation of prostitution in the city in 1899 as a means of curbing the threat of 'the activities of pimps, which are becoming ever more aggressive'.[88] The pimp was a threat to respectable male customers as well, complained a group of men in Hamburg at the turn of the century:

> Dressed in the most elegant manner, according to the latest fashion, in lacquered boots and kid gloves, he takes his whore for a stroll . . . He lurks in the background in her room, and leaps out without hesitation upon any visitor who has been remiss in his payment, to rob him, beat him up, and throw him out, indeed even to strike him dead.[89]

The pimp's very appearance – richly and fashionably dressed – was evidence for these men of the degree to which he exploited his girl by taking her earnings. The 'Louis', as he was colloquially known, lived exclusively off 'his' girl and maltreated her if she failed to keep him in sufficient funds. He

> takes devilish pleasure in knifing people. When he is likely to get in the way of his whore's carrying on her business, he goes out and moves around in the company of other people, loiters around on the street, or lurks in a dive, playing cards and billiards, and at the slightest excuse strikes out with his knife. And if such an opportunity does not present itself of its own accord, he will go out looking for it. He must have entertainment in his way. So he goes out onto the street, molests respectable ladies, jostles respectable gentlemen, and if he meets with the slightest resistance in word or deed, he will lunge out with his fists or strike out with his knife.

Prostitution, in the view of these Hamburg citizens, was the gigantic trade that held the underworld together and nurtured all other forms of violence and criminality.

Indeed, declared the Hamburg group, it was more than possible that in a period of political upheaval the forces of the sexual underworld would join with Social Democrats and the far left to form the shock troops of the revolution:

Prostitution and pimping in the current regulation of their circumstances are the first and transitional step to common criminality . . . How closely prostitution and crime are bound up with one another in Berlin can be judged from the fact that both speak the same language, the famous Berlin criminals' dialect which originally derived from Hebrew and subsequently became partly Germanized, partly adorned with German additions. That is the social danger of which we speak. And next to it there is also a sociopolitical danger. For if a time of serious hardship should ever come upon us, then we shall see unregulated prostitution, these thousands of vagabond pimps, standing on the side of the revolutionaries, and they will be terrible opponents, not because of their bravery, but rather because of their blood-lust and their bestiality, and even more because of the limitless importunity with which they will press themselves upon every group in society which is in any way accessible to them.[90]

This was doubtless an extreme view; but in a less hysterical form it represented the fears of social disorder that haunted all respectable people when they contemplated the mass of unemployed or casually employed in the great cities, above all perhaps in Berlin, where police control over prostitution was notoriously lax. There was, remarked a standard work on the subject published in the Weimar Republic, an 'inner connection between prostitution and criminality'.[91] Such connections were confirmed on the rare occasions when pimps themselves spoke out. In 1888, for example, the 39-year-old convict Joseph Kürper narrated to a prison chaplain, who then published his revelations as a warning to society, his story of a life of crime, which had begun with childhood begging in the company of his unmarried mother in the Palatinate. Graduating via petty theft to armed robbery, Kürper had also spent time as a 'Louis' in Mannheim. His tasks there had included protecting his 'girl' while attending horse-races and 'balls of a dubious character', accompanying her on the streets and in the park at night, forcing reluctant 'gentlemen' to pay up, and keeping a lookout for the police, whose task it was to suppress the 'free' and unregulated prostitution that was his business. Kürper added: 'I was armed with a dagger and a short American cosh and I was prepared for anything.'[92]

The fears which such sensational confessions aroused in respectable society were brought into lurid prominence in 1891 by a sensational murder case involving a pimp, one Heinze, and his wife, a prostitute. They had broken into a church in Berlin in order to steal the silver and murdered a nightwatchman who had interrupted them in the course of the robbery. Frau Heinze had 44 previous convictions for contravening the vice regulations; and Heinze had married her for purely professional purposes, he said. To the shocked fascination of the bourgeois public, Heinze was brazen enough to refresh himself occasionally in the dock with a bottle of champagne, and his defence was conducted to the plaudits of his underworld friends, who gathered in the public gallery to watch him. So great was the public outcry that the Kaiser himself issued a proclamation on 22 October 1891 condemning leniency in the courts and urging his government to introduce tougher laws against prostitutes and their hangers-on. The decree came at a significant moment, when respectable fears of social disorder were at their height following the lapsing of the Anti-Socialist Law the previous year and the consequent rash of marches, demonstrations and mass meetings held by the Social Democrats. These events unleashed a moral panic of considerable proportions. The government of Chancellor Caprivi could not let the Kaiser's proclamation go unheeded, and the matter was discussed in the Prussian cabinet on 2 November and again on 29 November 1891. Most ministers agreed that the spread of pimps and procurers across Berlin and other large cities was becoming a grave nuisance, and it was decided to use the opportunity to amend Clause 180 of the Criminal Code so as to allow police authorities to re-establish and extend the system of regulated brothels and thereby, it was thought, put an end to the pimping trade. As the Kaiser declared: 'The Heinze trial has demonstrated in a frightening manner that pimping, as well as the extensive trade in prostitution in the great cities, and especially in Berlin, has developed into a common danger for state and society.' He urged 'ruthless proceedings against the excesses of that depraved class of people'.[93]

And yet, despite the widespread view that police-regulated brothels prevented crime by suppressing pimping, there was abundant evidence that regulated brothels themselves were centres of criminal activity. In 1846, a liberal commentator, who disagreed with Stieber on almost everything else, seconded him on the connection he saw between prostitution and crime. He calculated that there were over 2000 'thieves' whores' in Berlin, who belonged to the 'organized world of thieving' and 'principally mix with criminals and share their haunts, help fence the ill-gotten gains, whose source is no secret to them, and even assist during thefts or commit crimes themselves.'[94] Many of them, he said, contradicting Stieber on this point, were based in state-controlled brothels, whose abolition he therefore welcomed. A few years later, Friedrich Avé-Lallement portrayed state-controlled brothels as the central institutions of the underworld, 'principal centres of villainy', places where thieves and robbers commonly stashed their loot and planned further outrages against respectable society.[95] Theft and deception were indeed the stock-in-trade of the brothel, whether regulated or not, in more senses than one. In Lübeck in 1876, for example, one Herr Schmidt complained that 'on 8 May this month, I met with the brothel-madam Bringezu, née Meyer, in Stockelsdorf, and her girls, and after being persuaded by them to use their services, I was robbed by them of: a. a gold watch, b. over 100 Marks in change, c. a pair of cufflinks, d. a 100-mark note and a five-mark note.' Evidently the total value of his losses was enough to overcome Herr Schmidt's embarrassment at the circumstances in which they had been stolen. This particular brothel was already known to the police for the fact that it was

levying illegal charges for drinks – no less than 4 Marks 20 for a bottle of red
wine, as another outraged client, the merchant Adolph Liegner, complained
on 25 November 1875.[96] Doubtless, similar activities went on in regulated
brothels all over Germany throughout the century, despite the ostensible
severity of police controls. In 1884, one writer echoed a widespread perception among their critics when he called them 'thieves' dens, and alarming
breeding-grounds for other vices'.[97]

Moreover, while opponents of regulation had to face the charge that they
were encouraging the dangerous social phenomenon of the pimp, others
argued that pimping was in many ways by no means as black a trade as it was
painted. Chief among the pimp's defenders was Hans Ostwald, who flatly
denied that Berlin's pimps were central figures in the criminal underworld. It
would damage their trade if they robbed the clients, he claimed, and would
frighten customers away. The bars they frequented were no 'robbers' caves'
but ordinary pubs. 'In the dives,' he wrote, 'things are not much different
from what they are in other bars. No louder, no rougher, no more vulgar.
The jokes the customers play are of exactly the same robust variety as in the
pubs and bars frequented by the workers and the lower middle classes.' Many
pimps indeed belonged to quite conventional clubs and societies, and around
the Alexanderplatz there were 'clubs whose members are almost exclusively
pimps', including male voice choirs (whose songs, said Ostwald, were 'pref-
erably patriotic') and athletics clubs. Few pimps worked full-time. 'Apart
from pimping, they are also: removal men, travelling booksellers, waiters,
dog-traders, bookmakers, professional gamblers, artistes, singers and athletes,
stone carters, dustbin-men, commissionaires, insurance agents, etc.' Ostwald
denied that they were evil parasites who forced inexperienced young girls first
to sell themselves and then to part with their earnings through verbal and
physical abuse. In his experience most pimps started, on the contrary, either
as innocent young workers who fell in love with girls not knowing initially
that they were prostitutes, or as students, soldiers, policemen or apprentices
whose mistresses started working the streets to earn more money. Many such
men became pimps gradually, without realizing it. As a rule, he argued, it was
clear 'that a prostitute is always a prostitute first and then gets herself a
pimp later on'. They needed such men both for company, and for protection
against the Morals Police. The pimp was useful in warning the prostitute of
approaching policemen, in looking after her room and possessions when
she was in custody and in helping her find her feet after her release. And
finally he prevented her from spending too much money on clothes (Ostwald
thought that all prostitutes above the lowest class were extravagant and
vain).

Ostwald was critical only of a minority of pimps. He strongly disapproved
of lesbian pimps ('the female pimp is a far more evil type, far more of a
bloodsucker, far more dangerous, than the male'), and of pimps who came
from outside the capital city:

The Berlin pimping scene has acquired a particular character through the numerous ex-sailors and the many south Germans and Viennese who have become part of it. These elements really are often rough and brutal. The south Germans are especially dangerous because of the way they play the gentleman. They dress in the latest fashion, currently with high wrap-around collars and tight trousers, their behaviour in itself is particularly conciliatory, and the greater half of them must be staying in Berlin without having registered their domicile.[98] The only purpose of much of this is for their whore to take advantage of some simple client – she almost only ever goes into hotels and bed-and-breakfast establishments, where she steals their wallets, purses, watches and anything else of value and vanishes with her pimp as quickly as possible.

Ostwald clearly knew many pimps personally and sympathized with their lot. He described them as 'vagrants of the big city', an appellation which betrayed a certain fellow-feeling in one who had spent much of his life as a vagrant of the conventional sort. 'Pimping', he observed further, was 'often only a transitional phase', rather like the artisan's tramping years, such as he had been through himself. Many of them, he claimed, eventually used their savings to set up as street-traders or to open a bar.[99] This pattern paralleled that of the lives of the women in their charge.

Ostwald's prejudices came through clearly in his claims about Berlin's pimps and their lifestyle, and much of what he wrote inevitably has to be taken with a good pinch of salt. His division of the world of pimps into innocent Berliners and rough, wicked outsiders does not convince, the more so since it was tinged with antisemitism (he thought that 20 per cent of Berlin's pimps were Jewish, against only 8 to 10 per cent of Berlin's prostitutes). Still less convincing was his attempt to argue that pimps were generally non-violent innocents corrupted by prostitutes with whom they fell in love. And there was plenty of evidence to connect them to the criminal underworld, for all his vehemence in refuting it. The notorious Heinze in Berlin was only one of many who clearly engaged in crime as a sideline, though relatively few pimps went as far as committing murder. The petty thieves who used the opportunity of the Hamburg suffrage riots of 17 January 1906 to raid the jewellery shops in the area where the disturbances took place also included a number of pimps.[100] The formal strictness of police controls over prostitution meant that most pimps devoted a large part of their energies to evading the law, and from here it was only a short step to breaking it. And while the social investigator Kurt Schneider was struck by the emotional warmth with which many of the prostitutes he interviewed in Cologne just before the First World War spoke of their 'Louis', there were surely quite a few such men, particularly lower down the social scale, who robbed and exploited the women, and treated them with the roughness and physical violence that were in any case common enough in working-class married life at this time.[101] Hans Ostwald, after all, reckoned that on average in Berlin there was one pimp to every five prostitutes, and while this undoubtedly meant that some girls worked on their own or in an organized brothel run by a madam, it must also have meant that many pimps lived off the earnings not of one prostitute but of two or three.[102] Police-regulated brothels altogether failed to reduce the number of pimps, even in a strictly regulated city such as Hamburg, because the extent of unregulated prostitution was so vastly greater. In 1896, for example, there were over 400 pimps on the files of the Hamburg Morals Police, who observed them closely but seemed unable in any way to curb their activities.[103] The numbers in Berlin must have been even greater. Even in smaller towns, pimps treated the Morals Police with open contempt. For instance, Joseph Kürper, serving a lengthy sentence for armed robbery in the late 1880s, told the prison chaplain Otto Fleischmann, that, when he had been a pimp in Mannheim some years before, he had found it all too easy to evade the attentions of the police. As far as the control of people like him was concerned, he said, it was clear 'that – at least in my day – the police were not in the slightest way equal to their task'.[104]

On the other hand, there seems no reason to distrust Ostwald's observation that many pimps had other, more legitimate sources of income besides prostitution. And his belief that police controls and the confinement of prostitutes to officially sanctioned brothels had no effect in reducing either the numbers or the importance of pimps was an interesting comment on one of the principal justifications commonly given by the police for these measures.[105] As one who for a long time lived on the semi-criminal margins of society himself, Ostwald was not inclined to demonize those whose lives he described in his work. His attempt to rescue the pimp from the status of a folk devil betrayed a strong gender bias, in which the women involved in prostitution were consistently described in more negative terms than the men. But the evident familiarity with the milieu which made him into something of a spokesman for such people also meant that some of his comments at least have to be taken seriously. Like other sources, Ostwald's writings make it clear enough that there was no justification in the common claim by defenders of police-regulated brothels that the system of regulation lowered crime rates and protected prostitutes and public alike by curbing the phenomenon of the pimp.

There is little doubt that the pimp was demonized into a kind of 'folk devil' in the moral panic of the early 1890s.[106] It was above all the Kaiser's stigmatization of these men which prompted the Prussian cabinet into putting a draft law before the Reichstag for the legalization of police-controlled brothels. The wording of the necessary amendment to Paragraph 180 of the Criminal Code caused some difficulty, since, as the Prussian Minister of Justice put it, such a step 'would superficially appear to be a legalization and facilitation of prostitution, and it would not be pleasant if this appeared to be a consequence of the All-Highest Decree.'[107] Moreover, the legislation, which became known as the Lex Heinze, ran into further trouble when it was debated in the Reichstag, for the original issue at stake quickly became obscured by an attempt on the part of the Catholic Centre Party to use the bill as a vehicle for the imposition of strong measures of censorship and repression against 'pornographic' art, literature and entertainment. In the ensuing uproar, which reached its climax only at the end of the century and resulted after a titanic struggle both within the Reichstag and without in the defeat of the bill, the original idea of curbing the activities of pimps by legalizing police-controlled brothels was virtually forgotten.[108]

The Failure of Regulation

Not only as far as pimps were concerned, but in other ways too, police regulations were unenforceable, and indeed largely unenforced. The detail in which they were composed was almost a confession of the extent of the police's impotence. Prostitutes were most frequently to be seen in the very streets, areas and institutions from which the regulations supposedly banned them. One writer noted in 1888 that 'the police edict of 1st July 1887, which banned the *demi-monde* from venturing upon the main traffic arteries of the great city, and at first seemed so terrible', had little effect beyond marginally reducing the 'shamelessness' of the prostitutes who plied their trade there.[109] On occasion, during a moral panic, usually inspired by political criticism of their system, the Morals Police did attempt to enforce the regulations strictly, as in Hamburg in 1894–95, following an attack launched on their operations by the Social Democratic leader August Bebel in the Reichstag. 27 brothels were closed for contravening the regulations by allowing the girls to tout for custom on the street outside, and 151 prostitutes were ordered to leave their lodgings for the same reason. Such purges were inevitably short-lived, however, and knowledgeable commentators all agreed that the police completely failed to enforce the rules on a long-term basis. In 1909, after renewed complaints, the Hamburg police acted again, issuing 222 official warnings and making 16 arrests. But the results were as transient and negligible as those of the previous purge in the mid-1890s.[110]

The strength of the Morals Police in most cities was pitifully inadequate for the proper exercise of the duties which the force was supposed to perform. In 1893–94, the number of officers in Hamburg's Morals Police was increased from 14 to 30, and by 1913 it had reached 46; but this was for a city which numbered 600,000 inhabitants in the early 1890s, over a million at the turn of the century, and a million and a half by the outbreak of the First World War. The increases altogether failed to keep up with the spread of casual and unregulated prostitution during this process of rapid urban growth.[111] Not only were the Morals Police failing to cope with the growth of casual prostitution – and there were said, implausibly perhaps, to be up to 200,000 prostitutes active in Germany at the turn of the century, a number which had supposedly increased to almost a third of a million by the outbreak of the First World War[112] – they were even by the 1890s failing to maintain control over the existing system of regulation itself. The police everywhere maintained strict rules about controlled prostitutes displaying themselves in public, yet, as a moderate Liberal newspaper, the *Hamburger Fremdenblatt*, reported on 20 December 1892:

> A charming nocturnal scene will unfold if one enters a street of the 'lost' in the evening after ten o'clock (frequently already after eight): 50 whores, one after the other, fall upon male passers-by, drag them by force into their house (often confiscating their hats as they do so), and swear and giggle without embarrassment on the street, until the call goes up: – 'the Morals!' – then all the windows with their white-painted lower panes (and what point is there in them?) are banged shut, and the guardian of morality marches at a measured pace through the now-silent alley, until he has turned the next corner, and the witches' Sabbath begins afresh.[113]

Not long after the turn of the century, the Berlin police in any case confessed themselves to be unwilling to enforce their regulations too rigorously, because the more difficult they made the situation of controlled prostitutes, the more prostitutes would be inclined to evade control altogether.[114] Moreover, the corruption and venality of the Morals Police were well known, and there were numerous and frequent cases of bribery, of which a notorious incident in Frankfurt-am-Main in 1914, when the head of the force was discovered to have been bribed by a madam to allow her to open a large brothel in a working-class area of the city, was only one of the most sensational.[115]

Police control was made more difficult by the fact that prostitutes seldom stayed in any one brothel for very long. In Hamburg each year, well over a thousand changes of address were registered – in 1863, for example, 1646, in 1866, 1294 – which meant that every officially controlled prostitute in the city changed her address twice a year on average. Moreover, many prostitutes took other employment and were deregistered. In 1862, for example, 610 new prostitutes were added to Hamburg's official register, and 573 were withdrawn. Of these, 234 were recorded as going home to their families, 159 left to become prostitutes elsewhere, 82 remained in Hamburg but were removed from the register, 78 absconded, nine married, ten died and one entered a 'Magdalens' Home' (thus underlining the numerical insignificance of 'rescue work' as far as registered prostitutes were concerned).[116] Similarly, a study of prostitution in Hanover at the turn of the century showed that over 200 of the 261 registered prostitutes surveyed had been registered for less than five years; 112 of them, indeed, for under 12 months, and 52 of these for less than three months. Most were reckoned to have left after a short period for other towns, to have obtained respectable jobs or to have married.[117] A similar pattern was recorded in Lübeck earlier in the nineteenth century, demonstrating that this was no new phenomenon. In 1843, Menzel's brothel in Lübeck, which generally employed between seven and eight girls at any one time, saw a typical turnover of prostitutes, with only one girl staying the whole year. Of those present on 1 January, one stayed six months, three left after four months, and one at the end of January. Six girls came and went at various points in the year, one staying a total of nine months, one eight, five four (one of them with a two-month gap in the middle of her stay), and one six. Four stayed for only a month. Of the eight prostitutes present at the end of the year, one had stayed the whole year, one had been there six months, one five, one four, one three, two two and one one month. Among those who left and did not return, one was said to have 'run away', two went to work in other brothels, and no fewer than ten were recorded simply as having 'left town'.[118] Schneider's study of the autobiographies of 70 prostitutes being treated in hospital in Cologne in 1913–14 showed that only one of them had been under police control for over ten years, five for between five and ten years, and three for between four and five years. The majority of them had only been registered prostitutes for a relatively short period – nine for between three and four years, 16 for two to three years, 20 for one to two years, and 16 for less than twelve months. The author's fear that few of them would ever be able to escape this lot was thus belied by his own statistics.[119] Many of the girls in the sample in Cologne expected their career of prostitution to end, just like a normal job, with marriage some time in their mid-to-late twenties (and 46 of the 70 women in the sample were under 25, 24 aged between 25 and 36).[120] And no doubt most of them, in Cologne as in other cities, did get married.

These figures suggest two conclusions. First, the idea that registered prostitutes were in any way imprisoned or forcibly confined in officially sanctioned brothels, as some contemporary critics maintained with their rhetoric of the 'white slave trade' and their attacks on regulated prostitution for encouraging it, is completely untenable.[121] Nobody ever troubled to ask the girls why they changed venue so frequently, but it can be surmised that it was not only because it was good for business, both for them and for brothel-keepers who wanted a constant supply of new prostitutes to satisfy clients' demands for variety, but also because it allowed the girls a degree of freedom to choose the conditions under which they worked. Brothel-keepers tried to counter this by keeping them constantly in debt for clothing, room rental and so on, but when these financial demands grew exorbitant, the girls seem to have had little hesitation in complaining to the authorities. Rather than produce permanent indebtedness, the most likely effect of the pecuniary demands of landlords was, the American investigator Abraham Flexner reported, to prevent prostitutes from accumulating any meaningful savings, despite the very large sums of money which a good proportion of them earned. The girls in one brothel in Bremen told him they needed to earn 10,000 Marks a year merely to survive, which, given average working-class earnings at the time, suggests that up to nine-tenths of what they earned went into other people's pockets.[122] In addition, brothels seem to have earned almost as much from the sale of drinks as from the sale of sex, which accounts for much of the disparity between what the prostitutes made and what the brothel-keepers pocketed. In Frankfurt-am-Main, for example, 'Madame' Bohnert, owner of a 16-room brothel in the Blücherstrasse, charged her girls an average of 15 Marks a day rent in 1914, which each of them could recover several times over in a single evening, enabling them to cover the cost of food and clothes and other living expenses; the sale of drinks must have netted 'Madame' Bohnert about 100 Marks a day in addition, which allowed her, among other things, to pay sweeteners to the Morals Police.[123] The girls could not have expected to save much on such an income, but neither could they be described as slaves.

Second, although claims made by prostitutes to the police that they were leaving to return home to their families must be treated with a degree of scepticism, it seems clear at least that it was not difficult for registered prostitutes to deregister if they wished to, and that many of them did in fact return, whether temporarily or permanently, to a life of relative 'respectability'. If this was true of those who were registered, then it was probably also true of those who, like 'Thymian Gotteball', were not; but the opportunities for achieving such 'respectability', of course, were likely to be strictly limited in scope. A return to the working-class or even petty-bourgeois milieu was one thing; going back unscathed to the world of the bourgeoisie was quite another. For someone like 'Thymian', who, it seems, could only have aspired to a life of middle-class propriety, marriage and a family were out of the question. However much such a woman might have been accepted as the companion of a wealthy old man in Nice or Monte Carlo, she would never have been accepted in any capacity in the polite society of Hamburg, Munich or Berlin, as the diary graphically demonstrated in recounting the failure of her career as a philanthropist once her background had been discovered. Yet if a former prostitute, registered or not, wished to return to a more modest style of life in due course, it certainly seems to have been possible. The ineffectiveness of the regulation system towards the end of the century, indeed, was underlined by the fact that the proportion of active prostitutes who were officially inscribed and confined to state-sanctioned brothels was small and in decline during this period. Some indication of the extent of illegal prostitution can be gained from arrest statistics. Following complaints from local inhabitants in 1898 that the Niedernstrasse and Steinstrasse, in one of Hamburg's run-down 'Alley Quarters', were being overrun with prostitutes, the Hamburg Morals Police set up a special watch in the area, and in the first 11 months of 1899 made 769 arrests for illegal prostitution. Such campaigns were inevitably short term, and intended as a deterrent or as a response to political circumstances, and achieved correspondingly meagre results. In 1897, there had only been 1654 arrests in the whole of Hamburg, so the fact that nearly half as many arrests were made in just two streets in a period of 11 months in 1899 gives some indication of the numbers of prostitutes operating illegally in the city – at least 3000 by the turn of the century, according to the best authority. This increased with the completion of the new main Hamburg railway station in 1905–06, which led to a rapid growth of unregulated prostitution in the nearby St Georg quarter. The spread of commercial entertainments, in the form of cheap concert-halls, dance-halls, *cafés chantants* and 'Viennese cafés' (whose number in Hamburg increased from seven in 1893 to 33 in 1899) also provided a growing variety of attractive, often up-market alternatives to the official brothel. In 1894, after complaints, the Hamburg police extended the licensing laws to cover 276 night cafés in which (supposedly) no alcohol was being sold. Fifty of these shut immediately, knowing they would not get a licence, and 36 more were closed down by the police. Beer-cellars also provided sexual services. In 1898 the Grand Beerhalls on the Spielbudenplatz, in St Pauli, were threatened with the loss of their licences if they did not expel the prostitutes who frequented their premises – 150 of them, according to one report. When the landlord reluctantly complied, his daily takings fell from 1000 to 250 Marks. The Hamburg police made over 700 arrests for prostitution in the first six months of 1898 in the Reeperbahn area, in response to complaints by the district's inhabitants, but were forced to admit that the prospects of effective control were minimal, and that the state of affairs in Hamburg was fast approaching that which existed in Berlin.[124]

In order to focus their resources more on combating illegal prostitution, the Hamburg Morals Police gradually closed down controlled brothels and concentrated the remaining ones in a smaller number of streets to allow easier supervision. From 1834 to 1874, the number of brothels sanctioned by the Morals Police had grown from 98 to 191, as the police kept faith with the idea that all prostitution in the city could and should be under their control. From this point onwards, however, they gradually abandoned this ambition. Between 1876 and 1879, police-concessioned brothels were removed from 11 streets in Hamburg, and in the latter year no fewer than 30 more were closed. By 1889 there was a total of 157 officially controlled brothels on only 16 streets in the city, and in 1895 police-supervised brothels were closed down in a further seven streets in the city.[125] The ineffectiveness of regulation was becoming apparent in other cities besides Hamburg too. In Frankfurt-am-Main, for instance, the brothels in the Rosengasse were closed down on 31 December 1913 and prostitutes allowed to live anywhere they chose thereafter; plans were simultaneously announced for the phased closure of all the other police-controlled brothels in the city at the same time, despite the protests of the landlords in the affected streets that they would not be able to rent or sell the vacated houses again, because of their immoral reputation.[126] 'In most cities', the American investigator Abraham Flexner concluded just before the First World War, 'regulation is moribund, and in many quite dead.' In 1909, for example, 140 women were inscribed at Munich, but during the same year the Munich Morals Police were keeping track of no fewer than 2076 'clandestine' prostitutes. The enrolment was thus less than 7 per cent of the total number of prostitutes known to the police, and even these were only a part of the whole.[127] In small and medium-sized towns, only a handful were registered by about 1908 or 1910: 45 in Mannheim, 63 in Karlsruhe, nine in Konstanz, nine in Baden-Baden (despite its reputation as a European centre for gambling), five in Freiburg and four in Pforzheim.[128] The vast majority in these towns operated outside police control. They had always done so everywhere. One estimate put the number of controlled prostitutes in Berlin in the mid-1850s at 300, and the number of those working clandestinely at no fewer than 6000.[129] The regulation system, one critic noted, was useless because it covered only a small fraction of the trade.[130] By 1870 the number of uncontrolled prostitutes in the city had grown to 20,000.[131] Just after the turn of the century, there were said to be 5000 prostitutes under police control in Berlin, 'some thousands more under observation as suspects', and between 30,000 and 50,000 operating outside the purview of the authorities.[132] In Hanover in the early 1900s it was estimated that only one in three to five prostitutes was under police control.[133] At the same time there were said to be 20 clandestine prostitutes for every controlled one in Cologne.[134] The truth was, as one Berlin prostitute told Flexner, 'only the stupid ones get registered'.[135] Here too, therefore, the experience of 'Thymian Gotteball', an intelligent woman who had no difficulty at all in evading the attentions of the police, seems to have been fairly typical.

Legal Problems and Community Protest

The problems of regulation were increased by the new legal situation which came in with the Reich Criminal Code of 1871. The state regulation of prostitution had been introduced to many German towns and cities by the French during the revolutionary and Napoleonic Wars or under the impact of the French example at roughly the same time. In Hamburg, for example, it was established in 1807,[136] while in Prussia it had been effectively allowed by Paragraphs 996–1026 of the General Law Code of 1794.[137] It had stayed in place until mid-century, when liberal pressure had led to its abandonment in Berlin in 1846 and its outlawing by the Prussian Criminal Code of 1851, ignored temporarily under the authoritarian regime of Berlin's police chief Carl von Hinckeldey in the reactionary 1850s.[138] The law of 1871, following this precedent, laid down imprisonment for anyone who provided through his own agency an opportunity for the exercise of prostitution and so countenanced and furthered it. The annexation of the province of Schleswig-Holstein to Prussia after the war of 1870 and its consequent subjection to the existing Prussian Code led to demands from Berlin for the closure of brothels in the province. The police in one of the province's major towns, Altona, which had hitherto followed the strict reglementary practice of the neighbouring city-state of Hamburg, contested the view in Berlin, and noted with alarm 'that the introduction of the Prussian Criminal Code must have the consequence that all the brothels in Altona which have hitherto been tolerated will be closed'. They observed that a form of reglementation had existed during the police regime of Carl von Hinckeldey even in Berlin under the 1851 Criminal Code, and took the view 'that the continued existence of police-sanctioned brothels in the province of Schleswig-Holstein cannot be ruled out under the provisions of the Criminal Code'.[139] In fact, the regime in Berlin had been changed in 1857 as a result of being in conflict with the Criminal Code, so the extension of the Code to Altona now led to 'peculiar conflicts' with the local police.[140] Moreover, the police in Kiel complained that the Prussian-appointed state prosecutor was constantly bringing the landlords of police-approved brothels before the courts under Paragraph 180, and even if the situation did lead judges to deal with the guilty parties leniently, it was still a considerable source of embarrassment. The local Morals Police gave in and closed the brothels in 1876, though they quietly reopened them three years later, no doubt after lengthy discussions with the state prosecutor.

Another German state annexed to Prussia, the former kingdom of Hanover, conquered in the war of 1866, also had to close its state-regulated brothels, as did Frankfurt-am-Main after its absorption into Prussia in 1867. Legal difficulties also led to the closure of police-approved brothels in Dortmund in 1873, Cologne in 1880, Erfurt in 1885 and Leipzig in 1889.[141] Some towns, like Bremen, where a single street was maintained with accommodation for 52 prostitutes under the supervision of the Morals Police, quietly disregarded Paragraph 180 and appealed to another clause in the Reich Criminal Code, Paragraph 361 Clause 6, which empowered the police to arrest and subject to medical examination any woman suspected of being a prostitute, claiming that the creation of supervised brothels was the only way that this could be done. Some, as in the grand duchy of Baden, found a way round the law 'by permitting several female persons who have been placed under police supervision by Paragraph 361 Clause 6 of the Reich Criminal Code to live together in the same house'.[142] But other Morals Police forces ran into trouble from civil servants and politicians in adopting this tactic. In Dresden, for instance, the chief of police complained that he had been prevented from confining prostitution to particular houses and streets by the opposition of officials in the Saxon Ministry of the Interior.[143]

More common, however, was opposition from ordinary citizens. Complaints from neighbours were a frequent cause of the closure of brothels, often on the grounds that there were children living in the street. The inhabitants of a street containing a brothel in Lübeck in 1862 objected to the excesses in particular of the public prostitution in which the inhabitants of the house allow themselves to indulge in the full light of day, together with the impudent advances and insults with which they approach passers-by, and finally the loud noise which they cause during the night, which indeed spills over onto the street because it has up to now been left out of the gas-lighting system in the town.[144]

In Bremen, neighbours of the state-controlled brothels in the Helenenstrasse were also increasingly hostile to their continued presence in the neighbourhood.[145] Property-owners in the south German town of Mannheim successfully objected to brothels operating in adjacent houses quoting the Civil Code introduced in 1900. Attempts by the local police to transfer the trade to a new working-class housing estate created 'a tremendous uproar in the Neckar suburb', the affected area, and the move was stopped. 'It has now become difficult for the whores to find somewhere to live,' noted the Baden government: 'the neighbourhood regards itself as very easily disadvantaged both in the value attaching to its property and indeed in its entire way of life.'[146]

Complaints by irate neighbours were sometimes backed up by radical-liberal opponents of the state regulation system. Such people managed to secure a judgment against the Hamburg authorities, after a lengthy series of court hearings, in 1876, when the Federal Council told the Hamburg Senate that it had to close the brothels or face prosecution under Paragraph 180.[147] The prospect of eminently respectable merchant Senators being hauled before the courts on a charge of procuring was sufficiently remote for the Hamburg police to feel safe in stopping at removing the drinks concessions from all brothels and changing the wording of their regulations, calling the brothel-keepers 'landlords' instead of 'owners', although their protests that they had no relationship with these people were unconvincing: the brothel-keepers were in fact one of the most important elements in Hamburg's system of control. Sometimes the Social Democrats supported local protests too. In Frankfurt-am-Main, a proposal in 1912 by the Morals Police to open 17 new brothels in the Gneisenaustrasse, near the main railway station, led to a protest meeting attended by 2000 working men of the area – women were excluded because the topic was deemed unsuitable for them to discuss in public. The protesters complained, in language that made it clear that the Social Democratic Party had had a hand in composing the document, 'that the exercise of public immorality is to be confined and approved in our part of town on the initiative of unscrupulous capitalists.' The protest was followed by a petition, and a debate was held in the Frankfurt town council. As a result, the scheme was dropped.[148] Such local protests had become a force to be reckoned with by the eve of the First World War. The fact that the authorities located brothels in working-class districts offended the respectable, usually steadily employed family men who formed the Social Democratic rank-and-file. Far from prostitution and left-wing politics being allied, as conservatives liked to argue, they were often bitterly opposed. Quite apart from the intrusion which police-controlled brothels represented into working-class everyday life, with their police raids and patrols, checks on drinks licences, visitors from outside the district and so on, the presence of prostitutes also offended the respectable morality to which the Social Democrats adhered, and which led them to claim, quite falsely as we have seen, that working-class men never used the services of prostitutes themselves.[149]

Moral Entrepreneurs and Feminist Campaigners

The division of opinion on the prostitution question in Imperial Germany to some extent cut across conventional political cleavages and alignments. The state-controlled Protestant Church, for example, though it was socially conservative and politically closely identified with the Wilhelmine monarchy, was critical of the police regulation of prostitution on the grounds that it gave the official approval of an allegedly Christian state to the maintenance of immorality and vice. At the same time, it was strongly in support of the pornography clauses of the Lex Heinze. The Kaiser's support for regulation rather inhibited the Church as such from taking a stand on the issue, but its views were made known by the General Conference of the German Morality Associations, an organization consisting mainly of lower middle-class Protestants, particularly schoolteachers, with a sprinkling of Catholics as well. Women were again excluded for reasons of delicacy. The Morality Associations formed an extra-parliamentary pressure-group of the kind which was growing in importance in the German political system towards the end of the nineteenth century. They were part of a widespread self-mobilization of the radicalized petty bourgeoisie, highly conservative on the one hand, but increasingly critical of the authorities for what they perceived as their weakness in upholding social stability, public morality and national pride on the other. Their leader, Pastor Ludwig Weber, was an ex-army officer and follower of the former court preacher and antisemitic demagogue Adolf Stöcker. In his autobiography, Weber wrote that his main purpose in life had been the defeat of socialism. He believed that the state had an important role to play as the moral educator of the working classes. If prostitution, along with 'immoral' plays, 'dirty' books and 'indecent' art, were stamped out, an important step would have been taken towards neutralizing the influence of Social Democracy and winning over the proletariat to the side of what Weber thought of as the national interest.[150]

For men like Weber, prostitution, as revealed by the Heinze affair, symbolized the threat of social disorder and political upheaval posed by the great cities and the growth of the urban proletariat. Immorality, the undermining of the family and the sexual emancipation of women were all part of this general social threat. Prostitutes were instruments of the Devil, immoral seductresses whom the state had the duty not to control but to persecute. Even before they united to form the Conference in 1888, individual Morality Associations had launched a number of attacks on the police toleration of prostitution, for example in Brunswick, Krefeld and Mühlhausen. In 1891, the leaflet which they issued on the occasion of the Heinze trial, printed in an edition of 65,000 and entitled *The Struggle against Immorality*, declared that Germany would follow Babylon, Assyria, ancient Greece, the Roman Empire and (of course) France into the ruin and collapse brought about by sexual immorality unless the German people rallied behind Jesus Christ to resist the works of the Devil.[151] The police, the pamphlet urged, should arrest, imprison or deport anyone they came across plying the ungodly trade of prostitution, instead of tacitly condoning it, as they were doing through the system of regulation. If women could control themselves, so should men, and the latter should therefore be punished by the law if they failed to.[152] To suggest that men were unable to control themselves was to reduce them to the level of animals. 'With the dying-out of chastity, all sense of law, all strength, all feelings of community and sacrifice perish as well.' A total police ban was the only solution.[153] This should be combined, as another conservative opponent of regulation added, with rigorous Christian education to encourage morality, especially among young girls, and discourage ideas of female emancipation and independence.[154] Clerical authorities were united in condemning sexual immorality, and a state which claimed to be Christian should not condone it.[155] Here, therefore, was another influence in bringing about the decline of police regulation in the Wilhelmine period.

This hostile stance towards both the police regulation of prostitution and the women it affected was shared by the Youth Protection Association, founded in Berlin by a woman, Hanna Bieber-Böhm, in 1888, the same year as the all-male Conference of German Morality Associations. An active feminist, Bieber-Böhm won the support of a wide variety of women's associations for the tireless campaigns which she waged throughout the 1890s. A petition she presented to the Berlin chief of police in 1895 demanded among other things the abolition of state-regulated brothels, the deportation of all foreign prostitutes and the imprisonment of all other prostitutes, including first offenders, for between one and three years. Women's prisons were to be reformed and special departments established to deal with the prostitutes and educate them into moral respectability. The Association also attempted preventive measures such as the founding of homes, clubs and recreational associations for female domestic servants, who, it considered, provided the main reservoir of recruitment for prostitution – a view which reflected among other things the fact that virtually all the bourgeois women who supported the Association were themselves employers of domestic servants and were anxious to exert as much control as they could over their lives.[156] Socially a cut above the Morality Associations, Bieber-Böhm's organization also had a distinctive feminist slant, as it asserted the right of respectable women to stand up in public and discuss sexual issues previously thought too indelicate to be mentioned in female company. Bieber-Böhm herself was a moving spirit in the foundation of the national feminist movement, the Federation of German Women's Associations, in 1894 and a leading figure in its campaigns for the rest of the decade. She did much to persuade the initially reluctant feminists that it was right and proper for them to take a stand on such matters in public.[157] Like many feminists of the time, she believed strongly that men should adopt the same standards of moral and sexual restraint as were conventionally expected of women; and her Association embarked on a campaign of public education along these lines, petitioning the Kaiser for example to provide sexual education courses for his troops which would aim to persuade them that the only way to stay healthy was to avoid sexual intercourse.[158]

While the Youth Protection Association differed from the Morality Associations in its insistence that women's voices should be heard on the issue of prostitution, and in its downplaying of the emphasis on religious regeneration and the fight against social disorder which was so central to the ideas of Pastor Weber, Bieber-Böhm shared with her male counterpart the fundamental assumption that prostitutes were wicked and immoral and should be punished if they refused to reform. It was precisely this assumption that aroused the wrath of a new and more radical generation of feminists who came to the fore towards the end of the 1890s. Led initially by Anita Augspurg and Käthe Schirmacher, both of whom had come into contact with British campaigners against the state regulation of prostitution while studying abroad, the new feminists were followers of Josephine Butler, who had led a successful campaign for the abolition of regulation in Britain in the 1880s. Butler had gone on to found an International Abolitionist Federation – the title of the German branch coyly avoided saying what the federation wanted to abolish – and in 1898, as the debate over the Lex Heinze reached its final and most widely publicized stages, Augspurg, Schirmacher and others founded a German branch. Like Butler, they believed that the state regulation of prostitution was an official endorsement of a dual standard of morality for men and women, for the male clients got off scott-free while it was the prostitutes who paid the price for men's lustfulness. The Abolitionists saw prostitutes as victims, and believed that if state regulation were abolished and men educated into self-restraint, the double standard would disappear and women would no longer be forced into prostitution through their own poverty and through men's lack of control over their own sexual impulses.[159]

Abolitionists such as Lida Gustava Heymann argued passionately for a single standard of sexual restraint. 'You should only ever have sex', she told a class of female high-school graduates in 1902, 'within marriage. Extra-marital intercourse often brings diseases with it; you cannot paint the consequences black enough.' She warned the girls in graphic terms to resist the advances of male seducers:

Male flatterers will address you on the street, ask you to drink a glass of beer with them, give you presents afterwards, pretend to be in love with you, lead you onto the dance-floor, into cheap variety shows and dubious restaurants. You will also be offered wine, and anyone who isn't used to it will soon get drunk and no longer know what they are doing. – Seducer and seduced, both in a state of intoxication, both aroused to the utmost, have sexual intercourse with one another. If the man is diseased, he will infect the girl.

Pregnancy would be another inevitable consequence of the encounter, she warned, and the seducer would equally inevitably abandon both mother and child and leave them to fend for themselves. As a result, she went on remorselessly, the mother would be forced into prostitution and the police would confine her to a brothel.[160] Heymann's narrative fell firmly into the pattern painted on a larger canvas in the *Diary of a Lost Woman*, the paradigmatic life-history of the 'fallen woman'. No doubt its dire warnings impressed many of her youthful listeners with its powerful insistence that it was women rather than men who paid the costs of extra-marital sexual intercourse. But the conventions of propriety which governed public life in Imperial Germany still prevented feminists like Heymann from speaking directly to the real addressees of their message of self-restraint – men. They were forced to watch helplessly as a debate in the Reichstag, sparked by their campaign, degenerated into an unseemly hilarity which showed, as one of them bitterly remarked, 'that a large section of the male population of Germany does not possess the moral maturity or the moral earnestness to treat such questions with the dignity they deserve.'[161]

For these feminists, prostitution was a symbol of the powerlessness of women in the society of their time. Liberal opponents of regulation earlier in the century had on occasion remarked that 'the brothel system is . . . only a consequence of the peculiar position of the female sex in general',[162] but the Abolitionists went beyond this general perception. The problem in their view was not that police regulation effectively confined prostitutes to 'restricted areas' in any literal sense – as we have seen, this was self-evidently not the case. The problem was that by creating such an elaborate set of rules and regulations, however seldom they were enforced, the police gave themselves the power to intervene arbitrarily in the lives of Germany's female citizens when they thought any of them was overstepping the invisible lines laid down by social and sexual convention. A prostitute walking up and down a major thoroughfare such as the Jungfernstieg in Hamburg or Friedrichsstrasse or Unter den Linden in Berlin, or plying her trade in a well-known restaurant or café, could perhaps feel that the possibility of arrest was an occupational hazard, that it was worth taking the risk, since arrests in these areas were rare enough events in practice. Any other woman on her own in these areas, however, was also at risk: exposed to the gaze of men trying to decide whether she was a prostitute or not, observed by the Morals Police if they were around and made to feel that they should not be there without a male chaperone. These, it is important to remember, were not out-of-the-way 'red light districts' but major thoroughfares, the central arteries of the urban public sphere. Thus regulation facilitated in the most direct possible way the intimidatory exercise of the male claim to monopolize this public sphere.[163]

It was precisely this claim that the feminists were contesting. 'I know', declared one of them in a public meeting in 1902,

> that one cannot go out on one's own in Hamburg. In Hamburg as in the other big cities of Germany, one cannot go on one's way unmolested. My acquaintances, highly respectable ladies, are often molested on the street as they make their way back home in the evening from the offices where they have been delivering their work, and Frau Louise Zietz has said in a public women's meeting here this very week that one cannot even be safe from uniformed police officers in the evening; on two occasions, she herself was molested in the most obscene manner by constables when she was out late in the evening.[164]

Louise Zietz was in fact a well-known organizer and speaker in the Social Democratic women's movement, who was subsequently to gain a seat on the party executive, so there may well have been some special political animus behind the police's behaviour towards her. Nevertheless, the general point stood. Even in the small towns of Baden, there were complaints in 1910 'that a respectable woman cannot walk along the streets any more at all in the evening or at night, without being molested . . . first by men . . . but also . . . by police officers.'[165] Radical feminist campaigners in Bremen attacked the regulation of prostitution in a similar way as a symbol of the regulation of women in general. Petitioning the city's ruling body, the Senate, in 1909, they portrayed prostitutes as victims of discrimination by men – whether police or clients – and criticized the dangerous medical treatments, often involving the forced application of mercury or arsenic remedies for venereal disease, to which they were subjected.[166] The growing independence of women in everyday life in Imperial Germany, presaging the much more far-reaching developments which were to take place in the Weimar Republic, was thus another influence behind the contestation of the police regulation of prostitution.

Feminists such as Augspurg linked police regulation not only to the subordination of women and the attempt to exclude them from the public sphere, but also to the dominance of an effete and immoral system of aristocratic and militaristic values in Imperial Germany. They took a radical stance on a whole number of other issues, from women's suffrage (not previously demanded by the women's movement in Germany) to imperialism, peace and democracy. The Abolitionists objected to the fact that prostitutes were punished and degraded, but 'not the men of the upper ten thousand' who patronized them. They expressed a notable degree of solidarity with the working-class women who formed the overwhelming majority of prostitutes under police control.[167] In taking this line, they placed themselves close to the political stance of the Social Democrats, who, as we have seen, regarded prostitution as an aspect of the social exploitation characteristic of capitalist society. Indeed, the radicalism of their campaigns was in every way as dynamic as that of the Social Democrats'. In Hamburg, led by Lida Gustava Heymann, the Abolitionists filed a series of lawsuits against the police under Paragraph 180 of the Criminal Code, backing this up with well-publicized mass public meetings. The Senate retaliated by prohibiting them from holding any further public assemblies, only lifting the ban in 1908. The ban led to a debate in the Reichstag, in which left-wing Liberals and Social Democrats joined in condemning the actions of the senate and the evils of regulation. Yet although they mounted similar campaigns in Baden, in Bremen and in Frankfurt-am-Main, and although they won the backing of the mainstream women's movement, ousting Bieber-Böhm from its leading circles in the process, the Abolitionists, perhaps unsurprisingly, failed to make any real headway in practical, legislative terms. Reich Chancellor and Prussian Minister-President Bernhard von Bülow spoke for many in authority when, he declared in 1908 that the traditional method of regulation was the best one. According to an official memorandum:

> The Minister-President gave it as his personal opinion that a satisfactory solution of the prostitution question would only be able to be achieved by the reintroduction of state-regulated brothels. Anyone who had lived abroad for a long time as he had would take a different line of thought on precisely this question than the current leading speakers in women's associations, synods, etc. In France, for example, where the brothels are minutely controlled by the police, such scandalous scenes as exist in Berlin, on the Friedrichstrasse, are unknown. However, he knew well enough at the moment that in view of the dominant prejudices, the introduction of state-controlled brothels could not be contemplated over here.[168]

Thus the Abolitionists did at least – along with the Morality Associations and the churches – create a climate of opinion in which no official attempt was made after the Lex Heinze to stop the continued decline of regulation or to amend Paragraph 180 of the Criminal Code. And they did succeed in sparking a widespread public debate on the issue of prostitution, and in persuading many people to regard prostitutes as victims rather than as perpetrators. It was this debate, indeed, which doubtless inspired Margarete Böhme to publish the *Diary of a Lost Woman* and which conditioned the massive and in general favourable public response which the book generated.[169]

Narratives of Sexual Deviance

By the time of the *Diary*'s appearance in 1905, the climate of the debate on prostitution was already beginning to change. Within the feminist movement, the 'radicals' were beginning to move towards a more sexually libertarian position under the influence of the sexual reformer Helene Stöcker. By 1908 they were campaigning for the abolition of Paragraph 218 of the Criminal Code and the consequent legalization of abortion, for the recognition of equal rights for unmarried mothers and for the acceptance that women as well as men had the right to sexual fulfilment. This not only undermined their previous arguments on prostitution, it also called forth increasingly vociferous opposition from 'moderate' feminists who felt that this was all going too far. In 1908, an attempt to commit the Federation of German Women's Associations to campaigning against Paragraph 218 was defeated at its annual general meeting, and soon the 'radicals' were being marginalized on this and other issues within the movement. They had in any case always been a minority in the feminist movement. In many towns, the 'moderates' had remained in control and had taken a very different line towards prostitution and its regulation. In Hanover, for instance, under the influence of the conservative Protestant women's movement, led by Paula Müller, who was to become a far-right member of the Reichstag in the Weimar Republic, the feminists had emphasized rescue homes and work schemes to prevent young women from falling into prostitution by training them for employment as domestic servants. While opposed to strict police regulation, they had studiously avoided portraying the prostitutes as innocent victims of uncontrolled male sexuality, and had co-operated closely with the municipal authorities in their rescue work. Their campaign of 1906 against a proposed tightening of the regulations governing state-controlled brothels was based on an increasing tendency to combat 'social degeneration' and gave rise in 1908 to the formation of the Cartel to Combat Public Moral Decay, in which the 'moderate' feminists were prominently represented, focusing on suppressing the sale of 'immoral literature' (including satirical magazines such as *Simplicissimus*) in local bookstores, putting pressure on local newspapers not to carry advertisements for abortionists and checking local art exhibitions for paintings which it considered unsuitable for children. The majority of Abolitionists in Hanover betrayed a marked reluctance to use the issue as a symbol of female oppression, and asserted that respectable women had nothing to fear on the street; a view which found the approval of a group of prostitutes who petitioned the police to be allowed to walk the streets between 11 pm and 3 am instead of being confined to brothels; at such a time, they said, respectable women never went out without an escort anyway. Unlike the 'radicals' in Bremen and Hamburg, therefore, the majority of 'moderate' feminists in Germany never showed much solidarity either with prostitutes or with working-class women in general; the creation of a united 'female cultural sphere', which some German feminist historians have seen as the principal feminist project of the Wilhelmine period, was always something of a myth.[170]

The growing influence of eugenics and Social Darwinism in German political culture also brought about a reorientation of the Abolitionist Federation, which by 1910 had been purged of its most radical libertarian elements. Persuaded by the propaganda of the German Society for the Combating of Venereal Diseases (founded in 1902) that the main problem posed by prostitution lay not in its degradation of women but in the threat it posed to the hereditary health of the German race through its role in spreading syphilis and gonorrhoea, the Abolitionists began to espouse a form of 'neo-regulationism' which took them further and further away from their fellow-Abolitionists in other countries. By the eve of the First World War they were campaigning not for the abolition of police regulation in the name of sexual equality, but for the introduction of prison sentences for anyone who had sexual intercourse knowing that they were infected with a sexually transmittable disease, a measure which of course implied a strong police control over prostitution and differed from the line formerly taken by Hanna Bieber-Böhm and the Morality Associations only in that it applied to male customers as well as to the women who served them. By 1910, there was a wider measure of agreement in government circles that control of venereal disease was the prime purpose of the police control of prostitution, and that the authorities – as the Minister of the Interior in the Grand Duchy of Baden declared – had the duty to arrest and medically examine all prostitutes, not just those under police control.[171] This policy was actually formally adopted by the German state during the First World War, backed up with further measures permitting the military authorities to register as a prostitute any woman known to have had sexual intercourse with more than one man (even without having demanded payment for it).[172]

The trend towards neo-regulationism which already made itself felt before the First World War reflected wider changes in attitudes towards criminality and deviance. The debate on penal policy was moving away from the more or less liberal idea which had been dominant for much of the nineteenth century of setting the punishment to fit the crime, and towards the idea that it was the criminal, not the offence, that should form the focal point of society's concern. Criminality was thought of increasingly as the product not of poverty, poor education or immoral influences, but of hereditary degeneracy. The idea of basing penal policy on deterrence was suited only to a rationalistic conception of human nature. If offenders were driven by hereditary forces beyond their control, then deterrence was useless. Social investigators and criminal anthropologists turned towards the detailed study of offenders' family trees and milieus, and discovered the existence of whole clans of deviants, whose refusal to conform to social norms they now ascribed to blood rather than morality. Such an idea bore a striking resemblance to

Avé-Lallement's view earlier in the century that the criminal underworld was largely the product of racial influences; but these influences were now sought not just in the role of Jews and gypsies in crime (though there were those who considered it to be just as important as Avé-Lallement had) but also in the insidious influence of degenerative factors within the German race as well. Penal policy began to be assimilated to 'racial hygiene'; and a legal model of criminality gave way increasingly to a medical and eugenic one.[173] In the debate on prostitution, the 'folk devil' of the pimp was increasingly portrayed as a racially degenerate or even alien figure, as attention shifted towards the role of the 'white slave trade', in which Jews and foreigners, especially from Eastern Europe, were alleged to play a particularly prominent part.[174]

With the emergence of this new penal discourse, it was not surprising that attitudes towards prostitutes began to change once more. The Minister of the Interior in the Grand Duchy of Baden reflected a widespread view among governments when he remarked in 1910 'that we are dealing in the cases of the great majority of these poor creatures with beings who are neither mentally nor morally normal' – a 'fact', he added, 'which is confirmed by many experts'.[175] Even the Abolitionists were coming to regard them in the last few years before the First World War as hereditarily tainted and degenerate. From this point of view, the narrative trajectory of the *Diary of a Lost Woman*, indeed, encapsulated a wider social trajectory; the decline and fall of an individual into prostitution, disease and death echoed the larger processes of decline and fall played out in the chain of heredity to which the prostitute was thought to belong. The prostitute became an object of medical, psychological and social investigation designed to pinpoint the exact nature, extent and origins of her social degeneracy. It was this spirit of enquiry that gave rise to projects such as that of the psychologist Kurt Schneider, with his belief that the prostitutes to whom he talked were mostly pathological degenerates with no hope of living a normal life. It was still a long way from here to the incarceration in concentration camps, forced sterilization and involuntary 'euthanasia' in the gas-chambers of asylums like Grafeneck and Hartheim which was to be their fate under the Third Reich. But the brief moment of social sympathy which they had experienced during the Feminist campaigns of the early 1900s, and which had been expressed both in the first-person narrative of the *Diary of a Lost Woman* and in the widespread and positive popular reception which the book had enjoyed, was not to be repeated.

During the Weimar Republic, to be sure, the *Diary* was filmed by the well-known director G.W. Pabst, with a script by Rudolf Leonhardt, which deviated in a number of respects from the written narrative. The role of Thymian was played by the popular American actress Louise Brooks. It received a couple of moderately favourable reviews. But the film's licence for commercial release, granted on 24 August 1929, was revoked on 5 December the same year by the Higher Film Examination Board of Berlin after protests from a number of Church organizations, women's societies and welfare agencies dealing with the prevention of prostitution. The censors took exception to the contrast between the film's negative portrayal of the girls' home from which Thymian escapes with the aid of Count Osdorff and its positive depiction of the brothel into whose practices the Count initiates her. They agreed with the protesters – many of them organizations devoted to running girls' homes themselves – that this contrast was likely to have a demoralizing effect on impressionable members of the cinema audience.

> The film illustrates life in a brothel very clearly, and not at all in a repulsive and therefore deterrent manner, and portrays it as easy, nice, comfortable and thus tempting and desirable . . . The Board has . . . confirmed in numerous decisions that an immoral effect is to be ascribed to a portrayal of a life of prostitution as something given, pleasant and easily to be thrown off, without such a life being shown as reprehensible and the prostitute's return to a respectable existence as one accompanied by many difficulties and disappointments. Herein an incitement to irresponsibility, sexual self-surrender and abandonment of morality must be seen, which will have the effect of robbing above all morally uncertain female spectators.[176]

Here the authorities were objecting to the representation of prostitution as in any way a positive choice made by women who engaged in it. More strikingly still, however, they were obviously outraged by the idea that women could move in and out of prostitution and work in a brothel, and cross the boundary between respectable society and the sexual underworld at will. Prostitution was not to be portrayed as something 'easily to be thrown off'. Respectable society continued to draw a sharp line between itself and the world of the deviant, whatever the reality might be, and in so doing, contributed itself to making that line harder to cross.

Pabst's film was only the latest in a long series of reworkings of the life-histories of prostitutes. Indeed, the original *Diary of a Lost Woman*, far from being a genuine prostitute's diary, was the invention of its 'editor', Margarete Böhme. To be sure, Böhme reproduced two handwritten pages of the 'manuscript' of the diary at the end of the book, in order to lend it an air of verisimilitude,[177] and the London *Times*, no less, pronounced of the English translation: 'There seems no doubt of the authenticity of this diary of a "lost" woman.'[178] However, by describing the sequel, *Dida Ibsen's Story*, explicitly as a 'novel', Böhme implicitly conceded the fictionality of its predecessor as well. The implication was there, too, in her confession in the *Diary*'s Foreword that she had originally intended 'after a while to rework the contents as a novel', but had been persuaded not to 'on the advice of my publisher, Herr Fontane'.[179] Many of Böhme's 30 other novels had a similar theme – the desperate situation of a woman ostracized by polite society as the result of a moral lapse, an illegitimate child or a divorce – and the polished language and carefully measured structure of the *Diary* mark it out as another of her literary compositions rather than a document she had come across written by some-one else. The fact remains that even in 1905, it was safer for Böhme to publish a book such as the *Diary* as if it were a document, rather than to risk damnation as immoral by admitting that she had written it herself. Such a reputation would then have attached itself to Böhme's other works – she was a well-known popular novelist of the day – with correspondingly disastrous results for sales. The widespread debate on prostitution, inspired largely by the Feminists, beginning in the early 1900s, would have suggested the topic. The two or three paragraphs of the *Diary* that were about prostitution in general could have been based on any one of the numerous social investigations published in this period. The confinement of the book's action to largely bourgeois milieus, its absence of any attempt to portray a real brothel and its refusal to go into any detail about the everyday life of the prostitute except in public pick-up places such as the opera testified to Böhme's personal ignorance of all of this, and reflected her wise decision to stick to scenarios with which she herself was familiar.

Böhme's narrative was only one of a number of contesting versions of prostitution in the early twentieth century, ranging from the Protestant portrayal of the prostitute as inherently wicked, corrupting and seductive, through the 'social hygienist' tale of the prostitute as a hereditary degenerate, to the Abolitionist version of innocent working-class women corrupted by male lust and police authoritarianism or the closely related Social Democratic vision which substituted capitalism and the bourgeoisie for men and the police. In the mid-nineteenth century, indeed, some commentators, as we have seen, viewed almost all working-class women as prostitutes. This con-trasted strongly with the predominant view at the turn of the century. By this time, prostitutes were generally regarded as a minority. Whether they were seen as symbolic female victims of male oppression or as eugenically tainted members of a hereditary class of deviants made little difference to this fact.[180] Böhme's narrative cleverly combined a number of these genres, organizing the events of Thymian Gotteball's life around the traditional motifs of the 'fall' of an innocent girl brought about by male lust and social prejudice, going on to show the knowing and cynical amorality that she displays after she has embarked on her life of prostitution, and ending with an element of moral regeneration in her love for the doctor and in the sympathetic language she uses about the elderly companion of the last phase of her career. By making the heroine of her novel middle-class, Böhme allowed her readers to identify with her in a way that would have been far more difficult had she located her, more plausibly, in the proletarian milieu from which the vast majority of prostitutes came. Throughout her narrative, a sharply ironic light is cast on the morals and mores of the 'respectable' society which it is

Böhme's principal purpose to criticize. The average reader, as a member of this society, would have found it difficult to come away from the novel without having gained a more critical perspective on the values by which that society and its members lived.

Conclusion

The French philosopher Michel Foucault argued that the nineteenth century saw the emergence of a 'carceral society' in which deviance from bourgeois norms became increasingly difficult, and surveillance by the police and other institutions became all-pervasive. Early modern penal practice, he claimed, had been based on making public examples of isolated offenders as a means of symbolically asserting the authority of the state. At the same time, society had many areas of tolerated illegality. The spectacle of physical punishment, at the pillory or the scaffold, often provided the occasion for the self-assertion of the common people in a saturnalian outburst of carnivalesque revelry. Round about the end of the eighteenth century, however, the European state began an ambitious project of making punishment more effective. Imprisonment, with its emphasis on breaking the offender's will through solitary confinement, the rule of silence, isolation from the outside world, hard labour and the treadmill, replaced the public mutilation of the body as the prime form of punishment. Areas of tolerated illegality were shut down; opportunities for the people to assert themselves were removed. The principle of equality before the law reduced everyone to a position ripe for investigation by the new classificatory sciences of psychiatry and criminology, like butterflies labelled and pinned to a board. New police forces, using a range of tactics from elaborate requirements for identity papers and registers of former offenders to undercover detectives, spies and *agents provocateurs*, infiltrated society until there were no zones of free action remaining. This economy of surveillance and control aimed to create a regimented proletariat that would be a disciplined and calculable instrument of industrial capitalism. Foucault argued that the new discourse of punishment and control divided the majority of the emerging proletariat from a deliberately created substratum of the marginal and the deviant, whose lives were to be lived within a world of totalizing institutions, from the orphanage and the workhouse to the asylum and the penitentiary. Incarceration and the threat of institutionalization became the means by which the whole of society was disciplined; power was devolved from the sovereign on to society at large, so that everybody supervised each other, internalizing the new scientific discourse of conformity and deviance so that they also, in the end, came to supervise themselves.[1]

Foucault's interpretation of the emergence of the modern police and penal systems was influential not least because it helped historians get away from the old liberal, optimistic history of punishment, which saw it in simple terms of a march from barbarism to humanitarianism, led by a dedicated band of enlightened reformers. It facilitated a more sophisticated, more critical view of the history of crime and punishment and contained some acute observations of the controlling impetus behind many of the institutions which it described. And in the German context, it helped give the lie to the argument, advanced in the 1970s, that liberal penal reformers were humanitarians whose relative failure helped perpetuate a harsh penal regime which other societies in Europe had long since abandoned. Foucault, indeed, laid bare a dark, bleak aspect of nineteenth-century liberalism which was much in evidence in the penal proposals of men like Carl Mittermaier, who was both a leading opponent of the death penalty and a leading advocate of solitary confinement, anonymity, silence and discipline within the prison.

At the same time, however, Foucault was not really interested in explaining why the discursive shift which he charted took place. His work evaded the question of agency: he said little or nothing about the forces which brought about change in penal practice. He presented the new carceral discourse as a unified body of language, ignoring the ways in which it was itself the site of contradiction and dispute. And he failed to address the possibility that the discursive shift was resisted from below.[2] Foucault wrote his work on crime and punishment in the early 1970s, at a moment when he was caught up in the disintegration of the radical impulses of 1968 and in a temporary shift of the far left towards a belief that the modern state was all-powerful and could only be overthrown by violent revolution and civil war. Its perspectives were correspondingly sweeping and extreme; in his subsequent work, indeed, Foucault distanced himself from many of them. His own life could in many ways be seen as living out possibilities of resistance whose existence he himself denied. Perhaps it was typical of an intellectual that his work affirmed the limitations of intellectual discourse in practice while denying that it had any such limitations in theory. Only in France, perhaps, a land where the influence of intellectuals has been unusually strong in the twentieth century, could an interpretation of history emerge which attributed to social science and philosophy the role of shaping and controlling the whole of society in the nineteenth century.[3]

The studies presented in this book may be seen among other things as a series of commentaries on Foucault's propositions. They are intended to demonstrate the power of 'micro-history', and to show how the detailed reconstruction of seemingly trivial past events from archival sources can revise arguments drawn from social science theory, historical philosophy and other, overarching general interpretations of the past. They also offer a series of glimpses of unknown historical actors in all their complexity, and powerfully suggest the recalcitrance of human nature in the face of subsequent attempts to reduce it to a formula or press it into the service of grand historical narratives. They reveal the ambiguities of criminality in modern German history, and the complexity of the relations between deviance and control. Simple models of state authoritarianism and popular resistance, insofar as they are still current in the literature, need to be revised. To some extent, indeed, they are closely related to deeper-rooted historical clichés about the German 'spirit of submission' to authority. Yet the image of the obedient German derives mostly from observations of the bourgeois world in the nineteenth century and neglects the mass of evidence that exists for rebelliousness and assertiveness in other parts of the social structure, among the lower classes, male and female. This assertiveness, as the chapters in this book have shown, was not solely directed against the authorities; it could also be aimed at the poor themselves. Ordinary people who evaded or disobeyed the instruments of policing did not necessarily do so out of a sense of solidarity with their fellow-citizens. Robbers were undiscriminating in their choice of people to steal from; prostitutes could exploit and fool working-class men as well as the bourgeois and the police, however close their everyday connections with the working-class milieu. Criminality was not a source of proletarian political mobilization; both the Marxist intellectual tradition and the political practice of the Social Democrats, were hostile to law-breaking, which they regarded as practised particularly by the politically pliant and volatile *Lumpenproletariat*. The underworld's hostility towards the authorities was never mobilized into a general assault on capitalism. The political stance of that characteristic *Lumpenproletarian* Franz Ernst was typical: he saw in the political tensions of the 1860s only the opportunity to make money, and was just as happy deceiving and betraying the revolutionaries as he was deceiving and betraying the authorities and the police.[4]

Punishment, as Foucault rightly saw, was undergoing a major transformation in the period covered by this book. But if we shift our gaze from the central features of his work, the decline of public executions and the rise of the penitentiary, and look instead at the margins – at corporal punishment, for example, or at transportation overseas – the contours of the transformation lose their sharpness. About the underlying processes of change there can be little doubt: the death penalty had already been severely restricted in its application in the course of the Enlightenment, while corporal punishment and transportation declined as instruments of penal policy, then vanished altogether in the second half of the century. What replaced them was indeed imprisonment, backed up by the spread of new, more intrusive forms of policing. In German society at least, the change took place in the course of a much wider shift from a status-bound society to a class-based society, in which honour and dishonour, on which public punishment had rested, gradually lost their importance. Consciousness of the ways in which the old social hierarchy was being undermined was central to the debates on both transportation and corporal punishment, as different groups came up with different recipes for dealing with the refusal of a significant number of people to know their place and obey the authorities. At no point was imprisonment seen as a panacea. Right through the nineteenth century, there was a widespread awareness that prisons were primarily engaged in the continual recycling of more or less the same body of persistent offenders, rather than doing what liberals believed was their proper task, namely improving their character and returning them to society as useful, law-abiding citizens. That is why alternatives to imprisonment such as whipping or transportation were constantly being canvassed.

There is much to be said, therefore, for Foucault's insight that prisons had a wider importance in the creation and perpetuation of a substratum of the marginal and the deviant whose existence was a constant reminder to respectable society both of the need to uphold its own values and of the fate that would await anyone who deviated from them. In a similar way, it is clear that the artificial creation of a whole class of registered prostitutes served as an instrument of control both over those who were not registered and over women in society at large, by framing an economy of the street that placed any woman walking on her own under suspicion and gave the police the right to stop her because she might be a prostitute plying her trade without proper authority. The attention devoted by the police to people such as those who lived in the 'criminal quarters' of cities like Hamburg and to ordinary individuals who lacked the necessary legitimation, or whose papers showed them to have a criminal record, restricted these people's opportunities to engage in anything other than a life of crime and deviance. The discourse of the pre-industrial *Gaunerwelt* of 'villains', or the urban-industrial 'underworld' of the late nineteenth and early twentieth centuries, in which criminals were portrayed as a separate social group shadowing respectable society at every level, as a race apart, equipped with its own language and customs, or as an assemblage of hereditary degenerates, helped create and perpetuate the very social threat it was seeking to identify and master.

Persuasive though they are, however, these points need some qualification. In the first place, it is doubtful how new all this was. The pre-industrial underworld was in many ways even more rigidly set apart than its nineteenth-century counterpart. As we saw in the case of several of the felons deported to Siberia, by branding and physically marking offenders in a very visible way, the early modern state in Germany contributed further to the creation of a social underworld whose members were clearly demarcated from the rest of society. The 'dishonourable people' we have encountered in this book – people such as the Siberian deportee Anton Leikowski the knacker and Franz Ernst the executioner's son-in-law – were destined for the underworld not just by their character but even more by their infamous social standing. In the pre-industrial social hierarchy, skinners, knackers and tanners, hangmen, ethnic groups such as gypsies and Jews, and categories of people such as bastards and 'dishonoured' women were deprived of civil rights, excluded from the guilds and the urban community, and frequently regarded as dangerous and polluting. It was especially from these groups in society that the hard core of robbers, beggars and vagrants was drawn, largely because their possibilities for earning an honest living were so limited.[5] The early modern state often portrayed the threat posed by such outcast groups in lurid terms, in order to justify the extension of its own powers; sometimes, indeed, it mounted huge purges of deviants, alleging that they were involved in vast conspiracies to subvert order and damage society.[6] In the light of all this, the idea that such discursive processes of stigmatization emerged with the growth of a 'carceral society' in the nineteenth century is difficult to sustain. Indeed, it could even be argued that the spread of ameliorative ideas in penal policy and administration, ineffective though they might have been in general, when combined with the gradual breakdown of status-bound social hierarchies and the institutions that sustained them, such as the guilds, weakened rather than strengthened the barriers that demarcated the underworld from respectable society in the nineteenth century.

Moreover, as the studies presented in this book have shown, resistance to these processes of stigmatization and control was offered at every stage and every level. The legal doctrine of 'special prevention', for example, which enabled the authorities to detain potential offenders indefinitely on suspicion, and which lay at the root of the policy of deportation to Siberia in 1802, was heavily criticized by early nineteenth-century legal theorists and had fallen into disrepute by the 1840s. The deportees themselves did everything they could to escape their fate; a number of them, notably the robber Franz Exner and the forger Wilhelm Aschenbrenner, succeeded. Corporal punishment of the most savage and repeated kind failed to have any effect on the behaviour of Gesche Rudolph. Police controls exercised through the creation of identity documents could, as the career of Franz Ernst demonstrated, easily be evaded. Even when they succeeded, their value to the police seemed questionable. The official registration of prostitutes and their confinement to state-sanctioned brothels was a fate that most prostitutes, including 'Thymian Gotteball', managed to avoid, and the elaborate and restrictive rules laid down by the police to govern the public behaviour of those who were inscribed were seldom observed by the women to whom they applied. The complexities of German society were far greater than can easily be subsumed under the discursive banners of 'respectable' and 'deviant'. They placed obstacles in the way of many of these policies. German colonists resisted the idea of sending convicts to join them; working-class neighbourhoods protested against police attempts to locate brothels within their territory; the democratization of concepts of honour led to widespread criticism of corporal punishment by those who refused to accept that some strata of society could automatically be regarded as infamous.

Political controversy was generated by many of these penal measures, as they were often – with a good deal of justification – regarded as symbolic or symptomatic of wider sociopolitical attitudes. Mid-century liberals and their successors fought the policy of corporal punishment for the lower orders because it violated the principles of ameliorative punishment and equality before the law and stood for a whole way of conceptualizing society that they found repellent. Feminists fought the policy of state-regulated prostitution because it embodied the principle of a dual standard of morality for men and women. The 1848 Revolution marked the culmination of a lengthy liberal campaign for penal reform and, as we have seen, the formal abolition of corporal punishment. The failure of projects to revive most of these policies in the reactionary 1850s signified the fact that the penal and criminal law reforms of the mid-century years, embodied above all in the Prussian Penal Code of 1851, rested on a series of compromises between the old order and the new, and that there was no going back despite the failure of the Revolution's larger aims. The massive extension of undercover political policing during the period of reaction created many injustices, but it also had its limitations, made clear among other things by the farcical plots hatched by the confidence trickster Franz Ernst. The Basic Rights of 1848 had been abolished, but many basic rights created by the Revolution still remained.

The judicial system was far more than a mere instrument of state control in all this. It provided a set of rules which gradually – as we saw in the case of corporal punishment – restricted the arbitrary violence of the upper social orders against their inferiors. In the case of prostitution, it placed severe restrictions on the police's powers of control, especially after 1871. Trial in open court, based on the formal presentation of evidence, imposed limitations on the ability of the authorities to authenticate their own interpretation of events. Equality before the law was more than a means of extending surveillance equally to all sectors of the population. It did, after all, enable punishment to be applied to the crime, not to the criminal. In the middle decades of the century, the law penetrated deeper into German society, and with it the rights of the ordinary individual. Yet it was counteracted by the persistent arbitrariness of police power. The deportation of felons to Siberia was justified as a 'police measure'; corporal punishment was similarly administered, at least in the earlier part of the century, by police powers as well as by sentence of the courts. Franz Ernst was arrested and detained for several weeks by the police without ever being brought to trial; the Morals Police acted wholly outside the purview of the judicial system in restricting the civil liberties of prostitutes. Observers such as the American Raymond Fosdick, author of a wide-ranging survey of European police systems published just before the outbreak of the First World War, were not wrong when they argued that the German police were more arbitrary, more intrusive and less subject to legal and political control than their counterparts in countries such as Britain and the United States.[7]

Change in these respects in nineteenth-century Germany was slow. It was slow too in the management of imprisonment. During the eighteenth century, the spirit of the Enlightenment made itself felt in the gradual replacement in most German states of capital sentences by custodial ones for serious offences such as robbery. By 1800, the death penalty applied in effect only to homicide and treason. At the same time, the extension of the state legal system to cover, then supersede patrimonial justice brought many more minor offenders within the purview of the courts. Increasingly, imprisonment was used instead of corporal punishment as the primary penal sanction. The extension of property laws to cover woodland, previously the source of free fuel and building material for millions of poor Germans on the land, in the wake of the emancipation of the serfs, created a whole new category of offences. Indeed, wood theft was by far the largest type of theft in the 1830s and 1840s, although poverty and deprivation drove many others to steal in order to live during these decades. Throughout the nineteenth century, moreover, Germany's population was growing at an unprecedented rate. Industrialization and the impoverishment of the artisans created a new class of the itinerant poor. All this meant that however many prisons the authorities built, there were never enough to keep pace with the growing population of offenders. From the beginning of the century to the end, complaints about the overcrowding of Germany's prisons scarcely ever ceased. Schemes to transport offenders overseas or to reintroduce corporal punishment were not least repeatedly put forward in reaction to this situation.

What this reflected was, among other things, the low priority which expenditure on prisons inevitably had in nineteenth-century government circles. The creation of a 'carceral society' cost money. Parsimony reigned in part because for much of the century crime rates showed few signs of any dramatic rise. In the first half of the century, while theft increased, crimes of violence decreased. During the Imperial period, the relationship was reversed, with theft declining and crimes of violence showing a distinct, if not particularly marked, upward trend. At some times or periods there were moral panics about particular offences – theft in the mid-1830s, for example, pimping and prostitution in the early 1890s, assault after the turn of the century; and these panics had the power to generate widespread critical reflection on penal policy and the nature and role of punishment. But while there were numerous short- or medium-term fluctuations in crime rates, there was never any marked long-term growth in criminality. The overall impact of industrialization and urbanization on criminality as a whole was, surprisingly perhaps, not very great in quantitative terms.[8] Hence the threat of increased crime, however serious it might appear in some places and at some times, was never consistent enough to generate sustained or large-scale expenditure on correctional institutions. Moreover, despite the ubiquity of the doctrine of ameliorative incarceration by mid-century, the training and rehabilitation of prisoners always came a poor second to discipline and the prevention of escape, just as the care and resettlement of offenders in society always came a poor second to their surveillance and control by the police. There was nothing peculiarly German in any of this. Other societies in nineteenth-century Europe also failed to push through projects of prison reform with any consistency or determination. The criminal population always had a low political priority.

By the turn of the century, long-term frustration with this situation – above all, with the overcrowding of the prisons and the extent of recidivism – was meshing with bourgeois fears of social and political disorder, symbolized above all by the anarchist assassinations and plots of the 1880s and 1890s – few of them, as it happened, taking place in Germany – to produce a new set of attitudes to crime. The Social Democrats, with their simplistic correlation of crime with poverty and exploitation and their windy rhetoric of revolution, unwittingly assisted this process of retreat from liberal penal theory by raising the kind of respectable fears which were articulated in their concept of the *Lumpenproletariat*. Social Darwinism and eugenics, in their various guises, were applied to the crime problem in the search for new solutions. Criminality began to be presented increasingly as the product of hereditary degeneracy. It was really only at this point that social deviants such as beggars, vagrants, prostitutes and thieves began to become the object of new classificatory sciences such as criminology and forensic psychiatry, which labelled them as abnormal and proposed a series of measures, ranging from perpetual incarceration to enforced sterilization, to deal with them. All of these involved new, more invasive curtailments of their civil liberties than before. Increasingly, too, the discursive representation of criminality was couched in a violent language that dismissed 'sentimentality' and implicitly advocated the exercise of physical force against the deviant.

It would be too simple, however, to regard this as a simple regression into earlier, 'uncivilized' forms of behaviour which had largely become outmoded in the rest of Europe, or as evidence of a long-term deformation of the 'civilizing process' in Germany. Penal practice in nineteenth-century Germany was certainly no less 'civilized' than in other countries and, in some respects indeed, the transition to the new penal regime based on incarceration had gone further in Prussia and the other states than elsewhere. Capital punishment was administered in England on a far wider scale than in Prussia up to the 1840s; public executions continued in France until 1939, while they had ceased in Germany after the end of the 1860s; transportation continued in England on a regular basis up to the 1850s and in France until well after the turn of the century; corporal punishment was still being carried out by court order in England in 1914, while it had been abolished in Germany half a century before; German prisons may have continued to use the whip as an instrument of discipline, but at least they did not introduce electric shock treatment, as some British prisons did in the late nineteenth century, however much some commentators might have speculated about its benefits. What was different in Germany was not so much the penal tradition as the militarization, autonomy and persistent violence of the police; and in the extent of the police's claim to control public morals and personal behaviour. The influence of Social Darwinist ways of looking at crime and deviance in the 1890s was also greater than in other countries.[9] An inegalitarian, selective eugenic discourse permeated the world of criminology and penal policy by 1914. Penal policy also occupied an important place in political debates. From the 1840s onwards, the left emphasized the role of circumstances – poverty and deprivation prime among them – in the causes of crime, while the right correspondingly placed its stress on the immorality, irreligion, ignorance and bestiality of the offender, later subsumed under the pseudo-scientific concept of hereditary degeneracy. The conflation of crime and revolution observable in the thinking of both traditional and neo-conservative commentators in various chapters in this book had serious consequences for penal policy, above all after the First World War and the subsequent revolution had polarized and radicalized German politics to an unprecedented extent. It was in this atmosphere that the violent invasion of the deviant body by the state became possible, and was eventually undertaken by the rulers of Hitler's Third Reich. And it was these wider forces, as much as any particular German peculiarities in the field of legal and penal policy, which lay behind Germany's deviation from the path taken by other European countries in tackling criminals and criminality in the first half of the twentieth century.

In the long run, therefore, the way people talked about crime and punishment in nineteenth-century Germany was as important as the way they dealt with it in practice. The narratives they constructed did not all, however, operate in one direction, as elements of a new discursive strategy of social control. On the contrary, a wider variety of narrative options was available. In the case of Wilhelm Aschenbrenner, for instance, and also – at least according to the lawyer Karl Grattenhauer – Franz Exner, popular and sensational literature offered a celebration of crime and deviance which presented them as adventure stories with the emphasis on the boldness, cunning, ingenuity and, in Aschenbrenner's case, the essential good-heartedness and romantic nobility of soul of the offender. They articulated popular resistance to the account of moral degeneration provided by official criminal biographies of the sort purveyed in Grattenhauer's comments on the life and crimes of the escapee Franz Exner. Other narratives, such as the lawyer Georg Wilhelm Gröning's account of the sufferings of Gesche Rudolph, or the novelist Margarete Böhme's description of the downward social path trodden by 'Thymian Gotteball', presented the offender as victim of official obtuseness or social prejudice. In the narratives, or tall stories, spun by the confidence trickster Franz Ernst, we see a variety of appeals directed at a variety of ends; presenting his life-story as that of a romantic traveller, nobleman, lover, doctor, scholar, scientist, political agent, intimate of the Berlin political police. In Ernst's hands, fiction became fact, as a whole series of people fell for his stories and acted upon them as if they were true; and fact became fiction, as he took up the details of his past life and spun them into a web of fantasy and deceit.

All these narratives are in some sense fragmentary: we do not know what happened to most of the convicts transported to Siberia, we do not know what happened to Wilhelm Aschenbrenner later on in his life, we do not know whether lawyer Gröning's solution to the problems of Gesche Rudolph was successful, we do not know what became of Franz Ernst after he left Bremen, we do not know in the end how far the experiences of 'Thymian Gotteball' were based on the experiences of real-life individuals. The limitations of the historical evidence mean that these individuals flit briefly across the historical scene, leaving a host of unanswered questions after they depart. In a sense, of course, the relation of all these narratives to historical reality is a question of secondary importance: they have their own kind of validity, and give their own kind of insights into contemporary discourses on crime and punishment. Nevertheless, in the end, they still have to be read against what else we can discover about the subjects with which they deal. Comparing fiction and semi-fiction with other kinds of historical source-material can generate further insights and enables us to explore the reasons why the stories with which we have been concerned are structured and told in the way they are. And micro-studies have to be undertaken with reference to wider contexts if they are to contribute to our understanding of history's wider issues. They are much more than mere 'case-studies' whose function is to illustrate previously arrived-at conclusions about historical issues on the larger scale: they can contribute, as the studies collected in this book have sought to demonstrate, to changing our vision of those issues by looking at them from an unfamiliar angle.

Notes

Introduction

1. For general reflections on this genre, see Carlo Ginzburg, *Clues, Myths and the Historical Method* (Baltimore, 1989), and Edward Muir and Guido Ruggiero (eds), *Microhistory and the Lost Peoples of Europe* (Baltimore, 1991). For classic examples, see Natalie Zemon Davis, *The Return of Martin Guerre* (Cambridge, Mass., 1983); Emmanuel Le Roy Ladurie, *Montaillou. Village occitan de 1294 à 1324* (Paris, 1978).

2. Quantitative work in the field includes Howard Zehr, *Crime and the Development of Modern Society: Patterns of Criminality in Nineteenth-Century Germany and France* (London, 1976); Eric A. Johnson, 'The Roots of Crime in Imperial Germany', *Central European History*, 15 (1982), pp. 351–76; idem, *Urbanization and Crime. Germany 1871–1914* (New York, 1995); idem and Vincent E. McHale, 'Urbanization, Industrialization, and Crime in Imperial Germany', *Social Science History*, 1 (1976–77), pp. 45–78 and 210–47; and Dirk Blasius, *Kriminalität und Alltag. Zur Konfliktgeschichte des Alltagslebens im 19. Jahrhundert* (Göttingen, 1978).

3. Dirk Blasius, *Bürgerliche Gesellschaft und Kriminalität. Zur Sozialgeschichte Preussens im Vormärz* (Göttingen, 1976); idem, 'Kriminalität als Gegenstand historischer Forschung', *Kriminalsoziologische Bibliographie*, 25 (1979), pp. 1–15; idem, 'Gesellschaftsgeschichte und Kriminalität', *Beiträge zur Historischen Sozialkunde*, 1 (1981), pp. 13–19; idem, 'Kriminalität und Geschichtswissenschaft. Perspektiven der neueren Forschung', *Historische Zeitschrift*, 233 (1981), pp. 615–27; idem, 'Kriminologie und Geschichtswissenschaft, Bilanz und Perspektiven interdisziplinärer Forschung', *Geschichte und Gesellschaft*, 14 (1988), pp. 136–49; idem, 'Recht und Gerechtigkeit im Umbruch von Verfassungs- und Gesellschaftsord-

nung. Zur Situation der Strafrechtspflege in Preussen im 19. Jahrhundert', *Der Staat*, 21 (1982), pp. 365–90. See the important critiques of Blasius's approach by John Breuilly, in *Social History*, 3 (1978), pp. 99–102, and Karl-Georg Faber, 'Historische Kriminologie und kritische Sozialgeschichte: Das preussische Beispiel', *Historische Zeitschrift*, 227 (1978), pp. 112–22.

4. For a sample of research on the history of crime and punishment in early modern Germany, see Richard van Dülmen, *Theater des Schreckens. Gerichtspraxis und Strafrituale in der Frühen Neuzeit* (Munich, 1985); Martin Dinges, 'Frühneuzeitliche Justiz', in Heinz Mohnhaupt and Dieter Simon (eds), *Vorträge zur Justizforschung*, Vol. 1: *Geschichte und Theorie* (Frankfurt am Main, 1992), pp. 269–92; Gerd Schwerhoff, *Köln im Kreuzverhör. Kriminalität, Herrschaft und Gesellschaft in einer frühneuzeitlichen Stadt* (Bonn and Berlin, 1991), pp. 17–48; Wolfgang Behringer, 'Mörder, Diebe, Ehebrecher: Verbrechen und Strafen in Kurbayern vom 16. bis 18. Jahrhundert', in Richard van Dülmen (ed.), *Verbrechen, Strafen und soziale Kontrolle* (Frankfurt am Main, 1990), pp. 85–132; Andreas Blauert and Gerd Schwerhoff (eds), *Mit den Waffen der Justiz. Zur Kriminalitätsgeschichte des späten Mittelalters und der Frühen Neuzeit* (Frankfurt am Main, 1993); Bob Scribner, 'The *Mordbrenner* Fear in Sixteenth-Century Germany: Political Paranoia or the Revenge of the Outcast?', in Richard J. Evans (ed.), *The German Underworld: Outcasts and Deviants in German History* (London, 1988), pp. 29–56; and idem, 'Politics and the Territorial State in Sixteenth-Century Württemberg', in E.I. Kouri and Tom Scott (eds), *Politics and Society in Reformation Europe. Essays for Sir Geoffrey Elton on his Sixty-Fifth Birthday* (London, 1987), pp. 103–20. For a recent, wide-ranging introduction to early modern criminality, see Gerd Schwerhoff, 'Devianz in der alteuropäischen Gesellschaft. Umrisse einer historischen Kriminalitätsforschung', *Zeitschrift für historische Forschung*, 19 (1992), pp. 385–414.

5. See, for example, Charles, Louise and Richard Tilly, *The Rebellious Century 1830–1930* (London, 1975), pp. 208–14; Rainer Wirtz, '*Widersetzlichkeiten, Excesse, Crawalle, Tumulte und Scandale.*' *Soziale Bewegung und gewalthafter sozialer Protest in Baden 1815–1848* (Frankfurt am Main, 1981); Arno Herzig, *Unterschichtenprotest in Deutschland 1790–1870* (Göttingen, 1988); and Heinrich Volkmann and Jürgen Bergmann (eds), *Sozialer Protest. Studien zu traditioneller Resistenz und kollektiver Gewalt in Deutschland vom Vormärz bis zur Reichsgründung* (Opladen, 1984). For a critique, see Richard J. Evans, *Proletarians and Politics. Socialism, Protest and the Working Class in Germany before the First World War* (London, 1991), Ch. 2.

6. For these points, see 'Police and Society from Absolutism to Dictatorship', in Richard J. Evans, *Rereading German History: From Unification to Reunification 1800–1996* (London, 1997), Ch. 6.

7. For a development of these arguments, see Norbert Elias, *Studien über die Deutschen. Machtkämpfe und Habitusentwicklung im 19. und 20. Jahrhundert* (Frankfurt am Main, 1992).

8. Michel Foucault, *Surveiller et punir: Naissance de la prison* (Paris, 1975); idem, *Discipline and Punish: The Birth of the Prison* (London, 1977). Michael Weisser, *Crime and Punishment in Early Modern Europe* (Hassocks, 1979), is a rather unspecific and unsatisfactory attempt to apply some of Foucault's ideas; see the critique in Dirk Blasius, 'Kriminalität und Geschichtswissenschaft. Per-

spektiven der neueren Forschung.' For Foucault's reception in, and applicability to, Germany, see Blasius, 'Michel Foucaults "denkende" Betrachtung der Geschichte', *Kriminalsoziologische Bibliographie*, 41 (1983), pp. 69–83; Martin Dinges, 'The Reception of Michel Foucault's Ideas on Social Discipline, Mental Asylums, Hospitals and the Medical Profession in German Historiography', in Colin Jones and Roy Porter (eds), *Reassessing Foucault: Power, Medicine and the Body* (London, 1993), pp. 181–212; Detlev J.K. Peukert, 'Die Unordnung der Dinge. Michel Foucault und die deutsche Geschichtswissenschaft', in Franz Ewald and Bernhard Waldenfels (eds), *Spiele der Wahrheit. Michel Foucaults Denken* (Frankfurt am Main, 1991), pp. 320–33. For a classic, if controversial, study of England along the same lines, see Michael Ignatieff, *A Just Measure of Pain. The Penitentiary in the Industrial Revolution 1750–1850* (New York, 1978).

9. For these arguments, see Richard J. Evans, *Rituals of Retribution. Capital Punishment in Germany 1600–1987* (Oxford, 1996), pp. 881–92.

10. Michel Foucault, 'The Subject and Power', in Hubert L. Dreyfus and Paul Rabinow, *Michel Foucault: Beyond Structuralism and Hermeneutics* (2nd edn, Chicago, 1983), p. 220.

11. For some preliminary reflections on these topics, see Richard J. Evans, *Rethinking German History. Nineteenth-Century Germany and the Origins of the Third Reich* (London, 1987), Ch. 5: 'In Pursuit of the *Untertanengeist*: Crime, Law and Social Order in German History', pp. 156–90.

12. Evans, *Rituals*, Ch. 4.

13. For this concept, see Karl Marx and Friedrich Engels, 'The Communist Manifesto', in *Collected Works*, Vol. 6 (London, 1976), p. 494. For a discussion of its use by Social Democrats in Hamburg, see Evans, *Rethinking*, Ch. 8: '"Red Wednesday" in Hamburg: Social Democrats, Police and *Lumpenproletariat* in the Suffrage Disturbances of 17 January 1906', pp. 248–90.

14. F.C.B. Avé-Lallement, *Das deutsche Gaunerthum in seiner social-politischen, literarischen und linguistischen Ausbildung zu seinem heutigen Bestande* (4 vols, Leipzig, 1858–62).

15. Martin Wiener, *Reconstructing the Criminal. Culture, Law, and Policy in England, 1830–1914* (Cambridge, 1990), studies these shifts in the British context; for Germany, see Richard F. Wetzell, 'Criminal Law Reform in Imperial Germany' (unpublished PhD, Stanford, 1991).

16. Natalie Zemon Davis, *Fiction in the Archives: Pardon Tales and their Tellers in Sixteenth-Century France* (Stanford, 1987).

17. Paul Anselm Ritter von Feuerbach, *Aktenmässige Darstellung merkwürdiger Verbrechen* (2 vols, Giessen, 1828–9); J.C. Hitzig and W. Häring, *Der neue Pitaval: Eine Sammlung der interessantesten Criminalgeschichten aller Länder aus älterer und neuerer Zeit* (Leipzig, 1842). 'Pitaval', derived from the French originator of the genre, was used to denote 'true crime' stories ('Newgate novels' being the English equivalent).

1   The Prussian Convicts' Journey to Siberia

1. Wilhelm Aschenbrenner, *Aschenbrenners authentische Geschichte bis zu seiner Deportation nach Sibirien. Freimuthig von ihm selbst geschrieben, und mit Hinsicht auf die, über ihn verhandelten Akten herausgegeben. Nebst seinem Bildnisse. Anhang: Einige Nachrichten über die Stadt und Festung Spandau* (Berlin, 1804), pp. 1–20.

2. Ibid., pp. 21–51.

3. Ibid., pp. 51–81.

4. Ibid., pp. 81–143.

5. Ibid., pp. 143–207.

6. Ibid., pp. 207–329.

7. GStA Berlin Rep. 84a/7794, Bl. 240–41: Verzeichniss der zur ersten Ablieferung designirten nach Sibirien zu deportirenden Verbrecher, Nr. 2; and (Anon.), *Allgemeine Nachricht an das Publicum über die aus den königl. preuss. Staaten nach Sibirien geschickten Bösewichter, nebst kurzer Schilderung ihres Lebens und ihrer Vergehungen, aus den Acten gezogen* (2nd edn, Berlin, 1803), No. 17.

8. GStA Berlin Rep. 84a/7794, Bl. 240–41, 70, 104–05.

9. Albrecht Heinrich von Arnim, *Bruchstücke über Verbrechen und Strafen, oder Gedanken über die in den Preussischen Staaten bemerkte Vermehrung der Verbrechen gegen die Sicherheit des Eigenthums; nebst Vorschlägen, wie derselben durch zweckmäßige Einrichtung der Gefangenanstaltenn zu steuern seyn dürfte. Zum Gebrauch der höhern Behörden* (Frankfurt and Leipzig, 1803), Anlage 4: Allerhöchste Cabinets-Ordre an den Gross-Canzler, Geheimen Etats- und Justizminister von Goldbeck, Berlin, den 28sten Februar 1801.

10. GStA Berlin Rep. 84a/7794, Bl. 104–05: Extract aus den Listen . . .

11. Ibid./7795, Bl. 36; ibid., Bl. 241: Schulenburg to Goldbeck, 19 April 1802.

12. Ibid., Bl. 69–77: Zweites Verzeichnis der zur Deportation qualificirten Verbrecher.

13. Ibid./7794, Bl. 265c–d: Übersicht der sämmtlichen jetzt zur Deportation aufgezeichneten Verbrecher, worin selbige nach ihrer Strafbarkeit und Gefährlichkeit rangirt sind.

14. Richard van Dülmen, 'Der infame Mensch. Unehrliche Arbeit und soziale Ausgrenzung in der Frühen Neuzeit', in idem (ed.), *Arbeit, Frömmigkeit und Eigensinn* (Studien zur historischen Kulturforschung, Vol. I, Frankfurt am Main, 1990),

pp. 106–40; Carsten Küther, *Räuber und Gauner in Deutschland. Das organisierte Bandenwesen im 18. Jahrhundert* (Göttingen, 1976); Otto Beneke, *Von unehrlichen Leuten. Cultur-historische Studien und Geschichten aus vergangenen Tagen deutscher Gewerbe und Dienste, mit besonderer Rücksicht auf Hamburg* (Hamburg, 1865); Kathleen Stuart, 'The Boundaries of Honor: Dishonorable People in Augsburg, 1510–1800' (unpublished PhD dissertation, Yale University, May 1993).

15. Evans, *Rituals*, pp. 252–53.

16. See Chapter 2, below, for more details, and also Dülmen, *Theater*, pp. 70–71.

17. For other examples of corporal punishment see Nos. 20, 22, 28 29, 35, 37 and 39 on the list in GStA Berlin Rep. 84a/7794, Bl. 265c–d: Übersicht . . .

18. Breaking with, or upon, the wheel was a particularly painful form of capital punishment, commonly used in Prussia at this time, in which the offender's limbs were smashed to pieces, in serious cases while he or she was still alive. See Evans, *Rituals*, pp. 27–28.

19. GStA Berlin Rep. 84a/7794, Bl. 265c–d: Übersicht . . . , Nos. 45, 46 and 48.

20. Ibid., No. 22; for Tarnow, see also Hitzig and Häring, *Der neue Pitaval*, Part II, pp. 362–85. Tarnow is not identified by Hitzig and Häring as one of the deportees, but the description of his crimes makes it clear that he is the same as the Tarnow on the list.

21. The last public burning at the stake took place in Berlin in 1813. See Ernst Rosenfeld, 'Die letzte Vollstreckung der Feuerstrafe in Preussen zu Berlin am 18. März 1813. Auf Grund amtlichen Materials zusammengestellt', *Zeitschrift für die gesamte Strafrechtswissenschaft*, 29 (1909), pp. 810–17.

22. Regina Schulte, 'Feuer im Dorf', in Heinz Reif (ed.), *Räuber, Volk und Obrigkeit. Studien zur Geschichte der*

Kriminalität in Deutschland seit dem 18. Jahrhundert (Frankfurt am Main, 1984), pp. 100–52.

23. GStA Berlin Rep. 84a/7794, Bl. 265c-d: Übersicht . . .

24. Ibid./7795, No. II: Zweites Verzeichnis der zur Deportation qualificirten Verbrecher.

25. Detlev Merten, 'Friedrich der Grosse und Montesquieu. Zu den Anfängen des Rechtsstaats im 18. Jahrhundert', in Willi Blümel *et al.* (eds), *Verwaltung im Rechtsstaat. Festschrift für Carl Hermann Ule zum 80. Geburtstag am 24. Februar 1978* (Cologne, 1987), pp. 187–208; Jürgen Regge, 'Strafrecht und Strafrechtspflege', in Jürgen Ziechmann (ed.), *Panorama der friederizianischen Zeit. Friedrich der Grosse und seine Epoche* (Bremen, 1985), pp. 365–75; Eberhard Schmidt, *Die Kriminalpolitik Preussens unter Friedrich Wilhelm I. und Friedrich II.* (Berlin, 1914).

26. For a useful recent collection of studies, see Jörg Wolff (ed.), *Das Preussische Allgemeine Landrecht. Politische, rechtliche und soziale Wechsel- und Fortwirkungen* (Motive – Texte – Materialien, Vol. 70, Heidelberg, 1995).

27. Eberhard Schmidt, *Einführung in die Geschichte der deutschen Strafrechtspflege* (3rd edn, Göttingen, 1965), pp. 225–53.

28. Arnim, *Bruchstücke*, Part I, p. 6.

29. A.G.F. Rebmann, *Damian Hessel und seine Raubgenossen. Aktenmässige Nachrichten über einige gefährliche Räuberbanden, ihre Taktik und ihre Schlupfwinkel, nebst Angabe der Mittel, sie zu verfolgen und zu zerstören* (3rd edn, Mainz, 1811), pp. 5–7.

30. For the economic situation in the late eighteenth and early nineteenth century, see for example Jürgen Bergmann, *Das Berliner Handwerk in den Frühphasen der Industrialisierung* (Veröffentlichungen der Historischen Kommission zu Berlin, Berlin, 1973) and William W. Hagen, 'The Junkers' Faithless Servants: Peasant Insubordination and

the Breakdown of Serfdom in Brandenburg-Prussia, 1763–1811', in Richard J. Evans and W.R. Lee (eds), *The German Peasantry. Conflict and Community in Rural Society from the Eighteenth to the Twentieth Century* (London, 1986), pp. 71–101.

31. Arnim, *Bruchstücke*, Part I, p. 30.

32. For the origins and development of prisons and imprisonment in Germany, see Eberhard Schmidt, *Entwicklung und Vollzug der Freiheitsstrafe in Brandenburg-Preussen bis zum Ausgang des 18. Jahrhunderts* (Berlin, 1915); Albert Ebeling, *Beiträge zur Geschichte der Freiheitsstrafe* (Breslau, 1935); R. von Hippel, 'Beiträge zur Geschichte der Freiheitsstrafe', *Zeitschrift für die gesamte Strafrechtswissenschaft*, 18 (1898), pp. 419–94, 608–66; idem, *Die Entstehung der modernen Freiheitsstrafe und des Erziehungs-Strafvollzugs* (Jena, 1932); Herbert Lieberknecht, *Das Altpreussische Zuchthauswesen bis zum Ausgang des 18. Jahrhunderts* (Charlottenburg, 1921); Albrecht Meyer, *Das Strafrecht der Stadt Danzig von der Carolina bis zur Vereinigung Danzigs mit der preußischen Monarchie* (Danzig, 1935); Ernst Rosenfeld, 'Zur Geschichte der ältesten Zuchthäuser', *Zeitschrift für die gesamte Strafrechtswissenschaft*, 26 (1906), pp. 1–18; Günther Seggelke, *Die Entstehung der Freiheitsstrafe* (Breslau, 1928); Hannes Stekl, *Österreichs Zucht- und Arbeitshäuser, 1671–1920. Institutionen zwischen Fürsorge und Strafvollzug* (Vienna, 1978); Adolf Streng, *Geschichte der Gefängnisverwaltung in Hamburg von 1622 bis 1872* (Hamburg, 1878); Pieter Spierenburg, 'The Sociogenesis of Confinement and its Development in Early Modern Europe', in idem (ed.), *The Emergence of Carceral Institutions: Prisons, Galleys and Lunatic Asylums 1550–1900* (Rotterdam, 1984), pp. 9–77.

33. Heinrich Wagnitz, *Historische Nachrichten und Bemerkungen über die merkwürdigsten Zuchthäuser in Deutschland. Nebst einem Anhange*

über die zweckmässigste Einrichtung der Gefängnisse und Irrenanstalten (2 vols, Halle, 1791); idem, *Ideen und Pläne zur Verbesserung der Policey- u. Criminalanstalten. Dem 19. Jahrhundert zur Vollendung übergeben* (Halle, 1801).

34. Blasius, *Bürgerliche Gesellschaft*, pp. 67–68, 86–87.
35. GStA Berlin Rep. 84a/7794, Bl. 205: Grundsätze, nach welchen die in der allerhöchsten Cabinets-Ordre vom 28. Februar 1801 befohlne Einrichtung der in sämmtlichen Preussischen Staaten anzulegenden Besserungs-Anstalten zu bewerkstelligen, p. 1.
36. Quoted in Arnim, *Bruchstücke*, Part II, pp. 179–80.
37. Ibid., pp. 178–79. Italics in original.
38. Ibid., p. 180.
39. Ibid., pp. 169–70.
40. Ibid., pp. 175–76.
41. Ibid., pp. 174–75.
42. Ibid., pp. 215, 222.
43. Ibid., pp. 202–04, 234.
44. Ibid., pp. 190–200, 205–09. Italics in original.
45. Ibid., pp. 237–39.
46. Ibid., *Anlage* 5 (pp. 68–69): Allerhöchste Cabinets-Ordre, Friedrich Wilhelm III to Arnim, 16 March 1801; ibid., Anlage 6: Allerhöchste Cabinets-Ordre, Friedrich Wilhelm III to Goldbeck and Arnim, 1 Feb. 1799.
47. Ibid., Part II, pp. 15, 27–28, 33–34, 45–46, 49–63, 84, 160; Part I, p. 7.
48. *Allgemeine Nachricht*, p. 4.
49. Blasius, *Bürgerliche Gesellschaft*, pp. 72–73; see also the correspondence between Arnim and Goldbeck printed in Arnim, *Bruchstücke*, Anlage 1–3. Arnim ended his final, 36-page missive to Goldbeck by admitting: 'My letter has become a treatise; I myself am amazed by the extent of it' (p. 47). Arnim was never sparing with words. Perhaps only a Prussian bureaucrat could give a four-part, 800-page publication a title beginning with the word 'Fragments' ('*Bruchstücke*').

50. GStA Berlin Rep. 84a./7794, Bl. 205–08: Grundsätze . . .
51. Ibid., Bl. 1: Promemoria vom 6. Juli 1800 betr. das Project zur Deportation (Kgl. Geheimrat Beyme); ibid., Bl. 7: memorandum from Grosskanzler von Goldbeck, 10 August 1800, also for the following.
52. Ibid.
53. Ibid.
54. *Publicandum wegen Deportation incorrigibler Verbrecher in die Siberischen Bergwerke* (Berlin, 7 July 1802).
55. GStA Berlin Rep. 84a/7794, Bl. 1: Promemoria vom 6. Juli 1800 betr. das Project zur Deportation (Kgl. Geheimrat Beyme); ibid., Bl. 7: memorandum from Goldbeck, 10 Aug. 1800.
56. Ibid., Bl. 7: Goldbeck memorandum, 10 Aug. 1800.
57. Ibid., Bl. 53: Arnim to Goldbeck, 26 Nov. 1800, p. 5.
58. Ibid., Bl. 13–14: Instructions to ambassadors.
59. Ibid./7795, Bl. 69–77: Zweites Verzeichnis.
60. GStA Berlin Rep. 84a/7794, Bl. 265c–d: Übersicht . . . , No. 8.
61. Ibid., Bl. 249–50: Übersicht . . . , Nos 24, 25 and 26.
62. E.J. Hobsbawm, *Bandits* (London, 1969), pp. 38–39.
63. Ibid.
64. Carsten Küther, 'Räuber, Volk und Obrigkeit. Zur Wirkungsweise und Funktion staatlicher Strafverfolgung im 18. Jahrhundert', in Reif (ed.), *Räuber*, pp. 17–42, here p. 37. See also Küther, *Räuber und Gauner*. For a more conservative view, drawing on the tradition of 'criminal biology' which reached its murderous apogee under the Third Reich, see Hermann Arnold, 'Ländliche Grundschicht und Gaunertum. Zur Kritik von Küthers Buch: Räuber und Gauner in Deutschland', *Zeitschrift für Agrargeschichte und Agrarsoziologie*, 25 (1977), pp. 67–76. An account of Arnold's work can be found in Joachim S. Hohmann, 'Die Forschungen des

"Zigeunerexperten" Hermann Arnold', *1999. Zeitschrift für Sozialgeschichte des 20. und 21. Jahrhunderts* 10 (1995), 3, pp. 35–49.

65. Carsten Küther, *Menschen auf der Strasse. Vagierende Unterschichten in Bayern, Franken und Schwaben in der zweiten Hälfte des 18. Jahrhunderts* (Göttingen, 1983).

66. Uwe Danker, *Räuberbanden im Alten Reich um 1700. Ein Beitrag zur Geschichte von Herrschaft und Kriminalität in der Frühen Neuzeit* (Frankfurt am Main, 1988); idem, 'Bandits and the State: Robbers and the Authorities in the Holy Roman Empire in the Late Seventeenth and Early Eighteenth Centuries', in Evans (ed.), *The German Underworld*, pp. 75–107. For a useful local study, though one employing concepts such as 'Asoziale' and 'Berufsverbrechertum' derived from Third Reich criminologists, especially Edmund Mezger, see Hermann Bettenhäuser, 'Räuber und Gaunerbanden in Hessen. Ein Beitrag zum Versuch einer historischen Kriminologie Hessens', *Zeitschrift des Vereins für hessische Geschichte und Landeskunde,* 75–76, (1964–65), pp. 275–348.

67. Danker, 'Bandits and the State', p. 103.

68. See Manfred Franke, *Schinderhannes. Das kurze, wilde Leben des Johannes Bückler. Nach alten Dokumenten neu erzählt* (Düsseldorf, 1984), for a detailed account of his career; cf. also B. Becker, *Actenmässige Geschichte der Räuberbanden an den beyden Ufern des Rheins* (2 vols, Cologne, 1804).

69. See, for example, Carl Philip Schwencken, *Actenmässige Nachrichten von dem Gauner- und Vagabunden-Gesindel, sowie von einzelnen professionirten Dieben, in den Ländern zwischen dem Rhein und der Elbe, nebst genauer Beschreibung ihrer Person* (Kasel, 1822); A.G.F. Rebmann, *Damian Hessel und seine Raubgenossen. Aktenmässige*
Nachrichten über einige gefährliche Räuberbanden, ihre Taktik und ihre Schlupfwinkel, nebst Angabe der Mittel, sie zu verfolgen und zu zerstören (3rd edn, Mainz, 1811); Ludwig Pfister, *Actenmässige Geschichte der Räuberbanden an den beiden Ufern des Mains, in Spessart und im Odenwalde* (Heidelberg, 1812); Friedrich Ludwig Adolf von Grolmann, *Actenmässige Geschichte der Vogelsberger und Wetterauer Räuberbanden, und mehrerer mit ihnen in Verbindung gestandener Verbrecher. Nebst Personal-Beschreibung vieler in alle Lande deutscher Mundart dermalen versprengter Diebe und Räuber* (Giessen, 1813).

70. GStA Berlin Rep. 84a/7794, Bl. 249–50: Übersicht . . . The numbered biographies on this list were published in an abridged form in the *Allgemeine Nachricht*, which mentions the physical examinations and the royal hand in the selections on page 7. (See note 7, above.)

71. Ibid., Bl. 23: Kgl. Stadtgerichts-Direktor Danzig to Goldbeck, 17 July 1800, and reply, 2 Aug. 1800.

72. Ibid., Bl. 127–28: Struensee memorandum, 22 March 1801.

73. Ibid., Bl. 47–48: report of 20 Nov. 1800, Berlin.

74. Ibid., Bl. 36.

75. Ibid., Bl. 48: report of 20 Nov. 1811, Berlin.

76. Ibid., Bl. 127–28: Struensee memorandum, 22 March 1801.

77. Ibid., Bl. 61: Auswärtiges Amt to Goldbeck and Arnim, 14 Feb. 1801, and Bl. 62: note on the Russian agreement, 18 Jan. 1801.

78. Ibid., Bl. 120–21 (Geh. Justizrat Grutzmacher, report of 10 March 1801), Bl. 162ff., 197: various notes.

79. Ibid./7795, Bl. 47: memorandum from St Petersburg, 31 Dec. 1801 (old style)/12 Jan. 1802 (new style); GStA Berlin Rep. 84a/7796, Bl. 2: letter from Procurer-General (St. Petersburg) to Vice-Chancellor, Berlin, 28 June 1802 (old style).

80. Ibid./7794, Bl. 266ff. (Dec. 1801).
81. Ibid./7796, Bl. 20.
82. Ibid./7794, Bl. 129–30: Struensee memorandum, 22 March 1801.
83. Ibid./7795, Bl. 55.
84. Ibid./7794, Bl. 266ff., Dec. 1801.
85. Ibid./7795, Bl. 167–76: certificates of arrival at Pillau, 235: report from Pillau, 243–49: lists of the prisoners, 273–74: receipt from the Russian authorities in Narva, 277–79: report of Friedrich Zimmermann. The same sources indicate that the escort party arrived back in Pillau on 8 July.
86. Ibid., Bl. 276: Rechnung über die von Pillau nach Narva transportirten incorrigiblen Verbrecher.
87. Ibid./7794, Bl. 241: Schulenburg to Goldbeck, 19 April 1802.
88. Ibid., Bl. 2: Procurer-General to Vice-Chancellor, 28 June 1802 (old style).
89. *Allgemeine Nachricht*, p. 8.
90. GStA Berlin Rep. 84a/7794, Bl. 141–50.
91. Ibid., Bl. 205: Grundsätze . . . , p. 1.
92. *Novum Corpus Constitutionum Prussico-Brandenburgensium Praecipue Marchicarum*, Vol. X (Berlin, 1801), pp. 958–59, edict of 7 July 1802.
93. GStA Berlin Rep. 84a/7796, Bl. 51–52: Ambassador in St Petersburg, reports of 18 Nov. 1802 and 14/26 Oct. 1802.
94. *Novum Corpus*, 1804, No. 8 (pp. 2145–46): Publicandum, wegen Entweichung der zur Haft gezogenen oder bereits zur Strafe verurtheilten Verbrecher aus den Gefängnissen, oder auf dem Transport nach den Besserungs-Anstalten, 3 April 1804; ibid., 1804, No. 62 (pp. 2787–88): Circulare an sämmtliche Ober-Landes-Justiz-Collegia, excl. des Geheimen Ober-Tribunals, wegen Verhütung des Entweichens der Verbrecher auf dem Transport, 6 Dec. 1804; ibid., 1805, No. 3 (pp. 1867–74): Publicandum, wegen besserer Organisation der Criminal-Collegium, 14 Jan. 1805; ibid., 1805, No. 59 (pp. 3057–58): Rescript an das Cammer-gericht, wegen der für Wiedereinbringung entwichener Festungsgefangene bewilligten Finanzgelder à 5 Rthlr, 13 Nov. 1805.
95. Ibid., 1804, No. 6 (pp. 2129–34): Circulare an sämmtliche Provinzial-Landes-Justiz-Collegia: wegen Einsendung der Listen von den entwischten Verbrechern, 17 March 1804.
96. Schmidt, *Einführung*, pp. 225–28; Richard Hartmann, *P.J.A. Feuerbachs politische und strafrechtliche Grundanschauungen* (Berlin [East], 1961), pp. 68–113.
97. Ernst Rosenfeld, 'Verschickung freiwillig auswandernder Insassen der Gefängnisse von Mecklenburg nach Brasilien in den Jahren 1824 und 1825', *Zeitschrift für die gesamte Strafrechtwissenschaft*, 24 (1904), pp. 412–25, here pp. 412–17. See also GStA Berlin Rep. 84a/7794, Bl. 1: Promemoria vom 6. Juli 1800 betr. das Project zu Deportation; and ibid., Bl. 7: memorandum von Goldbeck, 10 Aug. 1800.
98. See the relevant sub-file and exchange of diplomatic notes in LHA Schwerin Grossherzogliches Kabinett I/78.
99. Ibid. I/53, Bl. 1: Serenissimo Allerunterthänigstes Pro-Memoria, 12 May 1824.
100. Ibid., Bl. 64–68: In Untersuchungs Sachen wider die Inculpaten Rhode, . . .
101. Quoted in Rosenfeld, 'Verschickung', p. 412.
102. Küther, *Menschen*, passim.
103. Copy of the agreement in LHA Schwerin Grossherzogliches Kabinett I/54, Bl. 5.
104. Ferdinand Schröder, 'Die Deportation mecklenburgischer Staatsgefangener nach Brasilien 1824/25', *Der Auslandsdeutsche*, 15 (1929), pp. 497–98.
105. LHA Schwerin Grossherzogliches Kabinett I/53, Bl. 41–45: Nachweisung von denjenigen Arbeitern des Land-Arbeitshauses, welche unter den ihnen bekannt gemachten Bedingungen in Brasilien

106. Ibid., Bl. 98–103: Nachtrag zum General-Rapport für den Monat Juni 1824 betreffend die Transportirung der nach Brasilien auswandernder Landarbeitshäusler nach Hamburg.

107. Ibid. I/54, Bl. 70–75: Rectificirte-Liste derjenigen Sträflinge pp. welche am 6. Decbr. von Dömitz nach Brasilien abgegangen; ibid., Bl. 65: printed notice of 10 Dec. 1824. Schröder, 'Deportation', also claims that there were some 30 prisoners from the Correctionsanstalt in Rostock on the same ship. For another list, of 102 inmates from whom the eventual selection was made, see LHA Schwerin Kriminalkollegium zu Bützow 1127, Bl. 21–31.

108. LHA Schwerin Grossherzogliches Kabinett I/78, sub-file on appointment of consul.

109. Ibid. I/62, Bl. 56–57: Verzeichniss derjenigen Personen, welche in dem Criminal-Gefängnisse zu Bützow inhaftiert, und sich auf den Grund der dieserhalb erlassenen Allerhöchsten Bestimmung freywillig zur Auswanderung nach Brasilien erklärt.

110. Ibid., Bl. 63: Serenissimo Allerunterthänigstes Pro-Memoria, 26 July 1825.

111. Ibid. I/58, Bl. 69: Registratura, Güstrow, im Landarbeitshause, 12 Sept. 1828.

112. See the discussion on the Marlow brothers in LHA Schwerin Kriminalkollegium zu Bützow 1128, Bl. 55–58.

113. Although based on some of the relevant files, Rosenfeld's account ('Verschickung') is directed towards showing that the German colonists were deceived and badly treated by the Brazilians and is highly selective, omitting all the details about the emigrants' misconduct.

114. For the complaint about the lack of facilities for Protestant worship, see Schröder, 'Deportation'. Schröder's main concern was to counter criticism of the Mecklenburg government's supposed callousness in sending these people to Brazil, and he wanted to show therefore that it was not to blame if the transportees failed to practise their religion.

115. LHA Schwerin Kriminalkollegium zu Bützow 1130: Der Vortrag des Oberinspektors Ehlers und des Pastors Romberg aus Dreibergen auf Begnadigung mehrerer Sträflinge zur Auswanderung nach Amerika, 1847.

116. StA Hbg Gefängnisverwaltung A 41: Bericht über die nach Brasilien gegangenen Gefangenen, vom Verwaltender Vorsteher der Gefängnisse.

117. This last fact was considered particularly shocking, because it revealed to each of the men in advance what his own fate would be and so ran the risk of unnerving him. For this reason, officials at multiple executions in nineteenth-century Germany always took care to ensure that no offender had any chance of witnessing the dispatch of his companions (Evans, *Rituals*, p. 259).

118. StA Hbg Gefängnisverwaltung A 41: Holtermann letter, 20 Nov. 1825.

119. Ibid.: Senatsprotokoll 6 July 1832 and notes of 1 July 1832. The history of transportation from Hamburg to Brazil and the USA is also the main subject of an article by Günther Moltmann, 'Die Transportation von Sträflingen im Rahmen der deutschen Auswanderung des 19. Jahrhunderts', in idem (ed.), *Deutsche Amerikaauswanderung im 19. Jahrhundert* (Stuttgart, 1969), pp. 147–96.

120. See Chapter 2, below, for more details; also Moltmann, 'Die Transportation', pp. 150–53.

121. StA Hbg Gefängnisverwaltung A 41: Vogelsang letter of 10 Nov. 1832.

122. Ibid.: Vogelsang letter of 19 Dec. 1832.

123. Moltmann, 'Die Transportation', p. 155.
124. Jürgen Tampke and Colin Doxford, *Australia, Willkommen. A History of the Germans in Australia* (Kensington, New South Wales, 1990), pp. 14–19; Robert Hughes, *The Fatal Shore. A History of the Transportation of Convicts to Australia 1787–1868* (London, 1987), pp. 493–500.
125. Moltmann, 'Die Transportation', pp. 176–78.
126. GStA Berlin Rep. 84a/7797, Bl. 37–38: Von Jordan (ambassador in Dresden) to Ministerium der auswärtigen Angelegenheiten, describing an interview with the Coburg Staatsminister von Carlowitz, 22 Sept. 1837.
127. StA Coburg Min. D/469, Bl. 16–20: Gruner (Landes-Regierung), 29 Aug. 1826.
128. GStA Berlin Rep. 84a/7797, Bl. 34: *Allgemeine Zeitung* (Abschrift), 18 Oct. 1837.
129. StA Coburg Min. A/124: Landes-Regierung, 5 March 1846, and note of Prince Ernst, 14 March 1846.
130. GStA Berlin Rep. 84a/7797, Bl. 10–16: Votum of 29 Nov. 1835; ibid., Bl. 17–19: petition of the Stände der Mark Brandenburg, 6 April 1837; ibid., Bl. 35: report of 29 Nov. 1837.
131. StA Coburg Min.D/471, Bl. 145: Landes-Regierung, 24 April 1847.
132. Ibid., Bl. 133: Landes-Regierung, 25 Nov. 1845.
133. Ibid.: Landes-Regierung, 7 May 1856, and note of Prince Ernst, 15 May 1856.
134. Ibid. Min. D/471, 472 (see the lists at the beginning of each file).
135. Ibid. Min. D/472, Bl. 188–99: Landes-Regierung (Habermann), 20 Aug. 1855.
136. Ibid. Min. D/473, Bl. 243: Bericht des Landraths-Amts, 4 April 1867.
137. GStA Berlin Rep. 84a/7796, Bl. 65–74: Merckel, 6 April 1828, and copy of petition No. 19 of 2. Provinzial-Landtag, 28 Feb. 1828.
138. Ibid./7797, Bl. 2: Votum des Justiz-Ministers von Kamptz, 18 Jan. 1834.
139. Ibid., Bl. 11: Votum des Justiz-Ministers von Kamptz, 11 Nov. 1835: Abschrift of Staatsministerium Votum of 30 Oct.
140. Ibid., Bl. 12–14: Auszug aus der Wiener Zeitung, 6. Oct. 1835.
141. Ibid., Bl. 14–16: Votum Ancillon, 29 Nov. 1835.
142. Ibid., Bl. 20e–k: Oberpräsident der Provinz Brandenburg: Gutachtliche Äusserung des Landtags-Kommissarius zu der abschriftlich hier beigefügten Immediat-Vorstellung der Stände der Mark Brandenburg und des Markgrafthums Nieder-Lausitz, 6 April 1837.
143. Ibid., Bl. 21.
144. Ibid., Bl. 21–29.
145. Herrmann von Valentini, *Das Verbrecherthum im Preussischen Staate, nebst Vorschlägen zu seiner Bekämpfung durch die Gesellschaft und durch die Reform der Strafvollstreckung* (Leipzig, 1869), pp. 4–7, 65.
146. Heinrich Wagnitz, *Über die moralische Verbesserung der Zuchthausgefangenen* (Halle, 1787).
147. Herbert Schattke, *Die Geschichte der Progression im Strafvollzug und der damit zusammenhängenden Vollzugsziele in Deutschland* (Frankfurt, 1979), pp. 79–90.
148. Nikolaus Heinrich Julius, *Vorlesungen über die Gefängnis-Kunde, oder über die Verbesserung der Gefängnisse und sittliche Besserung der Gefangenen, entlassenen Sträflinge u.s.w., gehalten im Frühlinge 1827 zu Berlin* (Berlin, 1828), esp. pp. 216–22; see also Valentini, *Verbrecherthum*.
149. Carl Joseph Anton Mittermaier, *Die Gefängnisverbesserung, insbesondere die Bedeutung und Durchführung der Einzelhaft im Zusammenhange mit dem Besserungsprinzip, nach den Erfahrungen der verschiedenen Strafanstalten* (Erlangen, 1858), pp. 53–56, 74–76.
150. Carl Joseph Anton Mittermaier, 'Besserungsanstalten', in Carl von Rottek and Carl Welcker (eds), *Staats-Lexicon* (Altona, 1834), Vol. I, p. 504.

151. Blasius, *Bürgerliche Gesellschaft*, esp. pp. 70–92.

152. For a sensitive discussion of this aspect of nineteenth-century Germany liberalism, see David Blackbourn, *Marpingen. Apparitions of the Virgin Mary in Bismarckian Germany* (Oxford, 1994), pp. 282–302.

153. Norbert Finzsch und Robert Jütte (eds.), *Institutions of Confinement. Hospitals, Asylums, and Prisons in Western Europe and North America, 1500–1950* (New York, 1996).

154. B. Appert, *Die Geheimnisse des Verbrechens, des Verbrecher- und Gefängniss-Lebens* (Leipzig, 1851), Vol. I, pp. 97–101.

155. Mittermaier, 'Besserungsanstalten', pp. 504–14.

156. Mittermaier, *Die Gefängnisverbesserung*, p. 101.

157. Schattke, *Geschichte*, pp. 88–89.

158. Blasius, *Bürgerliche Gesellschaft*, p. 79.

159. C. Krohne, and R. Uber, *Die Strafanstalten und Gefängnisse in Preussen*, Vol. I (Berlin, 1901).

160. Evans, *Rituals*, pp. 380–81.

161. HStA Hannover Hann. 26a/7373, Bl. 38: Schreiben des Königlichen Gesammt-Ministerii vom 7. Januar 1860, die Reform der Strafanstalten bettreffend; and following documents.

162. Ibid. Hann. 9 Amerika 14, Bl. 14: Dudley Mann to Baron von Falcke, 15 Dec. 1847.

163. Moltmann, 'Die Transportation', p. 161.

164. HS+A Hannover Hann. 9 Amerika/4 Bl. 4–5: depositions of Moses Catzenstein and Amelia Blogg, Baltimore, 7 Feb. 1845.

165. Moltmann, 'Die Transportation', pp. 161–62.

166. Ibid., pp. 163–64. There were also reports of criminals arriving in New York from the Thuringian principality of Schwarzburg-Sondershausen, from the Duchy of Brunswick, and from the Kingdom of Württemberg at this time (ibid., p. 165).

167. HS+A Hannover Hann. 9 Amerika 14 Bl. 16–22. Ministerium des Innern to Ministerium der auswärtigen Angelegenheiten, 14 Jan. 1848. For the initial orders setting up the scheme towards the end of 1834, see ibid., Hann. 80 Hannover I A 626: Innenministerium to Landdrostei Hannover, 25 Nov. 1834 (No. 16075).

168. Ibid. Hann. 74 Hameln 4345: T. von Werlhof, Königliche Grossbritannisch-hannoversche Landdrostei an sämmtliche Obrigkeiten in dem Bezirke der Königlichen Landdrostei Hannover, 29 Juni 1835 (No. 8951); additional note of 27 May 1840, No. 5931 (marked 'Confidentiell'); ibid. Burgdorf I 1669: Ausschreiben der Landdrostei Lüneburg, 10 Dec. 1834. In 1844 the authorities expressed concern that the transportees were demanding 'uncommonly high travelling expenses and an uncommonly large amount of clothing', and introduced tighter controls. See ibid., Celle 1315, Bl. 6: Ausschreiben der Königlichen Landdrostei Lüneburg, 20 Aug. 1844.

169. Ibid.: Memorandum No. 5860, Feb. 1855.

170. Ibid. Hann. 80 Hildesheim I E 535: Innenministerium to Landdrosteien, 7 Jan. 1856; Edgecombe to Platen, 25 Dec. 1855.

171. Ibid. Hann. 9 Amerika 14, Bl. 47–49: Belgian ambassador in Berlin to Hanoverian government, 17 March 1855.

172. Ibid., Bl. 50–54: Ministerium des Innern to Ministerium für auswärtige Angelegenheiten, 26 March 1855.

173. Ibid. Hann. 9 Amerika 14, Bl. 28–31: President of Bremen Senate to Ministerium der auswärtigen Angelegeneiten, Hanover, 20 June 1851; Bl. 40–45: Bericht der Inspection der Mäkler im Senate, 16 Juni 1851.

174. Ibid., Bl. 32–33: memorandum of Innenministerium, 19 Aug. 1851.

175. Ibid., Bl. 35–39: Bericht des Amts Lehe, 11 Aug. 1851.

176. Ibid. Hann. 80 Hannover I A 626: Innenministerium to Landdrostei Hannover, 'vertraulich', 16 Jan. 1841.

177. Ibid.: Innenministerium to Landdrostei Hannover, 20 Jan. 1843.

178. Ibid. Hann. 74 Burgdorf I 1669: Landdrostei Lüneburg to Amt Burgdorf ('Vertraulich'), 17 March 1848.

179. Ibid. Hann. 9 Amerika 14, Bl. 35–39: Bericht des Amts Lehe, 11 Aug. 1851.

180. Ibid. Hann. 80 Hildesheim I E 535: Order of the Landdrostei Hildesheim, 1 Sept. 1851 (No. 13709).

181. Ibid. IE 1216: Gesuch des Sträflings A. Bock um Bewillgung einer Beihilfe zu den Kosten seiner Auswanderung nach Amerika, for one such example.

182. Ibid. IE 999: die beantragte Übersiedelung des im Strafarbeitshause zu Hameln detinirten David Fränkel aus Sarstedt nach Amerika, 1841. In this case at least, the Jewish community of Sarstedt refused.

183. Ibid., Bl. 60–62: Ministerium des Innern to Ministerium für auswärtige Angelegenheiten, 26 March 1855; see also ibid. Hann. 74 Hameln 4345: F. Mehlis, Königlich-Hannoversche Landdrostei to Obrigkeiten des Verwaltungs-Bezirks, 18 May 1855, No. 5955.

184. Ibid. Hann. 26a 7159: Species facti cum voto in Untersuchungsachen wider Heinrich Georg Hundertmark . . . , Bl. 148–49 (11 March 1836, No. 1); Charakteristik des Verurtheilten Heinrich Hundertmark (No. 2); Unterthänigster Begnadigungsgesuch von Seiten des Vollmeiers Wilhelm Hundertmark, 27 August 1841 (+ + +Handzeichen Wilhelm Hundertmark) (No. 20); 'Der Kettensträfling Hundertmark ist nicht zu begnadigen, Ernst August, 21sten September 1841' (No. 21); 'Bericht der Direction der Straf-anstalt zu Stade vom 2ten Januar 1852' (No. 43); note of local authorities in Pyrmont, 12 March 1854 (No. 59).

185. Ibid. Hann. 74 4345: Königlich-Hannoversche Landdrostei to Obrigkeiten des Verwaltungs-Bezirks, 20 July 1866 (No. 8754).

186. Ibid. Hann. 26a 7105: Untersuchung wider den Maler und Glaser Heyko Boelsen aus Timmel, wegen Brandstiftung, 1858–64.

187. Ibid. 7228: Pastoral-Zeugniss für den Sträfling Sander aus Powe, 5 Feb. 1865.

188. Ibid. Hann. 80 Hildesheim I E 1900. Bericht des Amts Einbeck, 11 April 1865.

189. Ibid. 7166: Freiting to Georg V, 20 Feb. 1864 (No. 439); Bericht der Direction der Kettenstrafanstalt zu Lüneburg, 16 Dec. 1865 (No. 58).

190. Ibid. 7236: memorandum of 17 Sept. 1865 and report of 14 March 1866. Unusually, his accomplice in the crime, Johann Schmidt, who had been pardoned two years previously for similar reasons, emigrated to Africa rather than the United States.

191. Ibid., Hann. 26a 7530 I: Knoop to Justice Minister, 30 Nov. 1856.

192. Ibid. II: Charakteristik des Heinrich Theodor Knoop aus Göttingen, Aufgestellt Lüneburg, 4 April 1862.

193. Ibid.: Pastoralzeugnis über den Sträfling Heinrich Theodor Knoop.

194. Ibid. Hann. 80 Hildesheim I E 826: Bericht des Magistrats Hildesheim, 17 June 1841.

195. Ibid. 1002: Bericht des Amts Hildesheim vom 31. August 1861; Reisepass-Ausstellung, 7 Oct. 1861.

196. Ibid. 1406: police report to Kultusministerium, Abteilung der Universitätsachen, 26 Feb. 1836 (No. 36).

197. Ibid.: Ministerium der geistlichen und Unterrichts-Angelegenheiten to Göttingen police, 12 March 1836 (No. 37).

198. Ibid.: Göttingen police report, 24 March 1836 (No. 38a).

199. Ibid. 7247: Bericht der Direction der Strafanstalt zu Lingen, 9 March 1856.
200. Ibid. 1440: Bericht der Polizei-Direction zu Göttingen, 3 Sept. 1841.
201. Ibid. 687: Rettstadt to Landdrostei Hildesheim, 4 June 1865; Bericht des Amts Gronau, 3 July 1865.
202. Ibid. 920: Charakteristik des Verurtheilten Carl Ritter. No. xiv.
203. Ibid. 923: Katharina Hartjen to Landdrostei Hildesheim, 5 Aug. 1840.
204. Ibid.: Magistrat to Landdrostei Hildesheim, 30 Aug. 1840.
205. *Foreign Criminals and Paupers*, 34th Congress, 1st Session, House, Report No. 359, 16 August 1856, cited in Moltmann, 'Die Transportation', p. 166.
206. Moltmann, 'Die Transportation', p. 167.
207. Haubold Freiherr von Spesshardt, *Handbuch über Straf- und Besserungs-Anstalten* (Hildburghausen, 1843), pp. 116–21.
208. StA Bremen 2-D 18.0: Verbannung, Transport, Zwangspässe, Ausweisung 1715–1873: Nr.6: Extract aus dem Senatsprotokolle 1852 – Mai 12 – p. 315: Transportirung von Verbrechern, Vagabunden etc. nach Bahia.
209. GStA Berlin Rep. 84a/7797, Bl. 63: report of the Kommission für Rechtspflege of the 1. Kammer, III. Leg. Per., No. 376, 26 April 1853.
210. Franz von Holtzendorff, *Die Deportation als Strafmittel in alter und neuer Zeit und die Verbrecherkolonien der Engländer und Franzosen in ihrer geschichtichen Entwicklung und criminalpolitischen Bedeutung* (Leipzig, 1859), esp. pp. 711–13.
211. HStA Hannover Hann. 74 Hameln No. 4345: Königliche Preussische Landdrostei Hannover to Obrigkeiten des Landdrostei-Bezirks, 21 April 1868.
212. BA Berlin 61 Re 1, Bd. 1: Deportation. Gefängnis und Gefängnisarbeit. Zuchthaus und Zuchthausarbeit. International. 1894–97; ibid., Bd. 2: Deportation, Zuchthaus und Gefängnisse 1897–1902. These are press clippings.
213. Wetzell, 'Criminal Law Reform', esp. Chs 3–4.
214. GStA Berlin Rep. 84a/7798: *Tägliche Rundschau*, 28 Feb. 1896.
215. Ibid.: *Hamburger Nachrichten*, 27 April 1904.
216. Johnson, *Urbanization and Crime*, esp. Chs. 2, 4.
217. GStA Berlin Rep. 84a/7797: Reichstagsdrucksache Nr. 823–118: Bericht.
218. Ibid.: Begründung der Petition des Deportations-Ausschusses des deutschen Kolonial-Bundes (1903).
219. Reported in HStA Munich M Inn 71567.
220. GStA Berlin Rep. 84a/7798: *National-Zeitung*, 15 Jan. 1908.
221. Ibid./7797: Reichstag, 104. Sitzung, 18. Feb. 1903, pp. 18,275–76.
222. Reported in HStA Munich M Inn 71567.
223. GStA Berlin Rep. 84a/7798: *Schlesische Presse*, 14 May 1881.
224. HStA Munich M Inn 71567 for reports of these negotiations.
225. GStA Berlin Rep. 84a/7798: *Norddeutsche Allgemeine Zeitung*, 2 Aug. 1896.
226. Ibid.: *Saale-Zeitung*, 27 July 1905.
227. Ibid.: *Tägliche Rundschau*, 28 Feb. 1896 (Beilage); ibid./7797, Bl. 94–96: memo by Landeshauptmann in Windhoek, 15 March 1896; ibid., Bl. 99–101: memo by Landeshauptmann in Togo, 10 April 1896.
228. Ibid.: *Danziger Zeitung*, 6 June 1896.
229. Ibid.: *Deutsche Tageszeitung*, 7 Aug. 1896.
230. Ibid.: *Deutsche Warte*, 8 Aug. 1896.
231. Ibid.: *Vossische Zeitung*, 29 March 1896.
232. Ibid.: *National-Zeitung*, 27 June 1906.
233. Ibid., Bl. 194: Reichstag, 106. Sitzung, 20. Feb. 1908; 108. Sitzung, 25. Feb. 1908; *Die Post*, 26. Feb. 1908.

234. Charles H. Cottrell, *Recollections of Siberia in the Years 1840 and 1841* (London, 1842), pp. 13, 281; Benson Bobrick, *East of the Sun: The Conquest and Settlement of Siberia* (London, 1992), pp. 272–73; Mrs Aga, *The Adventures of a Serf's Wife among the Mines of Siberia* (London, 1866), p. 119; George Kennan, *Siberia and the Exile System* (New York, 1891), Vol. I, pp. 109, 116, 143.

235. GStA Berlin Rep. 84a/7796; Ibid., Bl. 93: Borowski deposition; ibid., Bl. 124, report of Jan. 1804.

236. For further evidence of the hostility of Russian peasants to foreigners, see C.C. Zimmermann, *Bis nach Sibirien. Erinnerungen aus dem Feldzuge nach Russland und aus der Gefangenschaft 1812–1814* (Hanover, 1863), pp. 17–20.

237. GStA Berlin Rep. 84a/7796, Bl. 93, 118, 144–45 (Borowski and Wisniewski's depositions and examinations).

238. Ibid./7796, Bl. 2, 91–93, 100, 118, 124, 130, 138, 144–45: reports of 14 Nov. 1803, 22 Nov. 1803, 15 Feb. 1804, depositions and interrogations of Borowski and Wiesniewski.

239. Carl Wilhelm Friedrich Grattenhauer, *Über die Nothwehr. Ein Beitrag zur wissenschaftlichen Behandlung des Kriminalrechts* (Breslau, 1806); idem, *Exners Tod. Ein merkwürdiger Kriminalfall rechtmässiger Nothwehr: Erkenntniss des Kriminal-senats der Ober-Amts-Regierung in Glogau wider den Harpersdorffer Müller Johann Gottlieb Meschter* (Breslau, 1805); further details in Hitzig and Häring, *Der neue Pitaval* (Part I, 2nd edn, Leipzig, 1857), pp. 305–30.

240. Grattenhauer, *Über die Nothwehr*, p. 29.

241. Ibid., p. iv.

242. Ibid., p. v.

243. Ibid., pp. 31–37.

244. Dirk Blasius, 'Der Kampf um die Geschworenengerichte im Vormärz', in Hans-Ulrich Wehler (ed.), *Sozialgeschichte Heute. Festschrift für Hans Rosenberg zum 70. Geburtstag* (Göttingen, 1974), pp. 148–61.

245. GStA Berlin Rep. 84a/7796, Bl. 93: Borowski deposition.

246. Ibid./7794, Bl. 241–42: Verzeichniss der zur ersten Ablieferung designirten nach Sibirien zu deportirenden Verbrecher, Nos 3–4.

247. Ibid/7796, Bl. 93: Borowski deposition; ibid., Bl. 118, Bl. 130, Bl. 100.

248. August von Kotzebue, *Das merkwürdigste Jahr meines Lebens* (2 vols, Berlin, 1801).

249. M. Masson, *Mémoires secrets sur la Russie, et particulièrement sur la fin du règne de Catherline II et le commencement de celui de Paul Ier; ou lettres en réponse à M. Kotzebue* (4 vols, Amsterdam, 1803); (Anon.), *Nöthige Erläuterungen zu der Schrift des Herrn von Kotzebue: das merkwürdigste Jahr meines Lebens. Von einem Freund der Wahrheit* (Leipzig, 1802).

250. *Die schrecklichsten Jahre meines Lebens. Meine Leiden und Verhaftung zu Königsberg und Spandau und Verbannung in die Bergwerke nach Sibirien, von Wilhelm Aschenbrenner* (2 vols, Berlin, 1804). Extensive library searches in Germany and elsewhere have so far failed to turn up a copy of this publication.

251. Rudolf Schenda, *Volk ohne Buch. Studien zur Sozialgeschichte der populären Lesestoffe 1770–1910* (Munich, 1977), is the classic study. See also J.W. Appell, *Die Ritter- Räuber- und Schauerromantik. Zur Geschichte der deutschen Unterhaltungs-Literatur* (Leipzig, 1859).

252. Aschenbrenner, *Aschenbrenners authentische Geschichte*, pp. iv–x.

253. Ibid, pp. 334, 330; italics in original.

254. Kotzebue, *Das merkwürdigste Jahr*, Vol. I, pp. 242–43. On passing a column of convicts going on foot to Nerchinsk, some of whom begged him for food as he went by, Kotzebue paused in a moment of arrogant and self-pitying reflection: 'Ah! Even though I was just passing by them in a coach, yet my condition was perhaps worse than theirs! – Only the

soul gives the measure of suffering' (p. 243).

255. *Allgemeine Nachricht* (n. 7, above), p. 6.

256. John Dundas Cochrane, *Narrative of a Pedestrian Journey through Russian and Siberian Territory, from the Frontiers of China to the Frozen Sea and Kamchatka* (2nd edn, London, 1824), Vol. II, pp. 146–52.

257. Cottrell, *Recollections*, p. 325.

258. Perry McDonough Collins, *A Voyage down the Amoor, with a Land Journey through Siberia, and Incidental Notices of Manchooria, Kamschatka, and Japan* (New York, 1860), pp. 115–18.

259. Mrs Aga, *Adventures*, pp. 252–55.

260. Harry Lansdell, *Through Siberia* (3rd edn, London, 1882), pp. 43, 408–12, 418, 429; Kennan, *Siberia*, Vol. II, pp. 279, 285, 300, 305–07.

2 'The Bailiff's Magic Rod'

1. StA Bremen 2.-D. 18. 0, No. 5: Gröning to Senate, 21 May 1845, pp. 1–2.

2. Ibid., pp. 3–9.

3. Ernst Dronke, *Polizei-Geschichten, sowie der Prozess gegen denselben vor dem Zuchtpolizeigericht zu Koblenz* (ed. Detlev Wagner, Berlin, 1980), pp. 76–83.

4. Wilhelm Breithaupt, *Die Strafe des Staupenschlags und ihre Abschaffung im Gemeinen Recht* (Jena, 1938).

5. See Blasius, *Bürgerliche Gesellschaft*; and, on Bremen, Johannes Feest and Christian Marzahn (eds), *Criminalia. Bremer Strafjustiz 1810–1850* (Beiträge zur Sozialgeschichte Bremens, Vol. 11, Bremen, 1988).

6. Reinhard Koselleck, *Preussen zwischen Reform und Revolution. Allgemeines Landrecht, Verwaltung und soziale Bewegung von 1791 bis 1848* (Stuttgart, 1967), Exkurs I: 'Über die langsame Einschränkung körperlicher Züchtigung', pp. 641–59; here pp. 641–43.

7. GStA Berlin Rep. 841/8312, Bl. 6: Neumärkischer Regierungs- und Kriegs- und Domänen-Kammer allergehorsamstes Gericht, 23 Sept. 1806

8. See *Allgemeines Landrecht für die Preussischen Staaten von 1794* (Textausgabe, mit einer Einführung von Hans Hattenhauer, 2nd edn, Frankfurt am Main, 1994). Hattenhauer's introduction to this edition is the best overall account of the Code, its origins and its influence. See also J.-U. Heuer, *Allgemeines Landrecht und Klassenkampf. Die Auseinandersetzungen um die Prinzipien des Allgemeinen Landrechts Ende des 18. Jahrhunderts als Ausdruck der Krise des Feudalsystems in Preussen* (Berlin [East], 1960), and Wolff (ed.), *Das Preussische Allgemeine Landrecht*.

9. Friedrich Malblank (ed.), *Geschichte der Peinlichen Gerichtsordnung Kaiser Karls V.* (Nuremberg, 1763), pp. 237–38, and Gustav Radbruch (ed.), *Die Peinliche Gerichtsordnung Kaiser Karls V. von 1532 (Carolina)* (4th edn, Stuttgart, 1975), Clauses cvi–clxvi. See also J. Kohler and W. Scheel (eds), *Die Carolina und ihre Vorgängerinnen. Text, Erläuterungen, Geschichte* (4 vols, Halle, 1900–15, repr. Aalen, 1970), and F.C. Schroeder, *Die Carolina. Die Peinliche Gerichtsordnung Kaiser Karls* (Darmstadt, 1986). For an important collection of legal-historical studies, see Peter Landau and Friedrich Schröter (eds), *Strafrecht, Strafprozess und Rezeption: Grundlagen, Entwicklungen und Wirkung der Constitutio Criminalis Carolina* (Frankfurt am Main, 1984).

10. See Evans, *Rituals*, pp. 109–21.

11. *Novum Corpus*, 1801, No. 40 (pp. 963–66): Circulare an die Regierungen, dass bei Criminal-Untersuchungen die Angeschuldigten durch thätliche

Behandlung nicht zum Bekenntniss der Wahrheit zu nöthigen.

12. Koselleck, *Preussen*, p. 644.

13. GStA Berlin Rep. 84a/8312, Bl. 1: Friedrich Wilhelm III to Goldbeck, 24 Dec. 1804; ibid., Bl. 2–6: Neumärkischer Regierungs- und Kriegs und Domänen-Kammer allergehorsamstes Gericht, 23 Sept. 1806; ibid., Bl. 9–13: order of Friedrich Wilhelm III, 12 Feb. 1810, and report of Oberlandesgericht Neumark, 23 March 1810; ibid., Bl. 18: Friedrich Willhelm III to Oberlandesgericht Neumark, 28 April 1810.

14. Ibid., Bl. 20: report of 21 Dec. 1816; ibid., Bl. 21: Regierung Breslau to Justizministerium, 3 Dec. 1816; ibid., Bl. 26–27: Oberlandesgericht Breslau to Justizministerium, 20 July 1818; ibid., Bl. 29–30: Regierung Breslau to Justizministerium, 23 July 1818; ibid., Bl. 44: Oberlandesgericht Naumburg to Justizministerium, 26 Nov. 1824; ibid., Bl. 45: report of 15 Dec. 1824; ibid., Bl. 47: Justizministerium memorandum for Justizminister, 28 Oct. 1832; Koselleck, *Preussen*, p. 650.

15. Jutta Nowosadtko, 'Die Ehre, die Unehre und das Staatsinteresse. Konzepte und Funktionen von "Unehrlichkeit" im historischen Wandel am Beispiel des Kurfürstentums Bayern', *Geschichte in Wissenschaft und Unterricht*, 43 (1993), pp. 362–81; van Dülmen, *Kultur und Alltag*, pp. 194–214. More generally, see Martin Dinges, 'Die Ehre als Thema der Stadtgeschichte. Eine Semantik am Übergang vom Ancien Régime zur Moderne', *Zeitschrift für historische Forschung*, 16 (1989), pp. 409–40; Susanna Burghartz, 'Weibliche Ehre', in Heide Wunder and Karin Hausen (eds), *Frauengeschichte – Geschlechtergeschichte* (Frankfurt am Main, 1992), pp. 173–83; and Gerd Schwerhoff, '"Mach, daß wir nicht in eine Schande geraten!" Frauen in Kölner Kriminalfällen des 16.

Jahrhunderts', *Geschichte in Wissenschaft und Unterricht*, 43 (1993), pp. 451–73. Schwerhoff, 'Verordnete Schande? Spätmittelalterliche und frühneuzeitliche Ehrenstrafen zwischen Rechtsakt und sozialer Sanktion', in Blauert and Schwerhoff (eds), *Mit den Waffen*, pp. 158–88, provides an interpretative overview.

16. See Kai-Detlev Sievers, 'Prügelstrafe als Zeichen ständischer Ungleichheit', in Karl Köstlin and Kai-Detlev Sievers (eds), *Das Recht der kleinen Leute. Festschrift für Karl-Sigmund Kramer* (Berlin, 1976), pp. 195–206.

17. GStA Berlin Rep. 84a/8180, Bl. 1a: Goldbeck memorandum of 15 Aug. 1804.

18. Ibid./8181, Bl. 55: Staatsministerium to King Friedrich Wilhelm IV, 4 March 1853; cf. also Koselleck, *Preussen*, pp. 646–49.

19. Corporal punishment ordered by the courts had to be administered either by prison warders or by court bailiffs (*Gerichtsdiener* or *Gerichtsboten*), and was carried out, as a result of a decree of 1808, 'ad posteriora' with a leather whip or a cane. It was felt that whipping on the back was dangerous to the offender's health, so it was banned. A prison or court doctor only had to be present if there were *prima facie* doubts about the offender's ability to withstand the punishment. In the old Prussian provinces, the cane was seldom used, since whipping was considered more effective. In 1828, the Ministry of Justice confirmed that the whip was preferable. The prison at Lichtenburg used 'leather whips and thin hazel canes always on the clothed posterior'. The whip was usually about 27 inches long and slightly less than an inch thick, and it was made 'from four to five layers of leather laid over one another'. The offender was made fast to a device specially designed for the purpose. See GStA Berlin Rep. 84a/8180, Bl. 11a, 12g, 21–35: Landgericht Traustadt to

Justizministerium, 15 Sept. 1831, and reply, 30 Sept. 1831; Criminal-Senat des Oberlandesgerichts Naumburg to Justizministerium, 3 Feb. 1832, and reply, 8 June 1832; Kammergericht Berlin to Justizministerium, 14 May 1832; King Friedrich Wilhelm IV to Justice Minister Mühler, 17 Nov. 1838.

20. GStA Berlin Rep. 84a/8180, Bl. 12a, 12b; for similar complaints from the Superior District Court (*Oberlandesgericht*) in Ratibor, in 1830, see ibid., Bl. 13.

21. Reported in ibid./8181, Bl. 55: Staatsministerium to King Friedrich Wilhelm IV, 4 March 1853.

22. Koselleck, *Preussen*, pp. 651–55.

23. GStA Berlin Rep. 84a/8182, Bl. 102: Materialien: betr. die Abschaffung der Prügelstrafe in Preussen, 23 Sept. 1898.

24. Ibid./8035, Bl. 91: Strafrechts-kommission, 29 Oct. 1845; see also, briefly, Koselleck, *Preussen*, p. 658.

25. GStA Berlin Rep. 84a/8180, Bl. 146: Einige Bemerkungen zu den Verhandlungen der fünften Sitzung des Vereinigten Ständischen Ausschusses – die Abschaffung der körperlichen Züchtigung als Strafe betreffend; ibid./8182, Bl. 103: Materialien: betr. die Abschaffung der Prügelstrafe in Preussen, 23 Sept. 1898.

26. Siemann, 'Deutschlands Ruhe', pp. 341–42.

27. GStA Berlin Rep. 842/8180, Bl. 145–55: Denkschrift of Polizei-präsident von Minutoli, 3 Feb. 1848.

28. Ibid., Bl. 156: Eingabe des Constitutionellen Clubs, Berlin, 24 April 1848.

29. Ibid., Bl. 138: *Gesetzes-Sammlung für die Königlichen Preussischen Staaten*, No. 21, No. 2967, 6 May 1848.

30. H. Föhring, *Noch ein Wort zur Prügelstrafe* (Hamburg, 1879), p. 6.

31. See StA Bremen 2.-D.18.p: Körperliche Züchtigung.

32. GStA Berlin Rep. 84a/8181, Bl. 3: Friedrich Wilhelm IV to Justizministerium, 7 Dec. 1852.

33. Ibid., Bl. 2: Friedrich Wilhelm IV to Justizministerium, 8 Dec. 1852.

34. Marx also suffered from the connection, which was used to try and compromise him by his enemy, the left-winger Karl Vogt. For the connection, see David McLellan, *Karl Marx. His Life and Thought* (London, 1973), pp. 65, 312, 327.

35. GStA Berlin Rep. 84a/8181, Bl. 46: Votum des Innenministers, 7 Feb. 1853.

36. Ibid., Bl. 257–58: Votum des Innenministeriums, 30 Nov. 1854; italics in original.

37. Ibid., Bl. 214–23: Votum des Justizministers Simons.

38. Ibid., Bl. 262–65: Magistrat zu Lützen, petition of 30 Jan. 1855; ibid., Bl. 297–98: Oberpräsident der Provinz Sachsen (Witzleben) and Provinziallandtag.; ibid., Bl. 317: Bericht der Kommission für das Justiz-Wesen über den Antrag der Abgeordneten v. Rosenberg-Lipinsky und Genossen auf Einführung der körperlichen Züchtigung als gerichtliches Strafmittel, und mehrere, denselben Gegenstand, sowie die Verschärfung der Freiheitsstrafen betreffende Petitionen, p. 2.

39. Ibid., Bl. 266–69: Petition to Kammer der Abgeordneten, 8 March 1855.

40. GStA Berlin Rep. 181/14056, Bl. 15.

41. Ibid., Bl. 25.

42. Ibid., Bl. 11.

43. Ibid., Bl. 42–52.

44. Ibid., Bl. 35–38.

45. Ibid., Bl. 44, 56.

46. Ibid., Bl. 47.

47. Ibid., Bl. 29–34.

48. Ibid., Bl. 54–56.

49. Ibid., Bl. 58–64.

50. Ibid., Bl. 20–22.

51. Ibid., Bl. 63–64.

52. Ibid., Bl. 72–81; italics in original.

53. GStA Berlin Rep. 84a/8181, Bl. 235–48: Staatsministerium 'An des Königs Majestät', Berlin, n.d. (1854, draft); ibid., Bl. 276–90 (fair copy of same); ibid., Bl. 291–95.

54. Ibid., Bl. 87: Staatsministerium to Friedrich Wilhelm IV, 4 March 1853.

55. Ibid., Bl. 78–86: Votum des Justiz ministers Simons den Allerhöchsten Erlass vom 8ten Dezember 1852 wegen Wiedereinführung der körperlichen Züchtigung, betreffend.

56. Ibid., Bl. 134–213: Zusammenstellung des wesentlichen Inhalts der von den Gerichten über das Bedürfniss und die Nothwendigkeit einer Wiedereinführung der körperlichen Züchtigung als Strafe für gewisse Gattungen von Verbrechern und Vergehungen, sowie für einzelne Klassen von Verbrecher abgegebenen Gutachten.

57. Ibid., Bl. 214–23: Votum des Justizministers Simons.

58. Ibid., Bl. 317: Bericht der Kommission für das Justiz-Wesen über den Antrag der Abgeordneten v. Rosenberg-Lipinski und Genossen auf Einführung der körperlichen Züchtigung als gerichtliches Strafmittel (Nr. 37 der Drucksachen) und mehrere denselben Gegenstand, sowie die Verschärfung der Freiheitsstrafen betreffende Petitionen (Preussischer Landtag, Haus der Abgeordneten, IV. Legislaturperiode, 1. Session, Drucksache Nr. 199: Berichterstatter: Abgeordneter Breithaupt), pp. 1–4.

59. Ibid., Bl. 326: 'Nicht die Verbrechern, nur die Gefangenen haben sich unverhältnismässig vermehrt', Der Publicist. Zeitung für Recht und Gerichtsverfahren, Vol. XI, No. 37, 9 May 1856.

60. Ibid., Bl. 317: Bericht der Kommission für das Justiz-Wesen, pp. 4–5, italics in original.

61. Ibid., pp. 6–10.

62. Ibid., pp. 10–15.

63. Ibid., pp. 16–21.

64. Föhring, Noch ein Wort, p. 5.

65. GStA Berlin Rep. 84a/8184, Bl. 47: Der Tag, 21 March 1901.

66. Paul Sauer, Im Namen des Königs. Strafgesetzgebung und Strafvollzug im Königreich Württemberg von 1806 bis 1871 (Stuttgart, 1984), p. 171.

67. GStA Berlin Rep. 84a/8184: Berliner Tageblatt, 1 Feb. 1908.

68. Arnim, Bruchstücke, Anlage 7, p. 77.

69. Ibid., Part I, pp. 83–84.

70. Reported in GStA Berlin Rep. 84a/8181, Bl. 55: Staatsministerium to Friedrich Wilhelm IV, 4 March 1853.

71. Ibid./8180, Bl. 8: Friedrich Wilhelm III, memo of 14 May 1811, italics in original.

72. Ibid., Bl. 21–35: Landgericht Traustadt to Justizministerium, 15 Sept. 1831, and reply, 30 Sept. 1831; Criminal-Senat des Oberlandesgerichts Naumburg to Justizministerium, 3 Feb. 1832; Kammergericht Berlin to Justizministerium, 14 May 1832; Justizministerium to Criminal-Senat des Oberlandesgerichts Naumburg, 8 June 1832; Friedrich Wilhelm IV to Justice Minister Mühler, 17 Nov. 1838; ibid./8181, Bl. 303 (extracts from prison regulations).

73. Ibid., Bl. 309: Haus-Ordnung für die Arrest- und Korrektionshäuser in den Rheinprovinzen, §89 (23 Oct. 1827).

74. Alfred Bergmann, Das Detmolder Zuchthaus als Stätte von Christian Dietrich Grabbes Kindheit und Jugend. Zugleich ein Beitrag zur Geschichte des Strafvollzuges in Lippe an der Wende vom achtzehnten zum neunzehnten Jahrhundert (Detmold, 1968), pp. 58–65.

75. Ibid./8180, Bl. 79–70 (Mühler to Friedrich Wilhelm IV, 19 March 1833), and 95a–c (Friedrich Wilhelm IV to Mühler, 21 Dec. 1833); see also ibid./8182, Bl. 101: Materialien: betr. die Abschaffung der Prügelstrafe in Preussen.

76. Evans, Rituals, Chs 5, 6.

77. GStA Berlin Rep. 84a/8180, Bl. 162: memorandum of Justizministerium, 16 June 1848.

78. Ibid., Bl. 174: Criminal-Senat des Appellations-Gerichts Königsberg to Justizministerium, 6 Dec. 1849.

79. Ibid., Bl. 170: Magistrat Breslau to Justizministerium, 12 Dec. 1849.

80. Ibid., Bl. 172: Justizministerium to Magistrat Breslau, 5 Jan. 1850.

81. Ibid., Bl. 180: Appellationsgericht Magdeburg to Justizministerium, 9 March 1850.

82. Ibid./8181, Bl. 66a: Simons memorandum of 7 April 1853.

83. Ibid., Bl. 300–301: Votum, dem Königlichen Staats- und Justiz-Minister Herrn Simons Excellenz vorzulegen; italics in original.

84. Ibid./8182, Bl. 1–2.

85. See Evans, *Rituals*, Chs 6, 7.

86. See ibid., Ch. 7.

87. GStA Berlin Rep. 84a/8182: *Preussisches Abgeordnetenhaus*, 18. Sitzung, 18. Dec. 1882, pp. 375–77.

88. See the instances cited by August Bebel in *Stenographische Berichte über die Verhandlungen des deutschen Reichstages*, 10. Legislaturperiode, 1. Session, 175. Sitzung, 23 March 1900, p. 4941.

89. GStA Berlin Rep. 84a/8182, Bl. 10–12.

90. Ibid./8184: *Breslauer Zeitung*, 15 Dec. 1882.

91. Ibid.: *Berliner Tageblatt*, 5 May 1893.

92. *Stenographische Berichte über die Verhandlungen des deutschen Reichstages*, 10. Legislaturperiode, 1. Session, 175. Sitzung, 23 March 1900, p. 4941: (As above, n. 88).

93. GStA Berlin Rep. 84a/8184: *Posener Zeitung*, 13 May 1894; *Berliner Volkszeitung*, 13 May 1894.

94. Ibid.: *Berliner Tageblatt*, 30 March 1896.

95. Ibid.: *Freisinnige Zeitung*, 17 Feb. 1899.

96. Föhring, *Noch ein Wort*, p. 6.

97. GStA Berlin Rep. 84a/8184: *Deutsche Tageszeitung*, 13 Feb. 1909; see also ibid.: *Die Grosse Glocke*, 14 April 1909.

98. Ibid.: *Westfälischer Merkur*, 20 Sept. 1898.

99. Ibid.: *Berliner Volksblatt*, 14 July 1886.

100. *Stenographische Berichte über die Verhandlungen des deutschen Reichs-* *tages*, 10. Legislaturperiode, 1. Session, 175. Sitzung, 23 March 1900.

101. GStA Berlin Rep. 84a/8184, Bl. 51: Entscheidungen des Preussischen Oberverwaltungsgerichts, Vol. 9, p. 437, Vol. 15, p. 444, Vol. 16, pp. 414–15, Vol. 30, p. 437, cited in *Strassburger Post*, 26 Nov. 1901 ('Einige Bemerkungen über die Prügelstrafe').

102. For a selection, see Helmut von Bracken, *Die Prügelstrafe* (Dresden, 1925).

103. C. Klett, *Der Lehrer ohne Stock. Gegen die körperliche Strafe in der Schule* (Stuttgart, 1869), p. 5.

104. A. Freimund, *Über körperliche Züchtigung beim Unterricht in Volksschulen* (Leipzig, 1875), p. 23.

105. *Stenographische Berichte über die Verhandlungen des deutschen Reichstages*, 10. Legislaturperiode, 1. Session, 61. Sitzung, 7 March 1900, p. 4497: Abg. Bassermann.

106. Klett, *Der Lehrer ohne Stock*, pp. 11, 25.

107. Freimund, *Über körperliche Züchtigung*, pp. 30–50.

108. (Anon.), *Die Abschaffung des Rechtes körperlicher Züchtigung in der Schule* (Erlangen, 1868), *passim*.

109. Freimund, *Über körperliche Züchtigung*, p. 73.

110. (Anon.), *Die Abschaffung*, p. 5.

111. *Stenographische Berichte über die Verhandlungen des deutschen Reichstages*, 10. Legislaturperiode, 1. Session, 61. Sitzung, 7 March 1900, p. 4494: Abg. Oertel.

112. Ibid., p. 4497.

113. Norbert Elias, *Über den Prozess der Zivilisation. Soziogenetische und psychogenetische Untersuchungen*, Vol. I: *Wandlungen des Verhaltens in den weltlichen Oberschichten des Abendlandes*; Vol. II: *Wandlungen der Gesellschaft. Entwurf zu einer Theorie der Zivilisation* (Bern, 1969); Pieter Spierenburg, *The Spectacle of Suffering. Executions and the Evolution of Repression: From a Preindustrial Metropolis to the European Experience* (Cambridge, 1984); idem, *The*

Broken Spell. A Cultural and Anthropological History of Preindustrial Europe (London, 1991), pp. 1–13.

114.   Elias, *Studien, passim.*

115.   GStA Berlin Rep. 84a/8184: *Vossische Zeitung,* 14 March 1880.

116.   Ibid.: *Norddeutsche Allgemeine Zeitung,* 24 Sept. 1880.

117.   Ibid./8182, Bl. 435: *Preussisches Abgeordnetenhaus,* 19. Sitzung, 13. Feb. 1885.

118.   Ibid./8184, Bl. 13: *Kreuzzeitung,* 15 June 1894.

119.   Ibid., Bl. 68: *Hamburger Nachrichten,* 18 Nov. 1905 (1. Morgenausgabe).

120.   Ibid.: *Das Volk,* 26 May 1894.

121.   Ibid.: *Ostpreussische Zeitung,* 6 May 1898.

122.   Ibid.: *Das Volk,* 26 May 1894; *Deutsche Tageszeitung,* 16 Sept. 1898.

123.   Ibid.: *Deutsche Tageszeitung,* 16 Sept. 1898 (italics in original); the same claim in ibid.: 1 March 1900; similarly in *Stenographische Berichte über die Verhandlungen des deutschen Reichstages,* 10. Legislaturperiode, 1. Session, 175. Sitzung, 23 March 1900.

124.   GStA Berlin Rep. 84a/8184: *Deutsche Tageszeitung,* 24 Jan. 1901.

125.   Ibid., Bl. 52: *Deutsche Tageszeitung,* 11 Oct. 1902 (Abendausgabe); ibid., Bl. 65: *Kreuz-Zeitung,* 4 June 1904 (Abendausgabe); ibid.: *Der Tag,* 26 June 1904; ibid.: *Deutsche Tageszeitung,* 13 Feb. 1909.

126.   Ibid., Bl. 59: *Hamburger Nachrichten,* 17 Nov. 1903 (Abendausgabe); ibid., Bl. 68: *Hamburger Nachrichten,* 18 Nov. 1905 (1. Morgenausgabe).

127.   Ibid., Bl. 60: *Deutsche Tageszeitung,* 8 Dec. 1903 (Morgenausgabe); ibid., Bl. 65: *Kreuzzeitung,* 4 June 1904 (Abendausgabe).

128.   Ibid.: *Deutsche Tageszeitung,* 16 Sept. 1898; see also ibid.: *Kreuzeitung,* 25 Aug. 1899.

129.   Ibid.: *Breslauer Zeitung,* 4 Feb. 1900.

130.   Ibid.: *Vorwärts,* 28 July 1899.

131.   Ibid.: *Vorwärts,* 13 March 1900.

132.   *Stenographische Berichte über die Verhandlungen des deutschen Reichstages,* 10. Legislaturperiode, 1. Session, 175. Sitzung, 23 March 1900, p. 4941.

133.   GStA Berlin Rep. 84a/8184: *Freisinnige Zeitung,* 12 Nov. 1885.

134.   Ibid.: *Berliner Zeitung,* 13 Aug. 1890.

135.   Ibid., Bl. 69: *Leipziger Tageblatt,* 22 Nov. 1905.

136.   Ibid., Bl. 64: *Freie Deutsche Presse,* 19 April 1904; ibid., Bl. 68: *Hamburger Nachrichten,* 18 Nov. 1905 (1. Morgenausgabe).

137.   Ibid.: *Hamburger Nachrichten,* 7 Dec. 1909.

138.   Ibid.: *Strassburger Post,* 3 Dec. 1910.

139.   Ibid.: *Hannoverscher Kurier,* 12 Jan. 1911.

140.   Ibid.: *Vossische Zietung,* 15 Dec. 1910, *Magdeburgische Zeitung,* 13 July 1911.

141.   *Stenographische Berichte über die Verhandlungen des deutschen Reichstages,* 10. Legislaturperiode, 1. Session, 61. Sitzung, 7 March 1900, p. 4500: speech of Abg. Müller-Meiningen.

142.   GStA Berlin Rep. 84a/8184: reported in *Deutsche Tageszeitung,* 7 April 1911.

143.   Clive Emsley, *Crime and Society in England 1750–1900* (London, 1987), p. 231.

144.   GStA Berlin Rep. 84a/8184, Bl. 53: 'Die Bekämpfung des gewerbsmässigen Verbrechertums. Von einem Richter', *Strassburger Post,* 3 Nov. 1902 (2. Mittagsausgabe).

145.   Ibid.: reported in *Deutsche Tageszeitung,* 7 April 1911.

146.   Ibid., Bl. 69: *Leipziger Tageblatt,* 22 Nov. 1905.

147.   *Stenographische Berichte über die Verhandlungen des deutschen Reichstages,* 10. Legislaturperiode, 1. Session, 61. Sitzung, 7 March 1900, p. 4500.

148.   Karen Halttunen, 'Humanitarianism and the Pornography of Pain in Anglo-American Culture', *American Historical Review,* 100 (1995), No. 2, pp. 303–34; Schenda, *Volk ohne Buch,* pp. 351–56.

149.   J. Zeisig, *Memoiren einer Prostituierten,*

oder die Prostitution in Hamburg (St Pauli, 1847), pp. 137–39.

150. Rudolf Quanter, *Die Leibes- und Lebensstrafen bei allen Völkern und zu allen Zeiten* (Dresden, 1901); idem, *Die Schand- und Ehrenstrafen in der deutschen Rechtspflege* (Dresden, 1901); similarly, Dr Ullo, *Die Flagellomanie. Ihre Erscheinungsformen bei Anwendung der Straf- und Erziehungsmittel. Aufzeichnungen aus dem Leben, der Litteratur und Vergangenheit* (Dresden, 1901).

151. Dr Med. Wilhelm Hammer, *Die Prügelstrafe in ärztlicher Beleuchtung* (Leipzig, 1906).

152. 'Bernadotte', *Die strenge Klavier-lehrerin. Rute, Stock und Peitsche als Züchtigungsmittel für faule und unaufmerksame Klavierschüler und Klavierschülerinnen* (Pressburg, 1910), and the endpaper advertisements for other, similar publications; Else Ramburg, *Die Zuchtrute von Tante Anna. Ein interessantes Kapitel zur häuslichen Strafdisziplin* (Pressburg, 1908); etc.

153. D.K. Korell, *Pädagogische Irrwege oder Sadismus?* (Berlin, 1904), p. 4.

154. (Anon.), *Bildersammlung zum Verständnis des Sadismus und Masochismus, mit neuen aufklärenden Berichten* (Philadelphia, 1908), p. 17.

155. Bram Dijkstra, *Idols of Perversity: Fantasies of Female Evil in Fin-de-Siècle Culture* (New York, 1986); Gail Finney, *Women in Modern Drama: Freud, Feminism, and European Theater at the Turn of the Century* (Ithaca, NY, 1989).

156. Richard J. Evans, *The Feminist Movement in Germany 1894–1933* (London, 1976), esp. Chs 1–3.

157. See Maria Tatar, *Lustmord. Sexual Murder in Weimar Germany* (Princeton, 1995).

158. Klaus Theweleit, *Männerphantasien* (2 vols, Frankfurt am Main, 1977).

159. StA Bremen 2.-D. 18. 0, No. 5: Gröning to Senate, 21 May 1845, pp. 10–13.

160. Ibid.: 'Gerichtliche Vollmacht'.

161. Ibid.: Genehmigt in Senatssitzung vom 21. Mai 1845; Blasius, *Kriminalität und Alltag*, p. 51.

3 *The Many Identities of Franz Ernst*

1. Staatsarchiv Bremen 4, 14/1 – VII B 1e: *Eberhard's Allgemeiner Polizei-Anzeiger*, Bd. LI, No. 4 (Dresden, 13. Juli 1864), pp. 19–20.

2. Ibid.: Rechnung, Hôtel du Nord, Bremen (sent to police by landlord).

3. Ibid.: police notes of interrogation on 31 May 1864.

4. Ibid.: *Der Demokraten-Congress in Brüssel, am 26. September 1863, und die Absichten des demokratischen Central-Comités in Genf, von einem Mitglied des Central-Comités dargestellt. Den regierenden und nicht regierenden Fürsten Europas ehrfurchtsvoll gewidmet*, p. 9.

5. Ibid., p. 17.

6. Ibid., pp. 21–24.

7. Ibid., pp. 25–27.

8. Staatsarchiv Bremen 4, 14/1 – VII B 1e: 'Fragen an einen deutschen Ehrenmann'.

9. Ibid.: Notes 'Von der Polizeidirektion 11. Juli 1864'.

10. Ibid. The names Adolf Hoch and Franz Hermann Ernst are crossed out on the cover, and the final title is Maltzan – v. Hoff. For the *Steckbrief*, see ibid.: *Eberhardt's Allgemeiner Polizei-Anzeiger*, Bd. LI, No. 4 (Dresden, 13 Juli 1864), pp. 19–20.

11. For the background and status of executioners, see Evans, *Rituals*, esp. Ch. 1. Gisela Wilbertz, *Scharfrichter und Abdecker im Hochstift Osnabrück. Untersuchungen zur Sozialgeschichte zweier 'unehrlicher' Berufe im nordwestdeutschen Raum vom 16. bis zum 19. Jahrhundert* (Münster, 1979); Albrecht Keller, *Der Scharfrichter in der deutschen Kulturgeschichte* (Bonn and Leipzig, 1921); and Helmut Schuhmann, *Der Scharfrichter. Seine*

Gestalt – *seine Funktion* (Kempten/Allgäu, 1964).

12. *Preussisches Central-Polizei-Blatt*, Vol. 41, Steckbrief 4178, 1859.

13. StA Bremen 4, 14/1 – VII B 1e: *Eberhardt's Allgemeiner Polizei-Anzeiger*, Bd. LI, No. 4 (Dresden, 13. Juli 1864), pp. 19–20.

14. Karl Marx, *Enthüllungen über den Kommunistenprozess zu Köln* (Basel, 1853, repr. in Karl Marx, Friedrich Engels, *Werke*, Vol. 8, Berlin [East], 1960), pp. 405–70.

15. Leopold Auerbach (ed.), *Denkwürdigkeiten des Geheimen Regierungsrathes Dr. Stieber. Aus seinen hinterlassenen Papieren* (Berlin, 1884), pp. 109–212.

16. Wilhelm Eichhoff, *Berliner Polizei-Silhouetten* (Berlin, 1860, London, 1861, 2 vols); August Ladendorf, *Sechs Jahre Gefangenschaft unter den Folgen des Staatsstreichs und der Kampf um's Recht in der 'neuen Ära'. Ein Beitrag zur geschichtlichen Charakteristik der Reaction und deren Handlanger* (Leipzig, 1862).

17. For a contemporary pamphlet conveying this atmosphere, see A. Vandermeulen, *Enthüllungen aus der höheren Region der politischen Spionage, in Berichten eines ungarischen Judas Ischarioth. Nebst sonstigen Aufdeckungen in Bezug auf das Treiben der geheimen Polizei* (Berlin, 1802).

18. StA Bremen 4, 14/1 – VII B 1e, police notes.

19. Karl Marx, Friedrich Engels, *Werke*, Vol. 30 (Berlin [East], 1972), p. 391: Marx to Engels, 19 April 1864.

20. For these assassination attempts and their effects, see Wolfram Siemann, *'Deutschlands Ruhe, Sicherheit und Ordnung'. Die Anfänge der politischen Polizei 1806–1866* (Tübingen, 1985), p. 328.

21. StA Bremen 4, 14/1 – VII B 1e: Dr von Hoff to Wilhelm I of Prussia, 20 June 1864.

22. Ibid.: Hanover Polizeibehörde to Bremen Polizeibehörde, 11 July 1864.

23. Ibid.: 4, 14/1. VII. B. 1: Heinrich Bauer.

24. Max Roderich, *Verbrechen und Strafe. Eine Sammlung interessanter Polizei- und Criminal-Rechtsfälle, nach den Acten bearbeitet* (Jena, 1850), pp. 67–147.

25. For an excellent study of these, see Siemann, 'Deutschlands Ruhe'.

26. GStA Berlin Rep. 84a/8489: Die Herausgabe öffentlicher Blätter zur Verfolgung von Verbrechern, esp. Bl. 18–21, 91–96, 193.

27. F.C.B. Avé-Lallement, *Das deutsche Gaunerthum in seiner social-politischen, literarischen und linguistischen Ausbildung zu seinem heutigen Bestände* (4 vols, Leipzig, 1858–62).

28. Ibid., Teil II, p. 3.

29. F.C.B. Avé-Lallement, *Die Krisis der deutschen Polizei* (Leipzig, 1861), esp. pp. 14–19, 39. For a reply defending the police, see Carl August Ackermann, *Für die deutsche Polizei. Wider Herrn Dr. Avé-Lallement* (Schwerin, 1861).

30. See for example Karl Wilhelm Zimmermann, *Die Diebe in Berlin oder Darstellung ihres Entstehens, ihrer Organisation, ihrer Verbindungen, ihrer Taktik, ihrer Gewohnheiten und ihrer Sprache. Zur Belehrung für Polizeibeamte und zur Warnung für das Publikum. Nach praktischen Erfahrungen* (Berlin, 1847).

31. StA Bremen 4, 14/1: Polizei-Direction: 2. VII. B. 4: Sitten- und Kriminalpolizei. Gemeingefährliche Personen. Kunden und ihr Treiben (Gauner und Gaunerverbindungen): 'Die Kunden und ihr Treiben' (MS., 1856).

32. Avé-Lallement, *Gaunerthum*, Part II, pp. 4–5.

33. Ibid., Part I, pp. 305–06.

34. Valentini, *Verbrecherthum*, p. 117.

35. StA Bremen 4, 14/1: Polizei-Direction: 2. VII. B. 4: Sitten- und Kriminalpolizei. Gemeingefährliche Personen. Kunden und ihr Treiben (Gauner und Gaunerverbindungen): 'Die Kunden und ihr Treiben' (MS., 1856).

36. Peter Becker, 'Randgruppen im Blickfeld der Polizei. Ein Versuch über die Perspektivität des "praktischen Blicks"', *Archiv für Sozialgeschichte*, 32 (1992), pp. 283–304; idem, 'Vom "Haltlosen" zur "Bestie". Das polizeiliche Bild des "Verbrechers" im 19. Jahrhundert', in Alf Lüdtke (ed.), *'Sicherheit' und 'Wohlfahrt'. Polizei, Gesellschaft und Herrschaft im 19. und 20. Jahrhundert* (Frankfurt am Main, 1992), pp. 97–132; idem, 'Wie sieht ein Verbrecher aus?', *Damals*, 26 (1994), No. 7, p. 45.

37. O. Klatt, *Die Körpermessung der Verbrecher nach Bertillon, und die Photographie als die wichtigsten Hilfsmittel der gerichtlichen Polizei, sowie Anleitung zur Aufnahme von Fussspuren jeder Art* (Berlin, 1862), p. 7.

38. Grolmann, *Actenmässige Geschichte*, p. 2.

39. Karl Marx and Friedrich Engels, *The Communist Manifesto* in *Collected Works*, vol. 6 (London, 1976).

40. Dr von Hoff, *Die deutschen Gelehrten, Kaufleute, Handwerker und Tagelöhner in England, Schottland und Irland, mit ihren Institutionen, in ihrem Leben und Treiben* (Mannheim, 1863), pp. 1–7, 11–12.

41. Richard J. Evans, 'Family and Class in the Hamburg Grand Bourgeoisie 1815–1914', in David Blackbourn and Richard J. Evans (eds), *The German Bourgeoisie. Essays on the Social History of the German Middle Class from the Late Eighteenth to the Early Twentieth Century* (London, 1991), pp. 115–39.

4 The Life and Death of a Lost Woman

1. Margarete Böhme (ed.), *Tagebuch einer Verlorenen. Von einer Toten* (Berlin, 1905).

2. Eadem, *Dida Ibsens Geschichte. Ein Finale zum 'Tagebuch einer Verlorenen'* (Berlin, 1907), pp. v–vii.

3. Susan Sontag, *Illness as Metaphor* (London, 1983).

4. August Bebel, *Die Frau und der Sozialismus* ([East], Berlin, 1964 edn), pp. 207–42.

5. Heinrich Lux, *Die Prostitution, ihre Ursachen, ihre Folgen und ihre Bekämpfung* (Berliner Arbeiterbibliothek, III. Serie, 4. Heft, Berlin, 1892), p. 12; see also Paul Kampffmeyer, *Die Prostitution als soziale Klassenerscheinung und ihre sozialpolitische Bekämpfung* (Berlin, 1905).

6. Richard J. Evans, 'Prostitution, State and Society in Imperial Germany', *Past and Present* 70 (February 1976), pp. 106–29.

7. Regine Schulte, *Sperrbezirke. Tugendhaftigkeit und Prostitution in der bürgerlichen Welt* (Frankfurt am Main, 1979), p. 94.

8. Alain Corbin, *Women for Hire. Prostitution and Sexuality in France after 1850* (London, 1990).

9. Franz Brüggemeier, '"Volle Kost voll". Die Wohnungsverhältnisse der Bergleute an der Ruhr um die Jahrhundertwende', in Hans Mommsen and Ulrich Borsdorf (eds), *Glück auf, Kameraden! Die Bergarbeiter und ihre Organisationen in Deutschland* (Cologne, 1979), pp. 151–73.

10. Hans Ostwald, *Dunkle Winkel in Berlin* (Grossstadt-Dokumente, Vol. 1, Berlin, 1905).

11. Magnus Hirschfeld, *Berlins Drittes Geschlecht* (Grossstadt-Dokumente, Vol. 3, Berlin, 1905), p. 66.

12. Hans Ostwald, *Vagabonden* (Berlin, 1901); idem, *Die Tippelschickse* (Berlin, 1901); idem, *Verworfene. Erzählungen und Skizzen* (Berlin, 1902); idem, *Die Bekämpfung der Landstreicherei* (Stuttgart, 1903); idem, *Berliner Nachtbilder* (Berlin, 1903); idem, *Lieder aus dem Rinnstein* (Berlin, 1903).

13. See Peter Fritzsche, 'Vagabond in the Fugitive City: Hans Ostwald,

Imperial Berlin and the *Gross-stadtdokumente*', *Journal of Contemporary History*, 29 (1994), pp. 385–402.

14. Hans Ostwald, *Das Berliner Dirnentum*, Vol. 6: *Prostitutionsmärkte* (Berlin, 1905), p. 14.

15. Ibid. See also Ostwald, *Berliner Tanzlokale* (Berlin, 1905), p. 7; Wilhelm Hammer, *Zehn Lebensläufe Berliner Kontrollmädchen* (Grossstadt-Dokumente, Vol. 23, Berlin, 1905); and (Anon.), *Norddeutsches Babel. Ein Beitrag zur Geschichte, Charakteristik und Verminderung der Berliner Prostitution. Herausgegeben von einem philantropischen Verein* (Berlin, 1870).

16. Ostwald, *Prostitutionsmärkte*, pp. 6–7, 9.

17. Ibid., p. 12.

18. Ibid., pp. 20, 27.

19. Carl Röhrmann, *Der sittliche Zustand von Berlin nach Aufhebung der geduldeten Prostitution des weiblichen Geschlechts. Ein Beitrag zur Geschichte der Gegenwart unterstützt durch die vollständigen und freimüthigen Biographien der bekanntesten prostituirten Frauenzimmer in Berlin* (Leipzig, 1846), pp. 36–40; for a similar assessment, see (Anon.), *Die Hamburger Prostitution, oder die Geheimnisse des Dammthorwalles und der Schwiegerstrasse* (Altona, 1858), pp. 54–60.

20. Schulte, *Sperrbezirke*, p. 55.

21. Sta Braunschweig D IV 4783: Polizeidirektion to Stadtmagistrat, 12 June 1868.

22. Quoted in (Anon.), *Norddeutsches Babel*, p. 24.

23. StA Lübeck Rep. 49/1 No. 746, report of 7 March 1873.

24. Ibid., No. 747: Militärherren to Polizeiamt, 16 Nov. 1856.

25. Ibid., No. 751.

26. GLA Karlsruhe 233/32128: 12. Sitzung der 1. Kammer der Abgeordneten, 7. Mai 1910, Abg. Troeltsch (p. 485); for student customs in visiting brothels, see also Iwan Bloch and Georg Loewenstein, *Die Prostitution*, Vol. II (Berlin, 1925), p. 423.

27. E. Hoffet, *Die Unzucht, Ihre Ursachen und ihre Bekämpfung. Mit besonderer Berücksichtigung ihrer Reglementierung durch den Staat. Vortrag gehalten im Instruktionskursus für Innere Mission in Karlsruhe (Oktober 1899)* (2nd edn, Colmar, 1900), p. 10.

28. (Anon.), *Die deutschen Frauen und die Hamburger Bordelle. Eine Abrechnung mit dem Syndikus Dr. Schäfer, Hamburg, wegen seiner Reichstagsrede am 28. Januar 1904. Referate in der Protestversammlung des Deutschen Zweigs der 'Internationalen Föderation' am 12. Februar 1904 in Berlin* (Pössneck, 1904), pp. 28–30, italics in original.

29. GLA Karlsruhe 233/32128: Stellungnahme der Grossh. Regierung zum Bericht der Petitionskommission der 2. Kammer (No. 101, Beilage der 124. öffentl. Sitzung der 2. Kammer von 12. Augu. 1908).

30. Lynn Abrams, 'Prostitutes in Imperial Germany, 1870–1918: Working Girls or Social Outcasts?', in Richard J. Evans (ed.), *The German Underworld. Deviants and Outcasts in German History* (London, 1988), pp. 189–209, here p. 194, with examples from Remscheid and Neuss.

31. See, for example, the allusions to 'Perversitäten' in GLA Karlsruhe 233/32128: Beilage zum Protokoll der 94. öffentlichen Sitzung der 2. Kammer vom 13. Juli 1910: Bericht der Petitionskommission (Drucksache No. 76).

32. Friedrich Wilhelm Müller, *Die Prostitution in Deutschland am Ende des 19. Jahrhunderts. Historisch-kritische Darlegung der Notwendigkeit einer diesbezüglichen Reform* (Regensburg, 1892), p. 47.

33. Quoted in Anon. (i.e. Wilhelm Stieber), *Die Prostitution in Berlin und ihre Opfer. In historischer, sittlicher, medizinischer und polizeilicher Beziehung beleuchtet* (2nd edn, Berlin, 1846), p. iii.

34. (Anon.), *Die Hamburger Prostitution*, pp. 50, 60. The Vierlanden was a rural district outside Hamburg,

known for its production of fruit and vegetables.

35. Quoted in (Anon.), *Norddeutsches Babel*, pp. 15–16.
36. J. Zeisig, *Memoiren einer Prostituierten, oder die Prostitution in Hamburg* (St Pauli, 1847), p. 146.
37. Cited in Lux, *Die Prostitution*, p. 13.
38. Kurt Schneider, *Studien über Persönlichkeit und Schicksal eingeschriebener Prostituierter* (Berlin, 1921), pp. 177–79 and 224–25.
39. Flexner, *Prostitution in Europe*, p. 63.
40. Urban, *Staat und Prostitution*, p. 103.
41. Schneider, *Studien*, p. 189.
42. *Zeitschrift für die gesamte Strafrechtswissenschaft* 23/103 (1902).
43. Urban, *Staat und Prostitution*, pp. 39–40; and Abraham Flexner, *Prostitution in Europe* (New York, 1914), p. 157.
44. Lux, *Die Prostitution*, p. 13.
45. GLA Karlsruhe 233/12640: Eingabe des Vereins der Freundinnen junger Mädchen zu Heidelberg an den Reichstag, 1895 (see also *Stenographische Berichte über die Verhandlungen des deutschen Reichstags*, 9. Leg. Per., 5. Sess., 1897–98, Drucksache No. 1, p. 123).
46. Schulte, *Sperrbezirke*, pp. 88–112.
47. Robyn Dasey, 'Women's Work and the Family: Women Garment Workers in Berlin and Hamburg before the First World War', in Richard J. Evans and W.R. Lee (eds), *The German Family. Essays on the Social History of the Family in 19th- and 20th-Century Germany* (London, 1981), pp. 221–55.
48. Stefan Bajohr, 'Illegitimacy and the Working Class: Illegitimate Mothers in Brunswick, 1900–1933', in Richard J. Evans (ed.), *The German Working Class 1888–1933: The Politics of Everyday Life* (London, 1982), pp. 147–73.
49. Abrams, 'Prostitutes', p. 196.
50. Robert P. Neuman, 'Industrialization and Sexual Behavior: Some Aspects of Working-Class Life in Imperial Germany', in Robert J.

Bzucha (ed.), *Modern European Social History* (Lexington, Mass., 1972), pp. 270–98, here p. 291.
51. Flexner, *Prostitution in Europe*, p. 79.
52. Karin Walser, *Dienstmädchen. Frauenarbeit und Weiblichkeitsbilder um 1900* (Frankfurt am Main, 1985). See also Karin Walser 'Prostitutionsverdacht und Geschlechterforschung. Das Beispiel der Dienstmädchen um 1900', *Geschichte und Gesellschaft*, 11 (1985), pp. 99–111.
53. Stieber, *Die Prostitution*, pp. 78–79.
54. Schulte, *Sperrbezirke*, p. 68.
55. Schneider, *Studien*, p. 192.
56. Flexner, *Prostitution in Europe*, pp. 79–80; Judith R. Walkowitz, *Prostitution and Victorian Society. Women, Class, and the State* (Cambridge, 1980), p. 20. See also the biographies in Röhrmann, *Der sittliche Zustand von Berlin*, pp. 67–218, and the similar verdict in (Anon.), *Die Hamburger Prostitution*, p. 4.
57. Quoted in Schulte, *Sperrbezirke*, p. 151; see also pp. 125–26.
58. Schneider, *Studien*, p. 221.
59. Robert Hessen, *Die Prostitution in Deutschland* (Munich, 1910), pp. 17, 29.
60. Stieber, *Die Prostitution*, pp. 208–10.
61. C.W. Schülke *et al.*, *An Einen Hochedlen Senat der Freien und Hansestadt Hamburg ergebenste Petition in Sachen und abseiten C.W. Schülke und Consorten, Grosse Michaelisstrasse 16. Belass des jetzigen Zustandes der Mädchenherbergung bis zur Erledigung der Angelegenheit im Reichstag* (Hamburg, n.d., [c. 1900]).
62. B.E. von O., *Die Ursachen der Prostitution und die Möglichkeit ihrer Verminderung, sowie ein Wort über Bordelle und Findelhäuser* (Berlin, 1870), pp. 3, 5.
63. Schülke *et al.*, *An Einen Hochedlen Senat*.
64. Ernst W.H. Paul, *Lex Heinze. Die Hamburger Prostitution und das Zuhälterthum. Ein Beitrag zur Sittengeschichte Hamburgs* (Hamburg, 1897), pp. 7–8.

65. Julius Kühn, *Die Prostitution im 19. Jahrhundert vom sanitätspolizeilichen Standpunkt aus betrachtet, oder die Prophylaxis der Syphilis. Vorlesungen, gehalten an der Universität zu Leipzig im Wintersemester 1869–1870* (Leipzig, 1871), p. 53.

66. Stieber, *Die Prostitution*, pp. 111–12.

67. (Anon.), *Die Prostitution und ihre Gefahr für die Gesellschaft lässt sich nicht völlig beseitigen, jedoch beschränken. Ernster Anruf einer warnenden Stimme an die Kgl. Staatsregierung und die Vertreter des Volkes, sowie an Polizei- und Sanitäts-Beamte und Philantropen. Von einem Arzte* (Augsburg, 1867), p. 6.

68. GLA Karlsruhe 233/32128: Beilage zum Protokoll der 120. öffentlichen Sitzung der zweiten Kammer vom 5. Juli 1904.

69. Schulte, *Sperrbezirke*, p. 182.

70. Abrams, 'Prostitutes', pp. 191–92.

71. Schulte, *Sperrbezirke*, pp. 181–82.

72. Sta Braunschweig D IV 4784: Regulativ enthaltend die polizeilichen Vorschriften für die wegen gewerbsmässiger Unzucht der polizeilichen Aufsicht unterstellten Weibspersonen (1885), §4, Abs. 8 (1885).

73. Sta Frankfurt am Main, Magistratsakten S31/1434: Bericht des Unterausschusses des Gesundheitsamts, 13. Feb. 1899.

74. Quoted in Stieber, *Die Prostitution*, p. iii.

75. B.E. von O., *Die Ursachen*, p. 20.

76. StA Lübeck Rep. 49/1 No. 737: Schreiben von Senator Lame an Senator Curtius, 19 June 1862.

77. Ibid., No. 750.

78. StA Hamburg Senat Cl. I Lit. T No. 7 Vol. 6 Fasc. 9 Inv. 6a: Anlage zu Nr. 10: Betrifft Prostitutionswesen – vertraulich!. See also GLA Karlsruhe 233/4793, No. 68: Beilage zum Protokoll der 120. öffentlichen Sitzung der zweiten Kammer vom 5. Juli 1904; criticisms in ibid., 233/32128:12. Sitzung der 1. Kammer am 7. Mai 1910, Troeltsch.

79. B.E. von O., *Die Ursachen*, p. 23.

80. (Anon.), *Die Prostitution in Berlin, und die Mittel, dieselbe zu beseitigen, beziehungsweise in ihre wenigstgefährlichen Schranken zurückzuweisen* (Berlin, 1856), p. 29.

81. Quoted in (Anon.) *Zur lex Heinze in Bezug auf die früheren Hamburger Bordelle und das jetzige freie Prostitutionswesen* (Hamburg, 1895), p. 18.

82. (Anon.), *Norddeutsches Babel*, p. 17.

83. Sta Braunschweig D IV: 4783: Polizeidirektion to Stadtmagistrat, 12 June 1868.

84. GA Karlsruhe 233/32128: Bericht der Petitionskommission der 2. Kammer (Nr. 101, Beilage der 124. öffentl. Sitzung der 2. Kammer vom 12. August 1908).

85. Friedrich Wilhelm Müller, *Die Prostitution in sozialer, legaler und sanitärer Beziehung, die Nothwendigkeit und der Modus ihrer Regelung. Eine sozialmedizinische Studie* (Erlangen, 1868), p. 31.

86. Anon. (Stieber), *Die Prostitution*, pp. 76–77.

87. See ibid., and more generally Urban, *Staat und Prostitution*.

88. Sta Frankfurt am Main, Magistratsakten S31/1434: Gesundheitsrat, Sitzung am 21. Feb. 1899, for this opinion of the town's health board.

89. C.W. Schülke *et al.*, *An Einen Hochedlen Senat*, p. 9.

90. Ibid., pp. 11–15.

91. Bloch and Loewenstein, *Die Prostitution*, Vol. II, p. 450.

92. Otto Fleischmann, *Deutsches Vagabunden- und Verbrechertum im Neunzehnten Jahrhundert* (Barmen, 1888), pp. 107–08.

93. BA Berlin Reichskanzlei 749: *Norddeutsche Allgemeine Zeitung*, 28 October 1891.

94. Röhrmann, *Der sittliche Zustand von Berlin*, pp. 39, 219–20.

95. Avé-Lallement, *Gaunerthum*, Vol. II, p.28. See also Appert, Vol. I, p. 83.

96. StA Lübeck Rep. 49/1 No. 741: police notes of 25 Nov. 1875.

97. Hermann Dalton, *Der sociale Aussatz. Ein Wort über Prostitution*

und Magdalenenasyle (Hamburg, 1884), p. 17.

98. All Germans were required by law – and still are – to register with the police on changing address.
99. Ostwald, *Zuhältertum*, p. 86.
100. See Evans, *Rethinking*, Ch. 8.
101. (Anon.), *Die Sinnenlust und ihre Opfer. Geschichte der Prostitution aller Zeiten und Völker mit genauer Darlegung ihrer gegenwärtigen Form und ihrer Ursachen in Berlin, Hamburg, Wien, Paris, London und den anderen Grossstädten, nebst zeitgemässen Vorschlägen zu ihrer Verminderung und Regelung. Herausgegeben von einem philantropischen Verein* (Berlin, 1870), p. 218.
102. Ostwald, *Zuhältertum*, p. 59.
103. Urban, *Staat und Prostitution*, p. 119.
104. Fleischmann, *Deutsche Vagabunden- und Verbrechertum*, p. 107.
105. Ibid., pp. 13, 22–23, 51–55, 64–66, 71–75, 86.
106. For these concepts, see Stanley Cohen, *Folk Devils and Moral Panics. The Creation of the Mods and Rockers* (London, 1972).
107. BA Potsdam Reichskanzlei 749: Sitzung des Staatsministeriums am 2. Sept. 1891, p. 28, and *Norddeutsche Allgemeine Zeitung*, 28 Oct. 1891.
108. R.J.V. Lenman, 'Art, Society and the Law in Wilhelmine Germany: The Lex Heinze', *Oxford German Studies*, 8 (1973), pp. 86–113; Gary Stark, 'Pornography, Society and the Law in Imperial Germany', *Central European History*, 14 (1981), pp. 200–20.
109. Ostwald, *Prostitutionsmärkte*, p. 8.
110. Urban, *Staat und Prostitution*, p. 109.
111. Ibid., pp. 119–20; (Anon.), *Zur Lex Heinze*; *Die Frauenbewegung*, 1 Jan. 1902, pp. 1–2, 45.
112. Hessen, *Die Prostitution*, and A. Neher, *Die geheime und öffentliche Prostitution in Stuttgart, Karlsruhe und München* (Paderborn, 1912). For the global estimates, see Flexner, *Prostitution in Europe*, pp. 27–30.

113. Urban, *Staat und Prostitution*, pp. 109–10.
114. Flexner, *Prostitution in Europe*, pp. 147–57.
115. Sta Frankfurt am Main, Magistratsakten S31/1434: *Volksstimme*, 15 April 1914.
116. Urban, *Staat und Prostitution*, pp. 34–40.
117. Heinrich Berger, *Die Prostitutionsfrage in Hannover* (Berlin, 1902), pp. 20, 30.
118. StA Lübeck Rep. 49/1, No. 749.
119. Schneider, *Studien*, pp. 177–79 and 224–25.
120. Ibid., p. 176.
121. Müller, *Die Prostitution in Deutschland*, p. 53; (Anon.), *Die Hamburger Prostitution*, p. iii.
122. Urban, *Staat und Prostitution*, pp. 41–42; Flexner, *Prostitution in Europe*, p. 56; (Anon.), *Die Hamburger Prostitution*, pp. 5–8.
123. Sta Frankfurt am Main Magistratsakten S31/1434: *Volksstimme*, 15 April 1914 (figures slightly recalculated).
124. Urban, *Staat und Prostitution*, pp. 106–17, gives details.
125. Ibid.
126. Sta Frankfurt am Main, Magistratsakten S31/1434: police notes and protest of the brothel-keepers of the Rosengasse, 16 Nov. 1913.
127. Flexner, *Prostitution in Europe*, p. 157, for these figures.
128. GLA Karlsruhe 233/32128: Stellung der Grossherz. Regierung zum Bericht der Petitionskommission der 2. Kammer (Nr. 101, Beilage der 124. öffentl. Sitzung der 2. Kammer, vom 12. Aug. 1908), p. 14.
129. A.W.F. Schultz, *Die Stellung des Staats zur Prostitution* (Berlin, 1857), pp. 4, 13–14.
130. Gustav Sentzke, *Die Prostitution unserer Zeit, der Gesellschaft und dem Gesetze gegenüber* (Berlin, 1867). This plagiarized Stieber's work of 1846, and both were plagiarized by *Norddeutsches Babel* (n. 15, above) and *Die Sinnenlust und ihre Opfer* (n. 101, as above); plagiarism seems to

have been a particularly common vice in writings on this subject, especially the more morally conservative ones. One surveillance officer in the Hamburg police even plagiarized his own reports on prostitution to make it look as if he were recording a new conversation in the pub on which he was spying, instead of merely copying out notes on an old conversation which he had already reported some months before: for details and references, see Richard J. Evans (ed.), *Kneipengespräche im Kaiserreich. Die Stimmungsberichte der Hamburger Politischen Polizei 1892–1914* (Reinbek bei Hamburg, 1989), pp. 19–20.

131. (Anon.), *Norddeutsches Babel*, p. 23.
132. GLA Karlsruhe 233/4793: Beilage zum Protokoll der 120. öffentlichen Sitzung der zweiten Kammer vom 5. Juli 1904.
133. Nancy R. Reagin, '"A True Woman Can Take Care of Herself": The Debate over Prostitution in Hanover, 1906', *Central European History*, 24 (1991), pp. 347–80, here p. 355.
134. Abrams, 'Prostitutes', p. 193.
135. Flexner, *Prostitution in Europe*, p. 157.
136. Urban, *Staat und Prostitution*, pp. 18–19.
137. Bloch and Loewenstein, *Die Prostitution*, Vol. II, p. 570.
138. (Anon.), *Die Geschichte der Prostitution und des Verfall der Sitten in Berlin seit den letzten fünfzig Jahren in ihren Ursachen und Folgen* (Altona, 1871), p. 43.
139. GStA Berlin Rep. 84a/10776, Bl. 143: Königl. Regierung, Abtheilung des Innern (Schleswig), to Justizministerium, memorandum of 23 Jan. 1870. See also ibid., Bl. 145.
140. Ibid., Bl. 161: Oberstaatsanwalt Kiel to Justizministerium.
141. StA Hamburg Senat, Cl. I Lit. T No. 7 Vol. 6 Fasc. 9 Inv. 6a: Anlage zu 86: Landgericht Hamburg, in Sachen A.D. Arnal Testament gegen Polizeibehörde, pp. 37–39.

142. GLA Karlsruhe 233/4793: Innenministerium Karlsruhe, 11. April 1899, N2. 12287.
143. StA Hamburg Senat Cl. I Lit. T No. 7 Vol. 6 Fasc. 9 Inv. 6a: Anlage zu Nr. 10: Betrifft Prostitutionswesen – vertraulich!. See also GLA Karlsruhe 233/4793, No. 68: Beilage zum Protokoll der 120. öffentlichen Sitzung der zweiten Kammer vom 5. Juli 1904. These are general surveys of regulation in German towns and cities.
144. StA Lübeck Rep. 49/1 Nr. 741: Ellenhusen and nine other (male) citizens to Senat, 22 May 1862.
145. Elizabeth Meyer-Renschhausen, *Weibliche Kultur und soziale Arbeit. Eine Geschichte der Frauenbewegung am Beispiel Bremens 1810–1927* (Cologne, 1989), p. 311.
146. GLA Karlsruhe 233/4793: Beilage zum Protokoll der 120. öffentlichen Sitzung der zweiten Kammer vom 5. Juli 1904.
147. (Anon.), *Zur Lex Heinze*.
148. Sta Frankfurt am Main, Magistratsakten S31/1434: police notes and reports, and 25. Sitzung der Stadtverordnetenversammlung, 2 July 1912.
149. A point repeated by Otto Rühle, *Illustrierte Kultur- und Sittengeschichte des Proletariats* (Berlin, 1930), Vol. I, p. 488; see Abrams, 'Prostitutes', pp. 200–201.
150. Ludwig Weber, *Lebenserinnerungen* (Hamburg, n.d.); see also B.E. von O., *Die Ursachen*, p. 7.
151. BA Berlin Reichskanzlei 749: (Anon.), *Der Kampf gegen die Unsittlichkeit* (Berlin, 1891).
152. C.B., *Keine Prostitution mehr! Oder: Motivirte Vorschläge zur unbedingten Unterdrückung, resp. Ausrottung der überhand genommenen Prostitution und Sittenlosigkeit* (Landsberg, 1858), pp. 10–12.
153. Müller, *Die Prostitution in Deutschland*, pp. 11, 20, 33.
154. Carl Fricke, *Die Frauenfrage in ihrer Beziehung zur Prostitution* (Berlin, 1885), pp. 45–49.

155. (Anon.), *Clerus, Kirche und Staat gegenüber der Prostitution. Kritische Beleuchtung der Kammerverhandlung vom 13. März 1868 über den Artikel 221 des bayerischen Strafgesetzbuches nebst einem Anhange über die Argumentation des Herrn Universitätsprofessors Dr. philos. et theolog. Heinrich W.J. Thierisch gegen Herrn Dr. Friedrich Wilhelm Müller* (Erlangen, 1868).

156. Archiv des Bundes Deutscher Frauenvereine 8/2: Vorschläge zur Bekämpfung der Prostitution, von Hanna Bieber-Böhm (1905); Else Lüders, *Der 'linke Flügel'. Ein Blatt aus der Geschichte der deutschen Frauenbewegung* (Berlin, n.d. [c. 1900]), pp. 12–14.

157. Evans, *Feminist Movement*, pp. 37–50, 64–66.

158. Archiv des Bundes Deutscher Frauenvereine 8/2: Allerdurchläuchtigster Grossmächtigster Kaiser und König, Allergnädigster König und Herr!' (Petition of Jugendschutzverein).

159. See Evans, *Feminist Movement*, pp. 35–70, and Theresa Wobbe, *Gleichheit und Differenz: Politische Strategien von Frauenrechtlerinnen um die Jahrhundertwende* (Frankfurt am Main, 1989), pp. 22–98.

160. Lida Gustava Heymann, *Aufklärung über das sexuelle Leben und hygienische Ratschläge für die heranwachsende Jugend* (Hamburg, 1902), pp. 12–16.

161. (Anon.), *Die deutschen Frauen und die Hamburger Bordelle*, p. 18.

162. (Anon.), *Die Hamburger Prostitution*, p. v.

163. For these arguments applied to England, see Judith R. Walkowitz, *City of Dreadful Delight. Narratives of Sexual Danger in Late-Victorian London* (London, 1992), pp. 15–39.

164. (Anon.), *Die deutschen Frauen und die Hamburger Bordelle*, pp. 31–32.

165. See also Stadtrat Boeckh, in GLA Karlsruhe 233/32128: 12. Sitzung der 1. Kammer, 7. Mai 1910, p. 504.

166. Meyer-Renschhausen, *Weibliche Kultur*, pp. 303–19; see also eadem, 'Die weibliche Ehre. Ein Kapitel aus dem Kampf von Frauen gegen Polizei und Ärzte', in Johanna Geyer-Kordesch and Annette Kuhn (eds), *Frauenkörper, Medizin, Sexualität* (Düsseldorf, 1980).

167. StA Hamburg Politische Polizei SA593/I, Bl. 240-1: Versammlungsbericht, 18. April 1902.

168. BA Berlin Reichskanzlei 750, Bl. 135: Sitzung des Staatsministeriums am 30. November 1908.

169. For a detailed study of the Abolitionist campaign, see Evans, *Feminist Movement*, Ch. 2.

170. Reagin, '"A True Woman"'; also eadem, *A German Women's Movement. Class and Gender in Hanover, 1880–1933* (Chapel Hill, 1995), pp. 147–72.

171. GLA Karlsruhe 233/32128: 12. Sitzung der 1. Kammer, 7. Mai 1910, p. 491 (Freiherr von und zu Bodman).

172. StA Hamburg Politische Polizei S 593/I: Internationale Abolitionistische Föderation: Zweck (1912). For an insider's account of these changes, see Anna Pappritz, *Einführung in das Studium der Prostitutionsfrage* (Berlin, 1926), esp. p. 226. See also Evans, *Feminist Movement*, pp. 162–68, and Ann Tayor Allen, 'Feminism, Venereal Diseases, and the State in Germany, 1890–1918', *Journal of the History of Sexuality*, 4 (1993), pp. 27–50.

173. See especially Wetzell, 'Criminal Law Reform', for these developments.

174. Marion Kaplan, 'Prostitution, Morality Crusades and Feminism: German-Jewish Feminists and the Campaign against White Slavery', *Women's Studies International Forum*, 5 (1982), pp. 619–27, outlining in particular the attempts of Jewish women's organizations to counter such claims.

175. GLA Karlsruhe 233/32128: 12. Sitzung der 1. Kammer, 7. Mai

1910, p. 491 (Freiherr von und zu Bodman).

176. Cited in Böhme (ed.), *Tagebuch*, pp. 268–72.

177. Ibid., p. 308.

178. Eadem (ed.), *The Diary of a Lost One* (London, 1907), p. 2.

179. Eadem (ed.), *Tagebuch*, p. 3.

180. For a discussion of the variety of discourses around prostitution in the Scottish context, see Barbara Littlewood and Linda Mahood, 'Prostitutes, Magdalenes and Wayward Girls: Dangerous Sexualities of Working-Class Women in Victorian Scotland', *Gender and History*, 3 (1992), pp. 160–75, and, more generally, Linda Mahood, *The Magdalenes. Prostitution in the Nineteenth Century* (London, 1990).

Conclusion

1. Michel Foucault, *Discipline and Punish. The Birth of the Prison* (London, 1977).

2. Blasius, 'Michel Foucaults "denkende" Betrachtung der Geschichte', gives an historian's critique of Foucault's work; see also Michelle Perrot (ed.), *L'impossible prison. Recherches sur le système pénitentiaire au xixe siécle* (Paris, 1980), which includes a debate between Foucault and the historians; and Lawrence Stone, 'An Exchange with Michel Foucault', *New York Review of Books*, 31 March 1983, p. 42; Stephan Breuer, 'Foucaults Theorie der Disziplinargesellschaft. Eine Zwischenbilanz', *Leviathan*, 15 (1987), pp. 319–37; David Garland, *Punishment and Modern Society. A Study in Social Theory* (Oxford, 1990), pp. 153–63.

3. James Miller, *The Passion of Michel Foucault* (London, 1993), for the background. For a fuller elaboration of these arguments, see the Conclusion to Evans, *Rituals of Retribution*.

4. For speculations on the political consequences of popular criminality, see Blasius, *Kriminalität und Alltag*, pp. 75–78; Küther, *Räuber und Gauner*, p. 120.

5. See especially Küther, *Räuber und Gauner*; Werner Danckert, *Unehrliche Leute. Die verfehmten Berufe* (Berne, 1963); van Dülmen, 'Der infame Mensch' and Nowosadtko, 'Die Ehre, die Unehre und das Staatsinteresse'.

6. Scribner, 'The *Mordbrenner* Fear'; Michael Kunze, *Highroad to the Stake: A Tale of Witchcraft* (Chicago, 1987).

7. Raymond B. Fosdick, *European Police Systems* (New York, 1914).

8. Blasius, *Bürgerliche Gesellschaft*; Johnson, *Urbanization and Crime*.

9. Richard J. Evans, 'In Search of German Social Darwinism: History and Historiography of a Concept', in Manfred Berg and Geoffrey Cocks (eds), *Medicine and Modernity. Medicine and Public Health in 19th- and 20th-Century Germany* (New York, 1996).

Bibliography

A. Manuscript Sources

1. Bundesarchiv Berlin

61 Re 1 Pressearchiv des Reichslandbundes
  1523 Deportation. Gefängnis und Gefängnisarbeit. Zuchthaus und Zuchthausarbeit. International. 1894–97, Bd. I
  1524 Deportation, Zuchthaus und Gefängnisse 1897–1902, Bd. II.
Reichskanzlei
  749 Massregeln zur Bekämpfung der Unsittlichkeit, Vol. I
  750 Massregeln zur Bekämpfung der Unsittlichkeit, Vol. II

2. Geheimes Staatsarchiv Preussischer Kulturbesitz Berlin

Rep. 84a Preussisches Justizministerium
  7794 Die Deportation der Verbrecher
  7795 Die Deportation der Verbrecher 1801–02
  7796 Die Deportation der Verbrecher 1802–30
  7797 Die Deportation der Verbrecher 1834–1910
  7798 Äusserungen der Presse, betr. die Deportation der Verbrecher
  8035 Die Deportation der Verbrecher
  8180 Die Züchtigung der Verbrecher 1832–52
  8181 Die Züchtigung der Verbrecher 1852–58
  8182 Die Züchtigung der Verbrecher 1863–1923
  8184 Äusserungen der Presse, betr. Die Züchtigung der Verbrecher
  8312 Die Züchtigung der Verbrecher
  8489 Die Herausgabe öffentlicher Blätter zur Verfolgung von Verbrechern
Rep. 181 Regierung Marienwerder
  14056 betr. die Wiedereinführung der Prügelstrafe insbesondere für jugendliche Verbrecher
Rep. 84a/8312 Die Abschaffung des Halseisens, Bock, Ganten, Fiedel und ähnlicher Strafen

3. Bayerisches Hauptstaatsarchiv München

M Inn Innenministerium
  71567 Reform des Gefängniswesens und des Strafvollzugs

4. Niedersächsisches Hauptstaatsarchiv Hannover

Hann. 9 Ministerium für Auswärtige Angelegenheiten
 Amerika 14: Auswanderung verurtheilter Verbrecher oder entlassener
  Sträflinge nach den Vereinigten Staaten 1845–55

Hann. 26a Ministerium der Justiz
 7105 Untersuchung wider den Maler und Glaser Heyko Boelsen aus Timmel, wegen
  Brandstiftung 1858–64.
 7159 Heinrich Georg Hundertmark aus Versen, Tödtung des Häuslings Bosselmann
 7166 Hans Heinrich Hammann aus Westercelle, Todtschlag
 7228 Sander, Johann Heinrich aus Powe, Brandstiftung
 7236 Schmidt, Theodor Heinrich Rudolf zu Lüneburg, Raub
 7247 Schultz, Margarethe Sophie Friederike aus Krummasel – Brandstiftung und
  Verleumdung
 7373 Reform der Strafanstalten 1860–66
 7530 Knoop, Heinr. Theod. aus Göttingen, Diebstahl

Hann. 74: Ämter
 Burgdorf I   1669 Die Verschickung einzelner, sowohl den Strafanstalten als auch
           dem Gemeinwesen zur Last gehenden Personen nach Amerika,
           1834–90
 Celle   1315 Die Übersiedelung von Verbrechern oder sonstigen Personen auf
           Kosten der öffentlichen oder Gemeinde-Kassen nach Amerika,
           1834–69
 Hameln   4345 Vermittlung der Übersiedelung übelberüchtigter Personen nach
           Amerika, Generalia 1836ff.
 Hannover I A   626 Die Übersiedelung unnützer Individuen nach Amerika, 1834–
           68

Hann. 80 Hildesheim I E
 526 Stadt Moringen: Die beantragte Übersiedelung des Werkhausgefangenen
  Heinr. Thielebörger nach Amerika, 1854
 535 Die Übersiedelung der den Straf- und Besserungs-anstalten wie den
  Gemeindewesen überhaupt zur Last fallenden Personen nach Amerika, 1834–
  68
 687 Stadt Elze: Die Bewilligung einer Beihilfe zu den Kosten der Auswanderung des
  Sträflings W. Rettstadt nach Amerika, 1865–66
 920, 923, 926 Stadt Hildesheim: Übersiedelung von Sträflingen etc. nach Amerika,
  1840–50
 999, 1002 Stadt Saarstedt: Übersiedelung von Sträflingen nach Amerika, 1841, 1861
 1213, 1216 Stadt Dransfeld: Übersiedelung von Sträflingen nach Amerika, 1837, 1865–
  66
 1406 Stadt Göttingen: Die Bestrafung der Johanne Marie Ernestine Angerstein wegen
  liederlichen Lebenswandels, 1821–31
 1426, 1440 Stadt Göttingen: Übersiedelung von Sträflingen etc. nach Amerika, 1821–
  63
 1900 Amt Einbeck: Gesuch des Kettensträflings H. Mund behufs seiner Auswanderung
  nach Amerika, 1865

5. Mecklenburgisches Landeshauptarchiv Schwerin

Grossherzogliches Kabinett I (1763–1849)
 53 Die Abführung von Landarbeitshäuslern nach Brasilien, 1824–25

54 Die Abführung von Stock- und Zuchthaus-Gefangenen nach Brasilien, 1824–25
58 Die Nachrichten über die Schicksale der aus Güstrow, Dömitz und Bützow in den
   Jahren 1824 und 1825 nach Brasilien ausgewanderten Colonisten, 1828
62 Die Abführung von Sträflingen und Vagabunden aus Dönitz, Bützow und Güstrow
   nach Brasilien durch den Rittmeister Hanfft, 1825–27
78 Auswärtiges: Brasilien 1825–28

Kriminalkollegium zu Bützow
   1127 Die Deportation von in Dönitz inhaftierten Häftlingen nach Brasilien und die
        Auslieferung ihrer Papiere und Barschaften, 1824
   1128 Die aus dem Landarbeitshaus zu Güstrow und dem Zuchthaus Dömitz zum
        Zwecke der Auswanderung nach Brasilien entlassenen Gefangenen und die
        Massnamen bei deren eventuellen Rückkehr, 1825, 1830
   1130 Der Vortrag des Oberinspektors Ehlers und des Pastors Romberg aus Dreibergen
        auf Begnadigung mehrerer Sträflinge zur Auswanderung nach Amerika, 1847

6. Badisches Generallandesarchiv Karlsruhe

233/4793 Die im Grossherzogtum bestehenden Vorschriften über Prostitution
   12640 Das Kellnerinnenwesen
   32128 Die Prostitution und die Internationale Bekämpfung des Mädchenhandels

7. Staatsarchiv der Freien- und Hansestadt Hamburg

Gefängnisverwaltung
   A 41 Transportation von Gefangenen nach dem Ausland

Senat
   Cl. I Lit. T No. 7 Vol. 6 Fasc. 9 Inv. 6a Prostitution

Politische Polizei
   S 593/I Deutscher Zweig der Internationalen Abolitionistischen Föderation

8. Staatsarchiv der Freien- und Hansestadt Bremen

2-D 18. Strafarten und Strafanstalten
      o Verbannung, Transport, Zwangspässe, Ausweisung 1715–1873
      p Körperliche Züchtigung

4, 14/1 Polizei-Direktion
      VII B 1   Schwindler, Hochstapler etc.
      VII. B. 1e Franz Ernst (von Vietinghoff, Marzahn, von Hoff, etc.)
      VII. B. 4 Sitten- und Kriminalpolizei. Gemeingefährliche Personen.
                 Kunden und ihr Treiben (Gauner und Gaunerverbindungen)

9. Staatsarchiv der Freien- und Hansestadt Lübeck

Rep. 49/1 Polizeiamt
      737 Massnahmen zur Verfolgung der Lohnhurerei (1825) 1862–73
      741 Bordelle 1852–81
      742 Bordelle 1854–91
      746 Kontrolle der Bordellmädchen, Aufrechterhaltung der Ordnung, Verbote,
          1873–86
      747 Nächtliche Besuche der Bordellhäuser, insbesondere auch seitens des hier
          garnisonirenden Militairs 1838–1900
      749 Zahl der Bordellmädchen 1843–72

750 Bordellwesen
751 Bordellwesen

10. Staatsarchiv Coburg

Staatsministerium A
124 Auswanderungsgesuche nach Amerika, Polen usw. und Unterstützungen dafür
1846–61
Staatsministerium D
469   Gesuche um Erlaubnis zur Auswanderung in fremde Weltteile und die
dagegen erlassenen Vorkehrungen, 1817–77
471–473 Auswanderung nach den Vereinigten Staaten von Nordamerika 1833: Gesuche
um Erlaubnis und um Unterstützung, 1834–49; Beförderung der
Auswanderung 1833–52; dgl. 1852–56, 1856–73

11. Stadtarchiv Braunschweig

D IV 4783 Die Bordellwirtschaften in hiesiger Stadt
D IV 4784 Die Bordellwirtschaften in hiesiger Stadt

12. Stadtarchiv Frankfurt am Main

Magistratsakten
S31/1434 Bordelle und die polizeiliche Überwachung der Prostituierten

13. Archiv des Bundes Deutscher Frauenvereine (Landesarchiv Berlin)

8/2: Bekämpfung der Prostitution

B. Printed Primary Sources

ANONYMOUS PUBLICATIONS

*Allgemeine Nachricht an das Publicum über die aus den königl. preuss. Staaten nach Sibirien
geschickten Bösewichter, nebst kurzer Schilderung ihres Lebens und ihrer Vergehungen, aus den
Acten gezogen* (2nd edn, Berlin, 1803).
Allgemeines Landrecht für die Preussischen Staaten von 1794 (Textausgabe, mit einer Einführung
von Hans Hattenhauer, 2nd edn. Frankfurt am Main, 1994).
*Bildersammlung zum Verständnis des Sadismus und Masochismus, mit neuen aufklärenden
Berichten* (Privatdruck, Philadelphia, 1908).
*Clerus, Kirche und Staat gegenüber der Prostitution. Kritische Beleuchtung der Kammerverhandlung
vom 13. März 1868 über den Artikel 221 des bayerischen Strafgesetzbuches nebst einem Anhange
über die Argumentation es Herrn Universitätsprofessors Dr. philos. et theolog. Heinrich W.J.
Thierisch gegen Herrn Dr. Friedrich Wilhelm Müller* (Erlangen, 1868).
*Der Demokraten-Congress in Brüssel, am 26. September 1863 und die Absichten des demokratischen
Central-Comités in Genf, von einem Mitgliede des Central-Comités dargestellt. Den regierenden
und nicht regierenden Fürsten Europas ehrfurchtsvoll gewidmet* (Geneva, 1864).
Die Abschaffung des Rechtes körperlicher Züchtigung in der Schule (Erlangen, 1868).
*Die deutschen Frauen und die Hamburger Bordelle. Eine Abrechnung mit dem Syndikus Dr.
Schäfer, Hamburg, wegen seiner Reichstagsrede am 28. Januar 1904. Referate in der
Protestversammlung des Deutschen Zweigs der 'Internationalen Föderation' am 12. Februar 1904
in Berlin* (Pössneck, 1904).

Die Frauenbewegung. Zeitschrift der Verbandes fortschrifflicher frauenvereine.

Die Geschichte der Prostitution und des Verfall der Sitten in Berlin seit den letzten fünfzig Jahren in ihren Ursachen und Folgen (Altona, 1871).

Die Hamburger Prostitution, oder die Geheimnisse des Dammthorwalles und der Schwiegerstrasse (Altona, 1858).

Die Prostitution in Berlin, und die Mittel, dieselbe zu beseitigen, beziehungsweise in ihre wenigstgefährlichen Schranken zurückzuweisen (Berlin, 1856).

Die Prostitution und ihre Gefahr für die Gesellschaft lässt sich nicht völlig beseitigen, jedoch beschränken. Ernster Anruf einer warnenden Stimme an die Kgl. Staatsregierung und die Vertreter des Volkes, sowie an Polizei- und Sanitäts-Beamte und Philantropen. Von einem Arzte (Augsburg, 1867).

Die Sinnenlust und ihre Opfer. Geschichte der Prostitution aller Zeiten und Völker mit genauer Darlegung ihrer gegenwärtigen Form und ihrer Ursachen in Berlin, Hamburg, Wien, Paris, London und den anderen Grossstädten, nebst zeitgemässen Vorsvohlägen zu ihrer Verminderung und Regelung. Herausgegeben von einem philantropischen Verein (Berlin, 1870).

Keine Prostitution mehr! Oder: Motivirte Vorschläge zur unbedingten Unterdrückung, resp. Ausrottung der überhand genommenen Prostitution und Sittenlosigkeit (Landsberg, 1858).

Norddeutsches Babel. Ein Beitrag zur Geschichte, Charakteristik und Verminderung der Berliner Prostitution. Herausgegeben von einem philantropischen Verein (Berlin, 1870),

Nöthige Erläuterungen zu der Schrift des Herrn von Kotzebue: Das merkwürdigste Jahr meines Lebens. Von einem Freund der Wahrheit (Leipzig, 1802).

Novum Corpus Constitutionum Prussico-Brandenburgensium Praecipue Marchicarum (Berlin, 1801ff.).

Publicandum wegen Deportation incorrigibler Verbrecher in die Siberischen Bergwerke (Berlin, 7 July 1802).

Stenographische Berichte über die Verhandlungen des deutschen Reichstages.

Zeitschrift für die gesamte Strafrechtswissenschaft 23/103 (1902).

Zur Lex Heinze in Bezug auf die früheren Hamburger Bordelle und das jetzige freie Prostitutionswesen (Hamburg, 1895).

Ackermann, Carl August, *Für die deutsche Polizei. Wider Herrn Dr. Avé-Lallement* (Schwerin, 1861).

Aga, Mrs, *The Adventures of a Serf's Wife among the Mines of Siberia* (London, 1866).

Appell, J.W., *Die Ritter- Räuber- und Schauerromantik. Zur Geschichte der deutschen Unterhaltungs-Literatur* (Leipzig, 1859).

Appert, B., *Die Geheimnisse des Verbrechens, des Verbrecher- und Gefängniss-Lebens* (Leipzig, 1851).

Arnim, Albrecht Heinrich von, *Bruchstücke über Verbrechen und Strafen, oder Gedanken über die in den Preussischen Staaten bemerkte Vermehrung der Verbrechen gegen die Sicherheit des Eigenthums; nebst Vorschlägen, wie derselben durch zweckmässige Einrichtung der Gefangenanstaltenn zu steuern seyn dürfte. Zum Gebrauch der höhern Behörden* (Frankfurt am Main and Leipzig, 1803).

Aschenbrenner, Wilhelm (?), *Die schrecklichsten Jahre meines Lebens. Meine Leiden und Verhaftung zu Königsberg und Spandau und Verbannung in die Bergwerke nach Sibirien, von Wilhelm Aschenbrenner* (2 vols, Berlin, 1804).

―――, *Aschenbrenners authentische Geschichte bis zu seiner Deportation nach Sibirien. Freimuthig von ihm selbst geschrieben, und mit Hinsicht auf die, über ihn verhandelten Akten herausgegeben. Nebst seinem Bildnisse. Anhang: Einige Nachrichten über die Stadt und Festung Spandau* (Berlin, 1804).

Auerbach, Leopold (ed.), *Denkwürdigkeiten des Geheimen Regierungsrathes Dr. Stieber. Aus seinen hinterlassenen Papieren* (Berlin, 1884).
Avé-Lallement, Friedrich Christian Benedikt, *Das deutsche Gaunerthum in seiner social-politischen, literarischen und linguistischen Ausbildung zu seinem heutigen Bestande* (4 vols, Leipzig, 1858–62).
———, *Die Krisis der deutschen Polizei* (Leipzig, 1861).

Bebel, August, *Die Frau und der Sozialismus* (Berlin [East], 1964 edn).
Becker, B., *Actenmässige Geschichte der Räuberbanden an den beyden Ufern des Rheins* (2 vols, Cologne, 1804).
Beneke, Otto, *Von unehrlichen Leuten. Cultur-historische Studien und Geschichten aus vergangenen Tagen deutscher Gewerbe und Dienste, mit besonderer Rücksicht auf Hamburg* (Hamburg, 1865).
Berger, Heinrich, *Die Prostitutionsfrage in Hannover* (Berlin, 1902).
'Bernadotte', *Die strenge Klavierlehrerin. Rute, Stock und Peitsche als Züchtigungsmittel für faule und unaufmerksame Klavierschüler und Klavierschülerinnen* (Pressburg, 1910).
Bloch, Iwan, and Georg Loewenstein, *Die Prostitution*, Vol. II (Berlin, 1925).
Böhme, Margarete (ed.), *Tagebuch einer Verlorenen. Von einer Toten* (Berlin, 1905).
———, *Dida Ibsens Geschichte. Ein Finale zum 'Tagebuch einer Verlorenen'* (Berlin, 1907).
——— (ed.), *The Diary of a Lost One* (London, 1907).
Bracken, Helmut von, *Die Prügelstrafe* (Dresden, 1925).

Cochrane, John Dundas, *Narrative of a Pedestrian Journey through Russian and Siberian Territory, from the Frontiers of China to the Frozen Sea and Kamchatka* (2nd edn, London, 1824).
Collins, Perry McDonough, *A Voyage down the Amoor, with a Land Journey through Siberia, and Incidental Notices of Manchooria, Kamschatka, and Japan* (New York, 1860).
Cottrell, Charles H., *Recollections of Siberia in the Years 1840 and 1841* (London, 1842).

Dalton, Hermann, *Der sociale Aussatz. Ein Wort über Prostitution und Magdalenenasyle* (Hamburg, 1884).
Dronke, Ernst, *Polizei-Geschichten, sowie der Prozess gegen denselben vor dem Zuchtpolizeigericht zu Koblenz (1847)* (ed. Detlev Wagner, Berlin, 1980).

Eichhoff, Wilhelm, *Berliner Polizei-Silhouetten* (Berlin, 1860, London, 1861, 2 vols).
Evans, Richard J. (ed.), *Kneipengespräche im Kaiserreich. Die Stimmungsberichte der Hamburger Politischen Polizei 1892–1914* (Reinbek bei Hamburg, 1989).

Feuerbach, Paul Anselm Ritter von, *Aktenmässige Darstellung merkwürdiger Verbrechen* (2 vols, Giessen, 1828–92).
Fleischmann, Otto, *Deutsches Vagabunden- und Verbrechertum im Neunzehnten Jahrhundert* (Barmen, 1888).
Flexner, Abraham, *Prostitution in Europe* (New York, 1914).
Föhring, H., *Noch ein Wort zur Prügelstrafe* (Hamburg, 1879).
Fosdick, Raymond B., *European Police Systems* (New York, 1914).
Freimund, A., *Über körperliche Züchtigung beim Unterricht in Volksschulen* (Leipzig, 1875).
Fricke, Carl, *Die Frauenfrage in ihrer Beziehung zur Prostitution* (Berlin, 1885).

Geider, Egon, *Die Strafbarkeit des Erwachsenen bei Züchtigung des ungezogenen Jugendlichen* (Breslau, 1918).
Grattenhauer, Carl Wilhelm Friedrich, *Über die Nothwehr. Ein Beitrag zur wissenschaftlichen Behandlung des Kriminalrechts* (Breslau, 1806).

————, *Exners Tod. Ein merkwürdiger Kriminalfall rechtmässiger Nothwehr: Erkenntniss des Kriminal-Senats der Ober-Amts-Regierung in Glogau wider den Harpersdorffer Müller Johann Gottlieb Meschter* (Breslau, 1805).

Grolmann, Friedrich Ludwig Adolf von, *Actenmässige Geschichte der Vogelsberger und Wetterauer Räuberbanden, und mehrerer mit ihnen in Verbindung gestandener Verbrecher. Nebst Personal-Beschreibung vieler in alle Lande teutscher Mundart dermalen versprengter Diebe und Räuber* (Giessen, 1813).

Hammer, Wilhelm, *Zehn Lebensläufe Berliner Kontrollmädchen* (Grossstadt-Dokumente, Vol. 23, Berlin, 1905).

————, *Die Prügelstrafe in ärztlicher Beleuchtung* (Leipzig, 1906).

Hessen, Robert, *Die Prostitution in Deutschland* (Munich, 1910).

Heymann, Lida Gustava, *Aufklärung über das sexuelle Leben und hygienische Ratschläge für die heranwachsende Jugend* (Hamburg, 1902).

Hirschfeld, Magnus, *Berlins Drittes Geschlecht* (Grossstadt-Dokumente, Vol. 3, Berlin, 1905).

Hitzig, J.C., and W. Häring, *Der neue Pitaval. Eine Sammlung der interessantesten Criminalgeschichten aller Länder aus älterer und neuerer Zeit* (Leipzig, 1842).

Hoff, Dr von (i.e. Franz Ernst), *Die deutschen Gelehrten, Kaufleute, Handwerker und Tagelöhner in England, Schottland und Irland, mit ihren Institutionen, in ihrem Leben und Treiben* (Mannheim, 1863).

Hoffet, E., *Die Unzucht, Ihre Ursachen und ihre Bekämpfung. Mit besonderer Berücksichtigung ihrer Reglementierung durch den Staat. Vortrag gehalten im Instruktionskursus für Innere Mission in Karlsruhe (Oktober 1899)* (2nd edn, Colmar, 1900).

Holtzendorff, Franz von, *Die Deportation als Strafmittel in alter und neuer Zeit und die Verbrecherkolonien der Engländer und Franzosen in ihrer geschichtlichen Entwicklung und criminalpolitischen Bedeutung* (Leipzig, 1859).

Julius, Nikolaus Heinrich, *Vorlesungen über die Gefängnis-Kunde, oder über die Verbesserung der Gefängnisse und sittliche Besserung der Gefangenen, entlassenen Sträflinge u.s.w., gehalten im Frühlinge 1827 zu Berlin* (Berlin, 1828).

Kampffmeyer, Paul, *Die Prostitution als soziale Klassenerscheinung und ihre sozialpolitische Bekämpfung* (Berlin, 1905).

Kennan, George, *Siberia and the Exile System* (New York, 1891).

Klatt, O., *Die Körpermessung der Verbrecher nach Bertillon, und die Photographie als die wichtigsten Hilfsmittel der gerichtlichen Polizei, sowie Anleitung zur Aufnahme von Fussspuren jeder Art* (Berlin, 1862).

Klett, C., *Der Lehrer ohne Stock. Gegen die körperliche Strafe in der Schule* (Stuttgart, 1869).

Kohler, J., and W. Scheel (eds), *Die Carolina und ihre Vorgängerinnen. Text, Erläuterungen, Geschichte* (4 vols, Halle, 1900–15, repr. Aalen, 1970).

Korell, D.K., *Pädagogische Irrwege oder Sadismus?* (Berlin, 1904).

Kotzebue, August von, *Das merkwürdigste Jahr meines Lebens* (2 vols, Berlin, 1801).

Krohne, C., and R. Uber, *Die Strafanstalten und Gefängnisse in Preussen*, Vol. I (Berlin, 1901).

Kühn, Julius, *Die Prostitution im 19. Jahrhundert vom sanitätspolizeilichen Standpunkt aus betrachtet, oder die Prophylaxis der Syphilis. Vorlesungen, gehalten an der Universität zu Leipzig im Wintersemester 1869–1870* (Leipzig, 1871).

Ladendorf, August, *Sechs Jahre Gefangenschaft unter den Folgen des Staatsstreichs und der Kampf um's Recht in der 'neuen Ära'. Ein Beitrag zur geschichtlichen Charakteristik der Reaction und deren Handlanger* (Leipzig, 1862).

Lansdell, Harry, *Through Siberia* (3rd edn, London, 1882).

Lüders, Else, *Der 'linke Flügel'. Ein Blatt aus der Geschichte der deutschen Frauenbewegung* (Berlin, n.d. [c. 1900]).

Lux, Heinrich, *Die Prostitution, ihre Ursachen, ihre Folgen und ihre Bekämpfung* (Berliner Arbeiterbibliothek, III. Serie, 4. Heft, Berlin, 1892).

Malblank, Friedrich (ed.), *Geschichte der Peinlichen Gerichtsordnung Kaiser Karls V.* (Nuremberg, 1763).

Marx, Karl, *Enthüllungen über den Kommunistenprozess zu Köln* (Basel, 1853, repr. in Marx, and Friedrich Engels, *Werke*, Vol. 8, Berlin [East], 1960).

———, and Friedrich Engels, *Werke*, Vol. 30 (Berlin ([East]), 1972).

———, 'The Communist Manifesto', in *Collected Works*, Vol. 6 (London, 1976).

Masson, M., *Mémoires secrets sur la Russia, et particulièrement sur la fin du règne de Catherline II et le commencement de celui de Paul Ier; ou lettres en réponse à M. Kotzebue* (4 vols, Amsterdam, 1803).

Mittermaier, Carl Joseph Anton , 'Besserungsanstalten', in Carl von Rottek and Carl Welcker (eds), *Staats-Lexicon* (Altona, 1834), Vol. I, p. 504.

———, *Die Gefängnisverbesserung, insbesondere die Bedeutung und Durchführung der Einzelhaft im Zusammenhange mit dem Besserungsprinzip, nach den Erfahrungen der verschiedenen Strafanstalten* (Erlangen, 1858).

Müller, Friedrich Wilhelm, *Die Prostitution in sozialer, legaler und sanitärer Beziehung, die Nothwendigkeit und der Modus ihrer Regelung. Eine sozial-medizinische Studie* (Erlangen, 1868).

———, *Die Prostitution in Deutschland am Ende des 19. Jahrhunderts. Historisch-kritische Darlegung der Notwendigkeit einer diesbezüglichen Reform* (Regensburg, 1892).

Neher, A., *Die geheime und öffentliche Prostitution in Stuttgart, Karlsruhe und München* (Paderborn, 1912).

O, B.E. von, *Die Ursachen der Prostitution und die Möglichkeit ihrer Verminderung, sowie ein Wort über Bordelle und Findelhäuser* (Berlin, 1870).

Ostwald, Hans, *Vagabonden* (Berlin, 1901).

———, *Die Tippelschickse* (Berlin, 1901).

———, *Verworfene. Erzählungen und Skizzen* (Berlin, 1902).

———, *Die Bekämpfung der Landstreicherei* (Stuttgart, 1903).

———, *Berliner Nachtbilder* (Berlin, 1903).

———, *Lieder aus dem Rinnstein* (Berlin, 1903).

———, *Das Berliner Dirnentum*, Vol. 6: *Prostitutionsmärkte* (Berlin, 1905).

———, *Berliner Tanzlokale* (Berlin, 1905).

———, *Dunkle Winkel in Berlin* (Grossstadt-Dokumente, Vol. 1, Berlin, 1905).

Pappritz, Anna, *Einführung in das Studium der Prostitutionsfrage* (Berlin, 1926).

Paul, Ernst W.H., *Lex Heinze. Die Hamburger Prostitution und das Zuhälterthum. Ein Beitrag zur Sittengeschichte Hamburgs* (Hamburg, 1897).

Pfister, Ludwig, *Actenmässige Geschichte der Räuberbanden an den beiden Ufern des Mains, in Spessart und im Odenwalde* (Heidelberg, 1812).

Quanter, Rudolf, *Die Leibes- und Lebensstrafen bei allen Völkern und zu allen Zeiten* (Dresden, 1901).

———, *Die Schand- und Ehrenstrafen in der deutschen Rechtspflege* (Dresden, 1901).

Radbruch, Gustav (ed.), *Die Peinliche Gerichtsordnung Kaiser Karls V. von 1532 (Carolina)* (4th edn, Stuttgart, 1975).

Ramburg, Else, *Die Zuchtrute von Tante Anna. Ein interessantes Kapitel zur häuslichen Strafdisziplin* (Pressburg, 1908).

Rebmann, A.G.F., *Damian Hessel und seine Raubgenossen. Aktenmässige Nachrichten über einige gefährliche Räuberbanden, ihre Taktik und ihre Schlupfwinkel, nebst Angabe der Mittel, sie zu verfolgen und zu zerstören* (3rd edn, Mainz, 1811).

Roderich, Max, *Verbrechen und Strafe. Eine Sammlung interessanter Polizei- und Criminal-Rechtsfälle, nach den Acten bearbeitet* (Jena, 1850).

Röhrmann, Carl, *Der sittliche Zustand von Berlin nach Aufhebung der geduldeten Prostitution des weiblichen Geschlechts. Ein Beitrag zur Geschichte der Gegenwart unterstützt durch die vollständigen und freimüthigen Biographien der bekanntesten prostituirten Frauenzimmer in Berlin* (Leipzig, 1846).

Rühle, Otto, *Illustrierte Kultur- und Sittengeschichte des Proletariats* (Berlin, 1930).

Schneider, Kurt, *Studien über Persönlichkeit und Schicksal eingeschriebener Prostituierter* (Berlin, 1921).

Schroeder, F.C., *Die Carolina. Die Peinliche Gerichtsordnung Kaiser Karls* (Darmstadt, 1986).

Schultz, A.W.F., *Die Stellung des Staats zur Prostitution* (Berlin, 1857).

Schwencken, Carl Philip, *Actenmässige Nachrichten von dem Gauner- und Vagabunden-Gesindel, sowie von einzelnen professionirten Dieben, in den Ländern zwischen dem Rhein und der Elbe, nebst genauer Beschreibung ihrer Person* (Kasel, 1822).

Sentzke, Gustav, *Die Prostitution unserer Zeit, der Gesellschaft und dem Gesetze gegenüber* (Berlin, 1867).

Spesshardt, Haubold Freiherr von, *Handbuch über Straf- und Besserungs-Anstalten* (Hildburghausen, 1843).

Stieber, Wilhelm, *Die Prostitution in Berlin und ihre Opfer. In historischer, sittlicher, medizinischer und polizeilicher Beziehung beleuchtet* (2nd edn, Berlin, 1846).

Ullo, Dr, *Die Flagellomanie. Ihre Erscheinungsformen bei Anwendung der Straf- und Erziehungsmittel. Aufzeichnungen aus dem Leben, der Literatur und Vergangenheit* (Dresden, 1901).

Unterlechner, Franz Xaver, *Prügel und Erziehung. Pädagogisches und soziologisches zum Erziehungsproblem* (Berlin, 1932).

Valentini, Hermann von, *Das Verbrecherthum im Preussischen Staate, nebst Vorschlägen zu seiner Bekämpfung durch die Gesellschaft und durch die Reform der Strafvollstreckung* (Leipzig, 1869).

Vandermeulen, A. (i.e. Arthur Müller), *Enthüllungen aus der höheren Region der politischen Spionage, in Berichten eines ungarischen Judas Ischarioth. Nebst sonstigen Aufdeckungen in Bezug auf das Treiben der geheimen Polizei* (Berlin, 1862).

Wagnitz, Heinrich, *Über die moralische Verbesserung der Zuchthausgefangenen* (Halle, 1787).

———, *Historische Nachrichten und Bemerkungen über die merkwürdigsten Zuchthäuser in Deutschland. Nebst einem Anhange über die zweckmässigste Einrichtung der Gefängnisse und Irrenanstalten* (2 vols, Halle, 1791).

———, *Ideen und Pläne zur Verbesserung der Policey- u. Criminalanstalten. Dem 19. Jahrhundert zur Vollendung übergeben* (Halle, 1801).

Weber, Ludwig, *Lebenserinnerungen* (Hamburg, n.d.).

Zeisig, J., *Memoiren einer Prostituierten, oder die Prostitution in Hamburg* (St Pauli, 1847).

Zimmermann, C.C., *Bis nach Sibirien. Erinnerungen aus dem Feldzuge nach Russland und aus der Gefangenschaft 1812–1814* (Hanover, 1863).

Zimmermann, Karl Wilhelm, *Die Diebe in Berlin oder Darstellung ihres Entstehens, ihrer Organisation, ihrer Verbindungen, ihrer Taktik, ihrer Gewohnheiten und ihrer Sprache. Zur*

Belehrung für Polizeibeamte und zur Warnung für das Publikum. Nach praktischen Erfahrungen (Berlin, 1847).

C. Secondary Literature

Abrams, Lynn, 'Prostitutes in Imperial Germany, 1870–1918: Working Girls or Social Outcasts?', in Evans (ed.), *The German Underworld*, pp. 189–209.

Allen, Ann Taylor, 'Feminism, Venereal Diseases, and the State in Germany, 1890–1918', *Journal of the History of Sexuality*, 4 (1993), pp. 27–50.

Arnold, Hermann, 'Ländliche Grundschicht und Gaunertum. Zur Kritik von Küthers Buch: Räuber und Gauner in Deutschland', *Zeitschrift für Agrargeschichte und Agrarsoziologie*, 25 (1977), pp. 67–76.

Bajohr, Stefan, 'Illegitimacy and the Working Class: Illegitimate Mothers in Brunswick, 1900–1933', in Richard J. Evans (ed.), *The German Working Class 1888–1933: The Politics of Everyday Life* (London, 1982), pp. 147–73.

Becker, Peter, '"Randgruppen" im Blickfeld der Polizei. Ein Versuch über die Perspektivität des "praktischen Blicks"', *Archiv für Sozialgeschichte*, 32 (1992), pp. 283–304.

———, 'Vom "Haltlosen" zur "Bestie". Das polizeiliche Bild des "Verbrechers" im 19. Jahrhundert', in Alf Lüdtke (ed.), *'Sicherheit' und 'Wohlfahrt'. Polizei, Gesellschaft und Herrschaft im 19. und 20. Jahrhundert*, pp. 97–132.

———, 'Wie sieht ein Verbrecher aus?', *Damals*, 26 (1994), No. 7, p. 45.

Behringer, Wolfgang, 'Mörder, Diebe, Ehebrecher: Verbrechen und Strafen in Kurbayern vom 16. bis 18. Jahrhundert', in Dülmen (ed.), *Verbrechen*, pp. 85–132.

Berger, Thomas, *Die konstante Repression. Zur Geschichte des Strafvollzugs in Preussen nach 1850* (Frankfurt am Main 1974).

Bergmann, Alfred, *Das Detmolder Zuchthaus als Stätte von Christian Dietrich Grabbes Kindheit und Jugend. Zugleich ein Beitrag zur Geschichte des Strafvollzuges in Lippe an der Wende vom achtzehnten zum neunzehnten Jahrhundert* (Detmold, 1968).

Bergmann, Jürgen, *Das Berliner Handwerk in den Frühphasen der Industrialisierung* (Veröffentlichung der Historischen Kommission zu Berlin, Berlin, 1973).

Bettenhäuser, Hermann, 'Räuber und Gaunerbanden in Hessen. Ein Beitrag zum Versuch einer historischen Kriminologie Hessens', *Zeitschrift des Vereins für hessische Geschichte und Landeskunde*, 75–76, (1964–65), pp. 275–348.

Blackbourn, David, *Marpingen. Apparitions of the Virgin Mary in Bismarckian Germany* (London, 1994).

Blasius, Dirk, 'Der Kampf um die Geschworenengerichte im Vormärz', in Hans-Ulrich Wehler (ed.), *Sozialgeschichte Heute. Festschrift für Hans Rosenberg zum 70. Geburtstag* (Göttingen, 1974), pp. 148–61.

———, *Bürgerliche Gesellschaft und Kriminalität. Zur Sozialgeschichte Preussens im Vormärz* (Göttingen, 1976).

———, *Kriminalität und Alltag. Zur Konfliktgeschichte des Alltagslebens im 19. Jahrhundert* (Göttingen, 1978).

———, 'Kriminalität als Gegenstand historischer Forschung', *Kriminalsoziologische Bibliographie*, 25 (1979), pp. 1–15.

———, 'Gesellschaftsgeschichte und Kriminalität', *Beiträge zur Historischen Sozialkunde*, 1 (1981), pp. 13–19.

———, 'Kriminalität und Geschichtswissenschaft. Perspektiven der neueren Forschung', *Historische Zeitschrift*, 233 (1981), pp. 615–27.

———, 'Recht und Gerechtigkeit im Umbruch von Verfassungs- und Gesellschaftsordnung. Zur Situation der Strafrechtspflege in Preussen im 19. Jahrhundert', *Der Staat*, 21 (1982), pp. 365–90.

————, 'Michel Foucaults "denkende" Betrachtung der Geschichte', *Kriminalsoziologische Bibliographie*, 41 (1983), pp. 69–83.

————, 'Kriminologie und Geschichtswissenschaft, Bilanz und Perspektiven interdisziplinärer Forschung', *Geschichte und Gesellschaft*, 14 (1988), pp. 136–49.

Blauert, Andreas, and Gerd Schwerhoff (eds), *Mit den Waffen der Justiz. Zur Kriminalitätsgeschichte des späten Mittelalters und der Frühen Neuzeit* (Frankfurt am Main, 1993).

Bobrick, Benson, *East of the Sun: The Conquest and Settlement of Siberia* (London, 1992).

Breithaupt, Wilhelm, *Die Strafe des Staupenschlags und ihre Abschaffung im Gemeinen Recht* (Jena, 1938).

Breuer, Stephan, 'Foucaults Theorie der Disziplinargesellschaft. Eine Zwischenbilanz', *Leviathan*, 15 (1987), pp. 319–37.

Breuilly, John, review of Blasius, *Bürgerliche Gesellschaft*, in *Social History*, 3 (1978), pp. 99–102.

Brüggemeier, Franz, '"Volle Kost voll". Die Wohnungsverhältnisse der Bergleute an der Ruhr um die Jahrhundertwende', in Hans Mommsen and Ulrich Borsdorf (eds.), *Glück auf, Kameraden! Die Bergarbeiter und ihre Organisation in Deutschland* (Cologne, 1979), pp. 151–73.

Burghartz, Susanna, 'Weibliche Ehre', in Heide Wunder and Karin Hausen (eds), *Frauengeschichte – Geschlechtergeschichte* (Frankfurt am Main, 1992), pp. 173–83

Cohen, Stanley, *Folk Devils and Moral Panics. The Creation of the Mods and Rockers* (London, 1972).

Corbin, Alain, *Women for Hire. Prostitution and Sexuality in France after 1850* (London, 1990).

Danckert, Werner, *Unehrliche Leute. Die verfehmten Berufe* (Bern, 1963).

Danker, Uwe, *Räuberbanden im Alten Reich um 1700. Ein Beitrag zur Geschichte von Herrschaft und Kriminalität in der Frühen Neuzeit* (Frankfurt am Main, 1988).

————, 'Bandits and the State: Robbers and the Authorities in the Holy Roman Empire in the Late Seventeenth and Early Eighteenth Centuries', in Richard J. Evans (ed.), *The German Underworld. Deviants and Outcasts in German History* (London, 1988), pp. 75–107.

Dasey, Robyn, 'Women's Work and the Family: Women Garment Workers in Berlin and Hamburg before the First World War', in Richard J. Evans and W.R. Lee (eds), *The German Family. Essays on the Social History of the Family in 19th- and 20th-Century Germany* (London, 1981), pp. 221–55.

Davis, Natalie Zemon, *The Return of Martin Guerre* (Cambridge, Mass., 1983)

————, *Fiction in the Archives: Pardon Tales and their Tellers in Sixteenth-Century France* (Stanford, 1987).

Dijkstra, Bram, *Idols of Perversity: Fantasies of Female Evil in Fin-de-Siècle Culture* (New York, 1986).

Dinges, Martin, 'Die Ehre als Thema der Stadtgeschichte. Eine Semantik am Übergang vom Ancien Régime zur Moderne', *Zeitschrift für historische Forschung*, 16 (1989), pp. 409–40.

————, 'Frühneuzeitliche Justiz', in Heinz Mohnhaupt and Dieter Simon (eds), *Vorträge zur Justizforschung*, Vol. 1: *Geschichte und Theorie* (Frankfurt am Main, 1992), pp. 269–92.

————, 'The Reception of Michel Foucault's Ideas on Social Discipline, Mental Asylums, Hospitals and the Medical Profession in German Historiography', in Colin Jones and Roy Porter (eds), *Reassessing Foucault: Power, Medicine and the Body* (London, 1993), pp. 181–212.

Dülmen, Richard van, *Theater des Schreckens. Gerichtspraxis und Strafrituale in der Frühen Neuzeit* (Munich, 1985).

———— (ed.), *Arbeit, Frömmigkeit und Eigensinn* (Studien zur historischen Kulturforschung, Vol. I, Frankfurt am Main, 1990).

———— (ed.), *Verbrechen, Strafen und soziale Kontrolle* (Frankfurt am Main, 1990).

————, 'Der infame Mensch. Unehrliche Arbeit und soziale Ausgrenzung in der Frühen Neuzeit', in idem (ed.), *Arbeit Frömmigkeit, and Eigensinn*, pp. 106–40.

Ebeling, Albert, *Beiträge zur Geschichte der Freiheitsstrafe* (Breslau, 1935).

Elias, Norbert, *Über den Prozess der Zivilisation. Soziogenetische und psychogenetische Untersuchungen*, Vol. I: *Wandlungen des Verhaltens in den weltlichen Oberschichten des Abendlandes*; Vol. II: *Wandlungen der Gesellschaft. Entwurf zu einer Theorie der Zivilisation* (Bern, 1969).

————, *Studien über die Deutschen. Machtkämpfe und Habitusentwicklung im 19. und 20. Jahrhundert* (Frankfurt am Main, 1992).

Emsley, Clive, *Crime and Society in England 1750–1900* (London, 1987).

Evans, Richard J., 'Prostitution, State and Society in Imperial Germany', *Past and Present* 70 (February 1976), pp. 106–29.

————, *The Feminist Movement in Germany 1894–1933* (London, 1976).

————, *Rethinking German History. Nineteenth-Century Germany and the Origins of the Third Reich* (London, 1987).

———— (ed.), *The German Underworld. Deviants and Outcasts in German History* (London, 1988).

————, *Proletarians and Politics. Socialism, Protest and the Working Class in Germany before the First World War* (London, 1990).

————, 'Family and Class in the Hamburg Grand Bourgeoisie 1815–1914', in David Blackbourn and Richard J. Evans (eds), *The German Bourgeoisie. Essays on the Social History of the German Middle Class from the Late Eighteenth to the Early Twentieth Century* (London, 1991), pp. 115–39.

————, 'In Search of German Social Darwinism: History and Historiography of a Concept', in Manfred Berg and Geoffrey Cocks (eds), *Medicine and Modernity. Medicine and Public Health in 19th- and 20th-century Germany* (New York, 1996).

————, *Rituals of Retribution. Capital Punishment in Germany 1600–1987* (Oxford, 1996).

————, 'Police and Society from Absolutism to Dictatorship', in Richard J. Evans, *Rereading German History: From Unification to Reunification 1800–1996* (London, 1997).

Faber, Karl-Georg, 'Historische Kriminologie und kritische Sozialgeschichte: das preussische Beispiel', *Historische Zeitschrift*, 227 (1978), pp. 112–22.

Feest, Johannes, and Christian Marzahn (eds), *Criminalia. Bremer Strafjustiz 1810–1850* (Beiträge zur Sozialgeschichte Bremens, Vol. 11, Bremen, 1988).

Finney, Gail, *Women in Modern Drama: Freud, Feminism, and European Theater at the Turn of the Century* (Ithaca, NY, 1989).

Finzsch, Norbert, and Robert Jütte (eds.), *Institutions of Confinement. Hospitals, Asylums, and Prisons in Western Europe and North America, 1500–1950* (New York, 1996).

Foucault, Michel, *Surveiller et punir: Naissance de la prison* (Paris, 1975).

————, *Discipline and Punish: The Birth of the Prison* (London, 1977).

————, 'The Subject and Power', in Hubert L. Dreyfus and Paul Rabinow, *Michel Foucault: Beyond Structuralism and Hermeneutics* (2nd edn, Chicago, 1983).

Franke, Manfred, *Schinderhannes. Das kurze, wilde Leben des Johannes Bückler. Nach alten Dokumenten neu erzählt* (Düsseldorf, 1984).

Fritzsche, Peter, 'Vagabond in the Fugitive City: Hans Ostwald, Imperial Berlin and the *Grossstadtdokumente*', *Journal of Contemporary History*, 29 (1994), pp. 385–402.

Funk, Albrecht, *Polizei und Rechtsstaat. Die Entwicklung des staatlichen Gewaltmonopols in Preussen 1848–1918* (Campus Verlag, Frankfurt am Main and New York, 1986).

Garland, David, *Punishment and Modern Society. A Study in Social Theory* (Oxford, 1990).
Gibson, Mary, *Prostitution and the State in Italy* (London, 1986).
Ginzburg, Carlo, *Clues, Myths and the Historical Method* (Baltimore, 1989).

Halttunen, Karen, 'Humanitarianism and the Pornography of Pain in Anglo-American Culture', *American Historical Review*, 100 (1995), No. 2, pp. 303–34.
Hartmann, Richard, *P.J.A. Feuerbachs politische und strafrechtliche Grundanschauungen* (Berlin [East], 1961).
Herzig, Arno, *Unterschichtenprotest in Deutschland 1790–1870* (Göttingen, 1988).
Heuer, J.-U., *Allgemeines Landrecht und Klassenkampf. Die Auseinandersetzungen um die Prinzipien des Allgemeinen Landrechts Ende des 18. Jahrhunderts als Ausdruck der Krise des Feudalsystems in Preussen* (Berlin [East], 1960).
Hippel, R. von, 'Beiträge zur Geschichte der Freiheitsstrafe', *Zeitschrift für die gesamte Strafrechtswissenschaft*, 18 (1898), pp. 419–94, 608–66.
——, *Die Entstehung der modernen Freiheitsstrafe und des Erziehungs-Strafvollzugs* (Jena, 1932).
Hobsbawm, E. J., *Bandits* (London, 1969), pp. 38–39.
Hohmann, Joachim S., 'Die Forschungen des "Zigeunerexperten" Hermann Arnold', *1999. Zeitschrift für Sozialgeschichte des 20. und 21. Jahrhunderts*, 10 (1995) 3, pp. 35–49.
Hughes, Robert, *The Fatal Shore. A History of the Transportation of Convicts to Australia 1787–1868* (London, 1987).

Ignatieff, Michael, *A Just Measure of Pain. The Penitentiary in the Industrial Revolution 1750–1850* (London, 1978).

Jessen, Ralph, *Polizei im Industrierevier. Modernisierung und Herrschaftspraxis im westfälischen Ruhrgebiet 1848–1914* (Kritische Studien zur Geschichtswissenschaft, Vol. 91, Vandenhoeck and Ruprecht, Göttingen, 1991).
Johnson, Eric A., 'The Roots of Crime in Imperial Germany', *Central European History*, 15 (1982), pp. 351–76.
——, *Urbanization and Crime. Germany 1871–1914* (New York, 1995).
——, and Vincent E. McHale, 'Urbanization, Industrialization, and Crime in Imperial Germany', *Social Science History*, 1 (1976–77), pp. 45–78 and 210–47.

Kaplan, Marion, 'Prostitution, Morality Crusades, and Feminism: German-Jewish Feminists and the Campaign against White Slavery', *Women's Studies International Forum*, 5 (1982). pp. 619–26.
Keller, Albrecht, *Der Scharfrichter in der deutschen Kulturgeschichte* (Bonn and Leipzig, 1921).
Koselleck, Reinhard, *Preussen zwischen Reform und Revolution. Allgemeines Landrecht, Verwaltung und soziale Bewegung von 1791 bis 1848* (Stuttgart, 1967).
Kunze, Michael, *Highroad to the Stake: A Tale of Witchcraft* (Chicago, 1987).
Küther, Carsten, *Räuber und Gauner in Deutschland. Das organisierte Bandenwesen im 18. Jahrhundert* (Göttingen, 1976).
——, *Menschen auf der Strasse. Vagierende Unterschichten in Bayern, Franken und Schwaben in der zweiten Hälfte des 18. Jahrhunderts* (Göttingen, 1983).
——, 'Räuber, Volk und Obrigkeit. Zur Wirkungsweise und Funktion staatlicher Strafverfolgung im 18. Jahrhundert', in Reif (ed.), *Räuber, Volk und Obrigkeit*, pp. 17–42.

Ladurie, Emmanuel Le Roy, *Montaillou. Village occitan de 1294 à 1324* (Paris, 1978).
Landau, Peter, and Friedrich Schröter (eds), *Strafrecht, Strafprozess und Rezeption: Grundlagen, Entwicklungen und Wirkung der Constitutio Criminalis Carolina* (Frankfurt am Main, 1984).

Lenman, R.J.V., 'Art, Society and the Law in Wilhelmine Germany: The Lex Heinze', *Oxford German Studies*, 8 (1973), pp. 86–113.

Lieberknecht, Herbert, *Das Altpreussische Zuchthauswesen bis zum Ausgang des 18. Jahrhunderts* (Charlottenburg, 1921).

Littlewood, Barbara, and Linda Mahood, 'Prostitutes, Magdalenes and Wayward Girls: Dangerous Sexualities of Working-Class Women in Victorian Scotland', *Gender and History*, 3 (1992), pp. 160–75.

Lüdtke Alf, 'The Role of State Violence in the Period of Transition to Industrial Capitalism: The Example of Prussia from 1815 to 1848', *Social History*, 4 (1979), pp. 175–221.

——, *'Gemeinwohl', Polizei und 'Festungspraxis'. Staatliche Gewaltsamkeit und innere Verwaltung in Preussen, 1815–1850* (Göttingen, 1982).

—— (ed.), *'Sicherheit' und 'Wohlfahrt'. Polizei, Gesellschaft und Herrschaft im 19. und 20. Jahrhundert* (Suhrkamp Taschenbuch Wissenschaft 991, Frankfurt am Main, 1992).

Mahood, Linda, *The Magdalenes. Prostitution in the Nineteenth Century* (London, 1990).

Merten, Detlev, 'Friedrich der Grosse und Montesquieu. Zu den Anfängen des Rechtsstaats im 18. Jahrhundert', in Willi Blümel *et al.* (eds), *Verwaltung im Rechtsstaat. Festschrift für Carl Hermann Ule zum 80. Geburtstg am 24. Februar 1978* (Cologne, 1987), pp. 187–208.

Meyer, Albrecht, *Das Strafrecht der Stadt Danzig von der Carolina bis zur Vereinigung Danzigs mit der preussischen Monarchie* (Danzig, 1935).

Meyer-Renschhausen, Elizabeth, 'Die weibliche Ehre. Ein Kapital aus dem Kampf von Frauen gegen Polizei und Ärzte', in Johanna Geyer-Kordesch and Annette Kuhn (ed.), *Frauenkörper, Medizin, Sexualität* (Düsseldorf, 1980).

——, *Weibliche Kultur und soziale Arbeit. Eine Geschichte der Frauenbewegung am Beispiel Bremens 1810–1927* (Cologne, 1989).

Miller, James, *The Passion of Michel Foucault* (London, 1993).

Moltmann, Günther, 'Die Transportation von Sträflingen im Rahmen der deutschen Amerikaauswanderung des 19. Jahrhunderts', in idem (ed.), *Deutsche Amerikaauswanderung im 19. Jahrhundert* (Stuttgart, 1976), pp. 147–96.

Muir, Edward, and Guido Ruggiero (eds), *Microhistory and the Lost Peoples of Europe* (Baltimore, 1991).

Neuman, Robert P., 'Industrialization and Sexual Behavior: Some Aspects of Working-Class Life in Imperial Germany', in Robert J. Bezucha (ed.), *Modern European Social History* (Lexington, Mass., 1972), pp. 270–98.

Nitschke, Peter, *Verbrechensbekämpfung und Verwaltung. Die Entstehung der Polizei in der Grafschaft Lippe 1700–1814* (Internationale Hochschulschriften, Waxmann Verlag, Münster and New York, 1990).

Nowosadtko, Jutta, 'Die Ehre, die Unehre und das Staatsinteresse. Konzepte und Funktionen von "Unehrlichkeit" im historischen Wandel am Beispiel ds Kurfürstentums Bayern', *Geschichte in Wissenschaft und Unterricht*, 43 (1993), pp. 362–81.

Perrot, Michelle (ed.), *L'impossible Prison. Recherches sur le système pénitentiaire au xixe siécle* (Paris, 1980)

Peukert, Detlev J.K., 'Die Unordnung der Dinge. Michel Foucault und die deutsche Geschichtswissenschaft', in Franz Ewald and Bernhard Waldenfels (eds), *Spiele der Wahrheit. Michel Foucaults Denken* (Frankfurt am Main, 1991), pp. 320–33.

Reagin, Nancy R., '"A True Woman Can Take Care of Herself"': The Debate over Prostitution in Hanover, 1906', *Central European History*, 24 (1991), pp. 347–80.

————, *A German Women's Movement. Class and Gender in Hanover 1880–1933* (Chapel Hill, 1995).

Regge, Jürgen, 'Strafrecht und Strafrechtspflege', in Jürgen Ziechmann (ed.), *Panorama der friederizianischen Zeit. Friedrich der Grosse und seine Epoche* (Bremen, 1985), pp. 365–75.

Reif, Heinz (ed.), *Studien zur Geschichte der Kriminalität in Deutschland seit dem 18. Jahrhundert* (Frankfurt am Main, 1984).

Rosenfeld, Ernst, 'Verschickung freiwillig Auswandernder Insassen der Gefängnisse von Mecklenburg nach Brasilien in den Jahren 1824 und 1825', *Zeitschrift für die gesamte Strafrechtswissenschaft*, 24 (1904), pp. 412–25.

————, 'Zur Geschichte der ältesten Zuchthäuser', *Zeitschrift für die gesamte Strafrechtswissenschaft*, 26 (1906), pp. 1–18.

————, 'Die letzte Vollstreckung der Feuerstrafe in Preussen zu Berlin am 18. März 1813. Auf Grund amtlichen Materials zusammengestellt', *Zeitschrift für die gesamte Strafrechtswissenschaft*, 29 (1909), pp. 810–17.

Sauer, Paul, *Im Namen des Königs. Strafgesetzgebung und Strafvollzug im Königreich Württemberg von 1806 bis 1871* (Stuttgart, 1984).

Schattke, Herbert, *Die Geschichte der Progression im Strafvollzug und der damit zusammenhängenden Vollzugsziele in Deutschland* (Frankfurt am Main, 1979).

Schenda, Rudolf, *Volk ohne Buch. Studien zur Sozialgeschichte der populären Lesestoffe 1770–1910* (Munich, 1977).

Schmidt, Eberhard, *Die Kriminalpolitik Preussens unter Friedrich Wilhelm I und Friedrich II* (Berlin, 1914).

————, *Entwicklung und Vollzug der Freiheitsstrafe in Brandenburg-Preussen bis zum Ausgang des 18. Jahrhunderts* (Berlin, 1915).

————, *Einführung in die Geschichte der deutschen Strafrechtspflege* (3rd edn, Göttingen, 1965).

Schröder, Ferdinand, 'Die Deportation mecklenburgischer Staatsgefangener nach Brasilien 1824/25', *Der Auslandsdeutsche*, 15 (1929), pp. 497–98.

Schuhmann, Helmut, *Der Scharfrichter. Seine Gestalt – seine Funktion* (Kempten/Allgäu, 1964).

Schülke, C.W., et al., *An Einen Hochedlen Senat der Freien und Hansestadt Hamburg ergebenste Petition in Sachen und abseiten C.W. Schülke und Consorten, Grosse Michaelisstrasse 16. Belass des jetzigen Zustandes der Mädchenherbergung bis zur Erledigung der Angelegenheit im Reichstag* (Hamburg, n.d. [c. 1900]).

Schulte, Regina, *Sperrbezirke. Tugendhaftigkeit und Prostitution in der bürgerlichen Welt* (Frankfurt-am-Main, 1979).

————, 'Feuer im Dorf', in Reif (ed.), *Räuber, Volk und Obrigkeit*, pp. 100–52.

Schwerhoff, Gerd, *Köln im Kreuzverhör. Kriminalität, Herrschaft und Gesellschaft in einer frühneuzeitlichen Stadt* (Bonn and Berlin, 1991), pp. 17–48.

————, 'Devianz in der alteuropäischen Gesellschaft. Umrisse einer historischen Kriminalitätsforschung', *Zeitschrift für historische Forschung*, 19 (1992), pp. 385–414.

————, '"Mach, daß wir nicht in eine Schande geraten!" Frauen in Kölner Kriminalfällen des 16. Jahrhunderts', *Geschichte in Wissenschaft und Unterricht*, 44 (1993), pp. 451–73.

————, 'Verordnete Schande? Spätmittelalterliche und frühneuzeitliche Ehrenstrafen zwischen Rechtsakt und sozialer Sanktion', in Blauert and Schwerhoff (eds), *Mit den Waffen*, pp. 158–88.

Scribner, Bob, 'The *Mordbrenner* Fear in Sixteenth-Century Germany: Political Paranoia or the Revenge of the Outcast?', in Evans (ed.) *German Underworld*, pp. 29–56

————, 'Politics and the Territorial State in Sixteenth-Century Württemberg', in E.I. Kouri and Tom Scott (eds), *Politics and Society in Reformation Europe. Essays for Sir Geoffrey Elton on his Sixty-Fifth Birthday* (London, 1987), pp. 103–20.

Seggelke, Günther, *Die Entstehung der Freiheitsstrafe* (Breslau, 1928).
Siemann, Wolfram, *'Deutschlands Ruhe, Sicherheit und Ordnung.' Die Anfänge der politischen Polizei 1806–1866* (Studien und Texte zur Sozialgeschichte der Literatur, Vol. 14, Tübingen, 1985).
Sievers, Kai-Detlev, 'Prügelstrafe als Zeichen ständischer Ungleichheit', in Karl Köstlin and Kai-Detlev Sievers (eds), *Das Recht der kleinen Leute. Festschrift für Karl-Sigismund Kramer* (Berlin, 1976), pp. 195–206.
Sontag, Susan, *Illness as Metaphor* (London, 1983).
Spierenburg, Pieter, *The Spectacle of Suffering. Executions and the Evolution of Repression: From a Preindustrial Metropolis to the European Experience* (Cambridge, 1984).
———, 'The Sociogenesis of Confinement and its Development in Early Modern Europe', in idem (ed.), *The Emergence of Carceral Institutions*, pp. 9–77.
——— (ed.), *The Emergence of Carceral Institutions: Prisons, Galleys and Lunatic Asylums 1550–1900* (Rotterdam, 1984).
———, *The Broken Spell. A Cultural and Anthropological History of Preindustrial Europe* (London, 1991).
Stark, Gary, 'Pornography, Society and the Law in Imperial Germany', *Central European History*, 14 (1981), pp. 200–20.
Stekl, Hannes, *Österreichs Zucht- und Arbeitshäuser, 1671–1920. Institutionen zwischen Fürsorge und Strafvollzug* (Vienna, 1978).
Stone, Lawrence, 'An Exchange with Michel Foucault', *New York Review of Books*, 31 March 1983, p. 42.
Streng, Adolf, *Geschichte der Gefängnisverwaltung in Hamburg von 1622 bis 1872* (Hamburg, 1878).
Stuart, Kathleen, 'The Boundaries of Honor: Dishonorable People in Augsburg, 1510–1800' (unpublished PhD dissertation, Yale University, 1993).

Tampke, Jürgen, and Colin Doxford, *Australia, Willkommen. A History of the Germans in Australia* (Kensington, New South Wales, 1990).
Tatar, Maria, *Lustmord. Sexual Murder in Weimar Germany* (Princeton, 1995).
Theweleit, Klaus, *Männerphantasien* (2 vols, Frankfurt am Main, 1977).
Tilly, Charles, Louise and Richard, *The Rebellious Century 1830–1930* (London, 1975).

Ulrich, Anita, *Bordelle, Strassendirnen, und bürgerliche Sittlichkeit in der Belle Epoque* (Zurich, 1985).

Volkmann, Heinrich, and Jürgen Bergmann (eds), *Sozialer Protest. Studien zu traditioneller Resistenz und kollektiver Gewalt in Deutschland vom Vormärz bis zur Reichsgründung* (Opladen, 1984).

Walkowitz, Judith R., *Prostitution and Victorian Society. Women, Class, and the State* (Cambridge, 1980).
———, *City of Dreadful Delight. Narratives of Sexual Danger in Late-Victorian London* (London, 1992), pp. 15–39.
Walser, Karin, *Dienstmädchen. Frauenarbeit und Weiblichkeitsbilder um 1900* (Frankfurt am Main, 1985).
———, 'Prostitutionsverdacht und Geschlechterforschung. Das Beispiel der Dienstmädchen um 1900', *Geschichte und Gesellschaft*, 11 (1985), pp. 99–111.
Weisser, Michael, *Crime and Punishment in Early Modern Europe* (Hassocks, 1979).
Wetzell, Richard F., 'Criminal Law Reform in Imperial Germany' (unpublished PhD dissertation, Stanford University, 1991).
Wiener, Martin, *Reconstructing the Criminal. Culture, Law, and Policy in England, 1830–1914* (Cambridge, 1990).

Wilbertz, Gisela, *Scharfrichter und Abdecker im Hochstift Osnabrück. Untersuchungen zur Sozialgeschichte zweier 'unehrlicher' Berufe im nordwestdeutschen Raum vom 16. bis zum 19. Jahrhundert* (Münster, 1979).

Wirtz, Rainer, '*Widersetzlichkeiten, Excesse, Crawalle, Tumulte und Scandale'. Soziale Bewegung und gewalthafter sozialer Protest in Baden 1815–1848* (Frankfurt am Main, 1981).

Wobbe, Theresa, *Gleichheit und Differenz: Politische Strategien von Frauenrechtlerinnen um die Jahrhundertwende* (Frankfurt am Main, 1989).

Wolff, Jörg (ed.), *Das Preussische Allgemeine Landrecht. Politische, rechtliche und soziale Wechsel- und Fortwirkungen* (Motive – Texte – Materialien, Vol. 70, Heidelberg, 1995).

Zehr, Howard, *Crime and the Development of Modern Society: Patterns of Criminality in Nineteenth-Century Germany and France* (London, 1976).

Zunkel, Friedrich, 'Ehre', in Otto Brunner, Werner Conze and Reinhart Koselleck (eds), *Geschichtliche Grundbegriffe. Historisches Lexikon zur politisch-sozialen Sprache in Deutschland*, Vol. 2 (Stuttgart, 1975), pp. 1–63.

Index